W9-DES-487

Praise for:

AUTISM through the LIFESPAN

"*Starting with a few children, families, and a mission, Dr. David L. Holmes and his colleagues have created one of the few programs for persons with autism that are models of humanity, effectiveness, and successful organizational development. AUTISM THROUGH THE LIFESPAN describes in detail all of the practical activities involved in serving individuals with autism from infancy through adulthood; the operation of the Eden Family of Services; the overarching mission and values and the evolving conception of psychosocial development that guide the change process. If professional educators, college students, parents, and administrators could read only one book this year, AUTISM THROUGH THE LIFESPAN should be the one.*"

—Martin Kozloff, Ph.D., Watson Professor of Education
University of North Carolina at Wilmington

"*AUTISM THROUGH THE LIFESPAN is an unparalleled book in our field. In chronicling Eden's story—its history, philosophy, methods, and inner workings—the book both inspires and instructs others in developing exemplary services for people with autism.*

"*It **inspires** the reader that such a comprehensive network of services can be created, elaborated across the lifespan, and sustained over the years. It **instructs** the reader in precisely how these supports can be provided, from Eden's effective use of behaviorally based treatment through its organizational operation and its collaboration with families.*

"*Eden's story brings into dramatic focus the meaningful differences that a solid, stable, and successful program can make in all facets and phases of the lives of people with autism.*"

—Judith E. Favell, Ph.D., C.E.O., AdvoServ

AUTISM
through the
LIFESPAN

AUTISM

through the

LIFESPAN

The Eden Model

David L. Holmes, Ed.D.

Woodbine House ◆ 1997

Library of Congress Cataloging-in-Publication Data

Holmes, David L., Ed.D.
　　Autism through the lifespan: the Eden model / by David L. Homes.
　　　　p.　　cm.
　　Includes bibliographical references and index.
　　ISBN 0-933149-28-X　(pbk.)
　　1. Autism.　2. Autism in children.　　I.Title
　RC553.A88H64　　1997　　　　　　　　　　　　　　　　97-42934
　616.89'82—dc21　　　　　　　　　　　　　　　　　　　　　CIP

Manufactured in the United States of America
10　9　8　7　6　5　4　3　2　1

To Karen, Paige and Corinne
and my Eden Family.

*You have all made
a difference in my life.*

Table of Contents

Acknowledgements

This book is the result of many years of dedicated service and efforts by many people. The children and adults with autism and their families are the core reason for Eden and, in turn, this book. Eden's staff, a group of dedicated, self-effacing professionals, are the vessels through which the good services that Eden offers are brought to reality. Eden's neighbors and friends have always extended their encouragement to enable all of us to "carry on" under sometimes overwhelming odds. Finally, Eden's patrons—the public school districts, the Division of Developmental Disabilities of New Jersey, individuals, corporations, and foundations—have extended their generosity of resources in many ways in order that we can secure the much needed services for our children, adults, and families. All of these fine people and organizations are part of the Eden Family and the fabric of Eden's legacy.

Eden's families, children, boards, and staff have their thumbprint on the pages in this book. Names that represent these fine people can be found throughout its pages. Thank you deeply for your part.

I remember well when I began pulling together the material for the book and weaving it all into a factual compendium of Eden's services. I thought it looked impressive until I enlisted the editorial assistance of Jessica A. Haile and Cheryl L. Bomba. These two remarkable writers are the reason the book reads so well and is documented with such great precision. Both Ms. Haile and Ms. Bomba labored long to bring to life the many theories and practices Eden has developed. Thank you Jessica; thank you Cheryl.

The ideas and ideals of Eden flow from dialogues held regularly with Eden's families, staff, board, and the community. Refinements come from intense daily exchanges among myself, Linda Arcadu, Andrew Armstrong, Patricia Cleary, Marlene Cohen, Peter Gerhardt, Anne Holmes, Carol Markowitz, and David Roussell—all key players at Eden. Thank you, my compatriots.

I would be remiss if I didn't acknowledge the many mentors in my life. My parents, Erwin and Teckla Larson Holmes, Dr. Ivan Z. Holowinsky, Dr. Bernard Rimland, Dr. Edward G. Scagliotta, and Dr. Eric Schopler. My collegial friends, Dr.

Ron Comer, Dr. Edward DeForrest, Dr. Sandra Harris, Dr. Martin Kozloff, Dr. Gary Mesibov, Dr. George Neimann, and Dr. Robert Nicholas. Your encouragement and support have meant a lot.

Finally, there is one organization that is responsible for the format of this book and its coming to be. Seven years ago, Woodbine House visited Eden and said, "We have to write about this...." After many years of writing and rewriting, I present you with *Autism through the Lifespan: The Eden Model* with a large dose of thanks to Woodbine House, a remarkable publishing company dedicated to ensuring that people throughout the world recognize individuals with disabilities as people first.

All royalties from the sale of this book will go to the Eden Institute Foundation and therefore to children and adults with autism whose heroic daily struggles deserve our support.

Foreword

by Eric Schopler, Ph.D.*

People with the autism diagnosis have been recognized and served only since the World War II era. Appropriate services have been experimented with and initiated only since that time. Many of these pilot studies have been discontinued or faded into obscurity. But the Eden Institute, founded by its director, David L. Holmes, is one of the programs that has grown and flourished. This book's valuable contribution is in answering the many *how* questions that apply to Eden: how does Eden provide services, how does Eden make critical treatment decisions, how does Eden commit to lifespan services and then deliver them, how does Eden sustain its efforts, and how does Eden involve the families of the people it serves?

Both social organizations and professional careers are formed and shaped in part by cultural beliefs and attitudes. Even in its brief history, the understanding and treatment of autism was first shaped and misinformed by psychoanalytic theories blaming the symptoms of autism on faulty parental child rearing. Gradually, these misleading assumptions were replaced by the more empirically based behavioral theory and eventually modified and broadened with an emphasis on cognition and developmental theory.

When the Eden Institute was born, behavior modification was in its ascendancy. A large volume of laboratory research had shown that rewards could reinforce, increase, and intensify desirable behavior, while punishment could reduce the intensity and frequency of undesirable behavior. The possibility that behavioral techniques could remove the symptoms of autism and recover normal functioning was pursued by many professionals, focusing on the youngest, preschool age children, who they felt were most open to intervention.

As these preschoolers became adolescents, however, it became apparent that even with the benefits of earlier and more effective intervention, a large number of individuals with autism would require on-going and perhaps lifetime support. It was this realization that led Eden to create its lifespan services. It is most noteworthy that Eden did not abandon the useful technology produced by behavioral intervention, but instead used it to create its "prosthetic environment"—the highly structured educational, residential, and employment settings that enable Eden's participants to reach their full potential. Both then and now, autism is seen as a continuum of disability. While early intervention services are critical to correct young children's developmental trajectory, a majority of individuals will need some degree of support throughout their lifespan to stay on course for a productive, independent life.

This pioneering intuition paved the way for the Eden's programs for infants, toddlers, and school age children, followed by the supported employment training program, the community-based group homes, and, of critical importance, the Foundation for support funds for all the programs. Here then is the instructive story of how this most difficult population can be served, the organization, attitude and staff morale that can be developed, and the obstacles that can be overcome for both the individuals and the community in which they live together. The Eden Family of Services is a monument to the commitment and collaboration of parents and professionals. This book offers clear guidelines for how to replicate this model in other communities.

* *Eric Schopler is a professor of psychology and psychiatry at the University of North Carolina, Chapel Hill. He is also the founder of Division TEACCH (Treatment and Education of Autistic and Communication-Handicapped Children) at the University of North Carolina School of Medicine.*

Chapter **1**

Introduction

• • • • • • •

While a fellow at the Graduate School of Education at Rutgers University, I had the opportunity to study at the Children's Psychiatric Center in Eatontown, New Jersey. At the Center, I became interested in a group of children there who did not seem to respond to treatment. They were the toughest group of children to work with at the center. They were hyperactive, they seemed frustrated, they were aggressive, many did not speak, and most of them displayed some type of self-injurious behavior. When I learned that these children had in common a condition called autism, I decided to focus my studies on finding a treatment approach that would help them.

I began studying the work of Ivar Lovaas, who was conducting research on children with autism at UCLA. He had found that using specific behavior modification techniques helped the children learn new skills, become more open to outside contact, and reduce their self-injury and aggression (Lovaas, Freitag, Gold & Kassorla, 1965; Lovaas and Simmons, 1969; interested readers are referred to Lovaas, 1993 for a narrative description of Lovaas's early work). When I applied similar techniques to the children at the psychiatric center, I was able to replicate his findings. The treatment Lovaas called behavior modification, later to be known as applied behavior analysis, was a more effective treatment for the children than any other treatment I had tried.

After receiving my degree, I joined with a family to start a new school in Princeton designed specifically for children with autism, the Princeton Child Development Institute. After a few years, I realized that some of the children at the Institute were going to need treatment services long after they graduated from the educational system. I wanted to provide those services because I felt deeply concerned for their future and for their families, but my goal was not, at that time, in keeping with the Institute's direction. So, in 1975 I began another school, this time in partnership with several families. We named the school the Eden Institute.

EDEN'S HISTORY

◆ ◆ ◆ ◆ ◆ ◆ ◆ ◆ ◆ ◆ ◆ ◆ ◆ ◆ ◆ ◆ ◆

"It is not what you have, but what you do with it."
—**Edward G. Scagliotta**

Eden was first housed in the basement of the Trinity Episcopal Church in Princeton, but soon moved to the nearby and recently vacated St. Andrews Presbyterian Church, which provided more space. The building was three stories tall. We had the Early Childhood Program on the first floor, the Middle Childhood Program on the second floor, and the Vocational Program on the third floor. We used the main sanctuary for group activities and holiday plays. Speech and Language Therapy was in the balcony.

Within three years, Eden had grown so much that we had to move the Vocational Program to another building. That was difficult, because teachers could not move as easily from program to program. But it was a healthy part of our evolution from a school to a multi-faceted service delivery organization. A few years later, we decided that Eden needed a building of its own. Through the support of private donors, the Robert Wood Johnson, Jr. Trust, the Kresge Foundation, and trustees and families, Eden was able, in 1983, to purchase a facility of its own.

> I know my son isn't going to be a brain surgeon. I've come to terms with that. But it's important for him to be a contributing member of society. If he can work, he will be able to contribute to society. I measure him by his productive abilities. They will be his diploma when he graduates.
>
> —**Meme Omogbai**

The Eden Institute still resides in this building. It offers twelve-month, individualized programming for people from age three to twenty-one. Each program is behaviorally oriented, with one-to-one, two-to-one, or small group instruction. Skills are taught respecting the unique developmental, cognitive, and behavior management needs of each student.

Other programs which evolved from the school now have facilities of their own. The first group home in Eden's residential program,[1] the Winsten House, was opened in 1980, even before we secured a building for the school. Some of the students at Eden Institute needed residential services, and we found an old farm house that we could buy for a fraction of its actual value. The farm house was overgrown and needed total renovation, but had fifteen acres of land. Our fundraising efforts were then only raising between eight and ten thousand dollars a year. However, we bought the place, with the help of two parents Gil and Harriet Winsten, who agreed to take out a mortgage on the building. The families, Board, and staff members worked throughout a cold winter to fix up the property, including building two large stair towers on either side of the house to satisfy building codes and meet the regulations set by state agencies. Since the establishment of Winsten House, Eden has opened six additional homes.

> When I came to Eden, we were just barely opening our first group home. We knew there was a large need for residential services. There still is, and that need is going to continue to grow. Eden continues to admit infants, so there is going to be an even bigger group of people, most eventually needing adult services.
>
> **—Marlene Cohen, Director of Support Services**

Eden's work program, called WERCs (Work, Education, and Resource Centers), began in 1983. One of the first graduates of the Eden Institute, Scott, was really the "founder" of the program. In 1982, he was graduated from the Eden Institute and entered a state-run employment program that served people with a

variety of disabilities. Scott had some very challenging behaviors. He was occasionally aggressive, generally hyperactive, and often very mischievous. For example, on his first day in Eden's residential program, he climbed out a second story window and dropped to the ground . . . without a scratch. When he was younger, similar behaviors occurred at home and his parents called Eden more than once for advice.

In the first few weeks at the state-run employment center, Scott's behaviors were so challenging that the state offered to help Eden set up a work program specifically for people with autism. The next year the Jo-

---

[1] Eden's residential program is called Eden ACREs (A Community Residence Experience). However, the first group home was purchased before ACREs' incorporation in 1980.

seph A. Bendas Center was opened as the first of Eden's now three employment centers. Each center serves people living in nearby group homes or with their natural or surrogate families.

In 1984, Eden established a foundation to secure funding for its services and to perform public education about autism and Eden. The Foundation recently moved from a small corner it had held in the Eden Institute for 12 years to a

property adjacent to Wawa House, which houses our program for infants and toddlers. We acquired the building for Wawa House in 1991.

During its first five years of existence, Eden operated a summer residential program in Cape Cod, at the summer home of one of our families, Lois and George Bonnell. By 1980 we established an educational camp program in Califon, New Jersey, leasing space in a camp operated by the Lutheran Church. Support for our summer educational camp program came from a generous grant from the Turrell Fund, and continues to this day. In 1993 Eden purchased a historic property in Connecticut to serve as our own summer residential program and year-round retreat center. Eden's Wawa Education and Retreat Center opened in 1995. It is open year-round as a retreat, and has a capacity to serve over 40 children or adults. The Wawa Education and Retreat Center was supported in large part by Wawa, Inc., the Dorothy B. Hersh Foundation, American Re-Insurance Company, Hoechst Celanese Corporation, trustees, families, and friends of Eden.

Wawa House was named in honor of Wawa, Inc. due to its generosity in enabling the development of Eden's services to infants and toddlers. Currently, Wawa House serves 62 children—13 in a formal program, and 49 in a supplemental program. Eden Institute serves about 50 children total. There are 10 children in the Early Childhood Program (7 of these in a preschool program within Early Childhood), 11 in the Middle Childhood Program, 6 in the Transition Program, and 23 in the Vocational Programs (9 in Prevocational, 14 in Vocational Preparation). Eden ACREs serves 42 people, and Eden WERCs serves 58.

EDEN'S PHILOSOPHY, MISSION, AND CREDO

As Eden grew, we realized that we needed to define exactly why we exist, and what we want to do. These definitions became our philosophy and mission.

Eden exists because most people with autism need specialized services over their entire lifetime. We wanted to provide those services. We then outlined how we were going to carry out our mission. This became our credo. We defined how we were going to carry out our mission by establishing our responsibility toward the people we serve, their families, the staff members at Eden, the community, and toward Eden's supporters. The text of our philosophy, mission, and credo appears below.

PHILOSOPHY

Our philosophy is that the majority of children and adults with autism will require a lifetime of highly specialized services.

Our philosophy came from the realization, during Eden's early years, that people with autism generally need some degree of support throughout their lives, even if they do become independent in many areas. Implicit in our philosophy is an additional belief: People with autism should be as independent as possible. This belief runs through all of our programs, and is discussed in several chapters of this book.

MISSION

Eden's mission is to offer community-based, lifespan services to children and adults with autism and their families.

Our mission is Eden's reason for being. We want to provide the services that people with autism need throughout their lives. By lifespan services, we mean a continuum of services, from birth to death, without breaks. However, because we want the people we serve to be as independent as possible, Eden provides services that are based in the community. We want the people we serve to have as normal a life as possible. We want them to attend their local schools as appropriate, go to community parks and shop in local stores, hold jobs in nearby companies, and live in homes located in the community. We want them to carry out these activities as much as they can on their own.

> Because our services span the lifetime, I can track the progress children make. I have been here for ten years and have known many of the children since they were very young. I follow them through school, graduating, and getting a job. I see the long-term effects of what I have done, and the part I have played in their progress. That is incredibly rewarding.
>
> —Lyn O'Donnell, Coordinator, Clinical Services

Eden's mission statement sets forth its general purpose, but each service within Eden has a more defined purpose. The most important of these are:

- ◆ to provide year-round educational services to children with autism. These services should prepare children to enter a regular school, a job, or a structured work program.
- ◆ to provide training in employment skills to adults with autism.
- ◆ to provide community residential services.

◆ to enable children and adults with autism to be integrated in their communities to the extent most beneficial for each individual.
◆ to educate the community about autism.
◆ to train professionals in disciplines to teach people with autism.
◆ to train parents of people with autism how to teach their child effectively.
◆ to advocate for the rights of those with autism and other disabilities.
◆ to offer assistance to other programs and organizations that serve people with autism.
◆ to support research into the causes of autism, and into the effectiveness of treatment procedures for people with autism.

Each of these points is discussed in later chapters of this book. They are the primary services Eden provides to people with autism—year-round educational services, vocational training and employment services, community based residential services and involvement, parent and teacher training, advocacy for services, support for other programs, and research about autism.

In order to ensure that the values of the people who work at Eden remain true to its philosophy and mission, we developed a credo.

CREDO

Our first responsibility is to Eden's children and adults with autism. Our challenge is to educate and train our young people in order that they reach their full potential and enjoy a quality life. Each must be considered an individual. We must respect their dignity and recognize their merit. We must keep abreast of current and well-established intervention strategies and tailor remedial programs to the unique learning styles of each child or adult.

Our second responsibility is to Eden's families. We must help them understand autism and how they can help their children reach their full potential. We must be ever cognizant of the stresses a family with an autistic individual encounters and must be diligent in our efforts to support the family members.

Our third responsibility is to the men and women who work for the Eden Family of Services. They must feel professionally stimulated and challenged. They must be trained to offer the highest quality of program possible. They must have a sense of security in their jobs. Compensation must be fair and adequate. Working conditions must be clean, orderly, and safe.

Our fourth responsibility is to the community at large. We must be good neighbors to those in whose communities we offer services. We must continue to educate the community about autism. We must offer community members opportunities to fulfill their spirit of volunteerism. We must also advocate for the community of families who have children with autism. We must offer them: support of research into the causes and treatment of autism, consultation services, and support of government policies that encourage the development of services to families and their children with autism.

Our final responsibility is to those who support Eden. If we meet the first four of our responsibilities with success, we believe those who have supported these programs will feel that their support has been merited.

We use our credo as a guide for decisions regarding funding and the development of new services. Along with our mission and philosophy, the credo helps us explain why we do what we do. Together they summarize our priorities and goals, and keep us precisely focused on our goal of providing lifespan services.

EDEN'S SERVICE SPECTRUM

Eden's philosophy, mission, and credo provide an explicit definition of the services it delivers. In addition, Eden combines many different services, which are usually offered separately, into one organization. For example, most schools for children with autism offer programming for the traditional 10-month school year; Eden offers programs to extend educational programming over twelve months, including a summer residential program, and a day program at the school. Most schools that serve children with autism do not extend their services past age eighteen or twenty-one, when state education mandates cease; Eden's services are extended into the adult years. Additionally, programs that serve adults usually do not offer school-aged programming. Eden has a broad-ranged continuum of services for both children and adults. For adults, Eden offers both work and residential programs, each of which is often found separately in other organizations.

In addition to the elements mentioned above, Eden also focuses on several other areas. First, because teaching children and adults with autism over their lifespan is hard work, Eden places great emphasis on fostering high staff morale and positive attitudes. Second, Eden's services encompass and involve the family deeply in our work with people with autism. Third, Eden tailors its programs to each person it serves individually. It avoids trying to make anyone fit into preset programs or approaches. Lastly, Eden's services push people with autism toward ever-greater independence and responsibility. Although many of these elements can be found in other programs, Eden places great emphasis on them collectively. They color the services Eden provides and the "feel" at Eden. This combination of attributes and services is what makes Eden a useful potential model for other organizations serving people with autism. Presenting Eden as a model for replication is one of the primary purposes of this book.

WHY THIS BOOK?

The purpose of this book is to enable parents and professionals to benefit from what has been learned at Eden over the years about designing and running an

The tangible things at Eden can be replicated rather easily. These include documentation for the different processes we have developed, behavior reduction procedures, skill acquisition procedures, and the training and support we give staff members. The intangible things are harder to replicate. Our philosophy, mission, and credo are intangible, but are extremely important. They keep us all on the same track. We know why we are here, we know what we are doing, and we believe in what we are doing. Both the tangible and intangible aspects of Eden are needed in order to make a service delivery organization work.

—Dave Roussell, Director of Residential Services

organization for serving people with autism. We hope that, through this book, parents and professionals will be encouraged to establish similar programs elsewhere or to use some of the elements or philosophy. We especially hope to encourage the establishment of programs which are committed to serving people with autism over their entire lifespan.

Providing lifespan services is challenging. It is challenging to Eden, to other service organizations, and to state agencies. But it can be done. We have worked, and are still working, step by step to provide programs needed by the people we serve. Eden will probably never reach a point where it has created all the programs needed, but that is not the goal. At Eden what is important is the commitment to provide service, and to continue to find ways to fill the needs of people with autism. We hope others are encouraged to do the same. The Eden model can be, and has been, duplicated elsewhere. Numerous organizations have consulted with us in designing their own programs.[2] This book can help introduce more people to our model of service delivery. Professionals in related fields and parents of children with other disabilities may find that much of what we have created can apply to their area. We invite all interested parties to come and see, first hand, how our programs are run.

The material presented in this book will be familiar to some, and new to others. Some will agree, some may feel uncomfortable, and others may vehemently disagree with our views on current areas of debate in the field of autism, such as the effectiveness of facilitated communication or the use of aversive interventions to modify behavior. We welcome questions and comments. It is only through open dialogue, disagreement, debate, and discussion that these controversial issues can be fully explored.

OUTLINE OF CHAPTERS
◆ ◆ ◆ ◆ ◆ ◆ ◆ ◆ ◆ ◆ ◆ ◆ ◆ ◆ ◆ ◆ ◆ ◆

The following chapter, Chapter 2, gives a short history and definition of autism and describes the symptoms associated with the disorder. It also describes in general the services available for people with autism. Chapter 3 presents Eden's treat-

---

[2]   Chapter 8 describes some of the programs that are based on Eden's model.

ment philosophy, and discusses some of the common treatment problems encountered serving people with autism. Eden's philosophy of lifespan treatment, along with its policy of not discharging anyone from its programs, is presented in Chapter 4. Chapter 5 discusses the most popular treatments available for people with autism. It also discusses the types of placement available, and describes Eden's view of the different treatment and placement options.

Chapter 6 describes Eden's treatment approach—applied behavior analysis—in detail, and includes the techniques used to both increase and decrease behavior. The use of any behavior modification technique is guided by the Eden Decision Model and Accountability Process. It provides a highly structured method to analyze behavior, develop effective intervention strategies, and monitor effectiveness over time. The Eden Decision Model and Accountability Process are discussed in Chapter 7.

Chapter 8 explains the structure of our services for children from birth to age twenty-one. These include Wawa House and the various programs of the Eden Institute. The chapter also describes Eden Institute's curriculum, progress monitoring, and troubleshooting procedures. Services for adults, including residential and work programs, are described in Chapter 9.

Because families are an integral part of our programs, Chapter 10 explains the role families play in choosing their child's treatment and advocating for services. The chapter stresses the importance of parents and teachers working as partners. The training and counseling families receive is also discussed.

Chapter 11 describes the organizational side of Eden. The chapter emphasizes the importance of clearly defined job descriptions and lines of responsibility, setting clearly defined goals, maintaining administrative clarity and quality control, and being involved in the local community. The benefits, as well as the dangers, of growth and funding are also discussed.

By the end of Chapter 11, Eden's attitude toward serving people with autism should be clear. The most important elements of our treatment attitude are: a commitment by staff and faculty members to stand by those we serve; clearly defined criteria not only for those we serve but for staff, faculty, and administration; support of effective treatment methodologies; a rigorous effort to provide those we serve with the least restrictive environment possible; and a strong respect for those we serve, their families, our staff and faculty members, and others serving people with autism.

Chapter 2

Understanding
Autism
Today

S ince its identification by Leo Kanner in 1943 as a condition "...markedly and uniquely [different] from anything reported so far...,"(p.27) autism has become a focus of research throughout the world. However, despite 50 years of scientific investigation, from fields as diverse as psychology and cellular biology, many questions remain about what exactly autism is, how it is caused, and what can be done to help those with the disorder. Answers to these questions are currently only partial answers, but they provide insights into a fuller understanding of a disorder which has mystified parents, professionals, and scientists alike.

WHAT IS AUTISM?

Autism is classified in the American Psychiatric Association's *Diagnostic and Statistical Manual of Mental Disorders—Fourth Edition* (1994) as a "pervasive developmental disorder," a disorder that manifests itself in infancy, severely affects the development of social interaction and communication skills and results in the presence of stereotyped behaviors, interests, and activities. Typically apparent before age three, autism affects four times as many boys as girls and is found in families of all races, religions and social classes. Autism is one of the most prevalent developmental disorders, affecting 1 in 1000 births to 2 in 1000 births if the full spectrum of autistic behavior is included (autism, PDD NOS, Asperger's Disorder, Rett's Disorder, and Childhood Disintegrative Disorder) (Alexander et al., 1996). Increasingly viewed as an expression of an unidentified neurological disorder, the exact cause or causes of autism is currently unknown, although recent research shows a spectrum of impairments at both the anatomical and microscopic levels.

> No two people with autism are the same; its precise form or expression is different in every case. Moreover, there may be a most intricate (and potentially creative) interaction between the autistic traits and the other qualities of the individual. So, while a single glance may suffice for a clinical diagnosis, if we hope to understand the autistic individual, nothing less than a total biography will do.
>
> —Oliver Sacks, in *An Anthropologist on Mars*, 1995 (p. 250)

The question, "What is autism?", however, cannot be fully answered by a description of its clinical symptoms. It is equally important to consider the question from the reference point of individuals with the disorder. To begin, it is important to consider the degree of heterogeneity possible among people with autism. Individuals with autism will vary in the number of symptoms they present, the severity of those symptoms, the degree of cognitive impairment they will experience, and the number and type of associated medical problems they will have. The individual's involvement in appropriate treatment and education also needs to be considered; although the majority of individuals with autism will require lifelong support services, research is indicating that early, behaviorally-based intervention and placement in highly structured, family-focused and community-based services is critical to obtain the best possible outcome (Edwards & Bristol, 1991; Lovaas, 1987). And it is also important to consider that autism is a disorder of development and, as such, will affect the individual in different ways during different stages of development. "Certain features will not become apparent until later; others disappear with time. In fact, there is enormous change" (Frith, 1989, p.1).

In the end, the answer to the question, "What is autism?", is quite complex. Depending on the individual, autism may be a disorder that makes the rules governing typical social exchanges incomprehensible, but, otherwise, imposes few limits. For others, autism plays a predominant role in determining major life decisions such as where they will live and the kind of work they will do. The rest of this chapter describes current issues surrounding autism in greater detail and discusses how they affect the lives of the individuals with this disorder.

Autism Check List

Individuals with autism usually exhibit at least half of the traits listed below. These symptoms can range from mild to severe and vary in intensity from symptom to symptom. In addition, the behavior usually occurs across many different situations and is consistently inappropriate for their age.

- ❏ Difficulty in mixing with other children
- ❏ Insistence on sameness; resists change in routine
- ❏ Inappropriate laughing and giggling
- ❏ No real fear of dangers
- ❏ Little or no eye contact
- ❏ Unresponsive to normal teaching methods
- ❏ Sustained odd play
- ❏ Apparent insensitivity to pain
- ❏ Echolalia (repeating words or phrases in place of normal language)
- ❏ Prefers to be alone; aloof manner
- ❏ May not want cuddling or act cuddly
- ❏ Spins objects
- ❏ Noticeable physical overactivity or extreme underactivity
- ❏ Tantrums—displays extreme distress for no apparent reason
- ❏ Not responsive to verbal cues; acts as if deaf
- ❏ Inappropriate attachment to objects
- ❏ Uneven gross/fine motor skills (May not want to kick ball but can stack blocks)
- ❏ Difficulty in expressing needs; uses gestures or pointing instead of words

From What is Autism?, *a brochure available from the Autism Society of America.*

KANNER'S IDENTIFICATION OF AUTISM

Kanner's identification of autism in 1943 is very similar to the definition of autism accepted today. The first group of children Kanner identified as autistic consisted of "a number of children whose condition differs so markedly and uniquely from anything reported so far, that each case merits—and, I hope, will eventually receive—a detailed consideration of its fascinating peculiarities"(p.217). Kanner defined the "outstanding, 'pathognomic,' fundamental disorder"(p.242) of autism as:

the children's inability to relate themselves *in the ordinary way to people and situations from the beginning of life. Their parents referred to them as having always been "self-sufficient"; "like in a shell"; "happiest when left alone"; "acting as if people weren't there"; "perfectly oblivious to everything about him"; "giving the impression of silent wisdom"; "failing to develop the usual amount of social awareness"; "acting almost as if hypnotized." This is not, as in schizophrenic children or adults, a departure from an initially present relationship; it is not a "withdrawal" from formerly existing participation. There is from the start an* extreme autistic aloneness *that, whenever possible, disregards, ignores, shuts out anything that comes to the child from the outside. Direct physical contact or such motion or noise as threatens to disrupt the aloneness is either treated "as if it weren't there" or, if this is no longer sufficient, resented painfully as distressing interference. (Kanner, 1943, p.242)*

The children of Kanner's study displayed very little or no language, although many were capable of articulation and phonation. They had difficult joining words in sentences, and often parroted or echoed what they were told. They had difficulty with pronouns, especially with the use of "I." They had excellent rote memory,

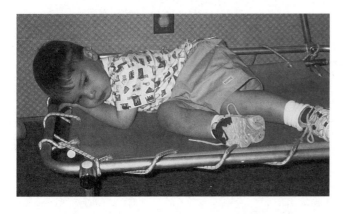

were often rigid in their eating habits, and had an obsessive desire for sameness in daily routines. They often displayed monotonous movements, such as rocking, and treated people as if they were simply objects.

Today, the children and adults with autism Eden treats display many of the same characteristics Kanner identified. Children entering Eden are often nonverbal and may lack even the most basic communicative gestures such as reaching their own hands toward an object that they would like to have. Individuals who develop verbal language often confuse personal pronouns, and initially use echoed phrases to communicate their needs and regulate their actions. It is not at all unusual to hear the classic phrase, "Do you want a cookie?", as individuals make requests of their teachers. Rote memory skills are seen in some individuals' ability to remember the birthdays of celebrities, or the year, make, and model of staff members' cars. And, insistence on sameness can be seen in individuals who must touch the number on the door of their school bus before boarding or turn around twice for every six steps taken.

Following is an example of an initial evaluation of a toddler with autism in Eden's Wawa House

Behavioral Observations
Kyle, 2 years, 6 months

SOCIAL INTERACTION

Kyle frequently appears unaware of others in his environment, although this may be a function of his disinterest in others. He is, however, clearly unaware of the affective states of others. One notable behavior that Kyle engages in is his consistent use of his parents as objects (i.e., he often uses their hands or arms to reach items he desires). Kyle also displays impaired imitation skills for his age and skill level, although he has recently begun to engage in smile-to-smile, nonverbal imitation as well as some emergent verbal imitation. His verbal imitation, however, seems more perseverative than imitative.

In terms of play, Kyle prefers solitary or parallel play to cooperative play and does not always play appropriately. Recently, he has become interested in peek-a-boo; however, his interest is limited to instances in which his parents are his playmates. He remains disinterested in play with children of his same age or his sisters, who are a few years older.

COMMUNICATION

Although Kyle has begun to use single words, his verbal language is inconsistent and both his receptive and expressive language abilities remain significantly delayed. There is also some indication of perseveration, as Kyle will repeat words or sing phrases from songs over and over. In terms of nonverbal communicative behavior, Kyle's eye contact is quite inconsistent. On occasion, if interested, it seems that Kyle will attend to a person and make adequate eye contact. However, Kyle primarily averts his gaze and seems to avoid making direct eye contact.

INTERESTS AND ACTIVITIES

Kyle's parents report that his range of interests is very narrow, and he seems preoccupied with parts of objects, especially cylinders. When directed to a toy box, Kyle looked through the toys one by one, as if he were searching for something specific. He retrieved each item, looked at it, and then put it aside. Kyle finally stopped looking after he found a cylindrical tube and a ball. Kyle placed the ball on top of the cylinder and seemed content with these toys.

DIAGNOSTIC RECOGNITION OF AUTISM

Autism did not receive diagnostic recognition until long after Kanner's study. In 1980, the *Diagnostic and Statistical Manual of Mental Disorders - Third Edition* (APA, 1980) included "Infantile Autism" as a diagnostic category for the first time. Categorized as a pervasive developmental disorder, the diagnostic criteria included the following characteristics:

◆ onset prior to 30 months of age;
◆ pervasive lack of responsiveness;
◆ language deficits including peculiar speech;
◆ bizarre responses to various aspects of the environment; and
◆ the absence of delusions, hallucinations, loose associations, and incoherence (in other words, the absence of any indication of a schizophrenic disturbance).

Two additional diagnostic categories, "Infantile Autism—Residual State" and "Childhood Onset Pervasive Developmental Disorder," were used to describe people who were experiencing disturbances in communication, social relations, and behavior, but did not meet the full criteria for "Infantile Autism."

This picture of autism was expanded in 1987 with the advent of the *Diagnostic and Statistical Manual of Mental Disorders - Third Edition (Revised)* (APA, 1987), which divided the criteria for autism into three major deficit areas:

◆ qualitative impairment in reciprocal social interactions;
◆ qualitative impairment in communication and imaginative activity; and
◆ a markedly restricted repertoire of activities and interests.

Onset was still recognized as occurring during infancy or childhood, but was not necessarily restricted to being prior to 30 months of age. The category "Infantile

Autism - Residual State" was abandoned while "Pervasive Developmental Disorder Not Otherwise Specified" replaced "Childhood Onset Pervasive Developmental Disorder."

Today autism is defined according to even more precise criteria. To allow for the identification and study of more behaviorally homogenous groups of individuals, the diagnostic criteria for autism were revised and separate diagnostic criteria were developed for Rett's Disorder, Childhood Disintegrative Disorder, and Asperger's Disorder in the fourth edition of the *Diagnostic and Statistical Manual* (APA, 1994). These newly-defined disorders are also categorized by severe impairments in socialization, com-

Behavioral Characteristics of Autism
(American Psychiatric Association, 1994)

Qualitative impairment in social interaction
- marked impairment in the use of multiple nonverbal behaviors such as eye-to-eye gaze, facial expression, body postures and gestures to regulate social interaction
- failure to develop peer relationships appropriate to developmental level
- lack of spontaneous seeking to share enjoyment, interests or achievements with other people (e.g., by a lack of showing, bringing or pointing out objects of interest)
- lack of social or emotional reciprocity

Qualitative impairments in communication
- delay in, or total lack of the development of spoken language (not accompanied by an attempt to compensate through alternative modes of communication such as gesture or mime)
- in individuals with adequate speech, marked impairment in the ability to initiate or sustain a conversation with others
- stereotyped, repetitive use of language or idiosyncratic language
- lack of varied, spontaneous make-believe play or social imitative play appropriate to developmental level

Restricted, repetitive, and stereotyped patterns of behavior, interests, and activities
- encompassing preoccupation with one or more stereotyped and restricted patterns of interest that is abnormal in either intensity or focus
- apparently inflexible adherence to specific, nonfunctional routines or rituals
- stereotyped and repetitive motor mannerisms (e.g., hand or finger flapping or twisting, or complex whole-body movements)
- persistent preoccupation with parts of objects

Delays or abnormal functioning in at least one of the following areas, with onset prior to age 3 years: (1) social interaction, (2) language as used in social communication, or (3) symbolic or imaginative play.

To receive a diagnosis of autism, an individual must exhibit at least six of the characteristics listed above, with at least two impairments in social interaction, at least one impairment in communication, and at least one restricted, repetitive behavior or interest.

munication and behavior, but have unique features not found in autism, such as the decelerated head growth seen in Rett's Disorder and the acquisition of age-appropriate skills across most developmental areas seen in Asperger's Disorder. The disorder most similar to autism, Pervasive Developmental Disorder Not Otherwise Specified, still remains as a diagnostic category for individuals who have qualitatively similar ("autistic-like") behaviors, but fail to meet the diagnostic criteria for any of the disorders listed above.

Although *DSM-IV* has been criticized for subgrouping autism and failing to define autism as a continuum or spectrum disorder (Gilman & Tuchman, 1995), it is important to note that the unique triad of deficits described by all three editions of the *DSM* have changed little since Kanner's incisive behavioral descriptions in 1943. People fitting his description have been reported from all parts of the world, and the core clinical features of his definition—social interaction, communication, and behavioral deficits—have proven remarkably robust, "...surviv[ing] the screening of different countries and languages, professional committees, courts and other social agencies" (Schopler, 1995, p. 8).

WIDE RANGE OF ABILITY

As mentioned earlier in this chapter, there is an extraordinarily wide range of ability among people with autism. Some have intact or even advanced cognitive abilities, but have difficulty moderating their behavior and developing social skills.

> Our specialty is the more severely involved kid. The kids that are readily accepted into regular education settings usually do not end up with us.
>
> —**Anne S. Holmes, Director of Outreach Services**

For example, Temple Grandin, a person with autism, has achieved a doctoral degree and an assistant professorship at Colorado State University, yet comments that she often feels like "an anthropologist on Mars" (Sacks, 1995, p. 259). On the other end of the spectrum are people who not only experience severe disturbances in their behavior and social skills, but mental retardation as well. Approximately 75 percent of individuals with autism will have an associated diagnosis of mental retardation, most often in the moderate range (IQ between 35 and 50) (American Psychiatric Association, 1994). This group presents the greatest challenge to parents and teachers.

This group is also the major focus of the Eden Family of Services. More often than not, Eden serves those who have been diagnosed as functioning in the lowest range of cognitive ability. And, of the 75 percent of people who are diagnosed both with autism and mental retardation, Eden serves the lowest 10 to 15 percent.[1] The people Eden serves are typically described as being "severely involved." This means they exhibit significant behavioral difficulties, often engaging in behaviors

---

[1]   Chapter 4 describes the people Eden serves in more detail.

that are harmful to themselves or others, such as self-injury or aggression, have limited abilities to understand and use language, and lack the cognitive skills needed to obtain meaningful scores on standardized measures designed to measure intelligence. In addition to these criteria, other researchers define severely involved people as individuals "...whose progress in existing programs is so slow or irregular that competent daily performance seems unlikely to result in the time avail-

What is Success?

I have been asked, on many occasions, "What success has Eden had with children with autism?" My response has always been, "All of our children are successes."

When Tiffany first came to Eden, she had no ability to talk or take care of her personal needs. The world was so confusing to her that she cried almost constantly. Ten years later, Tiffany can dress herself, feed herself, take care of her toileting needs and use sign language to communicate. She also has the biggest smile you could ever imagine. Is she "normal"? Will she ever attend a public school? Will she ever live a

life free of close supervision? No, on all counts. But is she happy? Does she enjoy her new-found skills? Is she a "success"? *Yes, on all counts.* She is no less successful than a typical child who has been blessed with all the typical attributes and will live a typical, independent life.

When Alan came to Eden, he had no academic skills and was unable to relate to his family or his teachers. But he already had some speech and could take care of many of his personal needs. After four years of hard work, Alan learned to use speech in a fluent, conversational fashion, work on grade-level academically, and develop warm, personal relationships with his family and teachers who helped him reach his potential.

Alan now attends public school, full-time, due to his exceptional gains in all areas of development. Is Alan a success? On all counts, yes, but he is no more of a success than Tiffany, whose progress was much slower, and much more painstaking.

So, "What success has Eden had with its children with autism?" Same answer: "All of our children are successes."

—**David L. Holmes, President and Executive Director**

able," emphasizing that those severely involved require a high degree of special-ization in their education and treatment (Wilcox & Bellamy, 1987).

Even among those most challenged by autism, there is still quite a range of ability. At Eden, for example, some participants are able to read at grade level, obtain a driver's license, and work forty hours per week in the community with-out the support of a job coach. In the future, these individuals will move to super-vised apartments to acquire the more complex skills the less-structured setting will demand. Other participants will need continuing support to acquire skills such as independence in toileting, dressing, and completing one-step directions. Regardless of the level of support a participant needs, however, all participants receive treatment and programming that enables them to be successful.

WHAT CAUSES AUTISM?

There is as yet no clear consensus on the exact cause of autism. Most researchers believe that autism is caused by a combination of factors, but the relative weight of each factor is still under debate.[2] What research has been able to determine,

however, is that autism is a biologically-based disorder, correlated with several sec-ondary conditions, none of which can in itself fully ex-plain autism. These re-search findings are ex-plained in this section.

In the past, theories on the cause of autism focused on the psychological envi-ronment of the person with autism. Since Kanner's ob-servation in 1943 that "...there are very few really warmhearted fathers and mothers" of children with autism, psychodynamic theorists have proposed several working models of the causal factors in autism. Perhaps the most famous psychodynamic theory for the cause of autism was posited by Bruno Bettelheim in 1967. Bettelheim, a leading child psychiatrist, hypothesized that children with autism were the result of dys-functional families, in which an unemotional "refrigerator" mother was particu-larly to blame for the child's distress, and advocated for the child's separation

---

[2] Therapies based on the various causal theories for autism are discussed in Chapter 5.

from the family as part of his treatment.[3] Researchers, however, have been unable to prove the validity of any particular psychodynamic theory. Although empirical studies consistently find that being the parent of a child with autism is particularly stressful due to the unique challenges these children present (Harris, Boyle, Fong, Gill & Stranger, 1987), no factors in the child's psychological environment have ever proven causal for autism. Over the last few decades research has provided a great deal more support for biologically-based theories (Bauman, 1993; Courchesne et al., 1988; Rimland, 1964) and today autism is widely considered to be a biologically-determined syndrome (Gillberg, 1989).

Biological theories for autism currently cover a broad range of possible factors. Theories based on genetics, infectious diseases and metabolic disorders, neurological factors, and pre-, peri-, and postnatal trauma are all supported by significant empirical correlation with the development of autism.

GENETIC FINDINGS

Evidence from twin and multiple-incidence family studies strongly suggests that genetic factors can be implicated in some cases of autism (Spiker et al. 1994). Although the mode of inheritance is unknown, findings such as the significant sex difference between males and females (APA, 1994; Lord, Schopler & Revicki, 1982; Wing, 1981), the matching higher rates for autism among twins and siblings of individuals with the disorder (APA, 1994; Smalley, Asarnow & Spence, 1988), and the correlation between autistic behavior and identifiable genetic disorders (for example, fragile-X syndrome, Down syndrome, and tuberous sclerosis) (Lotspeich & Ciaranello, 1993; Rutter, 1990; Smalley, Asarnow & Spence, 1988) are regularly reported in the literature. Although genetic tests cannot definitively confirm or rule out a diagnosis of autism for a given individual, screening for the genetic disorders listed above may provide additional treatment information and may assist with family planning. And although the identification of a single autism "gene" that will explain all or even most cases of autism is highly unlikely, theories focusing on genetic heterogeneity—the possibility that several different genes are capable of causing the same disorder—and polygenic inheritance—the possibility that several genes acting together cause a disorder—are under investigation and may provide an answer to the question of cause for at least some people.[4]

INFECTIOUS DISEASES

Infectious diseases have long been known to affect human development; the relationship between maternal rubella (German measles) and birth defects including deafness, blindness, mental retardation, cerebral palsy, and congenital heart

---

[3] Interested readers can see *The Empty Fortress* (1967) for a detailed account of Bettelheim's treatment methods as well as *The Creation of Dr. B: A Biography of Bruno Bettelheim* (Polack, 1997), a book that largely discounts Bettelheim's work.

[4] Interested readers are referred to the Stanford University School of Medicine's Autism Genetics Program, Department of Psychiatry and Behavioral Sciences, Stanford, California 94305.

disorders is particularly well documented (Miller, Cradock-Watson & Pollock, 1982). Not surprisingly, research has identified several pre-, peri- and neonatal diseases that are associated with autism. The group of infections referred to as the TORCH infections (toxoplasmosis, rubella, cytomegalovirus, and herpesvirus) seem to have particularly strong correlations, with autism (Edwards & Bristol, 1991). Unlike the relationship between maternal rubella and deafness, however, the relationship between these and other infectious diseases and autism may or may not be causal. Further research is needed to determine if there is a causal relationship or if the infection and autism simply coexist. Like genetic screening, checking for these and other infectious diseases can be helpful in providing additional, medically-based treatment to affected individuals and may also provide some information about cause for a small percentage of individuals with autism.

NEUROBIOLOGICAL FINDINGS

A number of researchers have identified a host of neurobiological abnormalities in individuals with autism (Bauman, 1993; Bristol, 1996; Courchesne et al., 1988; Rimland, 1964). In the 1970s and early 1980s, computerized tomography (CT) scans were used to examine the brain structure of individuals with autism. Although enlarged ventricles (particularly the third and fourth) and cerebral asymmetries were seen in some individuals, other studies failed to replicate these findings (see Gillberg, 1989, for a review). Magnetic resonance imaging (MRI), a technology that provides a much more exact view of the brain, became available soon afterward and was used in an attempt to clarify some of the CT findings. Cerebral asymmetries and ventricle enlargement (Hashimoto et al., 1989; Nowell, et al., 1990) were again found to occur more often in subjects with autism than in controls, and further studies yielded some evidence of smaller cerebellar areas in subjects with autism (Courchesne et al., 1988; Murakami et al., 1989). However, like most research involving individuals with autism, the results of these studies are variable. Margaret Bauman, a pediatric neurologist at Boston City Hospital, appears to have identified a consistent finding. Although the brains of individuals with autism are typically well developed with no gross abnormalities or lesions (Bauman, 1991), microscopic examination reveals a number of common abnormalities in the limbic system, cerebellum, and cerebellar circuits. To date, these abnormalities have included: 1) a marked loss of Purkinje cells, 2) retention of the fetal "circuits" that connect key neurons with the rest of the central nervous system, and 3) increased numbers of neurons in specific regions of the limbic system, hippocampus, and amygdala. Based on these findings, Bauman hypothesizes that autism is a disorder of early brain development (probably before 30 weeks of gestation) that curtails the development of the limbic system. Because the limbic system is associated with normal behavior, cognition, and memory, these abnormalities may play a prominent role in the social interaction, language, and learning difficulties characteristic of individuals with autism (Bauman, 1991).

Neurochemical Causes

In addition to the structural and microscopic abnormalities described above, a growing body of research is identifying significant neurochemical differences in individuals with autism. The most consistent finding in this area to date has been the identification of high levels of serotonin, a neurotransmitter, in between 25 and 40 percent of children and adolescents with autism

(Schain & Freedman, 1961; Cook, 1990; Gilman & Tuchman, 1995). Further research has implicated other neurochemical systems as well, including the dopaminergic and endogenous opioid systems.

Despite the consistency of some of these findings, researchers are still unsure of their significance. Early attempts to reduce brain serotonin with fenfluramine (Geller, Ritvo, Freeman & Yuwiler, 1982), for example, were met with initial success, but follow-up showed that these results were not durable. Subsequent studies supported the conclusion that fenfluramine is not an effective treatment for most individuals with autism (McDougle, Price & Volkmar, 1994). These disappointing findings indicate that the relationship between elevated serotonin levels and behavior is not a simple one, and is likely controlled by other, still unidentified, factors.

Neurochemical research, however, is a logical extension of neurobiological research. Now that researchers have identified the locations of structural abnormalities in the brains of individuals with autism, they can begin to look at the neurochemical profiles of these areas, which are likely to be abnormal (Bauman, 1992), and hopefully gain a more comprehensive understanding of the causes of autism.

Prenatal, Perinatal, and Neonatal Trauma

Several studies have examined the relationship between prenatal, perinatal, and neonatal complications and autism (Bryson, Smith & Eastwood, 1988; Mason-Brothers, Ritvo & Pingree et al., 1990; Nelson, 1991). However, when frequencies of specific complications such as maternal age, post-maturity, delivery complications, low Apgar scores, respiratory distress, and hyperbilirubinemia are compared in groups of individuals with autism and matched controls, few clear findings emerge. Although problems with pregnancy, delivery, and the neonatal period may be the cause of autism for certain individuals, these complications also cause other developmental disabilities and do not appear to be useful predictors of autism.

Uta Frith (1989), a research scientist at the MRC Cognitive Development Unit in London, believes that the current research suggests "we should not just think about 'the' cause for Autism, but about a long causal chain" (p. 80) and proposes a "hazard, havoc, harm" model:

> *...the hazard can be of many kinds, including faulty genes, chromosome abnormality, metabolic disorder, viral agents, immune intolerance and anoxia from perinatal problems. We can assume that any of these hazards has the potential to create havoc in neural development. Owing to the upheaval, lasting harm may be done to the development of specific brain systems concerned with higher mental processes. The harm may be mild or severe, but always involves the developmental arrest of a critical system at a critical point in time. It is our hypothesis that only then will Autism occur. (p. 80)*[5]

Frith's conceptual model is a good one, because it is grounded in the theory that autism is a biologically-based disorder and accounts for the current diversity of research findings.

No matter what theory of causation one finds plausible, it is critical to remember that autism is neither "otherworldly" nor "extraterrestrial." Autism is of this earth and is comprised of many symptoms that can be clinically defined and observed in people who do not have autism. By perpetuating the "mysticism" of autism, we inadvertently detract from treating the symptoms or determining its causes. As our understanding of the brain and medical technology advances, it is likely that more and more pieces will be found to the puzzle of autism and its "mystical" nature demystified.

WHAT CAN BE DONE TO HELP?

◆ ◆ ◆ ◆ ◆ ◆ ◆ ◆ ◆ ◆ ◆ ◆ ◆ ◆ ◆ ◆ ◆ ◆

The most effective way to help people with autism is to make appropriate treatment available. With effective treatment, people with autism can become productive and responsible members of society. The following chapter describes Eden's philosophy of treatment.

Along with effective treatment, people with autism need highly specialized educational, residential, and employment programs. This means that they may need services separate from those offered to mainstream society and individuals with other types of disabilities. Although many services for people with autism

---

[5] Frith, U. *Autism: Explaining the Enigma.* Cambridge, MA: Blackwell Publishers, 1988.

are mandated by federal law, several needed services are available only sporadically, or are not regulated by state or federal agencies. In fact, in the United States today there is a distinct lack of services for people with autism. The consequences of this lack are profound and debilitating to people with autism.

LACK OF SERVICES
◆ ◆ ◆ ◆ ◆ ◆ ◆ ◆ ◆ ◆ ◆ ◆ ◆ ◆ ◆ ◆ ◆

Given the relatively large number of children and adults with autism (approximately 400,000-500,000 in the United States) services available for people with autism are surprisingly scarce. For example, in 1985 there were fewer than 70 programs in the United States established to specifically serve the needs of children and adults with autism (Lauries, 1985). Of these 70 programs, fewer than 25 were established to serve adults with autism, and only approximately 15 of these 70 programs afforded community based residential services. In 1996 things have not improved much. Although there are more school-based services (inclusion) and home-based services (Lovaas), there are many more children than there are appropriate services. In addition, among services for children with autism, especially preschool children, more are turning to providing generic services rather than the highly specialized services that are needed (Bristol, 1996).[6] And for adults, the number of services for them has not increased since the 1985 study. There are four general consequences to this dearth of services.

1. Many people with autism simply have no placement in a specialized educational, residential, or employment program. They often live at home with their mother and father, who have not received training in how to manage their child's behavioral and learning problems effectively.

2. People with autism are placed in secure or semi-secure programs in state institutions which cannot effectively address their specialized needs. Similarly, several of the programs available for people with autism are generic educational or employment programs which are not specialized enough to address their unique learning styles.

3. Many people with autism are placed in programs outside their home state. Although this type of placement may be most appropriate for the person with autism, it often ends up costing the home state as much as one to two hundred thousand dollars a year.

4. Due to the variety of theories concerning the cause of autism, many programs provide services that are not strongly based on scientific evidence. Myths surrounding the cause or causes of autism persist despite emerging scientific advances. These myths can lead to caring, but naive, services which are based on outdated methodological practices.

---

6 Bristol, Marie. (1996). "The State of the Science in Autism: Beyond the Silver Bullet," in *Proceedings of the Eden Institute Foundation Princeton Lecture Series on Autism: Affecting the Research and Service Agenda,* Princeton, NJ: The Eden Press.

ENTITLEMENTS

Although services have not kept up with demand, parents and professionals continue to advocate for services for people with autism, and the number of services entitled by law continues to grow. Currently, children with autism (individuals under the age of twenty-one) are entitled to free and appropriate educational services, and related services such as speech and occupational therapy, under IDEA, the Individuals with Disabilities Education Act. This comprehensive law, first enacted in 1975 as the Education for All Handicapped Children Act, vastly improved the educational services available to all children with disabilities and continues to mandate children's rights to these services.[7]

Services for adults are much more scarce, and typically are characterized by waiting lists measured in years. Cases being decided by the Supreme Court, however, are setting precedents for the provision of appropriate, community-based residential and employment programming for individuals with autism over the age of twenty-one.[8]

CONCLUSION

"While autism was described almost simultaneously by Leo Kanner and Hans Asperger in the 1940s, Kanner seemed to see it as an unmitigated disaster where

Asperger felt that it might have certain positive or compensating features—a 'particular originality of thought and experience which may well lead to exceptional achievement later in life' " (Sacks, 1995, p. 245). Although autism is certainly a lifelong disorder, the effect it will have on the individual is by no means certain. Eden believes that early identification and treatment lead to a much more positive prognosis for both the individual and his family and that with effective treatment, all individuals will experience their own "exceptional achievements" throughout their lives. The following chapters describe the philosophy and service delivery systems that make this possible.

---

[7]   Chapter 5 more fully describes the history of this law and its current entitlements for individuals with autism.

[8]   Please see Chapter 9, "Adults with Autism."

Chapter **3**

Eden's

. . . .

Philosophy of

. . . .

Treatment

. . . .

This chapter presents the principles Eden follows in treating people with autism, and discusses the ways Eden deals with some of the common treatment problems faced by agencies serving people with autism.

GENERAL TENETS OF TREATMENT

Treating people with autism is perhaps most difficult because of the moment by moment challenges they present. Teachers and parents have to be able to anticipate, redirect, and encourage the person's impulses during every exchange every day. They have to be caring but firm, demanding but patient, energetic but calming, and, above all they have to have respect for the person. They must be able to see each person as an individual who is capable of improving, and of taking an active part in that improvement. They must provide the support the person needs, but maintain his integrity as a valuable and responsible person.

Juggling these attributes is not easy, but it is essential to enhancing the self esteem and growth of people with autism. The sections below discuss these principles of treatment and how they are applied to the day-to-day teaching of people with autism at Eden.

INDIVIDUALS FIRST

People with autism are people first who happen to have a condition called autism. Just as every person is different, every person with autism is different, and so no single treatment program works well for all people with autism. As the parents of Spike, Eric, and Erica Lofgren put it:

> *Someone with autism may have, say, eight out of twelve characteristics in DSM IV—three from column 1, two from column 2, and three from column 3. With all the permutations, there can be very different people, all with a diagnosis of autism.*

It is tempting to look for those people with autism who "fit" neatly into a program, those with particular characteristics, deficits, or levels of ability. Eden adapts its program to fit the needs of the individual person with autism. Noreen Miele, Assistant Director of Employment Services at Eden:

> *Although the basic teaching approach is the same for every person at Eden, everything is individualized. We may use one technique for several different people, but the implementation of that technique is adapted to each person. For example, two students who are learning to set the table may have very different abilities. One may respond well to physical touch, while another finds touch extremely aversive, but follows simple verbal commands well. Teachers would use a prompting strategy for both students, but would use primarily physical prompts with one, and mostly verbal prompts with the other.*

Cyndy Grunning, Eden's Supervisor of Clinical Services:

> *The neurological problems of some of our students cause them to forget, in the middle of an assembly task, whether they are putting an item together or taking it apart. So we constructed a box with a slit on top. When they finish an item, they slide it into the slot, thereby signifying completion. That way, there is only one progression to the skill, so they do not get confused. Other students do not have that problem, and so do not need the specialized box as a prompt.*

Teachers at Eden design programs tailored to each individual. Once developed, these programs are flexible, but never chaotic. They change in a deliberate way as the needs of the person with autism change.[1] Parents, Eric and Erica Lofgren:

> *Spike's strengths and weaknesses are backward from some of the other children at Eden. He forms personal relationships easily enough, but has a difficult time learning language. His teachers at Eden used that in developing programming for him, rather than putting him into a*

---

[1]   The flexibility of Eden's behavior management programs is described in more detail in Chapters 6 (Modifying Behavior) and 7 (EDM). The flexibility of curricular programs is presented in Chapter 8 (Curriculum).

mold he did not fit in. They build on his strengths, rather than ask him to fit a program they had already designed. The program they designed for Spike was his program, totally individualized.

Because there is such a wide range of strengths and needs among people with autism, it is important to be able to see each person individually. Understanding precisely how the various characteristics of autism are manifested in a particular person allows a teacher to be more effective in designing programs to reach the person, to connect with him, and to get him on a learning track.

EXPECTATIONS AND SUCCESS

Individualizing programs for each person means that the expectations and definitions of success will be different. Some students at Eden have progressed very quickly, and have been able to graduate from Eden's programs into less specialized settings. Others, however, may require a lifetime of intensive supports. In setting expectations, teachers at Eden look at each person's abilities and deficits, and are guided by the person's history of skill acquisition.

> What Eden tries to do is find the personality inside of the child with autism, and then develop this personality. They know that socially and academically a child may be very different, and they build on these differences to find the child. The process is a very natural one.
>
> —Sasha and Dasha Polyakov

Expectations are outlined in each person's Individualized Education Plan (IEP), for students, or Individualized Habilitation Plan (IHP), mainly for adults.[2] The IEP or IHP provides a map which helps teachers guide the person's development. Because the therapeutic path each person needs to take is often different, no person's IEP or IHP should be identical to another's.

◆ ◆

Below is a summary of two students' IEPs for the 1993-1994 school year. Jaime and Tommy are about the same age, but have very different skills. Jaime is 10 years, 5 months old, and is in the Middle Childhood Program. Tommy is 10 years, 6 months old, and is in the Transition Program. The performance levels and goals outlined here are detailed in their IEPs.

SUMMARY OF PERFORMANCE FOR JAIME

- ◆ Jaime sits correctly for 2-3 seconds when given the *Sd* (discriminative stimulus) "sit quiet."
- ◆ Jaime places a washer on a bolt.
- ◆ Jaime flushes the toilet independently.
- ◆ Jaime is currently on a 40-45 minute toileting schedule.
- ◆ Jaime picks up one object and places it in a container.
- ◆ Jaime uses his augmentative communication device with gestural prompts.
- ◆ Jaime responds appropriately to simple one step commands.
- ◆ Jaime gives and maintains eye contact on command. *(continued)*

---

[2] The process of developing IEPs and IHPs at Eden is described in Chapters 8 and 9.

PROGRAM GOALS FOR JAIME

Attending:
- ◆ Jamie will sit appropriately in a chair for 10 seconds.
- ◆ Jaime will accurately follow six one-step commands.

Self-Care:
- ◆ Jaime will wash his hands.
- ◆ Jaime will use a washcloth and clean his face thoroughly.
- ◆ Jaime will move a toothbrush over his teeth with correct pressure.
- ◆ Jaime will increase his toileting schedule to 1 hour.

Vocational:
- ◆ Jaime will place four sets of objects into containers.
- ◆ Jaime will fill a pegboard with pegs.

Domestic:
- ◆ Jaime will complete table setting by placing cups on table.
- ◆ Jaime will retrieve a wet sponge and wipe tables until clean.
- ◆ Jaime will rinse silverware and place in dishwasher.
- ◆ Jaime will put clean plates away on a shelf.
- ◆ Jaime will swing a broom in a pendulum motion while standing still and looking at bristles.
- ◆ Jaime will manipulate vacuum back and forth over a section of rug.
- ◆ Jaime will load a washing machine.
- ◆ Jaime will place wet clothes in a dryer.
- ◆ Jaime will fold towels and place in a laundry basket.

Communication:
- ◆ Jaime will request preferred items and activities using a voice-output computer.
- ◆ Jaime will receptively identify common objects.
- ◆ Jaime will nod his head to indicate "yes" and shake his head to indicate "no."

Motor:
- ◆ Jaime will demonstrate appropriate balance reactions.
- ◆ Jaime will tolerate varying types and degrees of tactile stimulation.
- ◆ Jaime will manipulate therapy putty to develop grasping skills.
- ◆ Jaime will develop age-appropriate gross motor skills.
- ◆ Jaime will increase cardiovascular fitness and flexibility.

Activity distribution for Jaime in hours per week:

Speech and language therapy	1.5	Preacademics/academics	0
Physical education	3.5	Prevocational/vocational	7.5
Music/art activities	2.5	Socialization	.25
Domestics	3.0	Self-care skills	1.5
Meal preparation/consumption	2.25	Other:	1.0

• •

SUMMARY OF PERFORMANCE FOR TOMMY

In mathematics:

- ◆ Tommy performs two and three digit computations in addition and subtraction.
- ◆ Tommy performs multiplication operations with one digit multiplier.
- ◆ Tommy performs division operations with one digit divisor.
- ◆ Tommy recognizes and draws basic geometric shapes.
- ◆ Tommy finds the equivalency of dollars in coins and makes change up to $2.
- ◆ Tommy needs verbal cues to solve addition and subtraction story problems.
- ◆ Tommy knows fractional parts of a whole, and numerator and denominator.
- ◆ Tommy knows basic geometry concepts, including line segments, end points, angles, right angles, plane figures, and congruent figures.
- ◆ Tommy has learned about the metric system in measurement.

In written language:

- ◆ Tommy writes complete sentences, with basic capitalization and punctuation.
- ◆ Tommy fills out basic information forms.
- ◆ Tommy applies spelling skills in writing.

In language arts vocabulary:

- ◆ Tommy uses a dictionary to select the meaning of a word.
- ◆ Tommy has learned decoding and word structure skills in the following areas:

  use of long and short vowel sounds, consonant blends.
  use of all punctuation.
  alphabetical order, syllabication, compound words.
  use of suffixes and recognition of root words.
  vocabulary skills using synonyms, homonyms, and antonyms.

In reading comprehension:

- ◆ Tommy follows facts and details, and answers who, what, why, and how.
- ◆ Tommy identifies correct order of story events with minimal verbal prompts.
- ◆ Tommy fills in sentence blanks with words that match the context.
- ◆ Tommy reads and follows simple directions.
- ◆ Tommy needs verbal cues to infer main ideas in a paragraph.
- ◆ Tommy knows common vocabularies of space, weather, and plant science.
- ◆ Tommy uses a map and legends to answer questions.
- ◆ Tommy reads graphs and locates information on them. *(continued)*

PROGRAM GOALS FOR TOMMY

In mathematics, Tommy will:

- ◆ Increase computation skills and simple problem solving in a regular textbook.
- ◆ Increase measurement concepts following both customary and metric units.
- ◆ Increase money concepts by learning to compare money and make change.
- ◆ Learn to collect data and construct graphs, tables, and charts.
- ◆ Learn problem solving using a pictograph.
- ◆ Learn the basic meaning of fractions (halves, thirds, fourths, etc.)
- ◆ Identify and find perimeter of polygons (pentagon, hexagon, and octagon).
- ◆ Write fraction numerals, and know fractional parts of groups.
- ◆ Add fractions with common denominators.
- ◆ Recognize decimals to tenths.
- ◆ Measure length, capacity, and weight using metric and customary units.
- ◆ Identify plane region, and find area by counting squares.
- ◆ Create bar graphs, and read and interpret line graphs.

In written language, Tommy will:

- ◆ Recognize and develop complete sentences following activities of interest.
- ◆ Use complete sentences in developing short 4-5 line paragraphs.
- ◆ Practice cursive writing by copying facts and information.

In language arts, Tommy will:

- ◆ Review parts of speech, capitalization, punctuation, and language skills.
- ◆ Expand functional vocabulary by using vocabulary boosters.

In reading comprehension, Tommy will:

- ◆ Develop comprehension, thinking, and reading skills in analogies, classification, similarities and differences, and absurdities.
- ◆ Use charts to discover facts.
- ◆ Create/interpret tables/graphs by gathering and organizing information.

In science, Tommy will:

- ◆ Learn additional vocabulary of weather, plants, space, and the body systems.
- ◆ Develop map reading skills.
- ◆ Learn computer terms to develop computer awareness.
- ◆ Learn about good nutrition, exercise, and grooming.

(continued)

Additional goals for Tommy:
- ◆ Increase functional vocational skills.
- ◆ Increase clerical skills.
- ◆ Develop appropriate leisure skills with playing computer/ developmental games.
- ◆ Increase social and language skills through community outings.
- ◆ Increase cardiovascular fitness and flexibility, expand spatial awareness, gross motor skills, and balance and vestibular processing skills.

Activity distribution for Tommy in hours per week:

Speech and language therapy:	2.5	Preacademics/academics:	5.0
Physical education:	2.5	Prevocational/vocational:	2.0
Music/art activities:	1.0	Socialization:	2.5
Domestics:	3.5	Self-care skills:	0.5
Meal preparation/consumption:	5.0	Other (Computer):	0.5

SUCCESS

Just as what is expected of the person with autism is different, what is defined as success is also individualized. What is success for one student may be considered just a step in a bigger process for a different student, who is held to higher expectations. Cyndy Grunning:

> *Valerie, a young woman in the Vocational Preparation Program, got very excited when, for the first time, she collated ten sets of letters by herself. She is twenty-one, and we have been working on sorting for several years. Afterward, she signed on our reinforcer sheet that she wanted a snack box of raisins because she understood that she did them correctly.*
>
> *Someone else, like Eric, could be given pages of unsorted letters which required more refined abilities to sort. They might have to look for the page numbers, addresses, or zip codes in order to complete the task.*

When I go to other programs for consultations, I try not to read a child's IEP beforehand because I don't want to have any preconceptions. I want to look freshly at the child, his environment, and what techniques might be best for him. For example, I don't want to know that teachers have been employing several different techniques to get him to sit in his chair for group activities. I want to see him in the group activity, see how he reacts, and come up with my own ideas about why he squirms and what might help him learn to sit more appropriately. Maybe I'll see something the teachers didn't, or maybe, by seeing him in a different light, I'll be able to come up with solutions that work.

—Cyndy Grunning, Supervisor of Clinical Services

With different expectations for people working on the same skill program, each person's success can be measured relative to their level of functioning. For example, some students may learn how to brush their teeth without much difficulty, but one person may begin the program not even able to hold a toothbrush. It could take a number of years for him to learn all of the component skills necessary to brush his teeth independently. Teachers' expectations for him must be different. If toothbrushing is taught as a group activity, teachers must be able to help him hold his toothbrush, while helping other students work on the step of the skill they have been able to achieve, such as squeezing the toothpaste tube, rinsing, or putting their brush away. It is important that what teachers consider "success" is different for every student, even in group activities.

Expectations and definitions of success for each student must be set individually, but they must also be challenging for the student. They must be high, but within reach. Challenging the student with the right balance of ease and difficulty enables him to learn as much as possible while moderating frustration.

PARTICIPANTS VERSUS CLIENTS

Eden's philosophy of treatment is reflected in the way in which the people with autism it serves are referred. It first avoids using the term "client." The term "client" gives the impression of receiving, or even purchasing treatment, and implies a passiveness in the treatment process on the part of the individual with autism. The process of teaching skills to a person with autism and modifying the person's behavior, however, is not something that can be given to a person. The person himself has to play an active part in the process or the process does not work.

Faculty and staff at Eden prefer the term "participant." Participant implies that the person is a partner—an active partner—in the teaching process. A participant is a respected partner with everyone involved in the educational process. Although the purpose of the process is to achieve educational and behavioral goals for the person with autism, the teacher learns a great deal as well from the exchange. For example, more has been learned about how human beings acquire skills from research and interaction with those with autism than has ever been learned from rhesus monkeys, pigeons, rats, or other animal studies. People with autism have done more to improve the quality of teaching for all children and adults than any form of non-human research.

The differences between "client" and "participant," however, are not just matters of superficial impression. Treating members of a program as participants enables them to have a subtle, but important, role in the development of their programming. Treating people as participants forces teachers to pay more attention to the person when making programming decisions, even though their input is often not explicitly communicated. For example, Donald's programming changed as the result of his behavior. Donald was working in a ceramics production activity in an employment center. Ceramics is one of Eden's secure employment options.

He was becoming frustrated and angry because of his poor motor coordination. He tended to crush the pieces. He did not have the fine motor dexterity and concentration to handle them. He also started being aggressive toward others and himself. Teachers at the center tried to help him accommodate to the demands of the skill, but he still was not doing well. His teachers decided that, although ceramics production is a core part of the center's employment program, the work was not good for Donald. He was then given a job that enabled him to work more successfully and independently. His outbursts of unacceptable behavior went down significantly. His job now is to clean and do general maintenance around the employment center with a self-monitoring schedule and minimal supervision. Donald could not necessarily articulate his frustrations, but he knew that teachers had expectations of him that he could not meet. In response to his behavior—the only way Donald knew of to communicate his frustration—his teachers changed his work, and found something he was able to do, and he found it gratifying.

We perceive the people at Eden as actively participating in the learning process as opposed to just being served by the process. We don't have a lawyer-client type of relationship, where the client pays the lawyer and the lawyer performs a service for the client. It's a mutually productive experience. We help them learn, but we actually learn, literally on a daily basis, as much if not more from them than they learn from us.

For example, we have been taught so much about human learning and autism itself by watching the participants develop their own sense about things. In greater degrees of skill acquisition and independence, our goal is to challenge them, but if they demonstrate difficulties in a program, and can give us a good reason for not wanting to do the program, we give them a break. We can understand where they're coming from. One participant, for instance, was having problems learning to staple in his collating job. Through some of his other behaviors, we figured out that he didn't like to push the stapler down because of the loud noise it made. We said okay. Now he's using paper clips, and is doing just fine.

We're always learning, especially out in the community, what it takes to support participants. Even for the same person in the same job on a day-to-day basis, almost on an hour-to-hour basis, we are constantly learning what it takes to enable them to be as independent as possible.

—**Peter Gerhardt, Director of Employment Services**

"As If"

Eden believes that if a person is treated as if he is a respected member of society and has the potential to reach greater goals, he will rise to meet those expectations. Some goals may be high, like sustaining a job independently or being able to live without constant supports, but these goals are worked toward with smaller, shorter-term objectives, such as learning how to take a work break, or how to do laundry. Holding high goals for people helps keep the programs focused on what they need to do, because the bigger goal is always there to measure progress against. High goals help create an atmosphere of dynamic learning and progress in a program. They keep teachers challenging students to do their best.

It is especially important to have high goals in programs for adults with autism. Too often, programs for adults revert to a care-giving, less challenging approach because the adults are out of the school system, and are of an age when most people without disabilities turn their focus from education to other things, like a family or career. But people with autism can and need to keep learning throughout their lives. There will always be skills they could learn which would increase their level of independence, but they need to continually be presented with the opportunities to learn these skills.

> We recently discussed Eden's "as if" philosophy with a parent who thought we were pushing her son too hard. She didn't think he could succeed in a community job that we wanted to place him in, and thought we should change our expectations. We explained to her that once we do that, once we lower our expectations of what any person can do, we might as well quit. We have to believe that everybody is capable of maintaining community employment. If we pick and choose who can work in the community and who can't, we're doing them a huge disservice. It's our responsibility to find out how to make the situation work, what supports to give to enable the person to work in that job.
>
> —**Tyffini Dodge, Supervisor, Briggs Center**

The philosophy that people be treated "as if" they can accomplish their goals makes the atmosphere at Eden one of constant learning and encouragement. It helps teachers keep long-term goals in focus while setting short-term objectives to get there.

Treating a person as if he can do something, especially something difficult, gives him respect and dignity. It says "You can do this. You are a valuable person." It challenges him to accomplish his goals and respects his attempts at reaching those goals. Steven, for example, had been learning to tie his neck tie, and finally did actually tie it. It was a good attempt, but was not perfect. His teacher at the time, Cyndy Grunning, explains:

> Steven needs to wear a tie to work at a nearby Wawa food market, and we have been helping him. One morning I held the bottom part of it and was verbally guiding him through the movements. He did it, and did a

good job, but the back of the neck tie came out about five inches longer than the front part. However, it was the first time he had actually tied it without a hand over hand prompt, and his apron would cover the back part anyway, so we left it. The important thing was that he did it himself. He was very excited when he did it and said to another teacher who came in "Nina, I tied my tie." It was important to him, and helped increase his self-esteem.

What we provide is as much structure as our participants need, but can't create on their own. For some individuals it may be a tight structure, and for others a loose structure, but we're always going to have to provide some amount of structure, at least as much as we all have in our own lives. I live by my own personal schedule. I have my date book, and absolutely depend on it. For some of the individuals in our group homes, a calendar on the wall may be sufficient, or a monthly or daily schedule may be better. The amount of structure needed is assessed and reassessed regularly.

—**Annette Cavallaro,**
Assistant Director of Residential Services

The "as if" philosophy also makes a person responsible for his actions. For example, if a person is treated as if he is capable of sitting quietly at the table while food is being served, even though, because he is hungry and agitated, he upsets the table sending plates and utensils everywhere, he must expect to clean up the mess himself. He will now have to wait for his food while he helps clean the area and put the table straight again, then wait until everyone is again seated quietly before he is served. Treating him just as any typical person would be treated teaches him that his actions have consequences, and that he is responsible for what he does. This helps move the person toward the ultimate goal Eden holds for all people it serves: independence and a productive life with all the joy and sorrow that it brings. Oliver Sacks (1995) calls it the "full estate of man," the grandeur and misery of being human.

> *The qualities that a person needs to have to be helpful to a person with autism are many. First, see the person as an individual and realize that no two people with autism are alike.... Second, have patience with the person with autism. They are trying as hard as they can and often get frustrated.... Third, focus on the person's strengths and not their weaknesses. I most certainly know mine, but I also know that I have some strengths that Autism has given me. Fourth, be yourself with the person with autism.... We are people, not a label. I have autism, I am not autism. Jean-Paul Bovee[3] (1996, p. 9-10)*

---

[3] Jean-Paul Bovee is manager of the Missouri Developmental Disabilities Resources Center located at University of Missouri-Kansas City Institute for Human Development, a University Affiliated Program. He has his masters degree in Medieval and Roman History from the University of Kansas and a masters in Library and Information Sciences from the University of Missouri-Columbia. Jean-Paul is an adult who lives with the challenges of autism, and cares a great deal about helping others with disabilities.

PROSTHETIC ENVIRONMENT

The term "prosthetic environment" was coined at Eden to define the highly specialized therapeutic setting that has been created for the people Eden serves. They are provided with an environment that is highly focused and structured, with systematic expectations, and with consequences to behavior. It is designed to reduce the individual's confusion and anxiety, thereby increasing his willingness to step out into life, rather than fearing life's consequences. The supports offered in a prosthetic environment may be as simple as assistance in getting dressed in the morning so a person can go to work. Or, it could be more involved, with a person requiring around the clock encouragement and prompting to accomplish the tasks he needs to navigate through each day.

Most often, the prosthesis people with autism need is a structure for their lives. They need to know when things will occur and what they will have to do to accomplish something. This prosthesis enables them to live full, productive lives. Again, Oliver Sacks (1995) alludes to this prosthetic need because people with autism do not live in a so called "universe" but rather a "'multiverse': consisting of innumerable, unconnected though intensely vivid particulars...'a collection of moments'" (p. 242).

In the field of regular education it is generally expected that by the age of eighteen or twenty-one, an individual will be capable of living independently. For people with autism, however, this expectation is often unrealistic, and measuring their success against such norms is often unrealistic. People with autism who require some sort of prosthesis after graduation, such as a job coach or someone to organize their daily schedule, are not failures because they are not 100 percent independent. The fact that they are actually able to hold a job and follow a daily schedule are indications of success as a responsible member of society.

Without a prosthetic environment, people with autism who need extra support do not receive it. If they cannot dress themselves, for example, they will not be able to work. If someone has not learned by the time he leaves the school system how to do his laundry, how to shower, how to prepare meals, and even, perhaps, how to use and clean dentures, he will not learn how if he does not have a support system to help him learn these skills.

Even if a person has learned a variety of skills by age twenty-one, Eden's experience indicates that he may lose them if he does not continue to be in a supportive, learning environment. For example, when Claire turned twenty-one, she graduated from her school placement, but had no where to go. A place in a group home was not yet available, and there was no transportation to enable her to attend an employment center. Claire's mother worked, and there was not even a day program Claire could attend, so she spent her day in the house, watching TV. Claire's unacceptable behaviors, such as hitting herself, began to increase, and she became less active, less participatory in life. She spent more and more hours a day in bed. Claire was not capable of teaching herself, and no longer had an environment supportive of her daily living needs. She regressed rapidly and was generally unhappy.

—**Peter Gerhardt, Director of Employment Services**

Rather than disabling them in the "real world," the dependence they have in a prosthetic environment enables them to take part in that world to the greatest extent they are able. And, they are able, with the proper supports, to be members of the "real community," instead of being outside it.

There is an individual in one of our group homes who I've known as long as I've been at Eden, 12 years. I was initially his teacher. He has always had the potential, I feel, of achieving a great degree of independence. He is higher functioning, has fairly good verbal skills, and can pretty much follow directions. But when he started at Eden, he had not been working with personal schedules. He also had some behavior that was interfering with his learning, so we were addressing the behaviors as well as teaching basic skills. At this point, with consistent use of schedules and structure, and simply teaching with fading prompts, he now works completely with his own schedule. He needs minimal supervision from staff. In fact, the only time he seeks out supervision is when he wants someone to check what he's doing. He'll come over and say "Can you please check my work?" and then he proceeds to the next step. He's also working independently part time out of Eden WERCs at a Wawa store. I know that he is where he is because we have provided him with consistent supports which we continually monitor, and will continue to fade. It would be wonderful if we could get him to the point of a full time job; I don't believe that's out of the question. It's just a matter of consistency and reassessing the level and intensity of each specific prosthetic procedure he needs.

—**Annette Cavallaro, Assistant Director of Residential Services**

Educational and lifetime prostheses extended to people with autism are really no different from prostheses used by people with other disabilities. Just as a child with diabetes who receives insulin injections still needs them after graduating from high school, and just as a person who needs a wheelchair during his school years continues to use it after graduation, an individual with autism who requires a specialized environment during his school years will, upon becoming an adult, require a continuation of that environment in some form in order to continue learning the skills he needs to be more fully independent. Logic dictates

When Jaime was in the Early Childhood Program, he made great gains during the school year, but after summer vacation, teachers found that he had lost almost all of what he had learned. During his second year, as expected, the same thing happened. He learned so much, and then lost most of it after the brief break (two weeks) between the summer program and the regular school year. As Jaime moved into the Middle Childhood Program, we hoped that the increased demands placed on children in Middle Childhood would stimulate him to retain more.

When Jaime got to Middle Childhood, he just took off. He learned quickly, and maintained the skills he learned. The demand level was just right for him. If we had stuck with the prompting criteria we had set for him in Early Childhood, he would still be relying on us to help him complete skills that he now does independently and retains when not in the program.

—**Cheryl Bomba, Assistant Director for Technical Support**

We determine how much help somebody needs by assessing what skills they already have. There are a variety of ways in which we do that. When somebody enters into the group home, we do an assessment of the skills they have and we review previous medical, educational, and psychological records, look at the family history, skill levels, behavior histories, and so forth. We make an assessment based on the past, and then with our ongoing assessment procedures we're able to assess how much training they need.

There's a very delicate balance to be found in providing a prosthetic environment. There is a need for prosthetics, but it's our goal and our duty to determine what the appropriate type and intensity is. We continue evaluating and assessing each individual's needs to keep an appropriate balance of supports and independence in their environment.

—**Michelle Brooks, Coordinator of Group Home Operations**

that the prostheses must be available for as long as the individual requires them. The need does not change simply because the person turns twenty-one.

Although a prosthetic environment is crucial to help people with autism navigate their world, prostheses can be relied upon too much. For example, if someone were dressed every morning because he could not dress himself, he could learn to be helpless in the situation, and not even attempt it.

Teachers can make sure people do not become dependent on prostheses by constantly evaluating how much and what type of support is needed. At Eden, teachers review supports on a basic level during each teaching session. The larger supports, such as dressing or using the bathroom, are composed of many smaller steps, which are, again, assessed during each teaching session. It is through each of the smaller steps that a person is slowly weaned from support. For example, if a student's task is to carry verbal messages to a teacher, he will start by walking down the hall with another teacher, being brought to the correct room, and being prompted to give the verbal message. As he learns to do each of these steps on his own, he will need less and less support to be able to deliver messages.[4]

Eden's ultimate goal is to no longer be needed to provide supports. This goal is admittedly distant for most of the people Eden serves, but it is essential for teachers and families to keep in mind so they provide only the degree of prostheses required, and so those who can be independent are given the necessary resources to be so. Eden's Director of Employment Services, Peter Gerhardt, describes this goal as it pertains to adults:

Our goal is to get all participants out working independently in the community, and so is, in a sense, to work ourselves out of a job. But in

---

[4] However, there are some larger supports that most people with autism will always need, such as help scheduling doctor and dental appointments to maintain their physical health. Skills requiring foresight, judgment, creativity and flexibility, and other skills which people with autism do not usually learn to perform independently, such as taking care of their personal health needs, are discussed later in this chapter.

the back of our minds we realize that there are always going to be more people who need the services we provide. Transferring all the participants here to independent settings is not a daunting possibility; it is what we are trying to do. Realistically, it is probably not going to happen for the majority of participants, but that is the goal for all of us.

Most people with autism, especially those who are more severely challenged, do require some form of prostheses in order to function productively. They need an environment which, not unlike any prosthesis, enables them to feel more secure, less anxious, and better able to focus on learning.

PLAYING GOD WITH PEOPLE'S LIVES

Providing a prosthetic environment means that choices will be made for a person. Dressing one's self, for example, is taught at Eden if a person cannot dress himself, but the decision that dressing one's self is an important skill is not made by the person with autism. It is made by those helping him learn the skills he needs to be independent. Because providing supports to a person with autism means that at least some decisions are made for him, it could be described as "playing God" with the person's life. There are several reasons why Eden believes that such an intervention into a person's life is necessary.

Many people with autism, especially those more severely challenged, are unable to speak for themselves. Because of neurological or physical difficulties, or due to the communication difficulties people with autism have, they can often not voice their opinions, or do not have opinions. People with autism frequently cannot make appropriate decisions for themselves either, or would make decisions that would be considered nonfunctional, nonproductive, or even dangerous. For example, a person with autism could decide to engage in finger-playing instead of learning how to button a shirt, or may decide to stop in the middle of a crosswalk (as seen in the movie *Rain Man)* without understanding the consequences of the decision.

These are indeed "decisions," but people with autism have different "reality rules" upon which they make decisions. Their decisions often serve to alienate them from the larger community. Finger-playing excludes someone from participating in a family dinner, and sets them apart as different when it occurs in a community setting. For a person with autism, the rules of conduct are simply different, and so what the person decides to do will be different.

The different reality rules of a person with autism should not be confused with the person's individual choices and preferences. A person with autism may make decisions about his behavior that, because of his autism, alienate him from society, but the person also, just like anybody else, makes decisions about things he likes and dislikes. He may like chocolate ice cream better than vanilla, or may prefer jumping on a trampoline to walking on a treadmill. These are really more the individual's personal choices and preferences than decisions. They are expressions of his individuality, and must be respected. They are different in scope than choices such as eating only chocolate ice cream, because they bring the person into greater social reality, rather than separate him from it.

The choices and preferences of a person with autism should be encouraged, but nonfunctional, maladaptive decisions the person makes should not be encouraged. They may serve to avoid a difficult task or situation, to inappropriately express frustration, or to cause an upset the person finds amusing, and so they do serve a purpose of sorts, but these purposes are dysfunctional. They keep the individual from participating in his community, and so are self-limiting.

Because people with autism can often not speak or make decisions for themselves, their parents and teachers must make some decisions for them, especially regarding the direction and goals of treatment. Parents and teachers need to plan for what skills the person with autism will need. Job skills, self-care skills, and the ability to behave appropriately are things a person with autism needs, but would not necessarily learn on his own. Consequently, parents and teachers need to make a plan for him to learn these skills.

This plan is in the form of the person's Individual Education Plan (IEP) and Individualized Habilitation Plan (IHP), and should be designed with the person's individual strengths and weaknesses in mind. Some people need only generalized

long term goals to keep them learning, while others require highly specified step-by-step objectives. However involved parents and teachers need to be in planning for the future of the person, the goal of the plan must be to lead the person toward independence.

All people, with or without autism, are better off if they are able to provide for their own needs as much as they possibly can. They should have to rely on help from others as little as possible in their personal needs. Others may not always be around to help them take care of their needs, or funds may cease to be available for the services they rely on. For people with autism, this means that parents and teachers must intervene in their lives, prevent them from following dysfunctional choices, and teach them as much functional behavior as they can learn as soon as possible.

Because the people Eden serves may need support for their entire lifetime, it is especially important that teachers at Eden intervene and teach independence skills. For example, Eden does not have the option of focusing on academics instead of vocational skills because Eden must find the person a job when he is old enough to work. Because the person may be with Eden the rest of his life, Eden has a real stake in the person's functional knowledge.

INTERVENTION MEANS TEACHING VALUES

Some people may see Eden's intervention in the lives of people with autism as denying them the right to choose for themselves what to learn. Others believe that the only proper environment for a person with autism is a value-neutral environment, where a person decides for himself what is important. But can a value-neutral environment really be created? A value-neutral environment includes ideas such as "People exercise rights," "People decide how to use their free time," and "People perform different social roles." These all seem relatively value free, but what about "People have friends," or "People participate in the life of the community"? The idea that having friends is important is a value. And the idea that participating in the community is important is a value. Even the idea that someone should receive support when needed is a value. So, in order to have a truly value-neutral environment, a person with autism would have to decide for himself that he wants help, and what form that help should take. Unfortunately, many people with autism are simply not capable of making that decision.

Eden believes strongly in instilling basic values in the people it serves. Teachers at Eden teach students to appreciate physical contact as rewarding, to have a rudimentary work ethic, and to control unacceptable impulses. Eden teaches responsibility for one's behavior, respect for one's self and others, respect for property and the law, and respect for one's benefactor, such as one's employer, teacher, or parent.[5] Most of the people Eden serves do not consciously recognize these as values, but they can learn to follow them through consistent and encouraging teaching programs.

The values that Eden works to instill in the people it serves are values that most children learn with ease. These values, which are deliberately and specifically taught to the people Eden serves, are only the base from which typical children begin their education. For example, on entering regular education, a typical child knows that people are different, and may be given a project to teach him to appreciate people's cultural differences. A child with autism, on the other hand, may need to be taught even the most basic premise that people are different from inanimate objects. In addition, teaching responsibility for one's actions is a deeply held value at Eden. This comes with relative ease to a typical child, but for a child with autism it takes a great deal of effort. These basic values that many people with autism lack are one of the biggest obstacles to their involvement in their communities.

By teaching values, Eden does "usurp" the right of those it serves to choose their own values. But without these basic values, access to larger communities would be extremely limited. In teaching values, Eden promotes the more important right of those it serves to be productive, included members of their communities. Eden views intervention as its obligation.

---

[5] See Chapter 6 for a definition of these values, and a description of how Eden teaches some of them.

URGENCY VERSUS VIGILANCE

During the early years of a child with autism, teachers must have an urgent approach toward teaching if the child is to make as much progress as possible. Urgency means having a pressing need to help the child learn and grow. As the child gets older and enters his adult years, the approach to treatment should gradually shift to one primarily of vigilance, or keeping watch over skills that have already been learned.

Why this shift of focus? Using an urgent treatment approach at the outset of a diagnosis of autism enables teachers and families to quickly address the many unacceptable attributes that so often develop early in children with autism, such as temper tantrums, aggression toward others, or making loud disturbing vocalizations. Diane Van Driesen, Supervisor of Infant and Toddler Services, describes the urgent approach in use at Eden's program for infants and toddlers, Wawa House:

> At Wawa House, we start teaching urgently about two and a half weeks into the program. We get the children sitting, looking, and attending. We work through a lot of extreme tantrums, and work to eliminate any self stimulating behavior we see. We also get the parents actively participating. The children can move so fast because they are younger, and more malleable. And they often have less symptomatology than children identified at later ages. Rigid patterns of behavior are not usually habitual when the children are so young, or they have not actually developed, so we see much milder symptomatology, and we are able to teach the children appropriate responses to life's demands.

An urgent approach should be maintained for as long as a child continues learning new skills while maintaining skills he has learned. As with the Lovaas method (Boodman, 1995), the discrete trial teaching[6] used at Eden accelerates the child's progress, and enables that progress to be quantified. This allows teachers to know exactly how well the child is doing. If the data collected during training sessions begins to show that learning has slowed, teachers implement troubleshooting procedures[7] to determine the cause. Troubleshooting will either identify ways to remedy the problem, or indicate that teachers need to begin shifting to a more vigilant treatment approach to maintain the gains made by the student. This usually occurs around the time students have neared their peak performance in any given skill area.

For example, if a twenty-year-old student is making only minimal progress in speech and language programming, teachers would troubleshoot his program to look for causes. If changes made in the student's program still did not result in improvement, and there seems to be no specific reasons for the student's minimal progression, the student may have neared the limit of his communicative abili-

---

[6]   See Chapter 6 for a complete description of the discrete trial method.

[7]   Eden's Troubleshooting Process is described in Chapter 8.

ties. Teachers would then shift their approach away from teaching new words to maintaining and generalizing his current language skills. In our experience, with the severe language difficulties most people with autism have, they tend to "peak" in acquiring language skills as they approach adulthood (Lord & O'Neill, 1983).

Although there should be a general shift of focus in teaching from urgency to vigilance as a child grows older, he should not be treated entirely with urgency or vigilance at any given time. Rather, there should be a balance between the two. The treatment approach for each person should be comprised of both urgent and vigilant elements. Becoming vigilant on those skills which have already been learned (through an urgent approach) allows the student to accept an urgent approach toward learning a new skill. For example, if a person is learning how to brush his teeth through intense, high frequency training sessions, his previously learned hair-combing skills will be maintained through periodic reinforcement. Teachers will be vigilant about maintaining his ability to comb his hair, and urgent about getting him to brush his teeth.

The amount of vigilance or urgency that is best depends on each person's age, ability, and motivation. Although young children are usually able to maintain a highly urgent approach, older people, especially people employed in a job, will not benefit from such an urgent approach. They have already learned several skills which must be maintained, and they usually are not as able to change and grow as quickly as children (Lovaas & Favell, 1987).

A balance between urgency and vigilance is not only needed in special education. It is common in regular educational settings and in society as well. For example, a student has to learn how to count before he can add, but while he is learning to add, he must maintain his ability to count. And when people graduate from college, their learning environment goes from being one of urgency to one of vigilance, so they can use the knowledge they have acquired.

A proper balance in treatment between urgency and vigilance makes for a healthy learning atmosphere and greater gains. Treatment is never so urgent as to cause frustration and regression, nor is it ever so vigilant as to disregard possibilities for future growth. Finding that balance between the two approaches allows people to feel a sense of both accomplishment and challenge.

COMMON PROBLEMS IN TREATING PEOPLE WITH AUTISM

Teaching people with autism can be extremely difficult. Due to the very nature of the condition, people with autism generally resist allowing people to get close to them. They do not like or cannot make the personal or physical connections necessary to let someone teach them. The cognitive difficulties many people with autism have make teaching even more difficult. The challenge of teaching people with autism can be compounded by several problems the program or organization itself can encounter. Some of the challenges organizations most frequently confront are: keeping all the stake holders in the teaching process highly motivated (teachers and parents), inadvertently teaching a person to be helpless (over prompting), establishing a positive and stimulating yet challenging environment for the person with autism, and determining motivating systems for the individual with autism to learn and develop further. Approaches toward solving or avoiding these challenges are presented below.

TEACHING VERSUS CARE-GIVING: THE NURTURING PROCESS

People with autism learn and grow through ongoing training. However, because of their intense needs, it is tempting to provide more care than education. This may be due to an inadequate number of teachers, who simply cannot teach every member of a program individually. Or, it may be due to a program's philosophy. The program may strive to reduce the levels of anxiety, frustration, and stress for those they care for, rather than challenge them to learn new skills. The drawback to providing too much care is that it teaches people with autism to rely completely on their caregivers. Motivation to learn is removed.

LEARNED HELPLESSNESS

The condition of learned helplessness is not reserved for people with autism. It can occur in anyone learning a skill. For example, if a parent always tied the shoes of a child who would otherwise walk around with his shoes untied, the parent would be giving care to the child, but would not be teaching the child to care for himself. The parent would, in fact, be making the child oblivious to the need to care for himself. Most children would rather go to their parents to get their shoes tied than face the difficult task themselves.

If the parent instead expected the child's hands to be involved in the task of shoe tying, and expected the child to eventually tie his shoes himself, the child would be treated as if he were capable of learning to care for his own needs. At first, the child would probably not readily accept participating in tying his shoes, but if his parent was concerned about him learning how to care for himself, the parent would owe it to the child to teach him to care for his own needs.

> **W**hat we do in respite services and group homes is "Greek" to a lot of people, especially care-giving programs, where they dress, feed, and bathe the person. The idea of getting to independence is really different. We've had people come into our group homes and say "Oh, it's like a normal house." The way the houses run is geared toward helping participants be independent. We don't make their meals, although we help them with prompts and cues. They do their own laundry and help with upkeep. We teach them living skills and how to occupy their time appropriately, which are probably the hardest things for visitors to get over.
>
> —Jamie Klim, Coordinator of Respite Services

Eden has found that people with autism can learn to be helpless, and still achieve what they want. For example, if a person is fed, rather than taught to feed himself, or is not expected to accomplish even simple tasks, rather than being challenged to complete an employable work skill, he can come to expect that he does not need to learn skills. They are done for him. When assistance is given unconditionally, it sends the message that anything the individual does is accepted.

> **R**obert can dress himself now for the first time. It may take them a year to teach him how to button his shirt, but they stick with it, and now he can button his shirt. He zips his pants and does his belt, too. He is the neatest of all my children. He takes his clothes off, folds them up, and puts them in the drawer.
>
> **—Mike Walsh**

Being helpless is often an attractive condition for people with autism. It allows them to retreat into their own world, and relieves them of the anxiety, frustration, and stress that come with learning new skills. But being helpless robs them of their most basic human dignity. It excuses them for any unacceptable behavior, and it fails to teach the person to be responsible for his behavior. It says to the individual, "you are incapable as a human being; you are basically an incompetent."

Eden's goal of independence for people with autism helps steer them away from the condition of learned helplessness. Family and teachers keep in mind an old saying: "If you give a person a fish, he will eat for a day. If you teach a person to fish, he will eat for a lifetime." Put simply, Eden strives to make good fishermen out of its children and adults.

Instead of a care-giving approach, teachers at Eden have found a "mentoring" approach more successful. Mentoring refers to how a teacher nurtures an interest in a person, one-on-one, and then enables the person to broaden his skills through this interest. A mentor does more than just instruct. A mentor takes a personal interest in students, whether young or old, and offers much more than a simple instructional experience. A mentor is a trusted friend who treats his students as unique, and as capable of performing tasks which they may feel are insurmountable.

Mentors must be willing to work with a person for however long it takes the person to learn. And sometimes, a mentor has to be tough, just as parents are with a child behaving in unacceptable ways. Applying "tough love" means that the mentor must be willing to take the risks associated with correcting the person if his behavior is not in his own best interest. Using tough love means that the mentor must be willing to intrude in another person's life in order to "pierce their shell." That takes a great deal of courage. Just as a parent might have to refuse to tie his child's shoe in order to get the child to do it himself, a mentor might have to hold a child's hands down for a few minutes to keep him from throwing his around, and to teach him to control his impulses. The child will not like the situation in either case, but the mentor is guided by what is in the best interests of the child.

Carol Markowitz, Eden's Director of Educational Services:

When Sean came to Eden, he preferred to be left alone. He would sit by himself and flip objects all day. He had a lot of abilities, though. He had language, prevocational, and occupational skills, but would not perform them with teachers. When any demand was placed on him, he would aggress, tantrum, cry, or bang his head. Teachers have had to work through a lot of behavior with Sean to teach him skills he needs and get him to perform the skills he has when required. Teachers have had to restrain Sean, work through difficult behavior, and keep Sean working at a task that we knew, for his future independence, he needs to learn.

Cheryl Bomba, Eden's Assistant Director for Technical Support:

When I started working with Spike as a toddler, he was shut down 100 percent. I got no indication from him that he heard what I was saying, or that he was even aware of my presence. I talked to him, brought in his favorite toys, and offered him food. I got nothing. He was not just intentionally ignoring me, because he showed none of the typical signs of registering what I was doing or saying. It was like I did not exist.

I started by getting right in his face and talking to him, trying to get him to respond in any way. I worked with negative reinforcement: if he complied, I would go away. Through persistence, demands, and not letting up on those demands, he slowly began to respond more. He then began, gradually, to like our interactions.

Now, at age six, he actually seeks interaction. He will even become distracted from a task to engage with others. He plays with his sisters, and even leads them to their playroom to play with the dollhouse. He likes to talk about his favorite TV shows. He wants to tell people about things, and prefers to be with people. Spike is unlike many of the children at Eden because he has definite degrees of liking people. He prefers some people to others, and will check back with his favorites throughout the day. That is a very social response. But it is so different from the enclosed little boy I first worked with.

Although the mentoring process[8] encourages people to be as independent as possible, Eden has found that people need to be given some care as well. The balance between giving care and expecting independence is found through a nurturing process. People need to be both given help and encouraged to do for themselves. Eden has found that there are three general areas of nurturing in which a balance must be found: in the person's physical health, in his mental health, and in providing him appropriate social values.

---

[8] For more on the mentoring process, see Dr. Temple Grandin's book, *Emergence: Labeled Autistic*. Novato, CA: Arena Press, 1985.

A person's physical health depends on personal hygiene, proper nutrition and sleeping habits, and proper medical care. Family and teachers can teach self-care and personal hygiene skills, and can broaden the often narrow range of foods

a person with autism will eat, but there may be some things the individual cannot do for himself. For example, he may not be able to inform others when he is ill, schedule regular hair-cuts and medical or dental checkups, or regulate his own nutrition and sleeping patterns. These are things family and teachers must monitor, and must provide for most people with autism.

Maintaining a person's mental health is the second variable in the nurturing process. Mental health depends largely on self-esteem. Some of the people at Eden understand that they are being treated as dignified human beings, but some of them do not. Many of the people at Eden are so disengaged that they do not have the same sense of self-esteem that a typical person would. Over time, however, they develop a degree of social awareness. For example, students and participants tend to develop an awareness of other members in a group when working on a group activity.

Building Self Esteem

There is no magic formula for ensuring that heightened self-esteem actually takes hold in people with autism. But if teachers project a message of expected competence, people with autism will tend to be more competent, and their self-esteem will grow. Eden takes all the pieces of the formula that it knows to build self-esteem, and applies those pieces to people with autism knowing that some of it will have an effect, but some of it will not. If the person with autism is more engaged, or has a better sense of self, then the approach that Eden uses has a very positive effect on self esteem. An example of self-esteem building occurs when teachers do consultations on a child. In consultations, teachers talk with the child, not about the child, if the child is in the room. They treat the child as a real person. It is difficult to tell whether the child knows the difference, but if he does, the teachers will be building his sense of self, and in turn his self-esteem.

A person's self-esteem is best built by treating him as a dignified human being. This means recognizing his limitations, while dwelling on his strengths. It means accentuating his positive attributes, and cheering him on when tasks become difficult. Marlene Cohen, Director of Support Services:

> *Many of the students at Eden use a token economy system in which they have large buttons. The buttons hold a picture of what the students are working for, such as a can of soda. Having the picture*

reminds the student of what he is working for, and it lets teachers see immediately what the student's reinforcer will be. Teachers can then congratulate the student on the work he has accomplished so far, and encourage him to keep going and get that can of soda.

Eden also builds self-esteem by encouraging people to take risks. People with autism are characteristically averse to risk, and so try new things unwillingly. Trying new things, however, is essential for growth. Eden encourages people to take risks by creating an all-but-fail-safe learning environment. A teacher or parent is right by a person's side to help him through a task, using prompting if necessary to make sure the task is successfully completed. There is no room for failure in learning a skill. Because the threat of failure or harm is reduced, the person's self-esteem faces little threat, and the person is more willing to take risks. Lyn O'Donnell, Coordinator of Eden's Speech and Language Program:

We create a reinforcing environment for the people at Eden, and encourage them along the way. We always say, "You can do this, you can do this, you can do this." However, with autism there are often so many learning disabilities involved, in how they learn material, retain, and process information. One student could learn six signs, but every time we taught him a seventh sign he would lose one previously learned. Maybe his memory could not hold that many signs. We provide people with as fail-safe a learning environment as possible by prompting, giving them the right answers when they do not know them, and by teaching them the right answers. The prompting keeps them from failing. It keeps them stable. It also helps them realize, "OK, this is what they want from me." All this helps people understand their world, and take risks they might not otherwise take.

The third variable in the nurturing process is establishing social values. For example, people need to be taught self respect and respect for others, people need to be taught that they should be reserved in a restaurant, and that they must eat at a reasonable pace, and with the proper utensils. This is a type of social value that underlies appropriate social interactions. So too are values most typical people take for granted. However, pro-social values in general do not usually develop naturally in people with autism, and so must be taught. Teachers and parents must teach people with autism behavior that society deems appropriate. Teaching these values enables people with autism to take a greater part in social activities and reduces the chance of their being excluded because of unacceptable behavior.

Nurturing the physical and mental health of people with autism and teaching them appropriate social values are part of the care that teachers and family must provide. Finding that "very delicate balance" between care-giving and encouraging a person to do for himself gives him both the support he needs and the respect he deserves.

EMPATHY VERSUS PITY

Webster's Dictionary defines empathy as "identification with or vicarious experiencing of the feelings . . . of another." Pity is defined as "sympathetic grief or sorrow excited by the suffering or misfortune of another, often leading one to give aid or show mercy." In treating people with autism, it is important that teachers use empathy, rather than pity. Pity can perpetuate some of the problems faced by people with

> I know that if I had begun my work at Eden feeling pity for the children, I wouldn't have lasted a minute. I could not get through the day here feeling sorry for the children. Of course I have emotion for them. But I can't think about that when I'm teaching. I have to treat the children just as I would my friends. I am here because I want to help the children help themselves. I'm not here to feel sorry for them.
>
> **—Donna Vicidomini, Assistant Director for Educational and Retreat Support Services**

autism. Feeling pity encourages a care-giving approach, and as discussed previously, a care-giving approach can lead people to be helpless. An empathetic approach, on the other hand, leads to mentoring and progress. Cheryl Bomba:

> *Some of the children entering Eden Institute will only eat a few foods. They cannot usually eat with their families because the other foods upset them. They cannot go out to eat in the community, and they usually have poor nutrition. So, when they come here, we put them on a food toleration program to gradually introduce new foods.*
>
> *I helped two little boys through this program. They each came to Eden eating only two foods,. They had a rough time with the food toleration program. They would cry and get sick, but I kept working with them. If I had pitied them, I would have excused them, comforted them, and stopped the program. I did not do that. I knew it was important for them to learn to eat more foods. Now, they eat several foods, and are able to sit quietly through dinner. They can go out to eat in the community, too. Overcoming their resistance to different foods has opened a lot of doors for them.*

Feeling pity toward people with autism can also encourage their self absorption. The disorder of autism drives people to focus on themselves and what they want. This often means they learn how to manipulate those around them to get what they want. This is particularly true at home, where there is usually a less rigorous, less structured environment. Many families have been pushed to their limit by the demands of a young child with autism. People with autism can take quick advantage of an environment in which they are pitied. They learn they can dictate their environment when someone who feels sorry for them allows them the opportunity.

In contrast, a teacher who feels empathy toward people with autism will make demands which the person with autism must fulfill. Empathetic teachers have a better understanding of the importance of placing demands on someone

Before we learned to control our home environment, everything revolved around what Michael and Patrick wanted. Michael was not sleeping more than two or three hours a night, and when Michael did not sleep, nobody slept. He had the whole house in an uproar. We could not have any lamps standing, or anything on a table top, even a cup or dish. He would fling it like a Frisbee. We spent our time cleaning up after him. If we got upset, it amused him. We finally had recessed lighting put in the house so we did not have to keep buying lamps. When Michael and Patrick wanted to eat it was time to eat. And when they were finished eating, everyone had to be done because they would throw plates and food everywhere. The teachers at their state-run program asked me what to do when they, for example, knock over the bookcases and pull down the shades. If I had the answers I would have been employing them. Before our boys entered Eden, nothing was the way we wanted it. Everything revolved around their behavior problems. We had no control at all.

—Judy Farrell (Parent)

with autism, even if he does not like those demands, when the demands foster the person's growth and development. For example, Michelle's teachers placed some very difficult demands on her. Edha Majumdar, Coordinating Teacher of the Transition Program:

When Michelle was younger, she was terrified of blenders and motorcycles. She would not even play outside or ride her bicycle because she was afraid a motorcycle would pass by. She never went out to dinner with her family because of the blenders in the kitchen. Her parents and teachers decided she needed to overcome these fears because they were severely limiting her experience in the community.

Slowly, we worked through her fear. That was tough, because she was genuinely terrified. We understood her feelings, but knew she had to overcome them. Now, she still finds motorcycles and blenders a little distressing, but knows that the noise will pass. She is able to go with her father out to dinner. It is one of her favorite activities. She plays outside and even walks with her mom to the store. She never would have done these things if we had not persisted in working through her fears.

Empathetic teachers tend to be better detectives in determining what factors are involved in learning challenges because their analyses are not clouded by pity. They are better able to understand and assess a person's feelings, and can therefore be more effective in changing behavior problems the person may have.[9]

---

[9] See Chapter 7 on the Eden Decision Model for some of the most common reasons teachers have found behind behavior problems.

COMMITMENT MEANS NEVER GIVING UP

Organizations serving people with autism need to guard against "giving up" on those they serve. There are two ways in which organizations can "give up". One is by providing too much care. It is difficult to continue meeting the challenges of people with autism. They not only need highly specialized teaching environments, but they have behavior challenges as well. To top it off, their needs and challenges are constantly changing. Unfortunately, the easiest way around these challenges is to provide care. For example, if a person with autism does not know how to groom himself, it is relatively easy for a teacher to groom him herself. If he has a tantrum each time he is asked to eat something new, the easiest solution is to simply give him his preferred food. It is much more difficult to employ rigorous programs to teach him skills to groom himself and to get him eating different foods. That takes an extra effort. If an organization is committed to not giving up on him, it must make that effort. Being committed to helping people with autism means staying focused on their needs, and teaching them to learn to take care of themselves as much as possible.

Organizations can also "give up" on those they serve by discharging people from their program due to age, lack of progress, or behavior challenges without securing appropriate alternative services. Many organizations serve a particular subset of people with autism, such as those who have a certain amount of language, those who meet certain cognitive criteria, or those of a certain age. These organizations often provide the most appropriate services to the population they have defined. If these agencies decide that they cannot serve a person well, or cannot provide the level of service he needs due to emerging cognitive, behavior, or other challenges, they will "graduate" him or, worse, discharge him. In order not to fall into the trap of giving up, they then must be committed to securing appropriate alternative services for the person, services which the organization could not provide.

> **W**e have to constantly change in order to keep meeting the needs of the people at Eden. We can't relax, or fall into old habits. Something might have worked yesterday, but doesn't today, so we have to be on our toes at all times to constantly look at programs and make changes quickly. That's a real challenge for the teachers. They have to always be on top of things. If a program isn't working, we've got to be able to analyze it, and come up with something totally new, or present it in a different way. If we don't keep changing, our students will not succeed.
>
> **—Ken Dorfman, Coordinating Teacher, Vocational Preparation**

The Individuals with Disabilities Education Act (IDEA), the law governing educational services to children with disabilities, offers help to children in this respect. However, although it guarantees that children will receive an appropriate education, that education often is far from appropriate. For example, the child's local education agency (LEA) is responsible for making certain that all children in the district receive a free appropriate public education, but that could mean only five hours a week of home tutoring, or being put on a waiting list for specialized services. That is minimally what the law requires, but is not truly an appropriate education. It meets the letter of the law, but not its spirit.

Amy Rowley's case illustrates this. Amy was a deaf student in regular education who needed an interpreter to fully comprehend classroom instruction. The state declined. The family took the case to court, where their expert witness testified that without an interpreter, Amy comprehended less than 50 percent of the verbal content of classroom instruction when compared to what typical students comprehend. The court ruled that, even though minimal, 50 percent was some education, and some education was all that the law required. The court concluded that the IDEA "[does] not require [a] state to maximize the potential of each handicapped child commensurate with the opportunity provided nonhandicapped children" (*Board of Education v. Rowley,* 102 S.Ct 3024 (1982)).

For adults with autism, the picture is worse. There is as yet no legal guarantee of specialized services. As a result, adults are the group of people with autism who most often are left without appropriate services. Many of the adults at Eden were in questionably appropriate programs before entering Eden's residential and work programs. Pam Hileman, Coordinator of Group Home Operations:

> *Sharon had been in many programs before coming to live at Eden ACREs' Farley House. She had finally been placed in an institution because no other program could handle her. Her behavior challenges were too great. But she has many abilities. She would actually write letters saying she did not like the institution. Until Farley House opened, however, there were no other placement options for her. She is now living in the community, is mostly independent, and does subcontract work through Eden WERCs.*
>
> *Another one of our participants was living in a psychiatric hospital before he came to Eden. His aggression was so severe that the hospital had him on heavy doses of Thorazine. His main problem was biting, so the hospital was seriously considering removing his teeth to keep him from injuring himself or others. Eden was asked to intervene, and with the specialized services he has received at Eden, he has improved immensely. He now lives in Bonnell House at Eden ACREs, has a job in the community, and is on only low doses of a milder medication.*

Organizations serving people with autism, especially adults, must be careful when discharging a person from their programs. Even if organizations feel that their services are no longer appropriate for a person in their program, they should feel responsible for securing services that are appropriate. Again, being committed to helping people with autism means focusing on their needs, not the needs of the organization.

Because Eden serves challenging people with autism, there are extremely few programs to which it can refer people if its teachers feel overwhelmed. Eden cannot discharge people because there is no where else for most of them to go and because Eden has a lifespan commitment. For many people with autism, Eden is the end of the line. Teachers, therefore, look long and hard to find out ways to meet the challenges they are presented with, and Eden never abrogates its responsibility.

The expansive needs of those it serves have caused Eden to be very sensitive in providing a wide range of program options. For example, Eden has developed long-term one-on-one teaching programs, before and after school and home programming, respite care, a comprehensive curricula flexible enough to meet each participant's individual needs, and financial assistance programs for families who could not otherwise place their child at Eden. But most importantly, the needs of people with autism are the impetus behind Eden's commitment to not only provide appropriate services to people with autism, but to provide services over their entire lifespan.

Chapter **4**

Lifespan
· · · · · ·
Philosophy &
· · · · · · · · · ·
Zero-Reject
· · · · · · ·
Policy
· · · · ·

When Eden accepts someone into its programs, it commits itself to providing the full range of services that person may need for the rest of his life. With this commitment comes Eden's policy of not discharging anyone from its programs, no matter the behavioral challenges they present. Even if a person at Eden becomes entirely independent, Eden's services remain available should the person need them in the future. The lifespan philosophy and zero-reject policy at Eden govern every aspect of its services.

Lifespan services have an exciting positive impact on the lives of families who are responsible for the day-to-day needs of their child with autism. With

> **B**eing in a program that provides lifetime services gives me a sense that there are people out there who are working for me. There will never be enough funding, and there will never be enough programming, and there will never be enough space, but at least there's somebody out there trying to figure out what kinds of programs might be developed to help both me and my child.
>
> —**Helen Hoens (Parent)**

lifespan services, parents do not have to bear the burden of continually searching for appropriate placements for their child, and they do not have to worry about the time in their child's future when they are not capable of, or around to, take care of him.

State agencies have also seen lifespan services as a positive development. There is such a strong need for community based services to children and adults with autism that states usually welcome organizations that commit to providing such services over the lifespan.

QUESTIONS ABOUT LIFESPAN SERVICES

Not everyone views lifespan services positively. Some have raised questions and concerns. One concern people have had with lifespan services seems to lie in the emotional difficulty of raising a child with autism. Families of children with autism naturally hope that their child's autism will fade with time, or even be cured. The prospect of having to handle the challenges their child presents for the rest of his life is understandably daunting, especially during the fragile period when a family first learns that their child has autism. Reflecting on the time when their son was diagnosed with autism, Nancy Cantor and Steve Brechin said:

> It was a very emotional time for us. We did not know what was happening with Archie. We did not know how to think about Archie. We did not know how to frame his condition, or what steps to take.

Eden delays discussing lifespan services seriously with families until their child is ten or eleven years old. If a child is not well on his way to being in a regular classroom by then, the family should begin to accept that he may require specialized services to some degree for the rest of his life.

There are children at Eden who are five years old, and whose parents have them on the list to receive group home placement. Parents know they will need services, but it is still hard to do. Their child is practically in diapers and they are thinking about lifetime services for him. They do not want to think about their own mortality, let alone the mortality of their child.

Once, during an intake meeting for a four-year-old child, the family was being presented with some of the positive attributes of Eden. When the concept of lifespan services came up, the smile on the mother's face dropped. We asked why she appeared less than enthusiastic about this important attribute of the program, and she said "My child is too young for us to think about this being a lifetime problem."

—**Gary Montgomery, Operations Coordinator, Eden Institute**

Delaying serious consideration of lifespan services has an added benefit. It encourages the family to not accept their child's developmental delays. One of the strongest factors in the growth a child is able to make is the family's intense desire to help him catch up to his typically developing peers. Eden has found that families are willing to exert a lot of energy to help their child if there is a possibility that the severity of their child's autism could be mitigated. Delaying the consideration of lifespan services enables the family to focus that energy on teaching their child when he is most open to learning, during his younger years.

When a clinician meets parents who are engaged in the endless search for a "cure" for a condition which is chronic in nature, it becomes important to help the family shift their focus from searching for an answer to dealing with the problem. Looking beyond the fact of their search to the reasons why they need to continue searching may help the clinician in facilitating this shift of focus for the family. Such feelings as anger and guilt may be motivating parents to look for the magical solution to a problem which, sadly, has no ready answers.

—S.L. Harris, author of *Families of the Developmentally Disabled: A Guide to Behavioral Intervention* (1983)(79).

Funding agencies also have expressed concern over lifespan services. They have been skeptical that an organization providing lifespan services might not try hard enough to encourage people in its programs to make transitions to less specialized settings. Eden, however, has a "safety net" approach to services, which encourages its students and participants to make transitions to less specialized settings. The safety net approach, described in detail below, enables people to make transitions to less specialized programs with the knowledge that they can return to Eden if necessary. Parents, Eric and Erica Lofgren, describe how the safety net approach affects them:

> It would have been an easy mistake to provide lifetime services to people from day one straight through, which would mean less of an incentive to try to stretch a child's abilities. But at Eden, if there is another program that better fits our child's abilities, we can go to it, even if it is not at Eden. Eden's philosophy allows us to do that, while still providing us with support.

Another concern people have had about lifespan services is that they limit the number of people an organization can serve. Those who are accepted are given

The curriculum at Eden is really based on research we have done with students at Eden Institute. We developed the curriculum over several years, as we learned more about how children with autism learn, and what types of skills they need. Data from teaching sessions was used to determine what elements to include. Other agencies have now used that curriculum to develop their own programs. For example, the Southern Bergen Jointure Commission was one of the first public school districts we helped develop a public, but separate, school classroom for students with autism. They followed Eden's approach. They consulted us, used our curriculum, and asked us to help them start their program.

—Anne S. Holmes, **Director of Outreach Services**

lifetime support, but the number of people accepted is only a fraction of the number who could benefit from the organization's services. For example, although only two or three new people are accepted each year into Eden Institute, it receives about fifty to seventy applicants. It is therefore true that an organization committed to lifespan services must control the number of people in its programs in order to provide the services they will need in the future. Eden, however, has controlled for this limitation by establishing an "Outreach Division" whose responsibility it is to consult with families and organizations to replicate Eden's lifespan services model in order to help many others.

> Eden has made it clear that it will be there for the whole life of our son Steven, and that nobody will drop him when he is 16. That is how Eden has helped us most. We knew from the outset that was the intent of the school, but we wondered, of course, if they would be able to do it. More and more now we know they will, because they have done it so far, and with people of all ages.
>
> —Norm Greenberg, President, New Jersey State Society, Autism Society of America

Controlling the number of people in its programs enables Eden to monitor programs closely, and evaluate the effectiveness of behavioral interventions and skill acquisition. Several empirical studies have been conducted at Eden because of the stability of its population.[1] Findings from these studies are communicated to others through publication and consultation.

Another question has been raised about lifespan services, particularly those Eden provides. Eden's commitment to providing lifespan services arose because the people it served were among the most severely challenged by autism. But because Eden serves people who are more severely challenged, and operates under a zero-reject policy, some have questioned whether participants are given poor models for behavior. There are two ways that Eden makes sure that students and participants have appropriate models of behavior. Eden provides regularly scheduled activities in the community,[2] and all of its therapeutic programs are in settings located throughout the community, from infant and toddler services to group homes to employment opportunities. Further, by maintaining a low ratio of students or participants to teachers,[3] coupled with daily exposure to typical peers and siblings in the community, models of appropriate behavior are presented at a high frequency.

Providing services for the lifespan is a difficult task, and some wonder whether Eden will be able to live up to its promise. It has at times been challenging, but Eden

---

[1] See Chapter 8 for some examples of the type of research that has been conducted at Eden.

[2] Students and participants go shopping, go out to lunch, go bowling, and engage in many activities with their peers in the community. Chapter 11 describes further community activities.

[3] At the Institute, the ratio is often one or two students to one teacher. The ratio is about the same in residential programs. A low ratio is not needed in work programs because participants are often out in the community working. In addition, the average age of staff members in both the residential and work programs is about the same as that of participants: twenty-four.

has so far been able to do so. Services may not be available exactly when they are needed, but Eden is always planning for them. For example, Eden may not have a group home placement waiting for a graduate of the Eden Institute. He may have to wait until Eden can establish a placement for him. Until then, he will be given supports such as respite services. To avoid as much as possible any delay in providing services, Eden begins planning for services years before they are needed. [4]

> Some children at Eden Institute are only six or seven years old, but we are constantly asking what they will need ten years from now. A child may be at a certain level now, but we have got to start preparing him for the future. We can't just look at what is going to get him through the week.
>
> **—Denise Burns-Jennings, Coordinating Teacher, Early Childhood**

THE SAFETY NET APPROACH

The most important aspect of Eden's lifespan services is the security it gives people with autism and their families. They know they will have support for as long as they need it, and whenever they need it. They know they can work toward independence because Eden is there for them to fall back on, even if they have been away for some time. Eden is there permanently at whatever level of service is needed as a "safety net."

Peter Gerhardt, Director of Employment Services, describes the safety net for two participants in Eden's employment program:

> *We have two people in WERCs who just need to be dropped off and picked up at their jobs. They are two of the most independent people at Eden, but they are still part of WERCs. If their job demands change, or if something happens, we go right back in and work with them. For example, one person was working independently in a competitive job when the company laid her off for economic reasons. She came back to an Eden employment center and engaged in secure employment activities until another supported or competitive job could be found. So, even though they do not need as intensive services as other participants, they are not forgotten. We are there, and have to be there, to provide them with services should they need them.*

The safety net Eden provides is *not a hammock*. It is not meant for lying in and relaxing. The safety net is conceptually like the net under a high-wire act. It is there to catch someone if they fall. It supports him until he can climb the ladder again. And it gives him courage to try again, because he will not be hurt if he falls.

---

[4] See Chapter 11 on Eden's Strategic Planning Process.

Eden provides a safety net in another way as well. If teachers and family feel that another treatment approach would also benefit a child, Eden would consider altering its course of action with the child.[5] If Eden did not feel it could provide the services, teachers would give the family information about the services, and would

find an agency which did provide the services to supplement, and not supplant, the child's programming. Eden would then help the family monitor their child's progress with the new service, and would evaluate its effectiveness. If the service was not beneficial for the child, there would not be any interruption of his core services at Eden.

Specifically, if teachers and family felt that a student would benefit more from a regular education placement, or that a participant would do better in a more independent residential setting, Eden would help arrange the transition. Eden would then monitor how well the student or participant did in his new environment. If, for any reason, the student's or participant's environment became inappropriate, Eden would once again offer services. For example, Eden is providing services for one of its former students, Michael, who made the transition to regular education classes ten years ago. After graduating from high school, Michael found that he had not acquired enough vocational training to get a job. His family contacted Eden and worked out a plan for Michael to receive vocational training again through Eden. Michael needed to fall back on that support from Eden because he could not find it in his regular education setting.

The safety net approach frees families from having to worry about losing services, or from being pressured to choose one form of treatment over another. Eric and Erica Lofgren:

> *The safety net is there, so we can go to another program if Spike needs it, and come back. That is important. It is comfort. And it gives us the ability to concentrate on doing the best for our child now, rather than worrying about losing the program he has, or having to look for another.*

Equally important to this feeling of security is knowing that Eden will never "discharge" a person because of behavior challenges or degrees of disability.

---

[5]   Eden remains committed to applied behavior analysis as its primary method of treatment. However, treatments that are compatible with applied behavior analysis, such as vitamin therapy, have been tried at Eden when family and teachers thought the therapy would be beneficial.

THE ZERO-REJECT POLICY

As discussed above, when organizations are faced with the challenges of treating people with autism, they may reject those they cannot serve effectively. Eden does not do this. Once at Eden, the zero-reject policy ensures that services will always be available, and that those services will be appropriate. But Eden's zero-reject policy works another way as well: in who it accepts into its programs.

Eden's zero-reject policy means that it does not "screen" people who apply for entrance. Whereas other programs often "screen out" based upon the severity of an applicant's behavioral challenges, or have cognitive and functional criteria an applicant must meet, Eden offers help to everyone with autism who applies for entrance no matter his degree of behavioral or cognitive challenges. However, Eden cannot accept everybody. Because the number of applications each year greatly exceeds the number of spaces available, some applicants must be referred to other organizations rather than being entered into Eden's formal programs.[6]

Those who apply to Eden tend to be more severely challenged. DSM-IV states that in most cases of autism "there is an associated diagnosis of Mental Retardation, commonly in the moderate range (IQ 35-50). Approximately 75 percent of children with

> If someone has a diagnosis of autism, they're an acceptable candidate for Eden, independent of their cognitive level of functioning, behavioral level of functioning, or physical level of functioning. If we have an opening, they can be accepted. Other programs have somewhat different criteria for accepting people into their programs. They often do a wonderful job with the group of people in their program, but they work with a different group of people than Eden. I like the people Eden works with. But Eden is also no-discharge. Once someone's here, they're here. We're not giving up. A parent may want to try another program, which is fine, but we are not going to say that a person presents too big a challenge for us, or is too low functioning. Those words don't exist.
>
> **—Peter Gerhardt, Director of Employment Services**

Autistic Disorder function at a retarded level" (p. 67). Of the three fourths with mental retardation, Eden serves the lowest 10-15 percent. There are no standardized assessments done on entry into the Eden Institute, ACREs, or WERCs, but Eden's functional analysis of their level of development shows that most people entering the programs have minimal self care or learning readiness skills. The stan-

---

[6] The Outreach Division at Eden was created with the primary objective of helping those children Eden could not accept into its formal programs due to size limitations. Outreach refers to other programs available through their network of contacts. They provide families with information and research about what is available and they evaluate the child in order to suggest types of placement which would be most appropriate for the child.

dardized testing done for children entering Wawa House indicates that they have an average of 1-10 percent of the skills of their typically developing peers.[7]

There are several reasons for Eden's serving the lowest functioning students and participants. Because of their behavior challenges, applicants are more likely to need the lifetime of services Eden offers. Further, alternative placements can be more easily found for people with fewer challenges. The people Eden has come to serve are those who many public agencies and private organizations find too difficult to serve effectively. They require a high level of specialized service, and so cannot usually be served well along with people who are less challenged. If people are dismissed from other programs, or have difficulty finding the services they need in a public agency, they are often referred to Eden.

ADMISSIONS

In deciding which applicants to admit, Eden has four main criteria: 1) the age of the applicant; 2) what spaces are available in Eden's programs; 3) the willingness of the family to become involved in the treatment process; and finally, 4) the severity of the applicant's disability. If there are two applicants of the same age and

degree of involvement, with families that are equally committed to working with Eden, but Eden had only one space available, the applicant who applied first would be admitted. Usually, however, if Eden must choose one among a group of applicants, the applicant that is more severely challenged than the others is usually chosen. This is due in part to the fact that his family would have more difficulty finding an alternate program. If all other variables are equal, the eagerness of the family to work with Eden in support of our training and home programming becomes a deciding factor.

At Eden Institute, if a child is an appropriate age for a program that has an opening, then the family of the child is closely scrutinized to determine whether a partnership can develop between family and teachers. The family is interviewed by the Director of the program in the child's age group, and then by the Executive Director of Eden. The family must support the treatment methodologies Eden

---

[7]   Chapter 8 describes in more detail the skill levels of people entering Eden.

has established. They must be willing to be an integral member of the team in treating their child. They must agree to participate in training to learn how to best help their child. The family's partnership with the teachers at Eden is crucial for the child's skill acquisition and behavior modification. Each must hold the same expectations to ensure a consistent learning environment.[8]

Eden ACREs and WERCs primarily admit adults to their programs, but there is not the same rigorous admissions procedure that there is for children because many of the adults entering Eden's residential and work programs have been with Eden for years. Adults who come in, usually through state referrals,[9] have detailed profiles of their history, which provide Eden with a somewhat comprehensive picture of their needs and abilities. Family involvement is important with adults, but it is not as critical. Most of Eden's adults do not live with their family, and families of adults are not held to the same level of consistency between home and employment setting. Families also need a break from urgency to vigilance as the child, now adult, grows up.

Admitted applicants enter one of Eden's programs—the infants and toddlers program (birth to age three, at Wawa House), the preschool program (ages three to five at Eden Institute), the school age programs (ages five to twenty-one at Eden Institute), Eden's work (WERCs), or residential (ACREs) program.

Eden admits as many children as it can to Wawa House. Because the infant and toddler program is not regulated by the school year, it admits children throughout the year. Two children a year on average are admitted to Eden Institute, but a given program may have more than two children at any time. Younger children who have progressed well sometimes sit in on a more advanced group, and children who are making a gradual transition to a local public school are often in a program at Eden Institute part-time. Eden expects to admit about 15 people over the next five years to its work program for adults, and will admit to its residential program as many as it can, depending on funding for housing and services.

As mentioned earlier, Wawa House now has 13 children in its formal program, and 49 children in a supplemental program. Eden Institute serves about 50

---

[8] Chapter 10 describes the partnership between families and teachers at Eden. It also describes the training process for parents, which is the same training staff members receive.

[9] See Chapter 9.

children. There are 10 children in the Early Childhood Program (7 of these in the preschool portion of Early Childhood), 11 in the Middle Childhood Program, 6 in the Transition Program, and 23 in the Vocational Programs (9 in Prevocational, 14 in Vocational Preparation). Eden ACREs currently serves 42 people, and Eden WERCs serves 58.

Eden does not expect to increase the number of people it serves through Eden Institute. The infants and toddlers program, however, has been growing over the past few years,[10] and Eden's work and residential programs naturally grow as more people graduate from Eden Institute and require employment and residential housing.[11]

---

[10] See Chapter 8.

[11] Eden's growth is described further in Chapter 11.

Chapter 5

Effective Placement

& Treatment of

People with

Autism

T he effective placement of people with autism in a learning environment is as critical as the effectiveness of the specific treatments they receive. Different options in placement and treatment, and the options Eden embraces, are discussed below.

TREATMENT OPTIONS

There are many approaches to treating people with autism. The more prevalent treatments include psychodynamic therapy (cf. Bettelheim, 1967; Mahler, 1952; Tustin, 1991), holding therapy (Tinbergen & Tinbergen, 1983; Welch, 1989), play therapy (Axline, 1964; Greenspan, 1992), sensory integrative therapy (Ayres, 1979), auditory integration training (Berard, 1982), vitamin therapy (cf. Rimland, 1988; Rimland, 1993), facilitated communication (Biklen, 1990), treatment following a developmental model (Baldwin, 1976; Haring & Bricker, 1976), treatment following a cognitive-developmental model (Miller, 1991; Miller & Eller-Miller, 1989), treatment following a cognitive-behavioral model (Harris, 1988; Meichenbaum, 1983), applied behavior analysis (cf. Lovaas, 1977, 1981), and intensive discrete trial training (Lovaas, 1987; Lovaas, 1993). Each of these approaches to treatment is described below.

PSYCHODYNAMIC TREATMENT

A psychodynamic treatment approach is based on the premise that children with autism withdraw from society at an early age because they have negative first interactions with their parents (Bettelheim, 1967). According to theory, the child with autism finds the external world frustrating and ungratifying, and so encloses himself in a world of fantasy. In order to draw the child out, teachers and parents have to unconditionally love and accept their child. They have to reverse the child's first impressions of the world by creating a safe and gentle environment in which he can emerge from his shell.

> The image often invoked to describe autism is that of a beautiful child imprisoned in a glass shell....[This] ... is misleading in more ways than one. It is incorrect to think that inside the glass shell is a normal individual waiting to emerge....Autistic people ...[have]... minds different from our own (p. 114).
>
> —Uta Frith in *Scientific American*, June, 1993

Purely psychodynamic approaches to treating autism are no longer common due to the strong evidence of a biogenic—biological and genetic—cause of the disorder (e.g., Huebner, 1992; Rimland, 1964; Rutter, 1968). Although some forms of psychodynamic therapy are still available, studies of the effectiveness of psychodynamically-oriented therapies have shown no advantages to this approach (Schopler, 1971).

HOLDING THERAPY

Holding therapy is a form of psychotherapy that focuses on the lack of bonding between a child with autism and his mother. Because the child withdraws from society at a very early age, the hypothesis is that he does not form strong bonds with his mother, and so does not feel safe in the world (Tinbergen & Tinbergen, 1983). The child with autism is instead plagued by an inner conflict; he wants the social contact he has missed with mother, but finds it too threatening.

In holding therapy, the mother holds her child tightly in her arms to try to establish the missed bond. When the child is upset or frustrated, it is especially important that the mother be there to love, hug, and help her child work through his negative feelings. As the bond with his mother grows, the child will slowly be drawn out of his autistic world by feeling accepted and safe.

Holding therapy is practiced by some agencies (e.g., Welch, 1989), but Eden does not offer it as a treatment option because there is no empirical evidence to support its effectiveness (Wimpery & Cochrane, 1991). Temple Grandin, a woman with autism who has written extensively about her personal experiences, proposes that for some tactilely-defensive individuals holding therapy may help desensitize them to touch. However, she also feels that the same results can be obtained from sensory integration activities, in a less stressful manner, and without the parents being made to suffer guilt about missing an opportunity to bond with their children (Grandin, 1989).

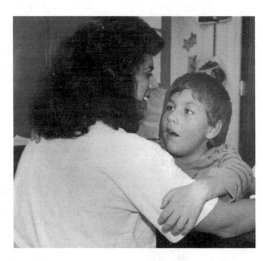

PLAY THERAPY

A slightly older psychodynamic approach to treating people with autism is play therapy. Through play, therapists would try to help children with autism work through their negative feelings and be more accepting of loving interactions (Axline, 1964). Proponents of play therapy today, however, generally work from the premise that children with autism withdraw from society because of an innate dysfunction in processing sensory information (Greenspan, 1992; Kalmanson, 1992) rather than because of a learned response to their environment.

Modern play therapy attempts to connect with the child on an emotional level by encouraging small interactions and communications while playing with toys or other objects. The goal of play therapy is to draw the child out of his solitary world with these interactions, and to eventually make the child aware of himself as a distinct and important identity (Greenspan, 1992).

Although Eden does not employ play therapy, the ability to play is taught as an important social and recreational skill. Preschool-age students are taught to play in order to interact with their family and peers; fundamental social skills like eye contact and turn-taking are taught within the context of age-appropriate games. For older students, play translates into games and leisure activities, both with other students and out in the community. No psychodynamic interpretations are made during play sessions; instead, students are systematically taught to use toys appropriately, interact with others, and occupy their free time in a productive, enjoyable way.

I visited a school recently following the open classroom approach. A teacher in the class told me that she can't contain the playroom because the kids have to be free to explore the entire room. For children with other disabilities that may make sense, but children with autism aren't exploring in these situations. They may be spinning a toy or running around, but don't suddenly decide to sit down and play. They need boundaries. They need to be taught to play, and reinforced for playing.

—**Anne S. Holmes, Director of Outreach Services**

SENSORY INTEGRATIVE THERAPY

Sensory integrative therapy (Ayres, 1979) is another treatment based on neural reorganization, this time focusing on the processing of sensory information in children with autism. Therapists believe that children with autism do not register or regulate sensory input correctly, especially tactile and vestibular input, and do not have an inner drive strong enough to overcome their sensory dysfunctions.

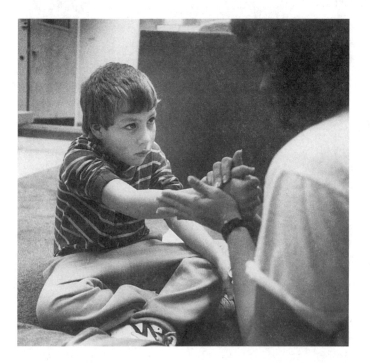

The environment for sensory integrative therapy gives the child with autism opportunities to swing, spin, slide, crawl, and perform other motor activities. These activities are designed to reorganize the child's still flexible brain in a way that better integrates sensory input. When the child is better able to integrate various sensory stimuli, the world will seem less threatening, and so the child will feel more comfortable interacting with people in his environment. As the child is positively reinforced for interacting with others, his inner drive to participate in the world around him will grow stronger. Proponents of sensory integrative therapy postulate that the motoric reorganization a child achieves through therapy sessions will carry over into other areas, like speech and language.

Eden uses the techniques of sensory integrative therapy in its adaptive physical education programs, but does not embrace it as a separate treatment method. Students and participants at Eden need to be better able to integrate sensory input, but Eden has found that progress in this area does not necessarily enable individuals to acquire functional skills in other domains. So, Eden incorporates some of the activities proposed by advocates for sensory integration therapy to enhance individualized instruction. For example, tactile stimulation activities (pouring water, finding objects hidden in rice, etc.) may be part of a tactilely-defensive student's programming, with the goal of reducing the learning-interfering, behavioral reactions. As the student becomes more and more able to integrate and tolerate tactile activities, instruction in functional skills with a tactile component—bathing, dressing, and feeding, for example—becomes less aversive to the student and success much more likely.

PATTERNING

Other forms of therapy are based on the premise that something about the brain of a child with autism is innately disorganized. To treat a child's autism, these therapies try to reorganize the dysfunctional aspect of the autistic brain. Patterning is one such treatment (Delacato, 1974; Doman, 1974). Although largely unsubstantiated, patterning claims to reorganize dysfunctional areas of the brain. Practitioners of the patterning approach to treatment believe that a child with autism has failed to pass through particular motoric stages in developing, and so cannot continue his development.

Treatment consists of having therapists, parents, and volunteers move the arms and legs of the child in specific patterns, such as crawling. Treatment is thought to reorganize the motor area of the brain by giving the child the motoric experience he missed earlier (Freeman, 1967). Patterning treatment is intense, with several hours of therapy each day, and must follow a rigorous schedule. The benefits a child receives from therapy will hopefully transfer to other areas of the brain, and improve language, reasoning, and social skills.

Patterning therapy is rarely implemented today. Studies have found no beneficial effects of the therapy (American Academy of Pediatrics, 1983), and the therapy is extremely difficult to implement. In a policy statement on patterning therapy, the American Academy of Pediatrics (1983) states:

> The regimens prescribed by [patterning therapy] are so demanding and inflexible that they may place considerable stress on parents and lead to their neglect of other family members' needs (p. 40).

The difficulty parents have in implementing patterning therapy has often been blamed for the failure of the treatment. Proponents of the treatment claim that the regimen must be followed exactly in order to be effective (Freeman, 1967), and that any small deviation from the regimen will result in failure. However, studies comparing the efficacy of patterning to other treatments for groups of children with severe disabilities have found that, although all children showed some improvements over the course of the study, there were no significant differences among the groups and no empirical evidence to recommend the rigorous techniques of patterning over other treatments (Neman et al., 1975; Sparrow & Zigler, 1978; Zigler & Seitz, 1975).

AUDITORY INTEGRATION TRAINING

An older therapy that has experienced recent popularity is auditory integration training. Auditory integration training for people with autism was first developed by Dr. Guy Berard in the 1960s. The treatment claims to reorganize areas of the brain so that the person with autism can shift his attention more easily and tolerate a greater variety of stimuli. This enables him to be more involved in and less overwhelmed by his environment. The reorganization of the brain is achieved through the auditory modality.

Treatment consists of several intense sessions. The person with autism listens to music which has been carefully filtered. The music has no frequencies which have been determined to be distressing to the person, and so will make him feel comfortable, rather than cause him to withdraw. The type of music is switched often to enable the person to shift attention quickly. As the person becomes more comfortable, the range of frequencies played is gradually increased. After treatment, the person should find his environment less threatening because he is more tolerant of change and variety, and can shift his attention to the activities in his environment without feeling overwhelmed.

No empirical evidence has validated auditory integration training, although a multi-phase, longitudinal study is currently being conducted by Bernard Rimland and Steven Edelson. To date, complete data have been collected for approximately 375 subjects (Rimland, 1993). Based on a preliminary analysis of their data, the researchers feel the results are "promising and encouraging, but not spectacularly positive" (Rimland, 1991).

VITAMIN THERAPY

Many studies have shown that vitamin therapy can be beneficial for some people with autism (e.g., Bonisch, 1968; Heeley & Roberts, 1965; Martineau et al., 1988; Rimland, 1964). Vitamin B6 has produced the most positive results. It is usually paired with magnesium to counter the nutritional deficits that can come with taking B6 alone. Subjects taking a B6-magnesium supplement have shown a decrease in negative behaviors (Bonisch, 1968; Rimland, 1964), a more normal metabolism (Heeley & Roberts, 1965; Martineau, Barthelemy & Lelord, 1986), increases in vocalization (Rimland, 1973, 1974), a decrease in general autistic symptoms (Rimland, 1964; Martineau et al., 1988; Martineau, Barthelemy & Lelord, 1986), and more normal eating and sleeping behavior (Rimland, 1973, 1974). Although vitamin therapy does not ever seem to cure a person's autism, it is especially attractive because it has none of the unwanted side effects of psychopharmacologic drugs (Martineau et al., 1988).

Vitamin therapy is based on the premise that people with autism have a nutritional disorder which is partially responsible for their autistic tendencies. Vitamin B6 is hypothesized to influence the metabolism of the brain, making for more normal neurotransmitter activity (Martineau et al., 1988).

Most of the families at Eden who have tried vitamin therapy have had negligible results, but some have found it effective. Judy Farrell found vitamin therapy helpful with her son:

> We tried a calcium-magnesium supplement because we heard it might help our son Michael sleep better, and it worked. Within twenty-four hours of when he started the supplement, he slept through the night. That was his first full night of sleep in months. He also started to verbalize for the first time in a year, and he started to sing.

Although Eden does encourage families like the Farrells to try vitamin therapy, Eden does not promote it as a primary treatment because not enough is known yet about its effectiveness. Vitamin therapy does not work for all people with autism (Rimland, 1988), and although there are theories, no one is quite sure why vitamin therapy works (Menage et al., 1992).

FACILITATED COMMUNICATION

Over the past several years, facilitated communication has been debated as a treatment for autism. Facilitated communication is an alternative communication strategy in which a person with autism communicates by typing messages on a computer or small keyboard. The person's hand, wrist or arm is physically supported by a facilitator who helps the person control his movements and focus on a task (Biklen, 1990). Proponents of facilitated communication believe that people with autism have typical cognitive abilities, but have problems in speaking or conveying words or ideas (Biklen, 1990; Crossley, 1990; Schubert, 1992). In other words, autism is viewed as a problem of expression, not understanding. Facilitated communication can therefore help all people with autism because it enables them to bypass their problem of expression by providing a mode in which they can communicate (Biklen, 1990; Crossley, 1990).

Proponents of facilitated communication often advocate for integrating children with autism fully into regular educational classrooms (Biklen, 1990). Since people with autism have typical cognitive functioning, they argue that there is no reason to segregate them into specialized classes. Many students with autism have indeed moved from specialized programs into regular classrooms with the help of a facilitator (Biklen, 1990).

Despite the allure of what seemed to be a miraculous cure for autism, facilitated communication has not been validated in any of a number of scientific studies (e.g., Green, 1994; Prior & Cummins, 1992; Bomba, O'Donnell, Markowitz & Holmes, 1996). In fact, out of the almost 350 individuals who have participated in the controlled, empirical studies of facilitated communication cited in the *Autism Research Review International* (Rimland, 1993), 316 were unable to communi-

> Although most participants in the study became tolerant of facilitation and some seemed to enjoy the instructional sessions, this did not impact their ability to communicate through [the computerized] system . . . [T]heir communicative competence was significantly greater when they used their familiar modes of communication.
>
> —**Bomba et al., (1996); study on the effectiveness of facilitated communication with fourteen students at Eden.**

cate through this method. And for the approximately 18 individuals who did show some ability to communicate, the messages were far less complex and much shorter than what proponents of facilitated communication claimed to achieve.

Studies cited by proponents of facilitated communication contain strictly anecdotal data, and are based on only a handful of subjects (Green, 1994; Holmes, 1992). The methods and procedures used are poorly described and difficult to replicate (Green, 1994; Holmes, 1992). Based on current reports, facilitated communication does not seem to be a treatment for all people with autism, as proponents have claimed (Crossley, 1990). The people described can only communicate "with certain facilitators, and in certain circumstances" (Biklen, 1990), and do not use their new language pragmatically. Finally, at odds with a decade of research which documents a strong correlation between increased communication and acceptable behavior (e.g., Carr & Durand, 1985; Durand & Carr, 1992), the "new ability to communicate" with facilitated communication does not affect other areas of performance, such as socially accepted behavior or work skills (Biklen, 1990).

TREATMENT FOLLOWING A DEVELOPMENTAL MODEL

Treatment following a developmental model is based on several assumptions. First, it is assumed that all individuals, including individuals with autism and other disabilities, will follow a predictable sequence of normal growth and development and achieve a sequence of developmental milestones. Second, it is assumed that these milestones serve as prerequisites for the development of higher order skills and that all individuals, regardless of their chronological age, must achieve these milestones in sequence. And finally, it is assumed that although individuals with disabilities may acquire developmentally-appropriate skills at a later age than

their peers, once these skills are acquired, they will be able to synthesize and use them in the same manner as their typically-developing peers (Gelardo, 1990). Skills which presumably occur first in typical development are taught first; when these skills are mastered, the sequence proceeds to skills that occur at progressively later ages (Brown et al., 1979).

Teaching within a developmental model can be a very comfortable framework for teachers, because a great deal of information exists on how young children develop and this information often forms the basis for training in special education (Gelardo, 1990). However, because individuals with autism often manifest significant skill deficits, a developmental model offers instruction only on those curriculum objectives usually mas-

An approach for treating people with autism that I see often is one that is generally used with children who have mental retardation, or delayed, but typical development. Children with autism are usually in these programs because there are no other programs for them.

It's not an effective approach for children with autism. The idea behind this approach is that a child is treated at the level he's functioning, but children with autism don't function at a developmental age. They function more at, maybe, five developmental ages. Socially they may be at three months, but with fine motor skills they may be at four years. When programs following this approach place children with autism at a particular level, I always ask what is that level. Even worse is that this approach leaves children at that level. If a child is diagnosed as functioning at a six month level, then he's six months. Period.

I recently visited a six-year-old child with autism in a program following this approach. The child was mouthing toys, and his teacher said, "Well, developmentally, he's at an age where mouthing is normal, so we've got to let him." Developmentally, that child isn't going anywhere. He could be twenty-two years old, and they're going to let him mouth toys and objects because, developmentally, he's still at eight months.

The approach is not just an accepting one, because teachers expect and hope that a child will grow developmentally, but they don't push the child. Children with autism not only need to be pushed, they occasionally need to be slam-dunked.

—**Anne S. Holmes, Director of Outreach Services**

tered by young children. As these individuals approach adolescence and adulthood, the outcome of this model is often instruction that is nonfunctional and inappropriate for the chronological age of the individual (Brown et al., 1979). Although individuals may show some progress with this model, "given the limited number of years [each individual has in school] . . . can the student possibly progress fast enough or far enough to acquire the skills needed for the most independent functioning possible in complex, heterogeneous, postschool environments?" (Brown et al., 1979).

For individuals with autism, the answer to this question is a resounding "no." The unique triad of deficits in social skills, communication skills, and repertoire of behavior and interests individuals with autism experience reduces their ability and motivation to learn the skills being acquired by their typically-developing peers (American Psychiatric Association, 1994). If a teacher were to wait for "signs of readiness" such as interest in toileting, dressing, and feeding to appear, some individuals would never acquire these skills. As a result, individuals with autism must initially be "pushed" into learning functional skills. Although Eden follows a developmental model—in that prerequisite skills are systematically identified and taught to ensure an individual's success in acquiring a skill and individuals are never pushed beyond what can reasonably be expected for a person of their chronological age—Eden actively engages all its students and participants in instruction that is community-based, functional, and chronologically-age appropriate. In this way, Eden ensures that its participants will be prepared, to the greatest extent possible, for demanding postschool environments.

TREATMENT FOLLOWING A COGNITIVE-DEVELOPMENTAL MODEL

Like the developmental model, the cognitive-developmental model also assumes that all children must progress through a certain sequence of development, but this model emphasizes the child's development of "reality systems"—the child's actions toward people, objects, and events (Miller, 1991). Cognitive-developmental theorists believe that for children with pervasive developmental disorders, such as autism, the normal infant processes of separation and individuation are disrupted, and as a result, the children ". . . become stalled at an early stage of development or . . . progress to more advanced stages in a disordered or distorted fashion" (Miller, 1991). Therapists attempt to identify each child's unique, subjective reality and implement strategies designed to resolve the child's reality problems.

Cognitive-developmental therapy is delivered through spheres— ". . . deliberately established repetitive sequences that, at first, closely simulate [the child's] nonfunctional rhythmic stereotypies" (Miller, 1991). For example, if a child persistently lacked an understanding of how he could use his own hands or body, he might be required to repetitively push over objects or pound pegs into a board. Initially, the spheres are controlled by the therapist (through hand-over-hand prompting, if necessary), but as the child progresses, it is hoped that he will be able to initiate and participate reciprocally in the spheres (Miller, 1991). The ultimate goal of cognitive-developmental therapy is to correct the aberrant manner in which children with autism orient toward and engage objects and events, and to teach flexible adaptation to people and surroundings (Miller, 1991). Because the cognitive-developmental model is based on changing an assumed, underlying dysfunction (a disrupted process of separation), it is not a model used at Eden.

TREATMENT FOLLOWING A COGNITIVE-BEHAVIORAL MODEL

Proponents of a cognitive-behavioral model of treatment advocate using a combination of behavior modification techniques and self-treatment methods such as self-monitoring, self-instruction, and self-evaluation to teach individuals to monitor and modify their own behavior. In a sense, these practitioners attempt to "teach thinking" (Meichenbaum,

Cognitive therapists view cognitions, or the "internal environment," as behaviors, subject to the same laws of development, modification and extinction as overt behaviors. Therefore, cognitive training procedures often frequently apply operant principles (e.g., shaping, positive reinforcement . . . and arranging for a high percentage of correct responses) to covert behaviors . . . Both [cognitive and behavioral] viewpoints emphasize a structured approach, methodological rigor and empirical support.

—K. Harris (1988, p.219)

1983) to "improv[e] students' self-control and self-awareness of their own learning processes" (Brown, Campione, & Day, 1981).

Like applied behavior analysis (discussed below), cognitive-behavior modification involves a careful analysis of both the task and the learner, and the formulation of operationalized goals (Harris, 1988). Training focuses on specific and concrete goals (as opposed to underlying deficits) and begins with "... simple sets of self-statements, self-instructions or self-controlled consequences" (Harris, 1988). For example, within this model, a student could be taught to monitor his own attending skills. After the teacher taught the student what behaviors comprised appropriate attending, he or she would then teach the student to self-assess whether or not he was paying attention. To cue the student to assess his attention, the teacher might ring a bell at random intervals. The student would then record his attending behavior on a score sheet, giving himself a plus for paying attention and a minus for not paying attention. As the student's attending behavior became more and more established, these prompts and cues would gradually be faded (Braswell, 1993).

For students and participants transitioning into less restrictive environments—a regular education classroom or a community work placement—cognitive strategies such as the one discussed above can decrease reliance on external supports (such as the continuous presence of a job coach) and increase independence. However, although these strategies are valuable and implemented whenever possible at Eden, they require a level of cognitive and communication skills that some students with autism may not attain.

> One of our students who had transitioned into a regular education program suddenly began crying and tantrumming in class. After observing him and talking to his teacher, we realized that he was becoming frustrated over difficult tasks. To help him control his behavior, we taught him to say to himself, "I'm having a hard time. I need to count to three and ask for help." Through a lot of guided practice and reinforcement, this student learned to use this strategy on his own. And once he realized that he had an effective strategy, the crying and tantrumming disappeared.
>
> **—Cyndy Grunning, Supervisor of Clinical Services**

APPLIED BEHAVIORAL ANALYSIS

Applied behavioral analysis is based on the idea that by manipulating stimuli surrounding a behavior, that behavior can be shaped and controlled (cf. Ferster, 1961; Lovaas, 1981). Therapists working with applied behavior analysis teach people with autism through repetitive, often one-on-one, sessions. Treatment is based heavily on data collected during the sessions. Therapists use reinforcements and punishments during the sessions to slowly build a skill such as dressing or writing one's name. The same principles are also used to reduce the negative behavior often exhibited by people with autism.

Applied behavioral analysis is becoming more and more popular as a treatment for people with autism. Studies continue to validate its effectiveness and dura-

bility in both teaching skills and reducing negative behavior (Lovaas, 1981; Lovaas, 1987; Lovaas & Smith, 1989). In 1987 Ivar Lovaas studied nineteen children who had been treated with intense behavioral modification. He found that 47 percent of the children who received the treatment had achieved normal intellectual and educational functioning (as opposed to 2 percent of the control group), 40 percent were in specialized classes for children with language delays (compared to 45 percent of the control group), and only 10 percent were in classes for children with autism or mental retardation (contrasted with 53 percent of the control group). Further, in a second follow-up study, McEachin, Smith, and Lovaas (1993) showed that 89 percent of these children continued to score within normal ranges on standardized assessments of intelligence and adaptive behavior.

Proponents of applied behavioral analysis continue to grow (e.g., Task Force on Autism in New Jersey, 1985). Lovaas and Smith (1989) state:

> *There is a remarkably close fit between learning theory [in applied behavioral analysis] and the behaviors shown by autistic children, establishing learning theory as an appropriate conceptual basis for behavioral treatment.*

Eden's programming is based on applied behavioral analysis.[1] Teachers work in small groups or one-on-one. They modify behavior and teach skills through a wide variety of reinforcement and aversive techniques[2] and keep careful data on each session.

As mentioned above, Eden does integrate elements of other treatment approaches, such as sensory integrative therapy, but these remain secondary to applied behavioral analysis.

INTENSIVE DISCRETE TRIAL TRAINING

Intensive discrete trial training (Lovaas, 1987) follows from the theory of applied behavioral analysis, but is a specific program of behavioral treatment. The intensive discrete trial training approach to treatment differs from the more global applied behavioral analysis in the expectations it holds for people with autism, and in the length of treatment it offers.

Intensive discrete trial training lasts between one and two years, and is indeed intensive. During treatment, teachers work up to forty hours a week

---

[1]   See Chapter 6 for a history of applied behavioral analysis and a description of how applied behavioral analysis is practiced at Eden.

[2]   Eden's use of aversive techniques is described in Chapter 6.

Eden and Discrete Trial Training

Eden uses discrete trial training throughout its programs as a means of jump starting skill acquisition. Although Lovaas (1993) prescribes 40 hours per week, Eden has found that for some children such intensity would be counterproductive. On average, children at Eden Institute receive approximately 20 hours per week of discrete trial training coupled with incidental and group training based upon a more global, applied behavior analysis in school and at home.

with a child with autism on a variety of skills, but focus especially on the development of verbal language (Lovaas, 1993). The theory of such intensive discrete trial training is that, by the end of treatment, the child will either be able to enter a regular education setting, or will need highly specialized, long-term services. An analysis of the data from the first group of children who began the program in the early 1980s indicates that children who are "auditory learners" (defined as children who acquire verbal imitation skills within the first three months of treatment) are most likely to achieve the best outcomes while the children who are "visual learners" (children who do not gain verbal imitative skills but show good ability in matching visual stimuli) are much less likely to do so (Lovaas, 1993). In the future, focus for this type of treatment will need to shift to the ". . . other half who did not achieve average and normal functioning," likely to be "a much more time consuming and challenging job than creating the best outcomes results" (Lovaas, 1993).

PLACEMENT OPTIONS

All people with autism can benefit from treatment, but it must be effective treatment. And effective treatment can only happen in an environment which is appropriate to the individual needs of the person being treated. To this end, the various placement options are discussed below.

There are several types of home and educational placements available to people with autism. Adults live in community group homes with other people who have disabilities. They live in supervised apartments, where they are more responsible for themselves. Some adults live in a skill development home, which is the home of a family who has been trained to work with people with disabilities. Adults can live on working farms, which provide both a home and a job. Some adults live in institutions.[3]

---

[3] Chapter 9 discusses in more detail the different residential placements available for adults with autism.

For children with autism, there is a similar variety of home placements. Many children live with their own families, but some live in foster homes with families trained to take care of their needs. Children live in institutions, and a few children live on working farms like those available for adults.

Although the home environment is important for children with autism,[4] what has received the most attention in recent years is their school placement. There is disagreement about how involved children with autism should be in regular educational classrooms. Some believe children with autism should be taught in regular education classrooms, and learn side by side with their typical peers (Biklen, 1992; Blackman, 1992; Gartner & Lipsky, 1989; Gaylord-Ross, 1989; Guralnick, 1979; Lipsky & Gartner, 1991; Simpson, 1987; Stainback & Stainback, 1991, 1992; Sailor et al., 1988). Others advocate for maintaining specialized services for children with autism, and prefer school environments which are tailored to the particular needs of children with autism (Chapman, 1992; Fuchs & Fuchs, 1994; Fuchs, Fuchs & Fernstrom, 1993; Jenkins & Heinen, 1989; Kauffman, 1993).

The concept of involving children with disabilities in the larger community has gone through several reincarnations. Since Wolfensberger's 1972 definition of normalization as "utilizing means, which are as culturally normative as possible, in order to establish and/or maintain personal behaviors and characteristics which are as culturally normative as possible," there have been many interpretations of what "normalization" is, and what it is not. Lakin and Bruiniks (1985) state that "[m]ost interpretations derive essentially from a human and societal value that the 'treatment' of developmentally disabled persons should occur within a larger context of recognizing their right to be respected as individuals and their natural membership in their native culture and community."

Terms that have sprouted from the idea behind normalization include mainstreaming, integrated education, regular education initiative, and supported inclusive education. There are important differences between these terms (Axelrod, 1992; Davis, 1989; Kauffman, 1993)[5] but more important are the similarities among them. James Kauffman (1993) summarizes:

---

[4] See Chapter 10 on how Eden works with the families of those it serves to improve and maintain a healthy home environment.

[5] Eden prefers the term "normalization." Since Eden provides lifetime services to people with autism, it has an interest in including people of all ages in the terms it uses. "Normalization" is a neutral term in this sense. Most other terms are focused specifically on educational concerns for school-aged children with autism, and thus exclude the large portion of adults with autism.

Nearly all advocates for students with disabilities want effective instruction in academic and social skills, appropriate education in the least restrictive environment, public education that accommodates students with special problems, labels that carry the least possible social stigma, parental participation in decisions to provide special services, and collaboration among all service providers.

INDIVIDUALS WITH DISABILITIES EDUCATION ACT

Public Law 94-142, the Education for All Handicapped Children Act, was passed in 1975 to address the educational needs of one million children with disabilities who were unable to attend school because their local school districts did not provide educational services for them. Now known as Public Law 102-119, the Individuals with Disabilities Education Act (IDEA), this law states that every child has the right to a "free appropriate public education" (FAPE). IDEA has several purposes: 1) to ensure that all children with disabilities have available to them a

free appropriate public education, which may mean specialized services designed to meet their unique needs; 2) to protect the rights of children with disabilities and their parents or guardians to receive these services; 3) to assist states and local governments to find the resources to provide for the education of all children with disabilities; and 4) to assess and ensure the effectiveness of efforts to educate children who have disabilities.

The debate around IDEA is on the interpretation of what an "appropriate" education for children is, in specialized educational settings or included in educational settings with typical students.

APPROPRIATENESS OF EDUCATION

"Appropriate" in "free appropriate public education" means what is most suitable to a student's particular educational needs. Although some children find full integration into regular educational settings the most beneficial (Fenske, Zalenski, Krantz & McClannahan, 1985; Lovaas, 1993), advocating integration for all children with disabilities is dangerous. Studies have shown that the regular educational system does not yet have the means to effectively educate all children with disabilities (Fuchs, Fuchs & Fernstrom, 1993; Jenkins et al., 1991; Jenkins et al., 1993; Wagner, 1993). Some children with autism find that partial integration best suits their needs (Tomchek, Gordon, Arnold, Handleman & Harris, 1992).

When Andrew first started school, he attended a specialized program for students with autism. He did very well there and was able to be mainstreamed into a regular elementary school. However, once he reached middle school, the demands in that setting became too much; he just wasn't able to learn in that setting anymore. At that point, he came to Eden. Andrew is in our vocational program now, and works in the community doing work study and volunteer work. When he graduates, he'll have a lot of "real world" experience, probably more than most high school students. For Andrew, having a continuum of placement options enabled him to be consistently challenged and reach his maximum potential.

—Ken Dorfman, Coordinating Teacher, Vocational Preparation

Others need highly specialized services, and may not do well in integrated settings (Harris & Handleman, 1986).

At a public policy conference in 1992, the Council for Administrative and Special Education Programs (CASE) reviewed the issue of inclusive education. The Council issued a statement saying that it believes in a full continuum of educational alternatives and services, and will neither support nor promote public policy which limits the range of educational opportunities or alternatives available to students with disabilities. The Council for Exceptional Children (1994) and the Autism Society of America (Torisky, 1990) support the same ideas.[6] Eden's philosophy is to use a full range of educational settings.

The appropriateness of a learning environment for a particular student should be based on the student's needs. The environment should provide him the specialized services he needs, but encourage him to learn and grow on his own. In other words, the most appropriate environment for learning is one which restricts the student as little as possible.

The best way to meet the differing needs of students with disabilities is therefore to keep all educational placements available, because narrowing the range of options available to a student limits his ability to find an education that matches his needs. For example, some students in Eden's Early Childhood program attend local preschool programs to benefit from the more challenging peer models these settings provide, and often do very well. However, as the cognitive, language, and behavioral demands increase across the later grades, not all students are able to keep pace. These students need to return to a specialized classroom in order to learn the skills they will need to compete in post-school environments. But as these students reach adolescence, many are able to return to less-specialized settings via work-study and community job placements.

Some, however, define the least restrictive environment for learning, and therefore the most appropriate environment, differently. They define the least restrictive environment not in terms of an appropriate educational experience,

---

[6]   See Chapter 3 on the type of environment Eden creates for its students and participants, and Chapters 8 and 9 for examples of how students and participants are involved in regular educational settings and their local communities.

but as the student's right to be involved in his community (Lipsky & Gartner, 1987; Stainback & Stainback, 1988). For example, Jeffrey Champagne (1992), Chief Counsel for the Pennsylvania Department of Education, sees the least restrictive environment as:

> *A measure of the degree of unrestrained opportunity a person has for proximity to, in communication with, the ordinary flow of persons in our society.*

The problem with this interpretation, and others which see the least restrictive environment in terms of a place in the community, is that it is contrary to the spirit of IDEA. The spirit of IDEA is about preparing students with disabilities to be fully included, productive members of society. This preparation is fostered through an educational experience that meets the child's unique needs, not merely through his exposure to social contacts. To participate in "the ordinary flow of persons in our society" (Champagne, 1992) requires an appropriate educational experience. To this end, every state has truancy laws that require *all* children to be properly educated at least until age 16 in order to prepare them to be productive members of society (and not merely more social).

Placing typically developing children in school every day is deemed appropriate because it prepares them to be productive members of society. The goal for students with disabilities is the same. What is required for them to reach this goal just may be different. IDEA was enacted to ensure students' rights to effective schooling, not to ensure their rights to participate in their communities (Davila, 1992).

Eden's view on the least restrictive environment for students with disabilities was summarized in a 1985 testimony before the Senate Education Committee on the Reauthorization of Public Law 94-142:

> *We contend that "least restrictive environment" cannot be interpreted as a segregation vs. integration issue, or a "proximity to the child's home" issue, nor a public vs. private issue. Rather, least restrictive environment must be interpreted based upon the educational needs of the child with autism. As such, we support all regulatory changes that relate to least restrictive environment that allow for a free and appropriate education based upon the child's specific special education needs. (Holmes, 1985)*

Students with Disabilities and Full Inclusion

Interpreting the term "supported inclusive education" to mean that students with significant educational, developmental, and social disabilities should be educated only in regular classes overlooks the sensitivity of students with disabilities, especially students with autism. Enabling people with autism to access normalized activities in the community takes a great deal of work, perceptiveness, and communication from all parties involved—parents, teachers, community members, and most importantly, the student himself. Students with autism are very sensitive to their environment. They need consistency, stability, and gradual change. The "just do it" approach advocated by many who believe in mandatory inclusion deposits the student into a completely novel and unfamiliar environment. An abrupt and total change in his environment would be highly confusing to a student with autism. Difficulty with change and transition and a desire to keep the environment as stable and familiar as possible are major characteristics of autism (American Psychiatric Association, 1994) and must be addressed systematically through structured teaching and a system of support.

Inclusive education received a large boost in the case of *Oberti v. Clementon School District,* decided by the United States Court of appeals on May 28, 1993. The Obertis sought to place their 8-year-old child with Down syndrome in a regular class in the neighborhood elementary school. The school district offered placement in a class for educable mentally retarded children. The Office of Administrative Law ruled for the district, but on appeal that decision was reversed.

Under the IDEA children with disabilities have a right to instruction specially designed to meet their unique needs, and that "to the maximum extent appropriate, children with disabilities are [to be] educated with children who are not disabled, and that special classes [are used] only when the nature and severity of the disability is such that education in regular classes with the use of supplementary aids and services cannot be achieved satisfactorily...."

To determine whether a district is in compliance with the IDEA's mainstreaming requirements, the Oberti court adopted a two part test asking (1) whether education in the regular classroom, with the use of supplemental aids and services, can be achieved satisfactorily, and (2) if not, whether the school has mainstreamed the child to the maximum extent appropriate by attempting to include the child in school programs with nondisabled children whenever possible. (H. Hinkle, 1995)

Although some specialized supports may continue to be offered, like an aide in the classroom or continued monitoring from clinicians, the total inclusion of students with autism into the regular educational system means cutting them off from at least some specialized support systems. These support systems are what enabled them to begin to be included in the first place. Reducing support before a student is ready to attempt more independence could lead to frustration, confusion, and ultimately regression for the student.

Some services are impossible to provide in the regular education class. Students with autism who have the cognitive skills to benefit from the instruction provided in a regular education class may continue to need a structured environment and a low student to teacher ratio in order to control their behavior and attend to classroom instruction. Additionally, a student may need to remain in a specialized environment to, for example, build social skills or gain adequate self-esteem. These may not be skills the student can adequately work on in a regular classroom. The full inclusion approach cannot be flexible enough in meeting each student's individual needs.

Although an inclusive setting may be appropriate for students with disabilities who do not have the serious cognitive challenges associated with autism, advocates for fully including students with disabilities into the regular educational system believe that the regular classroom is the best placement for any student, regardless of the student's level of ability. Such an absolute position does not just narrow the array of placement options available to students with disabilities, it eliminates it. For these advocates, only one choice is left—mandatory, full inclusion. If this choice does not happen to fit the particular needs of a student, no other options would be available.

REGULAR EDUCATION AND FULL INCLUSION

A further problem with fully including students with autism into classrooms with their typically developing peers is that the regular education system is not ready to handle the challenges the majority of students with autism present. It takes long, hard work to determine precisely how each student's special needs can best be met.[7] Teachers in special education have been working for decades since the founding of the special education system to find out which educational interactions work best for students with disabilities, how best to meet the students' challenges, and what each student's educational potential is.

Teachers in the regular education system know about IDEA and how special education is governed in general, but do not yet understand how to address the needs of students with disabilities in their regular classrooms (Wilson & Sailor, 1992). They have not been exposed to the types of educational interventions needed by students with disabilities, and often do not have the time to learn teaching methods specifically for the students with disabilities in their classroom (Semmel, Abernathy, Butera & Lesar, 1991).

Finally, when inclusion in the regular education system is mandatory and not a carefully selected option for an individual student, the result is not true inclusion, where the student is a full, active participant in the class, but rather "physi-

---

[7] See Chapters 3 and 6 for a description of how Eden teaches its students and participants.

We are trying to include Thomas, a fourth grader, in a regular educational setting, but are having problems with some of the staff there. They find some of his minor behavioral problems to be overwhelming. For example, Thomas does not like the school bell, and covers his ears every time. But he covers his ears by crossing his arms, then putting his hands over his ears. He also tantrums when he hears bells. The regular education staff thought this behavior was awful and appalling. It is a major challenge for us to help his teachers better understand and deal with his disruptive behavior.

—**Anne S. Holmes, Director of Outreach Services**

cal inclusion," where the student's physical presence in the classroom is the only way in which he or she could be considered "included."

Although it is possible to train teachers in regular education on what methods work best with students who have special needs, Kearney and Durand (1992) recently documented that schools of education are failing to provide sufficient coursework and field experience to enable general education students to work in integrated or mainstreamed settings. Dorothy Rubin, Professor of Education at The College of New Jersey, parallels this finding:

> *Unfortunately, regular classroom teachers are still often at a loss as to what to do with the disabled children who have been integrated into their classrooms for the full day. Most teachers are just not prepared for this role. Many are not receiving the special support they are supposed to be getting.... While at college, most regular classroom teachers have had to take less and less education courses and most did not have to take any special education courses. How well equipped are they to handle disabled children, especially severely disabled ones?*

For a challenging disability like autism, both training and ongoing support are necessary (Harris & Handleman, 1986; Holmes & Holmes, 1987; Lovaas, 1981). However, there is little likelihood that even the most motivated teachers will be able to obtain and more importantly *maintain* the supports they need for their students to be successful in this setting.

INCLUSION IS STILL NECESSARY

Although students with disabilities may need special supports to reach their goals, it would be a tremendous disservice to them not to support the concepts associated with inclusive education. If students are to become productive, they will need to be included in society. The special supports they need must therefore be geared toward including people with autism as much as possible in the regular world around them. So it is not the ideas behind supported inclusive education, but the narrow interpretation of what supported inclusive education means, that is detrimental to the education of students with disabilities.

Including students with disabilities in society could mean placing the student with his typically developing peers in a local public school, if the student's family and teachers decide it would result in an appropriate educational experience for him. Or, inclusion could mean that the student attends a highly specialized special education program, but visits a local regular education school once a week to participate in physical exercise activities, or to eat lunch in the cafeteria. Each of these inclusion options, as well as those in between, would provide the student with the educational supports he needs, but would also provide opportunities for him to interact with his peers in regular education.

The concept of full inclusion is important in another way as well. Holding full inclusion as an ideal goal for each student can give teachers inspiration to continue the often frustrating work of teaching students with autism. It provides teachers with the impetus to continue their efforts to find transitional opportunities for students in less specialized settings, even if both parents and teachers realize that full inclusion may be too large a goal for a child.

CHOOSING CAREFULLY

> *A painful question remains—whether parents and those who care deeply about autistic individuals are choosing to see them as they would like them to be, rather than respecting them for who they are.*
>
> **Frontline: Prisoners of Silence, October 19, 1993**

It is important to be slightly skeptical of the idealistic "solutions" in placement or treatment for people with autism. They are appealing because they feed the hope that a cure can be found for a pervasive, developmental disorder, or that a way can be found around a person's autism, but they usually offer only short-term solutions to the challenges faced by people with autism.

Incorporating elements of new theories or treatments must be done deliberately, and only after empirical proof of the effectiveness of the approach has been demonstrated. Doing anything less is a disservice to people with autism.

In the *Me Book*, Lovaas (1981) states that one of the first major mistakes he and his treatment team made in working with individuals with autism was to expect a breakthrough; he relates an analogy made by a former colleague, Ben McKeever of the University of Washington:

> *[R]esearchers [can be divided] into two groups, shaft sinkers and pyramid builders. A shaft sinker moves in relative isolation; he moves*

from one area to another, sinking shafts and hoping that he will strike a well of knowledge. When he does, a great number of problems will be solved at the same time. On the other hand, a pyramid builder feels that knowledge can best be gained by several persons working together, where each piece of information is sought to complement or strengthen the other pieces of information, where higher levels are built after lower levels and so on…. Personality theorists, psychopathologists and the like would be the shaft sinkers; behaviorists would be the pyramid builders. So far, the shaft sinkers haven't struck oil yet. The behaviorists have more going for them; the foundation of the pyramid under construction is more substantial and more reassuring than a dry well.

By being careful about which ideas in the sometimes fickle field of special education a service agency chooses to adopt, the agency is able to create a stable environment for those it serves. Some programs have quickly adopted new treatment methodologies, and have caused radical changes in the environments they provide. This has resulted in an extremely unstable environment for those in the programs.

This happened, for example, in many programs that adopted facilitated communication before any empirical studies of the treatment had been done. The Autism Program of Oswald D. Heck Developmental Center in Schenectady, New York is one well publicized example. In 1991, some clinical staff members became interested in facilitated communication and attended training sessions offered through Syracuse University. The staff immediately began using this technique with the individuals attending the program as well as training other staff members. "The use of facilitated communication proliferated rapidly during

> It was amazing to me to see how willing people are to abandon their beliefs and adopt a new belief without verification . . . and do that virtually overnight.
>
> —Douglas Wheeler, Clinical Coordinator, O.D. Heck Developmental Center, on *Frontline: Prisoners of Silence*, October 19, 1993

this period, with eventually 25 people with autism and 21 staff members actively involved" (Wheeler, Jacobson, Paglieri, & Schwartz, 1993). To document the validity of the participants' facilitated communications, the center designed and implemented a study protocol. When the results of this study were analyzed, they clearly showed that the participants' communications were under the "systematic and unknowing" control of their facilitators. In addition to the potential harm this technique could have caused the individuals in the program, the impact it had on the morale of the staff who had been implementing it was devastating. Marian Pitsas, a speech pathologist with the O.D. Heck Center, recalled:

> *It was devastating to see the data just there in black and white in front of you. It was mind-boggling…. It took me months, I think, before I could talk about it with some people without breaking down in tears (Frontline: Prisoners of Silence, October 19, 1993).*

The best way to ensure wise decisions in choosing placement and treatment for people with autism is to first look at the needs and abilities of each person individually. Each individual with autism will vary in terms of the number of symptoms he has, the severity of those symptoms, and his level of cognitive ability. Additionally, some individuals will experience other disabilities as well, including epilepsy, hearing impairment, and visual impairment (American Psychiatric Association, 1994). This great degree of variability necessitates careful assessment of the individual's complex learning needs. Schools must not only be sensitive to the needs of the student with autism when making placement or treatment decisions, but also consider the practitioner who will teach the student. Only after this assessment should placement and treatment strategies be considered.

Eden embraces the tenets of the Autism Society of America's "Priorities of Professional Conduct" (1996) in determining whether and how to use any treatment or educational theory, new or old, proven or unproven.

◆ ◆

Autism Society of America
Priorities of Professional Conduct

In order to distinguish a valid search for knowledge, interventions and/or practices from false advertisement and promotion, the Panel of Professional Advisors seeks to support the following priorities.

1. The generation of promising theories and hypotheses related to the understanding and treatment of autism.
2. The investigation of promising theories through scientific research.
3. The responsibility to identify clearly the investigation phase of such theories and/or interventions.
4. The full and free informed consent of consumers (self, parents, guardians, service providers and/or advocates) regarding the current status of such theories and/or interventions including:
   ◆ Potential Benefits/Risks   ◆ Costs
   ◆ Alternatives   ◆ Conflict of Interest
   ◆ Absence of Guaranteed Results

These priorities are adopted to address the vulnerability of consumers.

Approved July 15, 1993
Panel of Professional Advisors

◆ ◆

Being careful and thoughtful in choosing what sort of treatment and placement to provide people with autism gives them the effective treatment they deserve. It gives them the support they need in an environment that encourages their independence.

Guidelines for Theories & Priorities

Over the years, Eden has observed that the promotion of unproven theories and treatments has had a profound effect on the course of treatment for individuals with autism. There has been a relatively consistent pattern of events that play out when unproven theories and practices are promoted. Those events include:

- ◆ initial excitement;
- ◆ interest generated by the popular media;
- ◆ nonreplication of the theory or practice under controlled conditions;
- ◆ excuses proffered by proponents for nonreplication;
- ◆ accusations by proponents against those who voice concerns regarding the theories or practices;
- ◆ the development of an ardent group of true believers in the theory or practice; and
- ◆ the inevitable distraction of the development of effective treatments as these events play out, often upwards of four to six years before the excitement abates and the unproven treatments or theories find their proper leveling point.

Eden follows ASA's guidelines listed below for theories and treatments, not to discourage the development of new theories or treatments, but rather to encourage the full disclosure of the nature of the theory or treatment, its history, and its prospects for the future. The ultimate objective of these guidelines is to help our parents and teachers assess unproven theories and treatments and to limit their reckless promotion, a practice which has increased misunderstanding of autism and people with autism.

GUIDELINES

In assessing all theories and treatments parents and teacher need to answer the following:

1. Does the promoter adhere to the Priorities of Professional Conduct promulgated by ASA?
2. What is the purpose of this new theory/practice?
3. What do I have to do to benefit from the theory/practice and what are its lasting effects?
4. What is the status of this new theory/practice relative to controlled (scientific) investigation, and is there a reference list of publications?
5. How long must my child be involved in this new theory/practice to gain benefit?
6. Are there any physical or psychological harms that might come to my child as a function of participating in this new theory/practice?
7. What are the personal costs of time and money that I will have to endure, and will I be able to be reimbursed for these expenses?
8. How do I know that the costs for the implementation of this new theory/practice are fair and reasonable?
9. Are the theoreticians or practitioners competently and appropriately trained and prepared to implement the provisions of the theory/practice, and how is this competence assured?

10. What steps will be taken to protect my privacy?
11. Are there any legal actions, current or past, against promoters, consumers, or practitioners of the theory/practice?
12. How will the effects of this theory/practice be evaluated for my child?
13. By choosing this theory/practice, what alternatives (proven and unproven) are not being pursued?
14. Does this approach exclude other alternative approaches and does it mesh with my child's total program?
15. Which individuals with autism has this theory/practice positively benefited, and under what conditions?

GENERAL CONDITIONS

Proponents of theories and practices must inform participants that they are free to participate, free to decline to participate, or withdraw from the treatment; they must explain the foreseeable consequences of declining or withdrawing; they must inform participants of significant factors that may be expected to influence their willingness to participate, such as risks, discomfort, adverse effects or limitations, confidentiality; they must explain other aspects of which the prospective participants inquire; and they must protect the prospective participants from adverse consequences of declining or withdrawing from participation.

For persons who are legally incapable of giving informed consent, the proponents of theories and practices must provide an appropriate explanation to a guardian if substitute consent is permitted by law.

In offering inducements to participate in the theory or practice, proponents must make clear to each participant the nature of the services as well as the risks, obligations, and limitations. Proponents must not offer excessive or inappropriate financial or other such inducements to obtain participation. Proponents must never deceive participants regarding significant aspects that would affect their willingness to engage in or make use of the theory or practice, such as physical risks, discomfort, unpleasant emotional experiences, and/or financial demands. Theories and practices must not be presented in a misleading or fraudulent manner; either because of what is stated, conveyed or suggested, or because of what is omitted concerning research or practice.

IMMEDIATE PRESENTATIONS

Proponents of theories and practices in public lectures, demonstrations, radio or television programs, prerecorded tapes, printed articles, mailed material, or other media forms must ensure that statements are consistent with the ASA Priorities of Professional Conduct Statement (July 15, 1993)

TESTIMONIALS

Proponents of theories and practices must not solicit testimonials from current consumers or persons who, because of their particular circumstances, are vulnerable to undue influence.

Developed by the Panel of Professional Advisors and approved by the
Autism Society of America Board on January 17, 1997.

Chapter 6

Modifying

Behavior

Many things are taught at Eden: social skills, self management, domestic skills, communication and employment skills, and academic skills from learning readiness to grade level. Some individuals work primarily or exclusively on early learning skills, while others become proficient enough academically to be included in their local schools and to hold competitive employment in the community. Although academic subjects are taught at some level to all those Eden serves, working on skills that will enable the child to be as independent an adult as possible is the primary focus of Eden's programming. Initially children usually need to be taught how to learn and also how to self-manage their behavior. They need help in learning life skills, such as dressing and communicating their wants and needs. This chapter explains how Eden teaches these skills, and describes in detail Eden's approach to modifying behavior.

APPLIED BEHAVIOR ANALYSIS

Eden's approach to enabling people with autism to learn and become self-reliant is founded on the principle of applied behavior analysis. This approach uses a scientific basis for making decisions about the education and treatment of children with autism. It enables parents to more thoughtfully interact with children and adults with autism. Research and experience shows that children and adults with autism require a systematic approach to education and training; Eden has found that applied behavior analysis provides the precision that is needed.

In 1961 Ferster presented the first theory of autism based on a behavioral model (Ferster, 1961; Ferster & DeMyer, 1961). His premise: Autistic behaviors could be controlled and changed by the manipulation of stimuli before and after the behavior. He believed that autistic behavior resulted from the failure to learn the significance of social stimuli, and that a child's autistic behavior was his means of communicating in lieu of more appropriate responses. He hypothesized that manipulating the social reinforcers both before and after the child's autistic behavior would teach him more appropriate responses. Because Ferster focused on the child's behavior and the environment surrounding the behavior, his work bypassed the need to find a cause for autism before developing effective treatment. He was able to treat without having to know why the child behaved autisticaly.

Over the ensuing several years, Ivar Lovaas and his colleagues demonstrated that this behavioral theory worked in a natural environment through available social reinforcement. They found that the application of behavioral techniques could be broadened to teach not only social behavior, but speech, hygiene skills, play skills, and other behavior (Lovaas, Berberich, Perloff & Schaeffer, 1966; Lovaas, Frietag, Kinder, Rubenstein, Schaeffer & Simmons, 1966; Lovaas, Freitag, Nelson & Whalen, 1967). Lovaas and his colleagues also found that punishment such as an electric shock and a verbal "no" were extremely effective in modifying a child's autistic behavior. Although questioned on moral and ethical grounds,[1] they found aversive techniques critical to the success of the children in their program. Since the mid 1960s Lovaas has done more to advance and refine the behavioral treatment of autism than perhaps any one else in the field. His work continues to be central in the ongoing development of behavioral treatment methodologies (e.g., Lovaas, 1977; Lovaas, 1981; Lovaas, 1987; McEachin et al., 1993).

In 1967 Risley and Wolf formulated a series of training techniques to modify behavior that too were based on the principles of behavioral technology (Risley & Wolf, 1967). They developed the basic elements of behavior modification treatments used today: shaping, modelling, prompt fading, extinction, time-out from receiving reinforcement, and several reinforcement strategies to encourage acceptable behavior and discourage unacceptable behavior.

---

[1] For a review of the use of aversive interventions, see Repp, A.C. and Singh, N.W. (Eds), *Perspectives on the Use of Nonaversive and Aversive Interventions for Persons with Developmental Disabilities.* Sycamore, IL: Sycamore Publishing Co. 1990.

Evidence for the effectiveness of a behavioral approach to treating autism grew, and was firmly established as a treatment method by the end of the 1960s. Over the next few decades, discrete trial teaching (Lovaas, 1981) and task analysis techniques (Gold, 1976) created stronger, even more effective behavior modification treatment approaches. Today, behavior modification, or more formally, applied behavioral analysis (ABA), remains the treatment of choice for people with autism.[2]

The elements of ABA that are most important at Eden are the consistent and individualized treatment by parents and teachers, and the integral role of the family in choosing, with professionals, what treatment is appropriate for their child. In the treatment process, parents and teachers strive to foster compliance and impulse control, to teach successively more difficult skills, to enable the student to make decisions for himself, and to institute a work ethic.[3] These goals are fundamental components of Eden's approach to teaching people with autism. Each of them is outlined below.[4]

THE IMPORTANCE OF CONSISTENCY

The most critical element in the success of a program to modify behavior is the consistency with which it is applied. People with autism have a need for stability and a sense of order in their lives. They need to know what to expect and when. A consistent approach to treatment not only fills these needs, but uses them to further learning. The student is given rules and consequences for behavior, and therefore works in the predictable, stable environment he requires. Fortunately, following those rules results in skill acquisition and the modification of his behavior. What could be defined as a weakness—an intense desire for order—is thus used as a strength.

Because of the importance of consistency in treatment, Eden has clearly defined the parameters of its ABA approach. The data collected daily on each student is charted and analyzed regularly, and programs are developed through a rigorous step-by-step process. Procedures for teaching and maintaining skills are similarly established, and data is managed with a clear, precise system.[5]

Consistency in applying programs to modify behavior is ensured in other ways too. Faculty members from different programs regularly meet to make sure they

---

[2] See the Autism Society of America's Statement on behavior modification, given on pages 90-91.

[3] Note that although "student" is used in this chapter and the next, the material being presented applies to all people with autism at Eden, whether children, adolescents, or adults.

[4] These goals are pursued at the same time, and in harmony, with the principles underlying Eden's view of autism, as presented in Chapter 3: seeing students with autism as individuals, and as participants in the process of treatment; treating them as if they are capable of learning in a specialized "prosthetic" environment; making decisions for them only when necessary, but giving them as little care as possible; being empathetic to them; maintaining a balance of urgency and vigilance in treatment; and being committed unconditionally to helping them learn.

[5] See Chapters 6 and 7 for a complete description of each step of the process of developing strategies to modify behavior, and exactly how data on behavior modification programs are managed.

are working toward goals in a unified manner, and using techniques in the same way to reach those goals. In addition, the forms teachers use to evaluate skills or behaviors are standardized across programs, so that any teacher can quickly and easily see what each student is working on, what techniques are being used, and what progress has occurred.

Using standardized forms and holding group staff meetings is important not only in making sure that techniques are used in the same way across programs, but in making sure that they are used in the same way for each student. For example, the group home and work programs for adults teach many of the same skills, like sorting (laundry or assembling parts) or cleaning (washing dishes or tidying a work space). Faculty from each program create a participant's IHP together and coordinate their goals using similar techniques to reach those goals.

Consistency between the home and school environment is increased for students at Eden Institute through home training and respite services. Teachers come into the student's home and either teach parents the techniques used with the student during school, or actually teach the student at home, while parents observe and later participate. This gives parents a way to deal with the often frustrating behavior their child exhibits, and also helps the student learn more quickly, because what he is taught in school can be carried into the home.

Consistency is especially important in behavior modification programs which use aversive techniques. These techniques should be used for as short an amount of time as possible. Being consistent in using them is the best way to shorten the length of time they are needed. To make sure Eden's teachers are consistent in using an aversive procedure, each teacher working with the student goes through a role playing of the program before implementing it, and practices it until all teachers implement the program in exactly the same way. Once the program is implemented, checks are made regularly to ensure consistency.[6]

INDIVIDUATION
◆ ◆ ◆ ◆ ◆ ◆ ◆ ◆ ◆ ◆ ◆ ◆ ◆ ◆ ◆ ◆ ◆ ◆ ◆

Although people with autism often present strikingly similar behaviors, the reasons behind their behaviors are often quite different. For example, two students may have self-injurious behavior such as head banging, but one may do it to avoid a stressful situation, while the other does it because of a painful ear infection. The behavior exhibited is the same, but the motivation behind the behavior is very different. In order for a behavior modification strategy to work for each student, it must take into account the reasons behind a behavior. It must consider each student's behavior and environment individually. If the same strategy to modify behavior were used for both of the students mentioned above, such as lightly re-

---

[6] Again, see Chapters 6 and 7 for more on the development and use of behavior modification programs, including aversive interventions.

straining them when they begin their self injurious behavior, it might help the student who bangs his head as a way to avoid a stressful situation, but it would do nothing to cure the other student's ear infection.

A strategy to modify behavior for each student must be tailored. The student's needs, physical health, environment, and level of ability must all be taken into account to create a strategy that addresses not only the behavior, but what lies behind the behavior.[7]

No one strategy to modify behavior will work the same way for every student because every student has unique differences. Identifying these differences is crucial in finding the best approach to modifying behavior. For example, if one student finds cookies highly rewarding, they can be used as a motivator to change his behavior, but another student may not even like cookies, and so a behavior modification strategy using cook-ies as a reinforcer would not be effective with him. In fact, it would serve as a punisher. The second student may find social reinforcers highly rewarding instead. Knowing this is critical to developing an effective strategy to modify his behavior.

Strategies to modify behavior are part of a student's Individualized Education Plan (IEP) or Individualized Habilitation Plan (IHP). Each IEP and IHP at Eden is developed with a particular student in mind, but all IEPs and IHPs have several general themes in common. They aim to foster compliance and impulse control as values, they build on skills previously taught in a pyramid-like fashion, they enable students to make decisions for themselves, and they give students a work ethic, which helps to make them as independent as possible. The next several sections discuss these themes in detail.

FOSTERING COMPLIANCE AND IMPULSE CONTROL

The inability to follow directions can impede learning throughout a student's life. If someone cannot listen to and follow the most basic commands, he will not be able to achieve even minimal independence. And if he cannot control his impulses, he will not be able to concentrate on the most simple tasks. Even watching television requires the ability to sit for some length of time, which many people with autism do not naturally possess.

---

[7] See Chapter 7 for how Eden does this.

Compliance with directions is one of the first things taught to students at Eden, and continues to be a priority as new skills are taught. Each new student at Eden has a program in his IEP to teach compliance. These programs usually begin with basic commands like "sit down," "come here," and "look at me." By reinforcing the student for following these commands, he is slowly taught to value compliance.

Compliance is especially important for young students or students who have no prior schooling because people with autism tend toward noncompliance. Since people with autism generally prefer to remain in their own world, they resist contact or demands that infringe upon that world. They can be noncompliant simply by not paying attention to requests or commands that they know how to follow, or by deliberately exhibiting unacceptable behavior, like saying "no" repeatedly, self-injuring, refusing to speak, escaping (running), or responding with every possible alternative except the correct answer.

> **N**ot being able to follow directions can be a real problem, especially for the younger children. For example, if a child is darting around the room and doesn't sit down when teachers ask him to, he can cause the whole class to be disrupted. He often learns that darting around brings him attention, and so will make noncompliance into a game. He will dart around, disrupt the other children, and not be learning any productive skills. Teachers need to address noncompliant behavior right away so that it doesn't become a major problem.
>
> —**Denise Burns-Jennings, Coordinating Teacher, Early Childhood**

Teaching compliance as a value to people with autism also teaches them to control their impulses. Following a command consistently often means they have to restrain themselves from impulsive behavior. For example, if a student is supposed to be sitting in a chair, he cannot be running around. If he is being asked to name objects, he cannot also be having a tantrum. And if he is in an exercise program walking on a treadmill, he cannot simultaneously be aggressive toward someone else.

Although programs to teach compliance often teach impulse control at the same time, additional programs are

> **S**ean learned that he would get wanted attention by being noncompliant. When his teachers asked him to sit down, he would instead jump up and down. The more they asked him to comply, the more he jumped. For Sean, noncompliance was a way to manipulate his environment to get what he wanted—attention.
>
> —**Carol Markowitz, Director of Educational Services**

also employed to specifically teach impulse control. These programs focus on eliminating the need for the impulsive behavior, on replacing it with a more appropriate alternative, or on decreasing it by applying uncomfortable consequences to the behavior.[8]

---

[8] These programs are described in the sections below on increasing and decreasing behavior, and in the following chapter on the Eden Decision Model.

Programs to teach compliance and impulse control impose an external control and structure on behavior. The programs aim at gradually instilling this control and structure in the student himself, so he will be able to control his own behavior independent from a specialized setting. This process begins with teaching the student the skills he needs in order to effectively approach a learning situation, and continues by building on those basic skills.

LEARNING TO LEARN

Unlike their typically developing peers, students with autism seldom start school "ready to learn." They are often unable to sit quietly in a chair, attend to a teacher, imitate, or take care of basic needs such as toileting and feeding. Upon first entering Eden, students are started on programs to teach them the basic skills that they will need in order to learn.

Once learned, these basic skills are part of the student's skill repertoire, and so are part of any future formal or vicarious skill learning. For example, after learning the basic skill of sitting in a chair, a student would be able to work on eye contact with the teacher while sitting in a chair. Similarly, if a student had learned how to pronounce several different sounds, and knew the names of his mother and father, he might then be taught to call his mother and father by name. By incorporating previous skills into new teaching programs, a student's skills build up like a pyramid. This makes the student more capable and helps him toward greater degrees of independence.

Lovaas noted that the children with autism he taught learned, to some extent, the actual process of learning. For example, the children were able to learn new pronouns more quickly after having learned one pronoun. They understood something about the category of pronouns, although they did not verbalize this. What they had learned gave them a head start in learning new pronouns, and so they learned them more quickly. Lovaas also called this a "savings over tasks," and "positive acceleration."

The students at Eden also show this type of "learning to learn," however, some only in a limited way. For many children with autism, the severity of their disability and their level of neurological dysfunction generally make it improbable that they will achieve the abstraction of Lovaas' "learning to learn." However, the first interaction students at Eden have with their teacher is often a very basic form of Lovaas's "learning to learn." Nancy Guggenheim, Coordinating Teacher of Adaptive Physical Education:

The hardest thing is the first interaction, to get them to see that, really, it is not so bad to look at me for a second. Once they realize that what I am asking is not the end of the world, they start learning more quickly. They become more positively engaged with their environment.

Outside their first interaction, students' ability to make the rapid progress described by Lovaas is limited to very simple concepts. For example, they tend to learn temporal and spacial sequencing because these concepts are relatively basic and students work on sequencing in just about every skill. Temporally structured skills are those like making lunch (planning the meal, then taking out the food, then making it, then cleaning up) or assembling items (getting the parts, then going through the steps in order to complete the item). Spacial skills include finding one's way to the bathroom, knowing where food items are located in the grocery store, and remembering where to put the toys away.

Enabling Decision Making and Quality of Life Enhancement

Although the students at Eden have difficulty demonstrating the cognitive ability to comprehend abstractions, they can learn to make decisions for themselves. Being able to make decisions opens up many opportunities, and enables a student to have more control over his environment. Students and adults with autism who have been given the opportunity to make choices concerning their

daily schedule and activities have shown fewer social avoidance behaviors (Koegel, Dyer & Bell, 1987; Dyer, 1989), generally reduced problem behaviors (Dyer, Dunlap & Winterling, 1990), the ability to attend to a task for longer periods of time (Parsons, Reid, Reynolds & Bumgarner, 1990), more frequent spontaneous interactions (Peck, 1985), and more language learning (Koegel, Koegel & Surratt, 1992).

Choice-making at Eden is initially taught in a concrete manner. For example, a student may be given a choice between two edible reinforcers, and asked "Do you want cookies or chips?" while seeing the teacher holding them. The student's request or his reaching for either the cookies or chips is reinforced by receiving them.

The range of choices is expanded as the student becomes more proficient in choice-making, and concrete learning is supplemented by abstract learning. For example, real objects are represented by photographs, line drawings, written words, and other abstract representations of objects. The student's decision making is then expanded to activities in educational, vocational, and life skills programming, so he can begin to decide for himself how to spend his time.

Initially, choices are controlled to make sure students do not become confused or frustrated. Controlling choices also avoids any implication of right or wrong in choosing between options. For example, a student would not be offered a choice between doing his school work or going out to play. Instead, he would be offered a choice between two or three work related activities or between two or three play activities.

As the student becomes comfortable in making these types of decisions, teacher and parent control over decision-making begins to relax, and the student is expected to make choices about naturally occurring events. For example, if he is in the kitchen to prepare lunch, and sees both milk and juice in the refrigerator, the teacher will ask him which he wants. Under naturally occurring conditions, these are really incidental learning situations, because they are not set up or controlled by the teacher. As the student becomes even more proficient in making choices, he will be able to see the two choices and decide for himself spontaneously which one he wants, without any prompting.

Enabling a student to make acceptable choices fosters greater degrees of independence, and gives him more control over his environment and a higher quality of life. Choice-making skills enable him to decide what to do, when, and how, balancing his desires with those of society. This phenomenon becomes even more critical when the student enters adult services.

INSTITUTING A WORK ETHIC

The independence a student gains by being able to make socially acceptable decisions for himself is especially important in finding and maintaining employment. No employer would be willing to step in and coax an employee through every decision that had to be made throughout the day, like what side to put the staples on, whether to sharpen a pencil, or which soft drink to have with lunch. Decision making skills, along with a strong work ethic, are two of the most important factors in moving a student toward independence in adult life.

Students who are severely challenged with autism are capable of performing difficult and productive work, but only if training in basic employment skills is begun early. Teaching work-oriented skills at an early age begins to give the student the means and stamina he will need to sustain employment. He learns employable skills such as sequencing, assembly, disassembly, collation, and quality control, and gradually increases the amount of time he can attend to a work task. In learning such things, the student acquires a rudimentary work ethic. This work ethic is not like that of a typical worker. The student is not necessarily conscious of following a set of values for industry, and does not initially have the same concerns about his work that a typical worker would have. Most students do find work gratifying, and it is important to them to do a job to its completion.

The students' work ethic not only eases future vocational skill acquisition and eventual employment, but helps them obtain the self-care and life skills that enable them to be active participants in society. For example, in working on skills

such as assembling packs of pencils or collating pages of a book, a student learns how to organize objects. He also learns that the steps of a task have to be performed in a particular order, and that doing a good job means getting each step right. This knowledge helps the student in other areas, like dressing himself in the morning or washing his hands. He knows that there are steps to each of these tasks, and that he has to take each step in order. Initially, this knowledge may not be generalizable to new tasks, but students are able, after several years, to learn sequences of steps in a new task more quickly. This is evidence of the generalization of their knowledge, and of the emergence of their basic work ethic.

A work ethic is instilled gradually in students. Most begin by requiring continuous adult supervision to complete any task, and can work only on the simplest prevocational tasks. By the time students leave the Middle Childhood or Transition Programs, however, many are able to work at a task for up to a half hour without teacher intervention, and possess a range of skills. Each student's skill repertoire (number of skills they possess) and rate of productivity is expanded even further in vocational preparation programs, where real work is performed. Later, in supervised community work-study placements, students will be taught even more skills, and will work at closer to a normed rate and at more complex tasks.

These general themes—fostering compliance and impulse control, learning to learn, enabling decision-making, and instituting a work ethic—are common to all individualized education or habilitation plans developed for students at Eden. The IEPs or IHPs reflect these general themes through very specific behavior goals for each student. Following the model of applied behavior analysis, these goals are set by analyzing the function of a particular behavior. Behaviors that take the place of unacceptable impulses or result in skill acquisition are encouraged, while behaviors that isolate the student from more normalized settings or serve no productive function are discouraged. The methods used by Eden to increase or decrease behaviors, and the reasoning behind these methods, are discussed in the following sections.

Productivity Program for Tommy in the Transition Classroom

THE TARGET BEHAVIOR

Tommy will maintain a constant rate of work at 50% of the norm referenced rate for periods up to two one-half hour periods with a minimum of 95% accuracy. If normed rates for tasks are not available, several teachers will perform the task to determine an average rate.

PREREQUISITES FOR THE PROGRAM

Tommy will independently complete 10 trials of a given task with 95% accuracy for a period of 3 days.

THE CRITERION

The rate of work will be: 50% of the normed rate: constant for each half-hour, and performed with 95% accuracy.

THE MEASUREMENT

The rate of work for each half-hour period will be recorded, the percent of error will be figured, and the rate will be compared to normed rates.

THE PROCEDURE

1. Tommy will be given a task with all the necessary materials and specific instructions for completing the task for one half-hour period.
2. The length of time Tommy spends on the task will be increased by a one-half hour increment until he is able to perform the task at the established criterion for two one-half hour periods.
3. Tommy will perform a variety of tasks involving increasing levels of complexity (tasks involving one, two, and three or more steps) at the established criterion for two one-half hour periods.

PROMPTING TECHNIQUES

Ignore decreases in productivity, but reward stable or increased rates through a reinforcement schedule based on time with Tommy's favorite toy.

PRESENT STATUS OF PROGRAM FOR TOMMY, OCTOBER, 1993

Tommy has mastered steps 1-2 of the procedure, and can perform them independently.

Increased Task Duration Program for Tommy in the Transitions Classroom

THE TARGET BEHAVIOR
Tommy will work for up to two one-half hour periods with two or fewer teacher interventions per half hour.

PREREQUISITES FOR THE PROGRAM
Tommy will be able to independently perform the given task(s) for one half-hour period at 50% the normed rate.

THE CRITERION
Tommy will perform the task with 0-2 teacher interventions per half-hour session with at least 95% accuracy.

THE MEASUREMENT
Each intervention per half-hour session will be recorded.

THE PROCEDURE
1. For 15 minute sessions, the teacher presents an appropriate Sd (discriminative stimulus). When Tommy stops working for longer than a 10 second interval, the teacher will prompt him to stay on task.
2. Step 1 is repeated for one half-hour period.
3. Step 1 is repeated for one hour period.
4. Step 1 is repeated for one and one-half hour period.
5. Continue to increase work time until 2½ hours are completed with 0-2 teacher interventions per half hour.
6. Tommy will work up to 2½ hours on a variety of tasks in different locations, and with different teachers.

PROMPTING TECHNIQUES FOR ATTENTION TO TASK
1. Full prompt. Teacher says "Keep working, Tommy," and taps the table.
2. Teacher taps loudly on the table (no verbal prompt).
3. Teacher taps softly on the table (no verbal prompt).
4. Teacher makes eye contact and point prompts.

PROMPTING TECHNIQUES FOR OBTAINING ASSISTANCE OR ADDITIONAL MATERIALS
1. Teacher says, "What do you need," and prompts the response (e.g., "I need more cards.")
2. Teacher says, "What do you need," and fades the verbal prompt for the student's response, e.g., "I need…."
3. Continue to fade prompts until Tommy requests help independently.

PRESENT STATUS OF PROGRAM FOR TOMMY, OCTOBER, 1993
Tommy has mastered steps 1 and 2, and performs them independently.

INCREASING BEHAVIOR

◆ ◆ ◆ ◆ ◆ ◆ ◆ ◆ ◆ ◆ ◆ ◆ ◆ ◆ ◆ ◆ ◆

Eden uses a variety of reinforcement procedures along with discrete trial teaching to encourage behavior. Both methods are based upon the principles of applied behavior analysis. Because both reinforcement schedules and discrete trial teaching rely heavily on data collection and analysis, they provide a clear, objective picture of a student's behavior and how well the student is learning. Following the theory of learning underlying discrete trial teaching, Eden employs task analysis, shaping, and chaining as techniques to increase behavior. In addition, Eden makes use of incidental teaching opportunities, modelling, and reinforcement schedules to increase behavior. Further, generalization and maintenance programs are employed to broaden behavioral skills and keep them current. How Eden uses each of these approaches to increasing behavior is described below.

POSITIVE AND NEGATIVE REINFORCEMENT

People with autism often have cognitive abilities that are well below average. In fact, seventy percent of people with autism have IQ scores below seventy (Harris, 1989). The strategies used to teach them must therefore be highly structured, consistent, and concrete. Reinforcement is such a strategy for teaching. Eden uses two types of reinforcement: positive and negative. Both are designed to increase behavior. Negative reinforcement involves the removal of an aversive stimulus contingent upon performance of the desired behavior. For example, if a child is yelling, the teacher may cover the child's eyes and mouth until he is quiet. The covering of the eyes and mouth are the negative reinforcers, with desired behavior being the cessation of yelling. Negative reinforcement is considered only if the desired behavior is well established in the person's repertoire. In other words, it is not used to teach new behavior, but rather to bring out behavior that the person already knows. For this reason, negative reinforcement is rarely used.

In using positive reinforcement to encourage behavior, teachers follow a six point guideline. First, they determine what is rewarding to the child who is to learn a particular behavior. Teachers use both primary reinforcers, which are necessary to live, such as food, drink, and warmth, and secondary reinforcers, such as a smile, praise, and a token. Second, teachers define what reinforcement schedule they will use. There are four main types of reinforcement schedules used at Eden: a fixed ratio schedule, with reinforcement for every response, every second response, and so on; a fixed interval schedule, which rewards every correct response after a set length of time; a mixed ratio schedule, which rewards every correct response on a set ratio (such as every first, third, seventh, and ninth response); and a mixed interval schedule, with reinforcement at the end of a set time (such as at the end of one minute, three minutes, four minutes, and nine minutes). Third, teachers usually begin new teaching programs on a fixed ratio (continuous) schedule and move toward a mixed ratio schedule when the child appears to know the correct response. Fourth, teachers make sure to reward immediately following the correct response. There should be no delay. Fifth, teachers make sure to always give the secondary reinforcer before the primary so that the secondary reinforcer will take on reinforcing properties. Finally, teachers always have a variety of reinforcers available and present them randomly, so the child does not become satiated with a particular reinforcer. For example, a teacher might randomly reinforce a child with a piece of popcorn, a hug, and a back rub, all preceded by a "good answer."

DISCRETE TRIAL TEACHING

Discrete trial teaching is a highly structured, consistent, and concrete method for teaching. Over the years, it has been proven extremely effective in teaching people with autism (Lovaas, 1993; Mylee & Simpson, 1990; Lovaas, 1981), and continues to serve as a powerful tool for skill acquisition. Its clear components make it easier to apply consistently, and its data-based nature makes it a very concrete way to modify behavior and to track progress.

There are six basic components to a discrete trial teaching session. The first component is a clear, clean starting position, making sure the child is attending. Next is the presentation of the *Sd,* or discriminative stimulus. The *Sd* is the training cue, verbal or otherwise, a teacher uses to elicit behavior. Because language deficits are common among people with autism, and because people with autism often do not respond to environmental cues, *Sds* must be unambiguous, clear, and concise. The presence of a sink, for example, may not remind a student to wash his hands after toileting, so the teacher may use "wash hands" as an *Sd* to cue him to wash his hands. Similarly, "get dressed" may elicit dressing behavior that might not be triggered simply by the presence of the student's clothes on the bed.

The third component of discrete trial teaching is the prompt. Prompts for behavior are introduced if the student is unable to correctly respond to the *Sd.*

There are several types of prompts: physical prompts (actually manipulating the student's body), gestural prompts (cuing the student with a body movement such as a nod or a point), positional prompts (placing the correct materials closest to the student), and verbal prompts (simply telling the student the correct answer). The type of prompt used is that which best elicits the student's responses. Prompts are faded over time, and eventually eliminated altogether, so the student does not come to depend on them.

The fourth component of discrete trial teaching is the student's response, which should always be correct (errorless) in order for the child to feel a sense of accomplishment. Errorless responses are accomplished through effective prompting and prompt fading. This is followed by the fifth component, the consequence, which the teacher controls. Correct responses are immediately and lavishly rewarded, so it is clear to the student what behavior is being reinforced. If the response is incorrect, it is simply ignored and on successive trials the student is prompted to be correct.[9]

The sixth and final component of a discrete trial is measurement, otherwise known as data collection. The teacher records the student's response, and what sort of prompting was required. This data provides an accurate, objective record of the student's performance. The brief period of time in which the teacher records the data provides an interval between trials. This makes it even clearer to the student what behavior is being taught.

Trials are repeated several times in a session. Only correct responses are rewarded, and the student is given many opportunities to respond and receive reinforcement. The discrete trial method allows teachers to create a highly structured and predictable learning environment for the student, which maximizes his potential to learn.

SUPPORTING STRATEGIES TO DISCRETE TRIAL THEORY

The discrete trial teaching session allows a teacher to teach a student in small, specific steps. The tasks a student needs to learn, however, are often complex and involve several responses. For example, he needs to know how to put a button through a button hole and how to dress himself in the morning. To build more complex skills, three teaching strategies are used in conjunction with discrete trial teaching: task analysis, shaping, and chaining.

Task analysis is the process employed prior to teaching that breaks complex tasks down into a series of smaller, more easily mastered steps. These steps can be broken down even further, based on the ability of the student being taught. Dressing, for example, could be broken down into pulling on socks, putting on pants, putting on a shirt, and so on. If one of these steps, such as putting on a shirt, was too difficult, it could be broken down further into orienting the shirt correctly, putting one arm in, putting the other arm in, and buttoning each button.

---

[9] When teaching a skill or behavior, no punishment techniques are used at Eden. Punishment is used only to decrease behavior. See the following section for a description of how punishments are chosen and used.

Example of a Discrete Trial Teaching Session

Skill: Receptive Identification of Actions in Pictures

The teacher and student sit close together, face-to-face. The teacher uses a lap board to present the student's educational materials, in this example, pictures clearly depicting common actions. A nearby desk holds the teacher's clipboard with data sheet and reinforcers for the student.

Trial 1: The teacher places two picture cards, one showing a person jumping and another showing a person writing. The picture of jumping is on the right. The teacher places her hand on the top of her student's head, and prompts him to look at each card. "Look...look." She then prompts him to look at her by raising his chin. "Touch *jumping*." The student indicates the correct picture by pointing to it. The teacher reinforces him by saying enthusiastically, "Good job, all right!" She then takes away the distractor card (the picture of the person writing) and reinforces the concept by showing her student the jumping picture again. "Look, *jumping*." She then removes both cards, records her student's correct response on her data sheet, and presents the next trial.

Trial 2: The teacher places two cards on the lap board, a picture showing jumping and a picture showing building. This time the picture of jumping is on the left. The teacher prompts her student to attend to the pictures. "Look...look." She prompts eye contact by raising his chin. "Touch *jumping*." The student indicates the correct picture by pointing to it. The teacher reinforces him, "Good! Very nice work!" She pours a small amount of soda in a cup and hands it to him. He drinks the soda quickly, and returns the cup to the desk. As the student is drinking his soda, the teacher removes the cards, records his correct response, and gets the materials for the next trial.

Trial 3: The teacher places two cards on the lap board, the picture of jumping and a picture of writing. The picture of jumping is on the left. She prompts the student to attend. "Look...look. Touch *jumping*." The student indicates the correct card by pointing to it. "Good job! Give me five!" The teacher gives her student a "high five" and he smiles at her. The teacher removes the cards, records her student's correct response, and gets the materials for the next trial.

Trial 4: The teacher places cutting and jumping cards on the lap board; the jumping card is on the right. "Look...look. Touch *jumping*." Although prompted to attend, her student does not look as he points to the cutting card. Without saying a word or reacting to her student's incorrect response, the teacher removes the materials, records her student's incorrect response on her data sheet, and presents the next trial.

Trial 5: The teacher places the same cards on the lap board, exactly as they were before. She prompts her student to attend ("Look...look") and gives the *Sd* "Touch *jumping*." Immediately, she takes his hand and places it on the card that shows jumping. "Good job, *jumping*." She prompts her student's head down to make sure he is looking at the picture. She removes the materials, records her student's correct, prompted response, and gets the materials for the next trial.

Trial 6: The teacher places two cards on the lap board, writing and jumping. The jumping card is on the left. She prompts her student to attend ("Look...look") and gives the *Sd* "Touch *jumping.*" He responds correctly, indicating the jumping picture by pointing to it. "Good boy, you touched *jumping!* All right!" The teacher removes the distractor picture and holds up the jumping picture to further reinforce the skill. "Look, touch *jumping.*" The student touches the picture. "Good, nice job touching *jumping!*" The teacher removes the materials, records her student's correct response and begins to get the materials for the next trial. As she gets the cards, the student leans close to her and tries to grab the materials. Firmly, the teacher says, "Hands quiet," and immediately begins the next trial.

Trial 7: The teacher places the cards on the lap board, jumping on the left and ironing on the right. "Look...look. Touch *jumping.*" Her student looks at the cards, but indicates the ironing picture. The teacher removes the materials, records the incorrect response, and prepares the materials for the next trial.

Trial 8: Before the teacher can place the materials on the lap board, the student grabs the cards from her. Taking the cards from him, she tells him firmly, "Hands quiet," and places his hands on his lap. She puts the cards on the table, exactly as they were before, and prompts him to attend. "Look...look. Touch *jumping.*" She immediately takes his hand and places it on the correct card. The student touches the jumping card, then gets up from his seat. The teacher neutrally prompts him back to his chair by placing her hands on his shoulders. When he is seated, she neutrally tells him, "Good touching *jumping.*" She removes the distractor picture and holds up the jumping picture. "Look at the picture. Touch *jumping.*" The student looks at the picture and indicates it by pointing to it. "Good touching *jumping!*" The teacher removes the materials, records the student's correct, prompted response, and gets the materials ready for the next trial.

Trial 9: The teacher shows the student a piece of candy and asks, "Do you want this?" He nods yes. "Okay, you can earn candy for touching *jumping.*" She places the cards on the lap board, jumping on the right and opening a box on the left. "Look...look. Touch *jumping.*" The student indicates the opening card by pointing to it. The teacher removes the materials, records the student's incorrect response, and prepares the materials for the next trial.

Trial 10: The teacher places the cards, exactly as they were before, on the lap board. She prompts him to attend ("Look...look") and gives the *Sd* "Touch *jumping.*" She immediately takes the student's hand and places it on the correct card. "Good boy! That's right!" To end the session on a positive note, the teacher removes the distractor card and presents the jumping card alone. "Look, touch *jumping.*" The student looks and indicates the correct card by pointing to it. "Good job! That's good touching *jumping!*"

The student's percentage of correct responding for this program is 40%. The teacher will end the program and present a new skill for him to work on. However, the student will work on this program every day until his rate of correct responding increases to 90% or better. When he is able to indicate *jumping* with 90% accuracy across three consecutive days, his teacher will teach him a second action. When he masters the second action, the teacher will randomize the first action (jumping) and the second action, until he can identify both pictures, with 90% or better accuracy across three consecutive days. Then she will teach a third, and randomize all three when the third is mastered, teaching with this pattern until the student can receptively identify a wide variety of actions in pictures.

SHAPING

Shaping is a procedure in which a new behavior is taught by reinforcing successive approximations of the desired behavior. For example, if a student is being taught to clap his hands, the teacher might first reinforce him for just raising his hands off his lap. Then, he might be reinforced for raising his hands to his chest, and then for touching his hands together. As the shaping procedure evolves, the student will only be reinforced for responses that more closely approximate the desired behavior, clapping his hands.

Strategies to chain task analyzed skills together are probably the most important factor in enabling a student to perform complex skills. Chaining can be done either in a backward or forward fashion. In backward chaining, the component steps of a task, broken down through task analysis, are taught in reverse

Shaping Examples

EXAMPLE #1

A teacher and student are working on a gross motor imitation program. When given the *Sd* "Do this," and a model of clapping hands, the student raises his hands slightly off his lap. His teacher prompts him to complete the gross motor movement (clapping hands) and reinforces him. As teaching progresses, the student touches his hands together. His teacher prompts him to clap, then reinforces him. (The student is no longer reinforced for raising his hands slightly off his lap). As the shaping process continues, the teacher reinforces the student for behavior that is closer and closer to clapping. Once the student claps his hands, the student's approximate responses are no longer reinforced.

EXAMPLE #2

Teaching an individual to make a circle:

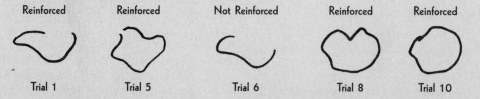

Reinforced	Reinforced	Not Reinforced	Reinforced	Reinforced
Trial 1	Trial 5	Trial 6	Trial 8	Trial 10

Some of the skills taught with a shaping procedure include sign language (the individual is reinforced for hand shapes that look more and more like the correct sign), verbal skills (the individual is reinforced for articulation that steadily improves), and handwriting (the individual is reinforced for forming letters that look more and more like the target letters).

order, so the last step in the task is taught first, then the next to last step, and so on until all the steps have been mastered. The student sees the finished product, like a well set table or a neatly made bed, after completing each step of the task, and is immediately rewarded. Because it is so immediately rewarding, and demonstrates task closure to the student, backward chaining is the most frequently used chaining procedure at Eden. See program on page 112.

Forward chaining is similar, except that teaching begins with the first step in the task's sequence. Forward chaining is especially useful in teaching more complex tasks. There is not immediate task completion reinforcement, so forward chaining is generally less effective in training toward independence on simple tasks, but tends to become more useful as the student matures, is able to understand task closure, and has more refined observation skills. Forward chaining is used for complex tasks that do not make as much sense when taught through backward chaining, like clerical collating. If backward chaining were employed, the student would begin with putting the last sheet on top of the pile (the final step of *many* steps), which does not really teach him anything about the process of collating. In forward chaining, though, the student begins by putting two separate sheets together, then adding another sheet, and another, and so learns from the start what collating is; generalization to varied collating tasks is more readily attained. See program on page 113.

OTHER TECHNIQUES FOR INCREASING BEHAVIOR

Incidental teaching, or teaching during unplanned, spontaneous situations, is used extensively at Eden to increase acceptable behavior. Taking advantage of incidental teaching opportunities is important because it helps the student learn to carry skills he has learned to other settings (generalization), outside the formal discrete trial session (McGee, Krantz, Mason & McClannahan, 1983). Cyndy Grunning describes one incidental teaching opportunity:

> *One day, John was handing out snacks that the children get during leisure time. There was one container of chips left, and the rest were pretzels. John wanted those chips, but the rules are that he had to ask everyone else what they wanted first before he could take his snack. When another student asked for chips, John gave him pretzels instead. A third student had been listening, and when he saw John do*

Hand Washing Program for Jaime in the Middle Childhood Classroom
(Backward Chaining Procedure)

THE TARGET BEHAVIOR
Within 3 seconds of the *Sd* "Wash hands," Jaime will wash and dry his hands.

PREREQUISITES FOR THE PROGRAM
1. Learning readiness skills
2. One-step commands

THE CRITERION
No prompts for each step for 2 consecutive days.

THE MEASUREMENT
Number and type of prompts needed for each trial.

THE (BACKWARD CHAINING) PROCEDURE
1. Jaime replaces cloth towel or disposes of paper towel correctly.
2. Jaime dries hands thoroughly with towel.
3. Jaime retrieves towel.
4. Jaime turns off water.
5. Jaime rubs hands together under water to rinse.
6. Jaime replaces soap.
7. Jaime retrieves soap and lathers hands (rubs hands together at least 10 times).
8. Jaime wets hands.
9. Jaime turns on water.
10. Jaime rolls up sleeves (if necessary).

PROMPTING TECHNIQUES
1. Full physical prompt—teacher takes Jaime's hands and helps him perform the activity.
2. Faded physical prompt—teacher moves Jaime's hands to begin the activity, and he finishes it.
3. Gestural prompt—teacher points to indicate the correct placement of Jaime's hands.
4. Above procedures are faded until no prompts are necessary.

WHEN THIS PROGRAM WAS IMPLEMENTED WITH JAIME, he could perform step 1 with gestural prompts, step 7 with full physical prompts, and step 9 independently.

OBJECTIVES FOR JAIME AS OF SEPTEMBER, 1993
Steps 1-7.

Clean-Up Program for Jaime in the Middle Childhood Classroom

(Forward Chaining Procedure)

THE TARGET BEHAVIOR

Given the Sd "Put away," Jaime will put cups and plates in their correct place and sort the flatware into bins.

PREREQUISITES FOR THE PROGRAM

1. The ability to attend to a task for at least 5 minutes.
2. Has begun sorting program.

THE CRITERION

No prompts for each step for 2 consecutive days.

THE MEASUREMENT

Number and type of prompts needed for each trial.

THE (FORWARD CHAINING) PROCEDURE

1. Jaime will pile plates correctly.
2. Jaime will place plates on shelf, plus above step.
3. Jaime will correctly stack cups, plus above steps.
4. Jaime will place cups on shelf, plus above steps.
5. Jaime will correctly sort flatware into the appropriate bin, plus above steps.

PROMPTING TECHNIQUES

1. Full physical prompt—teacher takes Jaime's hands and performs activity.
2. Faded physical prompt—teacher takes Jaime's hands, begins the activity, and Jaime completes it.
3. Gestural prompt—teacher points to indicate correct placement of Jaime's hands.
4. Probe—no prompt offered.

WHEN THIS PROGRAM BEGAN IN SEPTEMBER, 1993

Jaime could complete step 1 with full physical prompts.

OBJECTIVE FOR JAIME AS OF SEPTEMBER, 1993

Step 2.

this, he took back the pretzels and gave the student the chips instead. We congratulated that student for listening and for interacting with the other students, and we told John that if he wanted chips we would get him some later. This was their leisure time, and there were still opportunities to help them learn.

These students were taught skills formally, but even when they were relaxing during break time, their behavior mattered. Such incidental teaching opportunities help maintain an atmosphere of learning, no matter what activity students are working on. Incidental teaching opportunities extend the teaching session over the entire day, and so continue to encourage acceptable behavior.

Incidental teaching opportunities not only help encourage acceptable behavior, but also discourage unacceptable behavior. Although unacceptable behavior, such as tantrums, can be predicted in certain situations,[10] as a rule it is exhibited spontaneously by the student. Unacceptable behavior may occur more when the student finds something frustrating or distasteful, but the student's tantrum is not planned. It arises spontaneously from the student's frustration. Programs to decrease the

Destinations

Consider taking a long car trip. How do you go? You need to decide where you are going, make a route plan, lay out each day's driving, and leave time to visit interesting places you might come across. Taking a car trip is a good metaphor for how each of the elements in discrete trial theory—the discrete trial teaching session itself, task analysis, shaping, and chaining—work with one another. The discrete trial session can be viewed as the process of navigating the trip, task analysis as identifying the destination, vehicle, route, and various stops along the way. Shaping occurs in the various deviations from the route laid out through task analysis, deviations such as making a wrong turn and getting back on track, or taking a side road instead of the interstate, or maybe making a few interesting detours. Chaining occurs as each of the stops planned through task analysis is reached. The final destination is the developmental goal for the student, which, in a larger sense, is just another stop on an even greater trip toward independence.

Each of the elements of the trip is crucial for effectively modifying behavior, and the destination is the most important of all. Short and long term goals for each student must be clear, defined, and part of an overall vision of where the student is going, and how he can get there.

—Jessica Haille, Editorial Assistant

---

[10]   See the following chapter on how unacceptable behavior is analyzed to determine when and why it happens.

unacceptable behavior, then, are activated when the behavior occurs, and so are incidental in nature. Some programs, as discussed later, are more pro-active, but even these are based on the spontaneous occurrence of unacceptable behavior.

Another way behavior is encouraged is peer modelling. Peer modelling is difficult for many people with autism because of their general ineptitude in understanding the value of social skills and inability to relate to other people. Nevertheless, peer modelling can be very powerful in shaping social behavior. Although parents and teachers cannot have complete control over peer modelling, they can set up environments that encourage peer modelling. Nancy Guggenheim describes some of these situations:

> *Two of our children go to a regular nursery school to benefit from peer modelling, and we have play groups where children from other schools come in to Eden Institute to play.*
>
> *There is a child at Eden Institute right now, Gregory, who can benefit greatly from peer modelling. When we are in groups, I see him watching what other students do, and trying to imitate them as they are moving. When it is his turn, he knows what is going on and what is expected of him. He will often repeat what I say, like "roll!" as if to ask, "That is what you want, right?"*
>
> *I see peer modelling happening in Early Childhood too. When I am working with one child and give that child a reinforcer, often another child will see it and want it, and so will listen to the directions I give and try to model the behavior so they too can get the reinforcer.*

Nina Marcus, Coordinating Teacher of the Pre-Vocational program, describes another instance of peer modelling:

> *Students do all the photocopying for faculty members at Eden Institute. They enjoy it and it is a good, productive activity we can teach them. We were trying to teach Jimmy how to use the copy machine, but he was getting frustrated and was not learning. So, we decided to let him work on something else for a few weeks and then bring him back to the copying task. Jimmy's work station happened to be near the copier, and every time we worked on copying with another student, he would watch intently. When we then tried again to teach him copying, he had actually acquired some of the steps from watching the other students. He learned much more easily.*

Unfortunately, peer modelling can also have negative consequences. Just as a student can model acceptable behavior, he can model unacceptable behavior as well. Conditions must be carefully monitored to avoid this. Parents, Nancy Cantor and Steve Brechin:

> *Archie's teachers and we felt that he had come up with some unacceptable behaviors after watching some of the children in the Early Child-*

hood Program. He was doing disruptive things that he did not do before. We put him in a regular nursery school more often so he would get more productive behaviors to model, and it has worked fairly well.

Archie's teacher Denise explains the problems Archie had:

Archie imitates really well. So, during group time, when he saw another child get attention for doing something disruptive, he would do it himself to get attention. He did silly things, like fall off his chair or mat, and laugh inappropriately. We monitored the situation and determined that, due to his advancing peer modelling skills, he was now ready for transition to a regular nursery school. He does not participate in any groups at Eden now. His group time is at the regular nursery school.

Eden encourages students to model the behavior of other peers by having regular interactions with the local community. Peter Gerhardt, Director of Employment Services, explains:

The peer models out in the community can be much more appropriate than the models presented in our programs. Even we as teachers are not wholly appropriate peer models because we do not always act "normally." For example, we may be working with someone who has severe learning challenges, and who needs a very enthusiastic reinforcer once every minute. That is not a model of normal interaction. In addition, the community can present very inappropriate behavioral models; a balance must be struck.

Eden also uses token economy systems to encourage behavior. Token economies are used especially for tasks that may not be intrinsically rewarding, like dusting the furniture or vacuuming. For example, several students at Eden have a list of chores they must complete at home for which they receive tokens. They then exchange the tokens for activities they enjoy, such as watching their favorite video tape. Other students get a star for each work sheet they complete, and they can trade in their stars at the end of the week for a special treat at Eden's store.

Using token economies during the school years helps students understand the idea that if they work (complete a task requested of them), they will then be rewarded with a token (even a check) that can be exchanged for some desired item or activity. This understanding about work will bode students well in future employment placements.

Token economies being used at Eden can also be used to decrease or eliminate unacceptable behavior, rather than increase acceptable behavior. For example, a strategy used with Spike to decrease the unacceptable noises he was making was a response-cost token economy system. Spike's parents felt that the noises he made were excluding him from playing with the other children in the regular nursery school he attended. Spike was given a number of small toys at the beginning of the day that he could put in his pocket. When he made a noise, he would lose one of his toys. His noises soon diminished because he found the loss of one of his toys very distressing.

Another student was also on a token economy system to reduce the unacceptable noises he made. He was given small tokens, such as little round wooden blocks, that he would take to work, and he soon became aware that if he made his noise, he would lose a token, and if enough tokens were forfeited he would not have enough to purchase a preferred item from the store at the end of the day. His noises dropped off rapidly and have stayed at low rates. Thus, like incidental teaching opportunities, token economy systems can also be used to increase or decrease behavior. Occasionally, systems can be designed to do both. For example, the overall result of Spike's system was to decrease the number of noises he made, but it did so by simultaneously reinforcing him for not making noises, which was the desired behavior.

GENERALIZATION AND MAINTENANCE
◆ ◆ ◆ ◆ ◆ ◆ ◆ ◆ ◆ ◆ ◆ ◆ ◆ ◆ ◆ ◆ ◆ ◆

Mastering a skill is only the beginning of the learning process for students with autism. In order for a skill to be functional for them, they must be able to perform the skill in a variety of settings, with several different teachers, and with different materials, and they must be able to maintain their proficiency over long periods of time.

Although students with autism can learn, with difficulty, to generalize a skill to different settings and different people, they find it more difficult to generalize concepts (Lovaas & Smith, 1989). For example, they may be able to grasp the idea that one pencil is different from two pencils, and that one ball is different from two balls, but understanding the concept of plurals—that more than one of something means that it is plural—is much more difficult. Most students at Eden do not have the cognitive ability to grasp such an abstract idea.[11] For this reason, most programs to teach generalization do not include these concepts. They focus exclusively on generalizing skills across physical environments and materials; that is, across teachers and settings, and with different materials, with the expectation that the greater ease with which an individual can generalize the greater the refinement of generalization capacity.

The difficulty people with autism have in generalizing a skill they have learned to different settings is due to their tendency toward overselectivity, or attending to small or irrelevant aspects of skill or training stimulus (Lovaas, Koegel & Schreibman, 1979). They may be attending only to the particular materials they are using, the room they are in, or the characteristics of a particular teacher. If

---

[11] See the section above on "Learning to Learn" for more.

any of these elements are changed, the student may not be able to perform the skill, even though the recorded data indicate that he has mastered it. Generalization training aims to teach the student how to perform a skill regardless of the particular setting.

Generalization is not begun until a student has mastered a skill in a structured setting. Then, training is focused on only one area of generalization at a time. The goal is to eventually accomplish generalization across three areas: materials, environments, and teachers. In generalizing across materials, a student would be taught to apply a skill to different but related items. For example, a student who knows how to put on a pair of jeans would be taught how to perform the skill with dress pants or shorts. To generalize across environments, a student would be encouraged to perform the skill in different settings. For example, an adult who learned to prepare lunch at his group home would be taught to perform this task at his parents' home, or at a job in a restaurant. Finally, generalizing across teachers allows the student to perform the task with people other than the one who originally taught the task. This allows parents, siblings, substitute teachers, and employers to work as effectively with a student or participant as the original teacher did.

Once a student has generalized a skill, he must be able to maintain it. This means that he not only must keep his ability to perform the skill over the years, but that he must be able to perform it in more natural settings than the classroom, group home, or employment center. This is accomplished by establishing reinforcement systems with maintenance in mind.

> One day Andrew's mom woke up and heard him in the kitchen doing something, but she wasn't too concerned. A little while later, he came in her room, got on the bed, and started shaking her as if to say "get up, get up." She got up and he took her by the hand and led her into the kitchen. What she found amazed her. He had set a table with paper plates, and had gotten food out of the refrigerator, like strawberries and other breakfast foods. She saw the colander nearby where he'd even rinsed them off before putting them on the table. He had made her breakfast, and it was really great. We at school were shocked too. We make lunch at school, but he had obviously chained together a lot of different skills that he had learned separately, and then generalized them to his home. We had been teaching him table setting and how to prepare meals, but he had taken all these different tasks, put them together, and knew to get it all set up before going to get his mother.
>
> —**Donna Vicidomini, Assistant Director for Education and Retreat Support Services**

In teaching a skill initially, the student usually receives immediate reinforcement from the teacher, like a snack or pat on the back, but these reinforcements are not always available in nonteaching environments. An employer, for example, is not going to say "good job" each time his employee successfully puts together a packet of papers. To make natural reinforcement more motivating for the student, the schedule and type of reinforcement is varied once the skill is firmly mastered and generalized across settings. Intermittent schedules of reinforcement, in which the student receives reinforcers at varying or random intervals, are often used, and have been proven very effective (Charlop, Kurtz & Milstein, 1992).

Intermittent schedules of reinforcement imitate more natural reinforcements. In a natural setting, a good job is sometimes rewarded, but other times is not. For example, an employer might reward a well done job only when he happened to walk by, or when he was not too busy with other things. However, the employee would be expected to do a good job every time, whether or not he received praise. In gradually moving a student to more natural reward systems, the type of reinforcement is also varied, and is eventually re-

placed with one that occurs naturally. For example, if a student was initially reinforced with a soft drink (primary reinforcement) and verbal congratulations (secondary reinforcement) for setting the table, over time he will receive only verbal praise, then simply a smile. In pairing a nicely set table with praise and rewards, the student is encouraged to find the set table rewarding in itself, and may not need any other external reinforcement to maintain the skill. The more a student can rely on natural reward systems to motivate his behavior, the longer his skills will be maintained and even expanded upon.

DECREASING BEHAVIOR

The techniques described above to encourage a student to learn, generalize, and maintain a skill or behavior are the primary means by which Eden modifies behavior. However, at times behavior can be increased only by decreasing other behaviors. For example, a student may need to decrease body rocking behavior before eye contact can be learned. At other times, unacceptable behaviors in themselves are so detrimental to the student that they must be decreased as much as possible. Self-injurious behaviors fall into this category. People with autism can also have self-stimulatory behaviors such as hand flapping, gazing, or rocking.

They can have aggressive behaviors like pinching, biting, hitting, or kicking others. They may also have compulsive, ritualistic, or noncompliant behaviors. Self-injurious behavior is also often evident in people with autism.

The tendency to perform these behaviors is present to some extent in all people, but the severity of these behaviors in people with autism limits them. These behaviors prevent people with autism from adapting to social and learning environments. Thus Eden aims to decrease these types of behavior in order to enable the person with autism to have as much access as possible to typical environments.

Some students at Eden demonstrate these behaviors only in mild forms, while others present behaviors so severe that without effective treatment they would likely not acquire appropriate skills or, in some cases, live a life free from harm to themselves or others. In treating people with such a wide range of disability, Eden has found that using a full range of behavior modification techniques is most effective. These techniques are discussed below.

FULL-RANGE APPROACH TO TREATMENT

The treatment approach Eden uses, applied behavior analysis, provides that a behavior can be modified through the careful manipulation of events that precede and follow the behavior. These events shape behavior by either reinforcing it or punishing it, in much the same way that behavior is reinforced or punished in life. Good work is rewarded, and so encouraged, and unacceptable behavior is punished, and discouraged. As a theory of teaching, applied behavior analysis encompasses the full range of interventions to modify behavior, from those that are extremely reinforcing to those which the student finds quite aversive and punishing. Although it is not easy to decide that punishment is the best way to modify a particular behavior, that decision must sometimes be made.[12]

The term "full-range approach to treatment" is used at Eden to emphasize the importance of embracing, as a whole, the behavioral theory of treatment. Eden uses a full range of behavior modification approaches, and has found that each approach in the spectrum, from reinforcement to aversive, has at one time or another been the most effective and efficient strategy to modify a particular behavior with a particular student.

Because of the greater needs and generally lower levels of functioning in the students and participants Eden serves, the need to use the full range of treatment is even greater. Teachers at Eden are prepared to intervene intensely because of the severity of disability in those Eden serves, and because teachers know that Eden is committed to teaching the person to learn adaptive skills for as long as he needs training.

However, any program that is used to modify behavior must be carefully implemented. The environment in which behavioral modification programs are imple-

---

[12]   Refusing to use aversive interventions at all is also a negation of an important component of applied behavior analysis. The theory of ABA has a certain closure, it is a unit, and ignoring the options it offers is incongruent with the very basis of the theory and what is known about the learning process.

mented must by strongly positive, but the program itself may include punishment. Anne S. Holmes, Director of Outreach Services:

> *The research shows that sometimes, in addition to reinforcement, we need punishment. However, any program that uses a full range of behavior modification techniques also has the responsibility to focus on promoting behavior, and clinicians have the responsibility to replace every unacceptable behavior with an acceptable one. With every aversive program we employ, we document why teaching or reinforcement programs alone are insufficient, and why we're moving to a more intrusive step.*

Each program implemented at Eden is closely analyzed, supervised, and reviewed. Eden's General Procedures Manual includes strict guidelines for incorporating programs to modify behavior into IEPs or IHPs, and the Eden Decision Model and Accountability Process provides step-by-step instructions on how to develop, implement, and evaluate all behavior modification programs.[13]

People who are unfamiliar with the severity of the problems people with autism face may feel that some behavioral interventions are too harsh. However, these aversive techniques have demonstrated their effectiveness and, in some cases, superiority over other less intrusive techniques in achieving significant improvement in the behavior, health, and socialization of people with autism.[14] Still, controversy surrounds the use of interventions which are aversive in some way to the person with autism. This controversy is discussed below.

THE RISKS AND BENEFITS OF USING AVERSIVE INTERVENTIONS

A number of advocacy groups, including The Arc (1985) and The Association for Persons with Severe Handicaps (1986), have issued statements critical of the use of aversive interventions. Several groups, however, have also come out in support of using aversive interventions in controlled settings. The American Association on Mental Retardation (1990) reversed an earlier position and issued a statement supporting the use of aversive interventions. And, the Autism Society of America (ASA)(1990) rescinded an earlier statement critical of the use of aversives. The ASA now supports aversives when accompanied by parental choice in determining their use. Arguments for using aversive interventions have also been presented by the Association for Behavior Analysis (1989), the International Association for the Right to Effective Treatment (1994), and the National Institutes of Health (1989). There are arguments made by both sides on the effectiveness and ethical use of aversive interventions, but the sides differ importantly in their definition of what an aversive intervention, or punisher, is.

---

[13] See the following chapter for a detailed account of the Eden Decision Model and Accountability Process.

[14] See Lundervold & Bourland's 1988 review of aversive techniques.

What Is Punishment?

Those against using punishers to modify behavior define aversives according to the specific physical attributes of the stimulus. In other words, they place stimuli into aversive and nonaversive categories based upon the generally accepted value of each stimulus. For example, ice cream is generally nonaversive; a loud "no" is an aversive. There is a good deal of disagreement among opponents of aversives over which stimuli to classify as punishers (Axelrod, 1987), but the basis of classification is the same. It focuses not on how the student receiving the punishment views the stimulus, but on how society at large might view it.

> One of the things we looked for in a school was their willingness to use techniques that might be shied away from by other programs that were "politically correct." If a technique was right for a particular child, the school should use it. So rather than being one of the things we had to get used to, that was one of the things we actively sought out. We wanted a school that would have the courage to do what was right for the child, whether or not it looked pretty.
>
> —Eric and Erica Lofgren

Those in favor of using aversive interventions under controlled conditions define aversive stimuli according to the effect the stimulus produces, rather than on the particular attributes of the stimulus. This definition looks at the result of stimuli on a student's behavior, and so requires more individualization in defining what is and is not aversive. This definition also allows for more flexibility in categorizing stimuli, because it is not the stimulus that is the basis of the definition, but its effect. For example, in winter, a water spray may be aversive to a student whose behavior is being modified, and so would be classified as a punisher. But in the heat of summer, a water spray may actually be pleasing to the student, and so would be a stimulus to reinforce, rather than discourage, behavior. There are, of course, certain stimuli that are aversive to most students, such as pain, but these are rarely used at Eden.

Why Are Aversives Used?

Aversive strategies to modify behavior are used because they are effective.[15] Both those advocating for the use of aversives and those against their use recognize their effectiveness. Aversive strategies work by pairing an unacceptable behavior with an unpleasant stimulus either before or after the behavior. Over time, the student learns to associate the behavior and the stimulus. The unacceptable behavior then decreases for one of two reasons: the student wants to

---

[15] Numerous studies support the effectiveness of aversive interventions. For a thorough review, see Lundervold & Bourland's (1988) examination of 62 experiments on the effectiveness of aversive and reward-based interventions. All behavioral strategies used at Eden have been approved by the New Jersey Division of Developmental Disabilities. Additionally Eden's overall approach to modifying behavior has received tacit approval from several national oversight bodies.

avoid the aversive stimulus, or he no longer is reinforced for the unacceptable behavior. The student gradually learns to control or eliminate the unacceptable behavior. This enables him to be a part of his community, and it allows him to learn more appropriate behavior, such as self-care and work skills. By self-managing his behavior, the student's opportunities broaden. For example, he will more likely be able to access group homes or supervised apartments, and take part in a regular working community.

Aversive interventions are used in all cases to modify behavior that would otherwise be detrimental to the student's health or safety and a deterrent to continuous progress of the student, thereby limiting his social and personal options. However, the specific reasons for using aversive interventions differ for each student. The student's past history, the severity of his unacceptable behavior, and his personality and temperament are all factored in when deciding to use an aversive strategy.[16] The age of a student and his size are often additional factors to consider when deciding whether aversive interventions should be used. Adults, who are often larger and stronger, often require different strategies than children because their behavior is often more difficult to manage.

What Aversive Interventions Are Used?

The aversive procedures used at Eden are categorized by how restrictive they are to the student receiving them. A restrictive procedure is defined as one which meets one or more of the following criteria:

1. It restricts a student's freedom of movement;
2. It restricts a student's opportunity for acquiring positive reinforcement;
3. It causes the loss of privileges which a student enjoys;
4. It forces a student to engage in behavior which may be against his will (behavior he would not engage in given the freedom to choose);
5. It results in the application of a painful or unpleasant stimulus.[17]

Several questions guide the selection and level of restrictiveness of the intervention chosen. They are:

1. What are the possible side effects of the procedure, such as physical risks or the suppression of appropriate behaviors?
2. Is the procedure feasible, in terms of the time and number of staff involved?
3. What is the intensity of the procedure?
4. Has the procedure been proven effective in the literature?[18]

---

[16]   The following chapter describes in detail how decisions to use aversive interventions are made at Eden.

[17]   These criteria were developed in Holmes & Holmes (1987).

[18]   These questions were developed in Holmes & Holmes (1987).

When choosing an aversive intervention, we take the student's behavioral history and personal likes and dislikes into consideration. This is important because each aversive procedure works differently when used with different people.

For example, Sean was having tantrums which were accompanied by aggression and self injury, so we initiated a time-out procedure for him. Before the procedure, he had an average duration of twenty minutes a day in tantrums. Within four days of beginning the time-out procedure, however, the duration had jumped to forty minutes a day. We stopped the procedure immediately.

Time-out had a very different effect for Sasha. Before the time-out procedure, Sasha had an average of one tantrum a day, which would last about an hour. After three months, he was down to a rate of .4 tantrums a day. Within seven months of beginning the procedure, his tantrums were gone. He still does not tantrum.

—**Carol Markowitz, Director of Educational Services**

To serve as a guideline in selecting an aversive intervention, Eden has developed a hierarchy of a number of aversive interventions based on their general restrictiveness. Although these are listed below in order from least to most restrictive, they are not applied sequentially. Each of the interventions is given with a brief description.

1. Extinction—removing a reward from an unacceptable behavior to reduce its occurrence.
2. Selected reinforcement[19]—differential reinforcement procedures by which other behaviors (DRO), low rates of behavior (DRL), incompatible behavior (DRI), or alternative behaviors (DRA) are rewarded to take the place of the unacceptable behavior. Token systems and loss of reinforcement are also used.
3. Redirection/response interruption—giving a mild redirection of a behavior through a verbal reprimand, direction, or physical prompt (like a lip tap).
4. Contingent observation—a form of time out in which the student remains in the room, but is not allowed to participate in the activity during which the unacceptable behavior occurred.
5. Visual time-out—a visual screen, or blindfold; useful for visual self-stimulation behaviors, such as finger playing or looking at a light, and also for directed aggressive behaviors.
6. Time-out in a specified area—time out in an area of the room facing the wall, or behind a partition.

---

[19] The reinforcement procedures mentioned here are different from the positive and negative reinforcement schedules mentioned earlier. Whereas the previous are schedules for increasing behavior, the latter are techniques for decreasing behavior.

7. Time-out in a time-out room—time out in a more restrictive room, which is devoid of any reinforcing stimuli.
8. Mild contingent exercise—used for minor self-stimulatory behavior; includes moving the head, jaw, hands, or arms in a set way, sitting in a chair and standing, or using light weights.
9. Time-out on floor, without restraint—student simply lies on the floor; works well in calming down people showing aggression, or antecedents to aggression, especially adults or larger people.
10. Restitutional overcorrection—correcting the consequences of an unacceptable behavior and making the environment improved over its condition prior to the behavior; for example, having someone clean up his spilt milk and then wipe the counters off as well.
11. Positive practice overcorrection—similar to mild contingent exercise, student practices something incompatible with the unacceptable behavior; for example, a student might practice making lunch if he hoards food.
12. Negative practice overcorrection—practicing an unacceptable behavior over and over; used especially in speech and language programs to help students gain control over spontaneous verbalizations.
13. Moderate contingent exercise—used mainly for aggression; for example, doing sit-ups, push-ups, or walking on a treadmill or stairs.
14. Physical restraint—ranges from holding a student's hands at his sides to the basket-hold procedure, in which a student's arms are crossed in front of him and held from behind; used mainly for crisis intervention.
15. Partial mechanical restraint—head gear like a fencing mask, catcher's mask, or lacrosse helmet, used primarily for self-injury to the head.
16. Flooding—practicing an unacceptable behavior for an extended length of time; practicing it beyond boredom, to the point where the behavior is a burden.
17. Moderate to severe aversive conditioner—in general order of severity, these are: a lip tap, finger or hand squeeze, neck prompt, hair tug, hand or leg slap, noxious oral stimulus, water spray, cheek flick, rubber band snap, upper arm or cheek squeeze, tepid shower, or ammonia inhalant.
18. Negative reinforcement[20]—the removal of an aversive stimulus contingent on the performance of a desired behavior, and so used to increase behavior; includes hand, arm, or finger squeeze, neck prompt, or hair tug.

---

[20] Uses an aversive stimulus to increase the probability of acceptable behavior.

19. Time-out in chair with mechanical restraint—time out in a chair with wrists or hands restrained.
20. Time-out on floor with mechanical restraints—same as time-out on floor, but with restraints at the wrists or ankles.
21. Chemical restraint—medication; used as a last choice to manage or control behavior.

Although the list above does not represent an exact step-by-step order in which to employ aversive interventions, the least restrictive intervention determined by teachers, parents, and administrators to have a good chance of modifying a behavior is tried first. If it does not work, a more restrictive procedure may be tried, but must, again, be determined by clinical experience or literature review to have a high probability of successfully reducing or eliminating the unacceptable behavior. The most restrictive intervention on the list above—chemical restraint—is rarely used. The following section describes why.

Biomedical Services

Occasionally a student does not progress satisfactorily despite a thorough evaluation of his educational and behavioral needs. Eden's experience shows that educational and behavioral interventions will not be as effective when biomedical variables are present. A student's primary diagnosis of autism can be exacerbated by a secondary diagnosis such as depression or bipolar disorder. Accurate assessment is confounded by several challenges, including the inability of these students to self-report symptomology.

> In a program our son Sasha attended in Russia, he was very subdued, mainly because they fed him with neuroleptics. I cannot blame them too much, though, because they did not have many staff members to take care of the children. There was one teacher for the ten or twenty children in the program, so they had to drug them to keep things in order.
>
> —Sasha and Dasha Polyakov

In conjunction with START Clinical Services, Eden Institute staff collect the data for a START Comprehensive Psychiatric Evaluation (Sovner & Lowry, 1990). This evaluation involves determining behavioral equivalents in assessing the existence of a dual diagnosis. The evaluation also includes direct observation of the student, an in-depth review of medical and other diagnostic evaluations, and a parent interview that focuses on student and family history. This data is presented to START Clinical Services for interpretation, which may lead to a secondary diagnosis and pharmacological recommendations.

Using Medication

Although psychotropic medication is generally classed as an aversive intervention along with more physical interventions, the use of medication, and the reasons for choosing medication to control behavior, are quite different. Medication is more restrictive than physical intervention because it artificially eliminates behavior, rather than teaching the student not to perform the behavior, or teaching the student alternatives to the problem behavior.[21] Medication reduces the ability of the individual to be in control, and so can be like a "chemical straight jacket." In most cases, if the medication were removed, the student would return to the unacceptable behavior, because he has not been taught to behave acceptably.

However, medication is necessary for some of the people Eden serves. Without the use of medication, the behavior of some of the students would be too dangerous either to themselves or others. Medication is used at Eden only for behaviors like assaultiveness or self-injury, which threaten the safety of the student or those in his environment.[22] Medication is tried only after physical behavioral intervention strategies have been tried and found insufficient. Behaviors like noncompliance or hyperactivity that do not threaten either the student or others are never causes to medicate.

Most often, medication is used to control behavior in the home, where a family does not have the intense, around-the-clock support available at Eden. Carol Markowitz explains:

> In school, we can continue to change behavioral programs to find something that works for a child, but parents may not be able to really do that at home. They may have a limited repertoire of things they can use, or are physically capable of doing in the home. They may have other children, or are busy with their lives outside their child with autism. They may not have the luxury to just be a therapist for their child.

For students whose behavior is particularly challenging, or when parents simply feel out of control, medication may be the only option to get some control over behavior in the home. Again, Carol Markowitz:

> The decision to medicate turns on a crucial question: Can the family live with their child? Sean's family really have their backs against the wall. He is very aggressive, he bites, and he pinches. He is only eight years old, but he is a big, strong eight, and his mother is afraid of

---

[21] Medication has helped some students at Eden learn more. For example, a student who takes medication to control his hyperactivity at home has benefited from the overflow of the medication's calming effects during school. The medication has enabled him to pay more attention in teaching situations, and has reduced behaviors that result from impatience or frustration. Medication has also helped some students learn by decreasing the number of self-injurious behaviors they perform. It is understandably difficult to teach skills to a student who is intent on hurting himself. However, cases where medication has made learning easier are *rare*, especially with people whose behavioral problems are more severe, like those Eden serves.

[22] If a physical intervention strategy is used with a student, nothing else in the student's programming is changed. The effects of the intervention can then be clearly noted, and not confounded by other variables. Similarly, if a chemical intervention is implemented, nothing else is altered until the effects of the medication have been clearly identified.

him. He is also extremely self injurious, scratching his face and banging his head a lot. For several years, we have placed a great deal of effort into helping him acquire skills and changing his aggressive and self-injurious behavior, but his behavior at home remains unmanageable. Because of this, the family is looking for a medication to calm him down to some degree.

Deborah is in the Prevocational Program, and is now nineteen. She weighs about 220 pounds, and is often aggressive and can be very stubborn. She frequently drops to the floor when she does not want to do something, which causes a big scene because we cannot move her. We performed a functional analysis of her behavior implementing several different reinforcement and teaching programs with her, but she continued to show a lot of aggression. She is now on the medication Mellaril. Medication is appropriate for her because her parents want to keep her at home and do things with her, but she is too hard to manage without medication. With the medication, however, she can live at home instead of a residential placement. Her parents can do things with her in the community, and she helps with cooking and chores around the house.

Elaine's self-injury is very intense and frequent. She has around 1600 instances of self-injury in a five hour period, and averages around 320 instances an hour. She bangs her head on objects and hits herself with her hand. She has caused several hematomas on her head. The only thing her parents could really do at home was work through it and ignore it, which was not bringing it down. The things we do in school with her simply could not be carried over into the home. So even if her behavior became manageable at school, the family would not be able to do the programs with her at home. It would be too intensive. She is a candidate for medication for that reason. The family needs it, and they are going to need it even more because they have a third child on the way.

If the family and teachers decide to use medication in the home, teachers work with the family to monitor the medication's dosage, and to continue to teach the family behavioral reduction programs they may be able to use instead of, or along with, medication.

On rare occasions, Eden uses medication within its programs. If behavioral procedures have proven ineffective, and a behavior is extremely dangerous or disruptive, a student may simultaneously be given some medication to reduce the risk he poses to himself or others. Most people in Eden's programs who receive medication are adults in group homes, but some, like Elaine, are students at Eden Institute who exhibit such severe self-injury that no singular behavioral procedure has yet been effective.

Eden is extremely hesitant to use medication to control behavior because the effects of medication are extremely unpredictable. What works for one student may have the opposite effect on another student, or may have no effect at all. It is impossible to define exactly what makes certain medications work for certain people. Carol Markowitz:

> *Medication does not always work, and rarely works the same way for different people. Sometimes we get a behavior opposite from what we expected, or the unacceptable behavior gets worse. It is very difficult to determine what effect medication will have on individuals with autism.*
>
> *Andrew is eleven and in the Middle Childhood Program. His mother is a single parent with two other children, and cannot deal with Andrew's extreme behavior at home. He has begun destroying things in the house, like pulling cabinet doors off cabinets. Andrew's mother decided that she wanted to try medication to calm him down. She took him to a psychiatrist who prescribed a medication, but it did not work. If anything, she felt he was worse, so she took him off that medication and is now looking for something else. There is nothing we can point to and say "Yes, if you give him that he will calm down, or stop his unacceptable behavior." It does not work that way. We can never tell how medication will affect a child because every child with autism reacts differently.*

Research into the efficacy of psychotropic medications is equally indeterminate. It fails to prove any drug statistically useful to reduce the most disturbing type of unacceptable behavior—self-injury (see the National Institutes of Health, 1989). On neuroleptics, the National Institutes of Health have issued a statement saying:

> *[N]o solid conclusions can be drawn as to the usefulness of. . . neuroleptic drugs specifically for SIB [self-injurious behavior].... Particularly troubling is the amount of variability in response found among individuals studied with the various neuroleptic drugs. (1989)*

NIH drew similar conclusions for the effects of other types of psychotropic medications on self-injurious behavior. Very few studies have tested many of the drugs in use today, and the results from these few studies are conflicting or inconclusive (NIH, 1989). Psychotropic medications are still being used because they do work with some people, but much more research into how they work needs to be done.

The medications that are used at Eden are carefully monitored on a daily basis. Staff watch for negative side effects of psychotropic medications, and check for any habituation to the medication.[23] To avoid problems with medication, Eden uses a rotating schedule of medication, and regularly consults with physicians to discuss medication strategies.

---

[23] If a student becomes habituated to a medication, his body becomes used to the medicine's effects, and so does not respond to the medication in the same way.

Are Aversive Interventions Ethical?

The main argument of those against the use of aversive interventions surrounds the ethics of using punishment to modify behavior. Aversive opponents claim that aversive interventions dehumanize the student because they deny him full choice in conducting himself. They also argue that punishment strategies have too high a potential for abuse (LaVigna & Donnellan, 1986; McGee, Menolascino, Hobbs & Menousek, 1987; Meyer & Evans, 1989; TASH, 1981).

It is true that the use of aversives has resulted in abuse, but only in cases where there was insufficient monitoring of the aversive strategy, or where the strategy was improperly employed.[24] Aversive procedures are simply tools to use in modifying behavior; they are not treatments in themselves. Like any tool, they have the potential to be abused. However, the problem lies in the use of the tool, not in the tool itself. Cases of abuse are inexcusable and unfortunate misuses of a powerful tool. Finally, Eden has found that aversive interventions work only in a positive reinforcing environment. When only aversive interventions are used, the student grows accustomed to these types of exchanges and has no incentive to behave differently.

When only reinforcement strategies are used, teachers have no way to punish unacceptable behaviors like tantrums or self-injury. So, they tend to either ignore it or try to reason with the student to get him to stop. Most students with autism, however, do not respond well to verbal reasoning, but they do understand how to manipulate their environment. They learn very quickly that they can get a lot of attention for unacceptable behaviors if they can just wait out the teacher's patience. For example, a teacher can ignore self-injury only so long. When the teacher finally comes over to stop the injury and help the student work through the behavior, he or she hugs, holds, and talks soothingly to the student. The student learns how to court this attention. The teacher's attention ends up actually reinforcing the unacceptable behavior. When reinforcement strategies alone do not work at all, or well enough to modify behavior that could be harmful to the person with autism or others, then not using a tool that has been shown to be effective in treating that behavior is itself a case of neglect, and is unethical.

Ethical treatment must include the full range of behavior modification techniques, including punishment strategies. Not to do so is to abuse the student's right to receive effective treatment.[25] Parents, Charles and Nancy Richardson:

> *We do not like aversives, but there are circumstances where they are the best way to get results. Geoffrey reaches out and grabs other*

---

[24] Monitoring of the aversive strategies Eden uses is described in the following chapter.

[25] Several advocates for banning the use of aversive interventions argue that other more reinforcing interventions are just as effective, and should be used instead (McGee, Menolascino, Hobbs & Menousek, 1987). These alternative intervention strategies, however, have not proven as efficient in reducing negative behavior (Favell et al., 1982; Carr, Robinson, Taylor & Carson, 1990). Although they may be excellent at modifying mild behavioral problems, severe problems often respond only to strategies based on punishment (Simpson and Regan, 1986).

The following are examples of how a person's age affects the type of intervention used. The strategy for Jeffrey is different from the strategy used to modify Paul's behavior as an adult. Paul's is one of the most restrictive strategies Eden has ever used, but it was necessary to decrease behavior that was harmful both to himself and others. These cases show how important it is to have a full range of treatment options available.

Jeffrey has been with us a couple of years, and is in our Transition classroom right now at Eden Institute. For Eden, Jeffrey is a relatively advanced child, but has some very serious disruptive behavior. He will run away, throw things, or be aggressive to escape from a situation that he does not like. He also loves causing a commotion. If he runs out of the room and someone has to chase him, he thinks it is hysterical. The behavior maintained itself, because he was so reinforced by the consequences.

We did a functional analysis of the behavior, and decided to try to modify his behavior through a reinforcement system. We gave him reinforcement for not being aggressive, and prompted him to behave correctly. However, this proved to be ineffective.

After further determination that there were no medical or environmental indications for his behavior we decided to use an aversive package with him, from moderate to severe. We used a hand squeeze, leg slap, and hair tug, and alternated them so he would not get used to any particular one. Before treatment, the behavior was up to approximately fifty occurrences a day, and we brought it down to the point where it is not occurring at all anymore. He was able to go from a two-to-one setting in Middle Childhood to the more normalized six-to-one setting of the Transition classroom.

We never would have decided on that type of treatment package with an adult. For example, Paul is an adult in his twenties, who had developed some severely disruptive, aggressive behavior. He is rather astute, and knew when and where to create a really severe disruption. He would throw things, bite people, be physically assaultive, and toss tables over for many of the same reasons Jeffrey would, but Paul is close to six feet tall, weighs 180 pounds, and we could not simply go over to him, squeeze his hands, and tell him to sit down.

Again following a functional analysis of the behavior, we tried several things to modify his behavior, including time out and contingent restraints, but nothing worked. The frequency of his behavior was high and people were getting hurt. We ended up designing one of the most restrictive programs for him that we have ever used. We used a noncontingent mechanical restraint procedure, where he had to earn having the restraints removed for good behavior, rather than placing them on him when he became aggressive. We did this because we found that, with a contingent procedure, by the time we put the restraints on, all the reinforcement for the behavior had already taken place. The table was thrown, the juice was spilled, and the commotion was made, so we were not reducing the behavior at all.

Paul is socially motivated, and sought out interactions with people. The noncontingent restraints enabled us to keep up positive interactions with him, and begin teaching him more appropriate behavior. We employed that program only for a short while, but saw a big difference in his behavior. His disruptive behavior was very similar to Jeffrey's, and with similar motivations, but because of the differences in size, the treatments had to be very different.

—**Carol Markowitz, Director of Educational Services**

people's food off the table. That should not be tolerated. To get him to stop, we first tried a preventative strategy. Among others, we kept the table around him clear of food so he would not have the opportunity to take food. But the problem remained. That strategy did not work. So, reluctantly we moved to an aversive strategy which had immediate and long lasting positive effects of reducing his food stealing.

We feel there was nothing wrong with using an aversive procedure to discourage him. If it is not more unpleasant than the pleasure he gets out of the food, he is going to keep grabbing food. Breaking him of the habit is a worthy goal, and would make him more socially acceptable.

Geoffrey has another problem, too. He bites his hands when he is angry, so we restrain his hands when he starts to bite. We do not see anything wrong with that either. Parents do unpleasant things to their typical children in order to get them to behave well, and cause some emotional distress in the process. They might be given nonphysical punishments, like going to their room or not getting the car keys, but they have the cognitive abilities to perceive that as a negative consequence. Geoffrey does not, and so occasionally needs physical consequences for his behavior.

As legal questions have been raised about the use of aversive interventions, the law has supported their use, as long as proper monitoring and consent programs are in place. *Wyatt v. Stickney,* 344 F. Supp. 373, 344 F. Supp. 387 (M.D. Ala. 1972), *aff'd sub nom. Wyatt V. Aderholt,* 503 F.2d. 1305 (5th Cir. 1974); *Youngberg v. Romeo,* 102 S.Ct. 2452 (1982). The potential for abuse that exists with aversive interventions can be brought down to the absolute minimum by the application of rigorous, comprehensive guidelines for their use.[26]

Following these guidelines is crucial because

People who oppose aversives often use such extreme examples of aversive consequences, examples which are cruel. But these don't happen when behavior modification is used the correct way. We tried several things to reduce our son Geoffrey's self injury and tantrums, including ignoring them. But none of those strategies worked, so we went to an aversive procedure. We put a fencing mask on him so he couldn't bite his hand, which he did often in tantrums. With the mask, he still had to sit and do his work. The data show that his self injury has decreased significantly, and the tantrums that he used to exhibit are almost gone. He's much calmer and happier now.

—Charles and Nancy Richardson

---

[26] These guidelines include obtaining the proper consents, maintaining a human rights committee and behavioral management committee to oversee the implementation of the aversive strategy, and the careful definition of what interventions will and will not be used. See the following chapter for a description of the guidelines used at Eden.

the application of punishment strategies usurps certain freedoms of the student. When an aversive intervention is used, we are telling a student that he is not allowed to behave any way he wants. Instead, someone else, a parent or teacher, is deciding what his behavior should be. For example, it may be decided that a student needs to learn not to scream whenever a new food is introduced. Intervening in the student's behavior with an aversive strategy will not be pleasant to the student, and will likely go against his desire to scream, thereby communicating that he does not want to eat a more balanced diet. But parents or teachers intervene because they believe the behavior is not in the best interests of the student, and they believe that the student's right to effective treatment is more important than his right to behave as he pleases.

Because aversive strategies do override some of the student's freedoms, they must be as innocuous as possible. Providing conscientious treatment to people with disabilities means finding the least intrusive intervention that will effectively modify behavior. It also means weighing the risks and benefits of using aversive interventions at all. In "Aversive Treatment vs. Individual Rights: The Professional's Dilemma," Davis and Goldberg (1979) summarize this view:

> The use of aversives must be studied and used responsibly, balancing the interests and rights of all persons involved. The decision must be made individually in each case by the practitioner with the client and/ or the client's advocate, parent or guardian. An aversive stimulus must be applied not in anger but out of a concern and deep conviction that, for a particular individual, failure to use the available methodology would be more painful.

TREATMENT PACKAGES

If aversive intervention strategies are implemented at Eden, they are accompanied by teaching programs which increase desirable behavior.[27] This ensures that any aversive consequence is received within a highly positive learning environment. By accompanying aversive interventions with teaching strategies, Eden's students receive a "package" of different treatment methods. Although some programs are implemented to decrease behavior, the great majority encourage behavior, and teach various skills.

Behavioral reduction programs have been proven most effective when they are part of such a comprehensive treatment package. The NIH (1989):

> [A]lthough single treatment modalities are demonstrably effective, the most successful approaches are likely to involve multiple elements of therapy, environment, and education. Depending on the severity of the destructive behavior, therapy may require methods for enhancing desired behaviors; for producing changes in the social, physical, and

---

[27] Because many unacceptable behaviors originate from the frustration a student feels in not being able to communicate, these programs often include communication skills training.

educational environments in which the individual lives; and for reducing or eliminating destructive behaviors.

To be certain that behavioral reduction programs are part of an overall treatment package at Eden, and that a chosen reduction program is effective in modifying behavior, the Eden Decision Model (EDM) was developed (Gerhardt & Holmes, 1994). The EDM provides a framework around the process of deciding when and how to use behavioral reduction techniques. It is presented in the next chapter.

Chapter **7**

The Eden
Decision Model &
Accountability
Process

The Eden Decision Model (EDM) is a set of rules and procedures to guide decisions about the treatment programs Eden uses with its students. It follows the same objective as other strategies that have been developed to analyze, assess, and modify behavior (Evans & Myer, 1985; Groden, 1989; O'Neill et al., 1990; Parrish, Iwata, Dorsey, Bunck & Silfer, 1985; Touchette, MacDonald & Langer, 1985), but the EDM attempts to provide a more comprehensive analysis of the factors contributing to a behavior, and utilizes more input from staff and parents about the possible functions of a behavior. The EDM's Accountability Process enables teachers to track the effectiveness of behavioral interventions, and to modify them to achieve the greatest possible effectiveness. The Accountability Process, also a set of guidelines, ensures that the intervention chosen is the least restrictive intervention possible, and that the intervention meets clinical and human rights criteria.

Together, the EDM and its Accountability Process give staff members a concrete way to analyze and modify behavior. They provide a step-by-step outline of the questions that must be asked, and the decisions that must be made, to select the least intrusive, most effective intervention to modify a student's behavior.

The EDM consists of five related components: 1) determination of need; 2) analysis of environmental conditions; 3) analysis of curricular conditions; 4) differential reinforcement; and 5) analysis of behavior maintenance conditions—development of an aversive decelerative procedure. These five elements are closely related. They are discussed in the following sections.

COMPONENT I—DETERMINATION OF NEED

The first component of the EDM enables staff members to develop a data-based determination of need. Not all unacceptable behaviors need to be decreased through formal behavior reduction programs. To determine whether a behavior needs to be changed, and how pressing the need for change is, three questions are asked:

1. Is the behavior harmful to the student or to others?
2. Does the behavior interfere significantly with the student's work or learning?
3. Does the behavior seriously restrict the student's access to his community?

If the answer to all of these questions is "no," a formal program will not be developed. If, however, the answer to any one of these questions is "yes," an analysis is begun to change the behavior. Each of these questions refers to a critical area of behavior for the student. Any behavior that is harmful, interferes with the student's work, or significantly restricts the student's access to his community is a behavior that needs to be modified.

If it is determined that a behavior needs to be changed, an operational definition of the behavior is developed. The definition of the behavior is a written, objective description of the behavior that accurately describes the behavior and is easily and reliably understood by everyone involved in the student's treatment. This definition is field-tested by being given to several staff members who are not involved in authoring the description. If independent observers agree on the occurrence of the behavior based on the writ-

> We try to determine why behavior occurs. With self-injury, we start by asking why he hits his head every time we present a particular task. There must be something about that task he does not like or understand. Then we look at the different elements of the task, where it is taught, and what else is going on around the teaching session. Only by analyzing the situation in great detail, and trying several different strategies to get him to stop hitting his head, will we really understand the function of the behavior and be able to stop it.
>
> —Lyn O'Donnell, Coordinator, Clinical Services

ten description, the description is considered reliable. The operational definition of the behavior helps staff members address the behavior in a consistent manner, and increases the effectiveness of the intervention strategy.

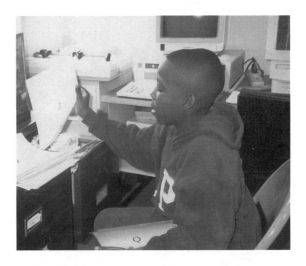

The next step is to collect baseline data on the occurrence of the behavior. This data provides objective information about the behavior before intervention strategies begin. The frequency and duration of the behavior is recorded, along with an antecedent-behavior-consequence (A-B-C) (Bijou, Peterson, Harris, Allen & Johnson, 1969) analysis. This analysis gives a general idea of the events that immediately precede and follow the behavior, and also includes other information that may affect the behavior, including environmental conditions, physical conditions such as the amount of sleep the student receives, what the student has eaten, and psychological conditions such as the student's affect.[1] The baseline period lasts a minimum of five days, or fewer for serious self-injurious or aggressive behaviors, until a stable rate has been achieved.

Gary Montgomery, Operations Coordinator, describes the process of collecting baseline data, and explains how important it is in developing an effective intervention strategy:

> *The analysis we do provides a good indication of what the motivation for a behavior is. We look at the behavior in different settings, note when it occurs—is the child alone or in groups, under stress, or in leisure time? Then we start to find out some interesting things about the child and the behavior. For example, we may think at first that a child screams because he does not want to help make lunch. The data, however, may show instead that the child screams whenever he has to enter the lunch room. With more analysis, we may be able to determine that the child dislikes crowded places in general. Knowing that enables us to develop much more effective intervention strategies. For this child, we would likely develop a program to gradually desensitize him to crowded places.*
>
> *Quite often a subjective observer, who is not using data, is wrong about behavior. Staff members who are inexperienced have said "I cannot believe his behavior. He is hitting all the time." But after a baseline of the behavior is done, it turns out that he actually hits maybe four times a day. It only seems to happen more often because hitting is a very disruptive behavior.*

---

[1] A systematic analysis of baseline and A-B-C data is conducted in Component II of the EDM.

Below is an example of the checklist teachers complete for Component I of the EDM. The analysis is being done for Sean in the Early Childhood Program. The behavior being analyzed here has been a problem of Sean's for some time, and so has been previously analyzed through the EDM. However, previous strategies to reduce Sean's behavior have not been sufficiently effective, so teachers have begun again at Component I to re-analyze Sean's behavior. The example below is from this re-analysis.

Behavioral Reduction Program Checklist
Component I: Determination of Need

TOPOGRAPHICAL CLASSIFICATION OF BEHAVIOR:
Aggression (hitting, grabbing, and pinching)

IS THE BEHAVIOR:

harmful to self or others?	Yes
highly work interfering?	Yes
restricting access to the community?	Yes

EXPLANATION:
Sean's aggression, especially if directed toward the other students, can be harmful. He seems to avoid work by being aggressive, and his aggression is not acceptable in the community.

OPERATIONAL DEFINITION OF THE BEHAVIOR:
Any aggression toward others with the exception of aggression accompanied by crying. (Reliability of definition established through previous analysis.)

BASELINE INFORMATION:
Date of baseline: March 26 through April 2.
Type of baseline: A measure of the frequency of the behavior.
Rate at baseline: 76 occurrences per day on average.
Antecedent-Behavior-Consequence analysis: see the following pie chart.

ADDITIONAL BASELINE INFORMATION:
Sean's aggression is often accompanied by self-injurious behavior and crying. His total aggression averages twenty minutes per day.

DOES THE BASELINE DATA VALIDATE A NEED FOR AN INTERVENTION PROGRAM?
Yes

Are there potential medical causes?

No. Sean has already been checked for ear infections and bladder problems, both of which have been causes of unacceptable behavior for him in the past.

Current rate of behavior:

76 occurrences per day, unchanged.

According to the data, is there a need for the decision-making process to continue from this point?

Yes

If yes, begin Component II analysis.

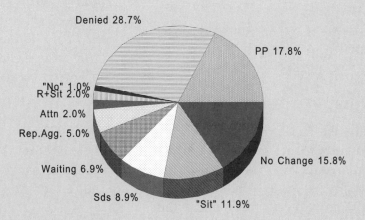

Aggression/SIB for Sean
% by Antecedent Event

Denied 28.7%

PP 17.8%

"No" 1.0%
R+Sit 2.0%

Attn 2.0%

Rep.Agg. 5.0%

No Change 15.8%

Waiting 6.9%

Sds 8.9%

"Sit" 11.9%

PP = Physical prompts were used   No Change = No change in activity
"Sit" = Told to sit   Sds = Variety of Sds
Waiting = While waiting   Rep.Agg. = Repeated aggression
Attn = Attention-getting behavior   R+Sit = Reinforced for good sitting
"No" = Told no   Denied = Denied a desired activity

When we have performed an analysis of a behavior, the program we develop is often successful. There are rare cases, however, in which we cannot do this analysis right away. A behavior may be so serious that we have to make a temporary clinical guess as to why it occurs, and initiate a behavior reduction program right away. We would then follow this up with more a careful analysis. We are not generally as successful when we have to make quick decisions. For example, if a child is hitting, we could initiate a temporary program to restrain his hands. At this point, we have not asked why he is hitting. He could be hitting to get attention. If so, we will likely reinforce, rather than reduce, his hitting because restraining his hands gives him attention.

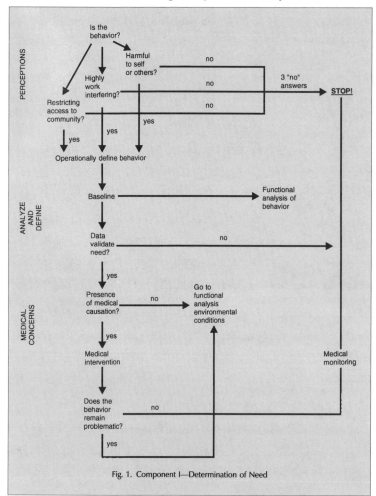

Fig. 1. Component I—Determination of Need

Occasionally, the baseline data reveal that the student's behavior does not occur with enough frequency or severity, or does not sufficiently limit learning or community opportunities, to justify intervention. In these cases, the decision-making process ends. If the data does indicate that intervention is necessary, however, the process continues, and possible medical causes for the behavior are investigated.

A wide variety of medical conditions, such as allergies, headaches, toothaches, viruses, and other infections, can adversely affect behavior, especially in people with autism. Because many people with autism lack the cognitive ability or language skills to effectively communicate that they are in pain or simply do not feel well, possible medical causes for a behavior are analyzed and eliminated before any behavioral intervention is begun. For example, several possible medical causes for Sean's aggressive behavior were explored. Carol Markowitz, Director of Educational Services:

Sean frequently has problems with ear infections, so we looked at them as a possible cause for his aggression. He was also having toilet accidents, so we did a urinalysis to ensure that he did not have a urinary infection. Medical tests revealed that he did not have either of these problems.

If a medical condition is found, appropriate treatment and monitoring are obtained, and the decision-making process ends. However, if no medical conditions are identified, or if a medical condition is treated and the behavior persists, the decision-making process proceeds to the second component of the EDM, an analysis of environmental conditions.

COMPONENT II—ANALYSIS OF ENVIRONMENTAL CONDITIONS

The second component of the EDM requires a more thorough examination of environmental conditions that surround a behavior. Teachers assess conditions in the student's environment, such as the amount of heat and light in a room, the type of furniture, the clothes a student wears, and other physical factors that could influence behavior. These are primary environmental conditions. They are assessed by asking if the student's environment is physically uncomfortable. Intervention at this level can be as simple as moving a student away from a drafty window or providing him with a different chair.

Secondary environmental conditions are also assessed. These are defined as conditions that might distract or confuse a student, such as excessive noise, an overcrowded work-place, or interactions with a teacher that involve complex responses. Inter-

> We have an ecological approach to behavior. We look at the whole environment the child is in, instead of just looking at the behavior itself. For example, knowing that a child hits himself twenty times a day doesn't tell us much about the behavior. We have to know why he hits himself, when, and what makes him stop. Figuring out why a behavior is done is where the EDM really comes in. A child often can't tell us why he does something, so we have to use other ways to analyze the behavior. We try to get as sophisticated an analysis as we can of every behavior we treat in order to determine the child's motivation for the behavior.
>
> **—Carol Markowitz, Director of Educational Services**

vention strategies for behavior related to secondary environmental conditions could include moving the student to a less crowded or noisy room, or the student could be allowed not to perform a task that requires multiple steps.

The second component of the EDM also provides an assessment of the student's ability to interact with his environment. Teachers ask if a student can communicate his responses to the environment in a functional and acceptable manner. If he cannot, he may become frustrated, which could be the cause of his behavioral problem. Research has clearly demonstrated a correlation between increases in communication and decreases in problematic behavior (Carr & Carlson, 1993; Durand & Carr, 1992; Wacker et al., 1990; Carr & Kemp, 1989; Bird, et. al., 1989).

This is the checklist for Sean in Component II of the EDM. This checklist is from an earlier analysis of Sean's behavior through the EDM. The intervention suggested here was not sufficiently effective in reducing Sean's aggression. However, it provides a good example of how teachers analyze a student's environment for possible causes of a problematic behavior.

Behavioral Reduction Program Checklist
Component II: Analysis of Environmental Conditions

WHAT CONDITIONS IN THE STUDENT'S PHYSICAL ENVIRONMENT MAY BE PERCEIVED BY THE STUDENT AS BEING UNCOMFORTABLE, AS INDICATED BY THEIR ASSOCIATION WITH THE TARGETED BEHAVIOR?
The A-B-C pie chart indicates that Sean's environment is comfortable.

WHAT CONDITIONS IN THE STUDENT'S LEARNING ENVIRONMENT MAY BE PERCEIVED BY THE STUDENT AS BEING DISTRACTING, AS INDICATED BY THEIR ASSOCIATION WITH THE TARGETED BEHAVIOR?
The A-B-C pie chart does not indicate that Sean's aggression is related to distracting conditions in the environment.

DOES THE STUDENT DEMONSTRATE AN ABILITY TO EXERT APPROPRIATE CONTROL OVER HIS ENVIRONMENT, WITH EMPHASIS ON SITUATIONS ASSOCIATED WITH THE DISPLAY OF THE TARGETED BEHAVIOR?
No. The A-B-C pie chart shows that Sean is more aggressive when he is told to do something, or when he is denied something.

IF "NO" WHAT ASSOCIATED PROGRAMMING IS INDICATED?
Sean may be trying to communicate so subtly that teachers are not able to pick up on his cues. Teachers will pay more attention to Sean's attempts to communicate.

Interventions to help the student interact more successfully with his environment could include teaching him functional communication, choice-making skills, or other ways to deal with a disturbing environment. For example, a student who finds bright rooms annoying may be taught to move himself away from the lights. A student who finds crowded and noisy places disturbing may be slowly desensitized to excessive noise and crowding.

Interventions to improve the control a student has over his environment include teaching communication alternatives to unacceptable behaviors, such as

Sean will also be given a greater variety of reinforcers, and teachers will be sure he gets the opportunity to choose among them. And, Sean will be able to choose from a variety of activities, so he has more control over his day.

DOES THE STUDENT HAVE APPROPRIATE ALTERNATIVES TO THE TARGETED BEHAVIOR?
Possibly not. Sean's reward system will be analyzed to ensure that the rewards he receives for communicating appropriately are greater than the reward he receives by hitting himself or his teacher.

RESULTS OF PROGRAMMING:
Sean is able to choose among a variety of reinforcers and activities, and his reward system has been analyzed. Teachers have also paid more attention to Sean's possible attempts at communication. However, Sean's behavior is still problematic.

AT THIS POINT, IS THE STUDENT'S PHYSICAL ENVIRONMENT COMFORTABLE AND CAPABLE OF PROMOTING THE DEVELOPMENT OF APPROPRIATE ALTERNATIVES TO THE TARGETED BEHAVIOR, AND IS PROGRAMMING IN PLACE TO TEACH APPROPRIATE ENVIRONMENTAL CONTROL?
Yes.

CURRENT RATE OF BEHAVIOR:
Approximately 70 instances per day.

ACCORDING TO THE DATA, IS THERE A NEED FOR THE DECISION-MAKING PROCESS TO CONTINUE FROM THIS POINT?
Yes.

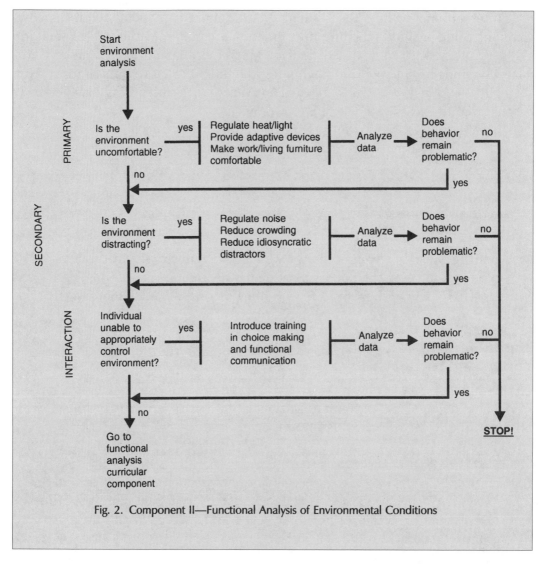

Fig. 2. Component II—Functional Analysis of Environmental Conditions

asking for help instead of throwing materials, or signing "go away" instead of becoming frustrated. Donna Vicidomini, Assistant Director for Education and Retreat Support Services:

> We try to show the children other ways to express themselves than being aggressive, and how they can channel their energy in a positive way. We do this by trying to help them work through their own misunderstandings. They might not know, for example, why they are feeling sad or frustrated, or what to do about it. They may show these emotions through aggression. We help them work out ways to deal with their feelings other than by being aggressive.

Other interventions which help the student interact successfully with his environment include choice-making skills, tolerance training, and relaxation techniques.

When Sean's teachers analyzed his aggression at a later date, they had a different answer to the question of whether Sean had appropriate alternatives to being aggressive. They responded:

> Sean may still not have appropriate alternatives to the targeted behavior. Therefore, a program will be developed to give him a more appropriate communicative alternative than aggression. Sean will be given an "escape" option on his voice-output computer and teachers will train Sean in what it means. When he asks to take a break, Sean will be excused from his work, and so will immediately reap the benefits of communicating. He will escape-avoid his work for a while to do something he loves, such as jump on the trampoline or climb on the climber.

After implementing this program, Sean's aggression decreased to about 60 instances per day. As Sean learned what the option meant, he began using it more to indicate his desire to quit working. However, teachers felt that his rate of aggression was still too high. So they proceeded to the next component of the EDM.

If one of these interventions significantly reduces the targeted behavior, the decision-making process ends. The student's physical environment is comfortable and he can adequately interact with his environment. If the data do not show a reduction in the targeted behavior, however, other factors must be causing the behavior. The decision-making process then proceeds to Component III.

COMPONENT III—A FUNCTIONAL ANALYSIS OF CURRICULAR CONDITIONS

The third component of the EDM is an analysis of the student's curriculum. It enables teachers to determine if something in the student's curriculum is causing the targeted behavior. The key question teachers ask is "Does a particular task always precede the behavior?" A task may cause unacceptable behavior because it is too difficult for the student, or involves some steps that have not yet been mastered. A task may take a long time to complete, and may be boring, or simply disliked. The A-B-C analysis done in Component III is used to determine whether the behavior is related to a particular task.

Sean's data indicated that he was not having a problem per se with the curriculum we had developed for him, but he was still showing a lot of aggressive behavior. When it became clear that our approach was not working, we looked at his reinforcement system. The staff members did several days of antecedent data collecting to see what preceded his aggressive behavior, and what was reinforcing to him. We also looked again at what reward choices we were offering him, and what activities he was given to choose from during the day.

—**Carol Markowitz, Director of Educational Services**

Below is the checklist completed by Sean's teachers for Component III.

Behavioral Reduction Program Checklist
Component III: A Functional Analysis of Curricular Conditions

DOES THE DATA INDICATE THAT A TASK PRECIPITATES THE TARGETED BEHAVIOR?
Yes. Sean is aggressive in teaching situations where he receives heavy physical prompts. Physical prompts are used with him mostly in adaptive physical education activities. Sean is also aggressive when he has to wait his turn.

CAN THE TASK BE REMOVED FROM THE STUDENT'S REPERTOIRE?
No. Sean needs adaptive physical activity and needs to learn how to wait his turn, i.e., be patient.

DOES THE TASK SEEM TOO COMPLEX OR DIFFICULT?
No. Sean is able to wait, and to participate in adaptive physical activity.

DOES THE TASK SEEM BORING?
Quite possibly. Sean at times seems bored with the equipment he works with. Adaptive physical education appears not to interest him, and he does not have a strong desire to participate in such teaching sessions.

INTERVENTION STRATEGIES:
In adaptive physical education groups, Sean will only need to stay in his preassigned place to be reinforced. He will not need to participate in the group, and so will receive fewer physical prompts. Teachers will also use more gestural, and fewer physical, prompts with him.

Teachers will also change the equipment Sean works with in teaching sessions, and will present the equipment to Sean in a different fashion to make it more interesting to Sean.

RESULTS OF PROGRAMMING:
Sean's participation in the group has dropped, but he is staying in place more. His interest in teaching sessions has not changed significantly, and his rate of aggression is about the same.

AT THIS POINT, IS THE STUDENT'S CURRICULUM INDIVIDUALIZED, FUNCTIONAL, AND APPROPRIATE?
Yes.

CURRENT RATE OF BEHAVIOR:
Remains at approximately 60 instances per day.

ACCORDING TO THE DATA, IS THERE A NEED FOR THE DECISION-MAKING PROCESS TO CONTINUE FROM THIS POINT?
Yes.

If a correlation between a task and the behavior is found, teachers evaluate how well the student and the skill are matched. The skill may be too difficult, and so may need to be broken down into smaller parts. Or, the skill may need to be made more relevant. For example, instead of teaching basic measurement skills, the student may need to be taught how to measure the ingredients for the day's lunch. Occasionally, a skill can be deleted from the curriculum, but only if the removal of the task of learning the skill does not inadvertently reinforce the targeted behavior. Skills that are essential for independent functioning in the future are never deleted.

After these interventions have been implemented, the frequency and duration of the behavior is again examined. If the behavior has been reduced successfully, the decision-making process ends. If not, the process proceeds to the next component of the EDM.

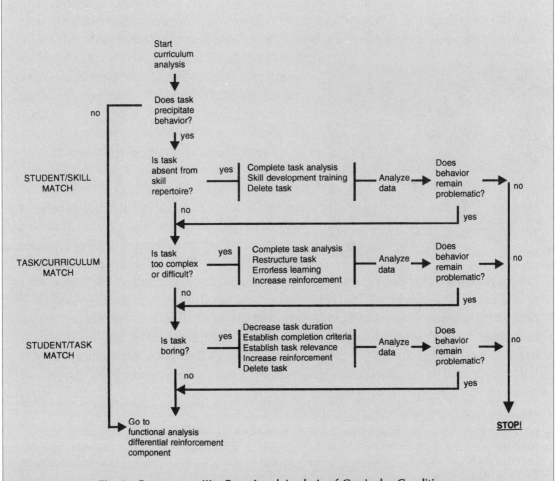

Fig. 3. Component III—Functional Analysis of Curricular Conditions

COMPONENT IV—BEHAVIOR REDUCTION THROUGH DIFFERENTIAL REINFORCEMENT

◆ ◆ ◆ ◆ ◆ ◆ ◆ ◆ ◆ ◆ ◆ ◆ ◆ ◆ ◆ ◆ ◆ ◆ ◆

The strategies developed to modify behavior through Component III of the EDM are "preemptive" in nature. They attempt to decrease the frequency and duration of the targeted behavior by manipulating the conditions associated with the behavior, and teaching the student how to accommodate those conditions. The intervention strategies in Components IV and V, on the other hand, are reactive in nature. These strategies react to the targeted behavior rather than try to change the conditions causing the behavior.

In Component IV of the EDM, procedures to modify the targeted behavior are developed around several structured differential reinforcement strategies. Differential reinforcement is a technique that involves reinforcing desired behaviors while ignoring unacceptable ones. Since most desired and unacceptable behaviors cannot occur simultaneously—working on an

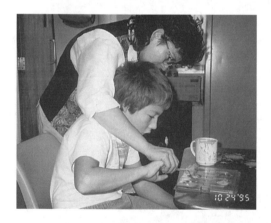

assembly task is directly incompatible with hand flapping, for example—differential reinforcement procedures teach people to replace unacceptable behaviors with desired ones.

There are many types of differential reinforcement procedures. Differential reinforcement of other behaviors (DRO) involves reinforcing for longer and longer periods of time in which a person does not engage in the targeted behavior, and so reinforces other appropriate behavior. In the differential reinforcement of low rates of behavior (DRL), a student is reinforced for lower and lower frequencies of the targeted behavior. A DRL procedure is often used as a precursor to a DRO procedure because each reinforces the student for gradually replacing the unacceptable behavior with desired behavior. The differential reinforcement of incompatible behaviors (DRI) reinforces the student for behaviors that are directly incompatible with the targeted behavior.[2] The differential reinforcement procedure chosen de-

---

[2] There are other differential reinforcement procedures, namely DRA, DRC, and DRH. In the differential reinforcement of alternative behavior (DRA), a student is reinforced for behavior that produces the same effect but is more acceptable than the defined behavior (for example, tapping someone on the shoulder to get attention rather than yelling). Through the differential reinforcement of communicative behavior (DRC), a student is reinforced for communicative behavior that serves the same function as the targeted behavior (for example, asking for a preferred activity rather than engaging in it without permission). DRC is often used in functional communication training. DRH, or the differential reinforcement of high rates of behavior, is used to increase behavior. It is therefore used in skill acquisition programs rather than as a behavior reduction strategy. DRH, DRC, and DRA are especially useful procedures to employ under incidental teaching conditions.

This is the checklist for Sean in Component IV of the EDM.

Behavioral Reduction Program Checklist
Component IV: Differential Reinforcement

DO THE DATA INDICATE ANY IDENTIFIABLE CONDITIONS WHICH ARE ASSOCIATED WITH, AND REINFORCE, THE TARGETED BEHAVIOR?
Yes. Sean often escapes from a task when he is aggressive. This is indicated by the high rates of aggression when Sean is asked to do something (including being asked to wait and to sit down).

When Sean is aggressive, he also receives attention from the teachers. This also seems to be reinforcing his aggression. The data indicate this with high rates of aggression even when there are no demands on Sean. During such times, his aggression is often identifiable solely as attention-getting.

It is fairly certain that Sean's aggression is not motivated by noncompliance. The proximity of his outburst to teachers' requests, and the nature of his aggression, indicate that his behavior is motivated by either the desire to escape a situation, or to get attention.

IS THE TARGETED BEHAVIOR A LOW FREQUENCY AND LOW INTENSITY AGGRESSION OR SELF-INJURIOUS BEHAVIOR?
No. In fact, the frequency of the targeted behavior has increased.

AT THIS POINT, IS DRO, DRI, DRL, DRA, OR DRC ALONE APPROPRIATE?
No. Sean also has other behavior problems which could be inadvertently reinforced by using only a DRO, DRI, or DRL procedure. His aggressive behavior is very intense, and is often accompanied by self-injury. However, his self-injury and aggression are not perfectly correlated. Therefore, using a DR procedure for his aggression could inadvertently reinforce his self-injury.

CURRENT RATE OF THE BEHAVIOR:
Approximately 70 occurrences per day.

ACCORDING TO THE DATA, IS THERE A NEED FOR THE DECISION-MAKING PROCESS TO CONTINUE FROM THIS POINT?
Yes.

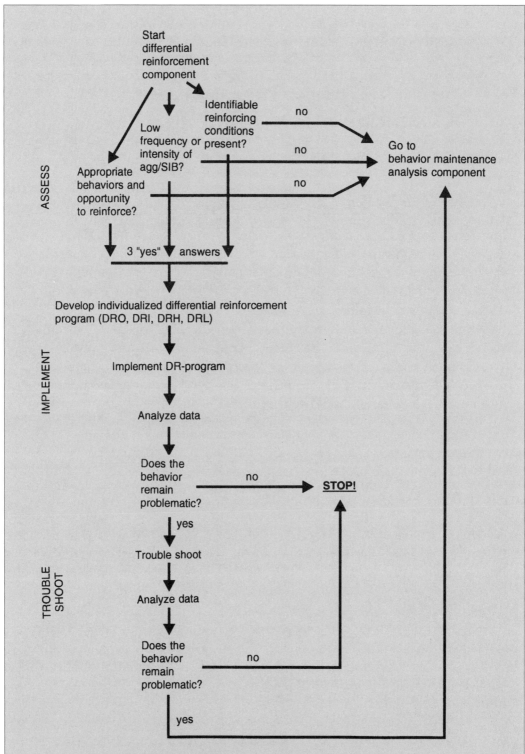

Fig. 4. Component IV—Differential Reinforcement

pends on the frequency, duration, and function of a student's behavior. Depending on the severity of the targeted behavior, other strategies may need to be used in conjunction with differential reinforcement strategies. For example, a student who talks loudly to himself when alone would likely be reinforced with a DRO strategy. But he would also need a program to teach him more appropriate leisure activities. Teaching programs are often combined with differential reinforcement procedures because students generally need to be taught the behaviors which are reinforced through DR procedures.

If a differential reinforcement procedure is effective in reducing the targeted behavior, the decision-making process ends. If these procedures are not effective, the reinforcement's effectiveness is analyzed before the process proceeds to the final component of the EDM. In analyzing the reinforcement, teachers look at the duration of the interval between reinforcement, how reinforcing the rewards offered are, and the consistency with which the procedure is implemented. If the targeted behavior is reduced after reassessing the student's reinforcement, the decision-making process ends. If not, the process continues to its final stage: the development of a more intrusive behavior reduction procedure.

COMPONENT V—BEHAVIORAL REDUCTION THROUGH PUNISHMENT

◆ ◆ ◆ ◆ ◆ ◆ ◆ ◆ ◆ ◆ ◆ ◆ ◆ ◆ ◆ ◆ ◆ ◆

Having progressed through the first four components of the EDM, teachers have determined that: 1) the student has no medical conditions that may be the cause of the behavior, 2) the student is living and working in a safe, comfortable environment, 3) the student has been taught or is being taught strategies that will enable him to manipulate his own environment, and the student's curriculum consists of tasks that are challenging yet commensurate with his abilities, and 4) reinforcement for appropriate behaviors is available on a regular basis. All four of these conditions must be met before any behavior reduction strategy based on punishment is implemented. If a punishment strategy is used, all the teaching and modification strategies developed through the first four components of the EDM continue to be monitored, and are not changed in any way until teachers can determine whether the punishment strategy has any effect on the targeted behavior.

When selecting a punishment procedure, the conditions discussed in the previous chapter must be met.[3] Just as important as those conditions in developing an effective intervention strategy, however, is the continuing analysis of what

---

[3] Again, these are: a) it restricts the student's freedom of movement; b) it restricts the student's opportunity for acquiring positive reinforcement; c) it causes the loss of privileges which a student enjoys; d) it engages the student in behavior which may be against his will (behavior he would not engage in given the freedom to choose); e) it results in the application of a stimulus viewed as painful or unpleasant by the student.

motivates the student to display the targeted behavior. Teachers have found that the motivation for unacceptable behavior generally falls into one of four categories: 1) as a way to get attention, 2) to escape something unpleasant, 3) the behavior is intrinsically rewarding, or 4) occasionally the student does not receive adequate reinforcement for engaging in alternative behavior.[4]

If the analysis from Component I indicates that the targeted behavior occurs more frequently when there is less teacher or peer interaction, the behavior may be maintained by positive reinforcement, or as a way to get attention. For example, if a student makes disruptive noises to get attention, and a teacher comes over to see why he is noisy, the teacher would be incidentally reinforcing the student's behavior by giving him attention. Intervention strategies to reduce attention-getting behavior are those which manipulate the positive reinforcement associated with the behavior, such as extinction,[5] time-out strategies, visual screening, and various token loss/earn strategies.

A behavior could also be motivated by the desire to escape. If a student made disruptive noises whenever he participated in speech therapy, his behavior would effectively exclude him from participating in speech training. Strategies that negate the efficacy of escape have had the most success in modifying behaviors motivated by the desire to escape. The student's disruptive noises, for example, could be redirected by the teacher; the teacher could then turn the noises into sounds the student uses in speech therapy. Other intervention strategies used for escape-motivated behaviors include simple correction, positive practice overcorrection, negative practice overcorrection, and restitutional overcorrection.[6]

If the behavior is maintained primarily by the reinforcement the behavior itself provides, as with most self-stimulatory and all compulsive behaviors, more typical punishment is usually appropriate. Aversive contingencies, such as verbal reprimands or a tap on the hands, are often effective. Visual screening, overcorrection procedures, brief restraint through temporary response interruption procedures, and occasionally contingent exercise are also used. Contingent exercise helps reduce anxiety and hyperactivity, and so is a good way to release excess energy which can drive compulsive behavior. For example, contingent exercise would be used with a student who runs around flapping his arms. Being placed on the treadmill for five minutes would give him a positive way to channel his energy, yet be a disincentive for arm flapping.

Finally, sometimes the student has been taught an appropriate alternative to the targeted behavior, but does not use it. The unacceptable behavior pro-

---

[4] However, some behavior does not fall into any of these categories. Behavior motivated by fear does not. If a student has what appears to be irrational fears—one student had a fear of stairs, another was terrified of blenders and motorcycles, and a third panicked at even the slightest touch—teachers implement strategies to desensitize him. The student may be gradually introduced to what he fears, or a more intrusive flooding procedure may be more appropriate.

[5] See the previous chapter for a description of each of the intervention strategies mentioned here.

[6] See Chapter 6 for descriptions of these procedures.

◆ ◆

This is the checklist for Sean in the final Component of the EDM. Sean's teachers proceeded to this point in the EDM more than once to try to modify his behavior. So, a summary of additional strategies tried with Sean is given after the early version of the checklist below.

Behavioral Reduction Program Checklist
Component V: Development of a Behavior Reduction Procedure

AS INDICATED BY THE DATA, IS THE TARGETED BEHAVIOR MAINTAINED BY POSITIVE REINFORCEMENT, OR TO GET ATTENTION?

Yes. This was determined in Component IV. The aggression that Sean exhibits when he is asked to do something often seems to be motivated by a desire for more attention. For example, when teachers prompt him to stay in place during adaptive physical education activities, Sean will often be aggressive in order to disrupt the session and have attention focused on himself.

INTERVENTION STRATEGIES:

Teachers will continue to use primarily gestural prompts with Sean, but if gestural prompts are not responded to, Sean will be prompted physically without teachers' eye contact, and without any verbal command. Teachers will also use fewer prompts, so that Sean has fewer opportunities to disrupt the group.

AS INDICATED BY THE DATA, IS THE BEHAVIOR MAINTAINED BY NEGATIVE REINFORCEMENT, OR THE DESIRE TO ESCAPE?

Yes. This was determined in Component IV.

INTERVENTION STRATEGIES:

A mild negative reinforcement strategy will be used. The physical prompting described above will be used to make sure Sean stays in place during adaptive physical education activities, and to make sure that he completes the trial. If he stays in place and completes the trial with or without prompting, he will receive reinforcement.

AS INDICATED BY THE DATA, IS THE BEHAVIOR MAINTAINED BY PERCEPTUAL REINFORCEMENT? IN OTHER WORDS, IS IT INTRINSICALLY REWARDING (SELF-STIMULATORY)?

No. If it were, Sean would show high rates of the targeted behavior when in low-demand situations. He does not.

(continued)

Have previous intervention strategies from Components II-IV failed to significantly decrease the targeted behavior?
Yes. The behavior remains problematic.

Results of programming:
Paying less attention to Sean's aggression and using the mild negative reinforcement procedure has reduced Sean's aggression somewhat. However, these strategies were designed to modify his aggression mainly during physical education activities, and Sean's aggression has been occurring more frequently in other teaching sessions.

Current rate of behavior:
60 instances per day.

Additional information:
Teachers suggest that the decision-making process return to Component I. A re-analysis of Sean's behavior is needed.

◆ ◆ ◆ ◆ ◆ ◆

Sean's teachers did begin a re-analysis of his behavior when the negative reinforcement strategy did not work. They tried more restrictive strategies. Carol Markowitz explains:

Sean was showing aggressive behavior in all prompting sessions, so we went through the EDM again. We decided to try putting a protective helmet on him so he at least would not hurt himself. We also tried putting him in time-out every time he became aggressive. That actually ended up reinforcing his aggression. His rate doubled in just a few days.

Sean began getting too big for us to work through his behavior, and the behavior was still occurring frequently. So, we began restraining his hands at his desk until he was calm. We would then continue with the task, so he was not actually allowed to escape. That worked very well. He has had several days of no aggression, and many more very low incidence days.

◆ ◆

vides a more efficient means of getting what he wants. Behavior falling into this category is usually motivated by a desire to communicate. For example, a student may know how to request a break, but finds that throwing a small tantrum is easier and more effective. Interventions for this type of behavior are designed to decrease the efficiency of the targeted behavior and increase the efficiency of

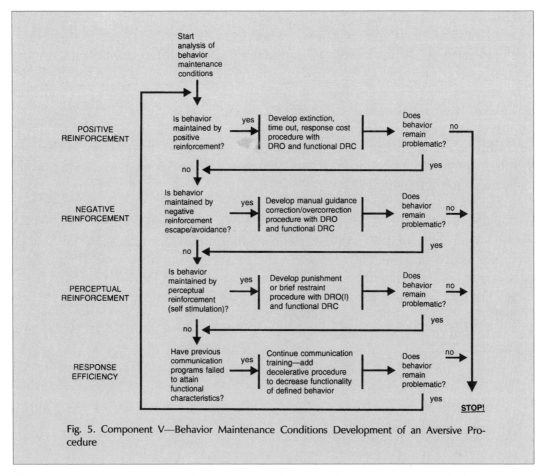

Fig. 5. Component V—Behavior Maintenance Conditions Development of an Aversive Procedure

the appropriate response. The student might be given more rewards for requesting a break, for example, and punished for having a tantrum. A student with this type of behavior is also given more functional communication training. He is taught appropriate alternatives to the unacceptable behavior, such as tapping a teacher on the shoulder or raising his hand. As he learns to communicate more effectively, the aversive procedures used to punish the unacceptable behavior can often be faded or eliminated.

Negative reinforcement strategies are also effective in modifying this type of behavior, especially when paired with functional communication training. Negative reinforcement strategies are based on the contingent removal of an aversive stimulus when a student exhibits the appropriate behavior, for example, not allowing the student to take a break until he functionally communicated the request to do so. Because a student with this type of behavior knows what the appropriate behavior is, negative reinforcement often modifies behavior quickly.[7]

The effectiveness of aversive procedures in modifying the targeted behavior is assessed regularly. It is compared to the original baseline and analysis of the

---

[7] See Chapter 6 on positive and negative reinforcement.

behavior from Component I. If the procedure is effective (i.e., the behavior is greatly reduced or eliminated), it proceeds while being monitored, and structured attempts are made to fade the intervention by replacing it with differential reinforcement strategies and strategies developed through the first three components of the EDM. The environmental and curricular conditions of Components II and III continue to be assessed to make sure the student's appropriate behavior is maintained.

If the targeted behavior remains problematic after implementing punishment procedures, and if efforts to refine the interventions have proven ineffective, the process returns to its beginning. New analyses are done, and new strategies are developed and implemented.

Sean's case described above provides a good example. Sean's behavior was especially problematic. The motivations behind his behavior were complicated, and changed somewhat over the course of evaluations. At first his behavior seemed to be primarily motivated by a desire to communicate, but after several months of analysis it became clear that his behavior was motivated more by a desire to escape. The first aversive contingencies tried with Sean were not effective enough in reducing his aggression. So, teachers returned to Component I to reanalyze his behavior and come up with new strategies to modify it. The length of time it took teachers to find a strategy that would work for Sean was unusual, but they kept reassessing his behavior and trying different intervention strategies. The EDM enabled them to do that in a systematic way.

ACCOUNTABILITY
◆ ◆ ◆ ◆ ◆ ◆ ◆ ◆ ◆ ◆ ◆ ◆ ◆ ◆ ◆ ◆ ◆ ◆ ◆ ◆

If, based on the results of the EDM, an aversive intervention is determined to be the most appropriate treatment, Eden's Accountability Process begins. The Accountability Process is designed to ensure that all behavioral interventions are safe and effective, and protect the student's human rights. It is a system of checks and balances that incorporates team review, analysis, and group decision-making. It remains in effect for the entire duration of the intervention. The Accountability Process consists of three stages: intervention, implementation, and monitoring.

INTERVENTION
The first stage, intervention, is the actual application of the Eden Decision Model. The student's teachers, administrators, and clinicians all review the data collected on the student's unacceptable behavior. Members of the Behavioral Management Committee[8] also review the data at this early stage. Once a behavioral intervention is chosen, the second stage of the Accountability Process, or implementation of the intervention, begins.

---

[8] The Behavioral Management Committee is comprised of, but not limited to, the Directors of Outreach Services, Support Services, Employment Services, Educational Services, and Residential Services, and the Clinical Support Specialist.

IMPLEMENTATION

The implementation of the intervention begins with the development of a behavioral management program. The behavioral management program describes the exact parameters of the intervention and how it should be implemented. The director of the student's program, along with both the supervisor and teachers, develops an initial draft of the behavioral management program. The Clinical Support Specialist is responsible for making sure that the Accountability Process is properly followed, and that all paperwork is completed. The behavioral management program then undergoes a five step review process: an initial administrative review, a clinical review, a parental review, an ethical review, and a final executive review.

During the initial administrative review, the behavioral intervention program is presented by the program supervisor to the director of the student's program. If any modifications need to be made, the director oversees them and gives the program to the Clinical Support Specialist for a last administrative review. Once the director approves the program, it is presented to the Behavioral Management Committee.

The Behavioral Management Committee conducts a clinical review through an open discussion of the program. It makes sure the program has been developed properly, is clinically appropriate for the student, and is consistent with good clinical practice. The Behavioral Management Committee must unanimously approve any behavioral intervention before it can be implemented.[9] In practice, less than 10 percent of proposed interventions are rejected on their first submission. If modifications, additional information, or clarification is required by the Behavioral Management Committee, the program is returned to the program director for revision and resubmission.

Throughout the entire decision-making process at Eden, parents are consulted about their child's behavior. They are part of the assessment of unacceptable behavior, and often propose behavioral intervention programs to modify their child's behavior. Once the Behavioral Management Committee approves a behavioral management program, the parents' formal approval is sought. The director of the student's program discusses the program in detail with the parents. The director brings any parental questions or concerns to the Behavioral Management Committee, which makes changes when appropriate.

---

[9] New Jersey law allows a behavioral management program to pass with one dissenting vote from a behavioral management committee. Eden requires a unanimous vote. Eden's Behavioral Management Committee decided on this policy because it felt that if even one clinician had strong enough doubts about a program to veto it, the program should be sent back for further review.

Once the parental review phase is complete, the behavioral management program is presented to the Human Rights Committee (HRC) for an ethical review. This committee is generally comprised of two members of the community not associated with Eden, two parents of students at Eden, one staff member either at the teaching or supervisor level, and the Clinical Support Specialist. The purpose of the Human Rights Committee is to ensure that the dignity and individual freedom of each student at Eden are protected. The Human Rights Committee weighs the relative risks of implementing the procedure with the benefits of the procedure. To guide their decisions, the Human Rights Committee addresses several questions. These are:

1. Does the student have a signed IEP or IHP in place?[10]
2. Has appropriate Behavioral Management Committee and parental consent been obtained?
3. Is the plan presented in accordance with the General Procedures Manual?[11]
4. What is the specific time frame for reviewing the program?
5. Is the student involved in productive work and home activities?
6. Have less restrictive procedures been tried prior to this program?
7. If the proposed procedure is not the least restrictive, why is it the most appropriate?[12]
8. What are the potential risks associated with the program?
9. Do the associated risks place the student at greater risk than does the targeted behavior?
10. What risks are foreseen if the program is not implemented, and what benefits will it give the student?
11. What alternative, appropriate behavior will be taught or reinforced to replace the behavior that is targeted for reduction?

---

[10] This is another check on the individualization of programming and the official status of the student's program.

[11] The General Procedures Manual outlines the procedures for all staff members in the use of teaching techniques, designing teaching programs, developing a behavioral reduction program, and implementing behavioral interventions.

[12] If several interventions have been proposed to modify a student's unacceptable behavior, but the behavior remains, the Behavioral Management Committee will usually present to the Human Rights Committee a procedure that is only slightly more restrictive. However, occasionally the Behavioral Management Committee presents a much more restrictive procedure. It would do this for one of two reasons. The Behavioral Management Committee is a group of clinicians who know the students at Eden well. They might feel that a less restrictive procedure would not be effective enough in reducing a particular student's behavior, and so would approve a more restrictive procedure. The Behavioral Management Committee can also decide to pass over a component of the EDM if they feel, based on their clinical experience with a student, that the conditions analyzed in that component have no bearing on the student's behavior. They do this generally only when an analysis of the student's behavior has previously been done through the component being waived. If the Human Rights Committee does not agree with the restrictiveness of an intervention proposed by the Behavioral Management Committee, it has the authority to recommend revision.

Programs must be approved by all but one vote of the Human Rights Committee, in contrast to the unanimous vote required by the Behavioral Management Committee. This is because the Human Rights Committee is composed of a variety of people, only some of whom have experience with the students at Eden.

Because of their clinical expertise, the Behavioral Management Committee requires a unanimous vote, but the Human Rights Committee is allowed one dissent.

If the Human Rights Committee has any questions or concerns, or recommends any modifications, the program is returned to the Behavioral Management Committee and the process begins again. Once the Human Rights Committee approves a program, it is presented to the Executive Director for final approval.

Only when the director of the student's program, the Behavioral Management Committee, the student's parents, the Human Rights Committee, and the Executive Director have all approved the intervention can implementation proceed. To ensure the consistent, effective, and ethical implementation of the behavioral management program, the Clinical Support Specialist reviews the approved program with the teachers who will implement the program. The Clinical Support Specialist answers any questions or concerns the teachers have, and often has them role-play the procedure to ensure its proper implementation.

MONITORING

The third and final stage of the Accountability Process is monitoring of the intervention. In general, a 75 percent decrease in the targeted behavior from the baseline rate must be achieved within the first two weeks of implementing the program. If the program is not decreased by 75 percent, it is either discontinued or reassessed at the same stage in the EDM. Decreased rates of the targeted behavior are analyzed through a variety of checks.

To measure change in the targeted behavior, once an intervention is implemented, data is taken and reviewed daily by the direct care staff, and weekly by the program supervisor.[13] In addition, the Clinical Support Specialist reviews each intervention at thirty day intervals for the first three months, and every ninety days thereafter. As another check, each division is also required to present a review of the data for every behavioral intervention to the Clinical Support Specialist once a month.

---

[13] The box on the next page gives an example of how this review process can lead to a change in an intervention designed to reduce hand-play behavior.

Jon's hand-play activity had excluded him from many community outings and was interfering with his skill acquisition, so teachers recommended a behavioral program to stop the behavior. Through the EDM, it was determined that his hand-play was driven by compulsion. This conclusion led teachers to the final component of the EDM. A behavioral management program was approved to grasp Jon's hands and give him a firm verbal "no" when he began hand-playing. This strategy seemed to work for several days. After the fourth day, however, it became clear that the targeted behavior had begun to return to the baseline rate. On the eleventh day, teachers determined that this intervention was not, and would not, significantly decrease Jon's behavior. The behavior was re-analyzed through Component V, and a new program was developed.

Teachers felt that after having paid so much attention to Jon's hand-playing with the previous intervention, Jon might have become more aware of his hand-playing. They conjectured that his hand-playing might have become more of a conscious, less compulsive, behavior. So, on day 12, teachers began treating Jon's behavior with extinction, or planned ignoring. This had a much more profound effect. The following is a graph of the gross data collected over the first four weeks of the intervention. The graph begins with the baseline period (days -2 to 0), and continues to day 25 of the intervention.

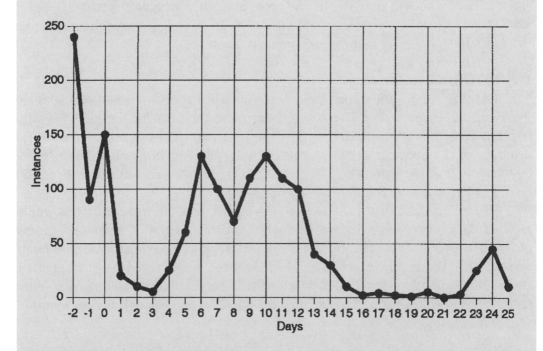

The complete package of interventions in use at Eden is reviewed several times a year during staff and general service evaluations. Each of the services at Eden is reviewed twice a year by directors and peer reviewers, and also through the Support Services Division. The purpose of these evaluations is to make sure that teachers are using proper teaching techniques and implementing behavioral management programs appropriately and consistently. These evaluations provide an effective indicator of the effectiveness of programs within Eden's services, and they also provide an additional check on the types of behavioral intervention procedures in use. The regular monitoring and rigorous structure for approving behavioral interventions help ensure the safe implementation of behavioral management programs.

BENEFITS OF THE EDM AND ACCOUNTABILITY SYSTEM

Both the EDM and Accountability Process are effective tools on their own, but used together they create an even more powerful and efficient system by which to manage the modification of behavior. The EDM-Accountability system has several benefits. They require that staff, administration, families, and the community be deeply involved in the development of intervention programs, and they require precise and efficient assessment of behavior. The system also allows fast decision-making when necessary.

Decisions made in the EDM-Accountability system are team decisions, involving everyone from the Executive Director of Eden to the direct line staff and parents who work every day with the people about whom the decisions are made. Decisions are made through hard work and detailed analyses. They are consensus decisions, and so take into account what staff members at all levels of service have to say. The input of teaching staff is especially important because they implement intervention programs and they likely know the student better

> **W**e get a lot of treatment questions from people outside of Eden, but we don't frequently receive attacks because we explain our methods to anyone who comes in and asks about our treatment procedure. For example, if a visitor sees a teacher slap a child's hand, and asks why, we explain to them the accountability system, the rigorous process we went through to have the program approved and the positive impact the procedure has had on the child.
>
> —**Cindy Bregenzer, Coordinating Teacher, Middle Childhood Program**

than specialists or administrators. Involvement of the parents and direct line staff in making behavioral decisions, therefore, increases the chance of success of the program developed. Involvement in the process also gives the staff and parents validation of their observations, and gives them a sense of ownership in the program, which also increases the potential for success.

The rigorous structure of the EDM-Accountability system also helps avoid teacher frustration. When staff members have questions or problems about behavior, they can look to the EDM and the Accountability Process to see what steps they need to take to answer their questions. No agency serving such a challenging population of people with autism can avoid frustration altogether, but a structured approach to treatment minimizes that frustration.

Another benefit of the EDM-Accountability system is the efficiency with which behaviors and motivations for behaviors are assessed. Because the steps of the EDM and Accountability Process are clearly delineated, there is little confusion about how to deal with problematic behavior. Cindy Bregenzer:

> One of the biggest benefits of the EDM is having a structured approach to treatment. In other places that serve children like ours, a problematic behavior will occur, and the staff will not know how to approach it. The behavior will cause a panic, and the staff will do crisis intervention. Every time the behavior happens, it will be a crisis. No behavior should ever be a crisis unless it is a behavior like none we have ever seen before. Even a destructive or assaultive behavior is not considered a crisis; it is a behavioral management challenge that we have to address. The EDM gives us a step-by-step procedure we can follow to deal with the behavior.

In providing a clear structure for understanding and dealing with problematic behavior, the EDM-Accountability system allows teachers to modify behavior effectively and efficiently. Because behavior is analyzed thoroughly, a detailed account of when and why it occurs in a variety of stimulus conditions is known. This enables teachers to sort out exactly which conditions are associated with the behavior, and what motivations exist for the behavior. This analysis results in the development of intervention programs that are tailored to the particular student. Not every analysis and not every intervention program will be exactly like another. Although many behaviors exhibited by people with autism may appear similar, each is unique.

The EDM-Accountability system not only takes into account a variety of different stimulus conditions in developing an intervention strategy, it also allows for the integration of several separate strategies to modify behavior into one comprehensive treatment package. In other words, the treatment is as detailed and efficient as is the analysis of the targeted behavior. *Quick fixes are often quicksand.* Therefore, most often a simple treatment, such as just squeezing a student's hands when he begins to hit, is less effective in modifying his behavior than one that is more complicated. For example, if the student hit in order to escape from a situation, treatment would be more effective if teachers both squeezed his hands (punisher) and taught him how to communicate his desire for a break. If he hit sometimes out of frustration, and sometimes to get physical contact, teachers might put him in time out for some occurrences of the behavior, and squeeze his hands for others. These different treatment approaches can be developed only because the EDM-Account-ability system is exacting in its assessment of unacceptable behavior. Together, the approaches make for a complicated but more effective intervention strategy.

The EDM-Accountability system takes the shortest possible route to the development of an effective intervention strategy, which means that behavior is modified as efficiently as possible. Peter Gerhardt, Director of Employment Services:

> *The EDM-Accountability system is efficient because it provides everyone in the process the tools to analyze a behavior, which gives them the best possible chance at developing an effective intervention. Without the EDM-Accountability process, teachers would at best be taking a guess as to which intervention would be most successful.*
>
> *Before the decision-making process is begun, teachers usually need to take a temporary guess as to why a behavior is happening. After the process is completed, it often turns out that teachers' initial perceptions were inaccurate. For example, one of the participants in Eden WERCs was having trouble with increasing outbursts of self-injury and aggression. Initially, teachers thought this behavior was a resurgence of a previously established behavior and treated it with a behavior reduction program. However, it turned out that his problem was due to a medical condition, oral thrush. We discovered that variable by using the EDM-Accountability system. Once his medical condition was treated, the self-injury and aggression decreased significantly.*

The EDM-Accountability system allows decisions to be made even more quickly if the behavior is extremely disruptive, or threatening to the student or others. These interventions can begin immediately, and are refined after a more detailed analysis of the behavior is completed. At Eden, protection from harm holds the highest priority. For example, if a behavior is extremely disruptive, or threatening to the student or others, an intervention can be approved and implemented within a matter of hours. These interventions are generally developed and approved as an "emergency interim procedure" by the Behavioral Management Committee, the Human Rights Committee, and the Executive Director.

Quick decisions can also be made to change intervention programs that are not working well. Provisions for changing intervention strategies are an integral part of the EDM-Accountability system. If an intervention has not reduced the targeted behavior by 75 percent by the end of two weeks, the answer to the final question in each component of the EDM— "Does the behavior remain problematic?"—is "Yes." The process then either proceeds to the next step (for Components I through IV) or returns to the beginning of the component (for Component V) for a re-analysis of the behavior and intervention.

If an intervention is successful in reducing the targeted behavior, data continue to be collected on the behavior long after the intervention program has worked and the official use of the EDM and Accountability Process is over. The original analysis from which the intervention strategy was developed continues to be noted. However, it now reflects changes in the effectiveness of the intervention or in the student himself. This ongoing analysis provides a foundation from which new interventions may be developed.

Continued monitoring also provides a basis from which existing interventions can be changed. Programs may need to be changed over time. People change. An intervention designed for a student at one point may not, at some time in the future, still be the best strategy to modify his behavior. The motivation for a behavior may change, as with Sean's aggression. Sean's behavior was originally motivated by a desire to communicate. Over time, it became a means to get attention and a means to escape. The interventions teachers used with Sean also had to change.

The ability to adjust intervention strategies is important with children to enable them to grow and learn. For example, Spike's behavior changed radically in just a short time. Eric and Erica Lofgren, Spike's parents, describe what happened:

> *Spike was making odd noises. They were stigmatizing him in the regular nursery school program he attended part time, and made it difficult for him to interact with the other children. Everyone thought hard about how to get him to stop, and Eden came up with a token system. It was based on his desire to collect things, and would give him a quiet way to hold these things and feel good about them. When he made a noise, he would have to give away one of these things. If he kept them, he could trade them in for something bigger and better after a certain amount of time. That system worked beautifully. Spike went from a hundred noises to five in a matter of days, as soon as he figured out that he could keep these things by keeping quiet.*

Carol Markowitz, Director of Educational Services:

> *Spike's system was working great. He was able to go for almost an hour without making a noise. Then, all of a sudden, the system stopped working completely. He did not care about the objects anymore. We tried changing the objects, but it did not work. The motivation behind his behavior became completely different. After careful analysis, we have now changed his system and are trying nonexclusionary time-out instead. That is beginning to work. Sometimes we think we have an answer, and we do have one for a while, but then the child changes.*

Carol Markowitz, in another example:

> *We got approval on a contingent exercise program with Alex in Early Childhood to decrease his aggression. Alex pinches. He seemed to be*

reinforced by people's reactions when he pinched them, and would pinch because he disliked an activity, or even if we just picked him up to hug him. We decided on a contingent exercise program. He would walk on the treadmill and do sit-ups or a push-up. That program decreased his aggression, but not to the extent we wanted, so we discontinued the program. We still had about eight behaviors a day, and eight contingent exercises a day is too much.

We then changed his program to make it less aversive. When he began to pinch, we simply took his hands and prompted them down. That minimized the amount of attention we were giving the behavior, and so did not give him the feedback he enjoyed so much. We then directed him back to task. We also instituted a reinforcement system for him similar to Spike's. He gets tokens, and loses one every time he pinches. If he still has three left at the end of his interval, which is up to about twenty or thirty minutes, he can trade the tokens in for a special treat. This has worked very well.

The ability to change intervention strategies is also important for adults. Behavioral problems tend to return in adults, because they have had much more time to practice the targeted behavior. The continued monitoring teachers do with intervention programs allows them to see immediately when a behavior returns.

The final benefit of the EDM-Accountability system is that decisions are mandatory. No problem is allowed to be tabled, or put aside when it gets difficult. As the flow charts given above for the EDM show, there is no "remove child from program" step, or "see if it goes away in time" step. Each problem has to be dealt with. There is no "exit" from the EDM-Accountability process unless the behavior no longer remains problematic.

These are the biggest benefits of the EDM-Accountability system: mandatory and fast decision making on behavioral issues, efficient and effective assessment of a behavior, and team decision making. But perhaps the greatest benefit of all is that the system works. The EDM-Accountability system has enabled parents and teachers to successfully reduce hundreds of problematic behaviors, and to keep those behaviors under control. The EDM-Accountability system is a decision model that can be, and has been, adopted by many public and private schools throughout the United States to treat the behavioral challenges presented by people with autism in a safe, humane, and effective manner.

The following shows how each step of the EDM works for an adult in Eden's services. Note that many of the concerns are similar to those in Sean's case, but presented in an adult context. *This case study was published previously in Gerhardt, P.F. & Holmes, D.L. (1993). "The Eden Decision Model: A Decision Model with Practical Applications for the Development of Behavior Decelerative Strategies," in E. Shopler & G.B. Mesibov (eds),* Behavioral Issues in Autism. *New York: Plenum Press. pp 247-276.*

EDM CASE STUDY

INDIVIDUAL DESCRIPTION

At the time of assessment, Oscar was a 29-year-old adult male with autism who functioned in the severe range of mental retardation. Oscar was verbal, but articulation often made comprehension difficult. He was, however, generally able to express most of his wants, needs, and interests. Oscar resided in a community group home for individuals with autism and was employed in a sheltered employment setting.

DETERMINATION OF NEED

Oscar entered the Eden Work Education Resource Centers (WERCs) program with a history of severe and directed aggression. Initially, aggression was brought under control through the use of relaxation training for times during which Oscar appeared anxious (anxious or anticipatory behaviors), a token-earn system for time on task and use of appropriate communication, and a restraint procedure for any occurrences of aggression or attempts at aggression. An EDM assessment was indicated, however, as the frequency of aggression had increased over previous weeks to a level where safety concerns became a factor. Aggression and anxious/anticipatory behaviors were defined as:

> Aggression—any directed biting, kicking, grabbing, hitting, or scratching of others, not to include any accidental or social contact.

> Anxious behavior—the taking of rapid short breaths or the repetition of the same question or statement more than twice within 2 minutes.

As a result of staff input regarding the defined behaviors, the applied functional analysis or baseline procedure consisted of the following measures: frequency of aggressive episodes; duration of time until calm following an aggression; an anecdotal assessment of the "intensity" of each episode of aggression; frequency with which Oscar was offered the option to relax; day of the week; number of people in the environment; time of day; and activities or curricular demands. An A-B-C log was also maintained to supplement this information. During the assessment, a medical evaluation was completed that failed to identify any potential medical correlates to Oscar's increased aggression.

Data collected during the assessment validated staff reports of a need to modify Oscar's existing behavioral programming. Aggression, during assessment, occurred at a rate of approximately 3 episodes per week (Figure 6), whereas anxious behaviors were displayed approximately 21 times per week (Figure 7). Following 9 weeks of assessment, the data collected on the potential environmental correlates to aggression were analyzed in accordance with the EDM.

ENVIRONMENTAL CONDITIONS

Two particular staff perceptions were validated by the applied functional analysis baseline data. First, Oscar was far more likely to aggress whenever there were more than 20 people in his immediate environment (Figure 8). Thirty-five percent of all aggressions were associated with this level of crowding. As Oscar spent only 8 to 10% of his time at this

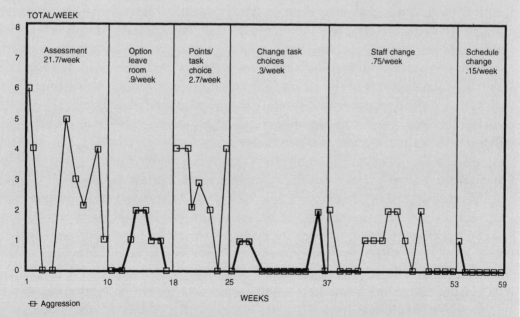

Fig. 6. Aggression as a function of EDM-directed modifications.

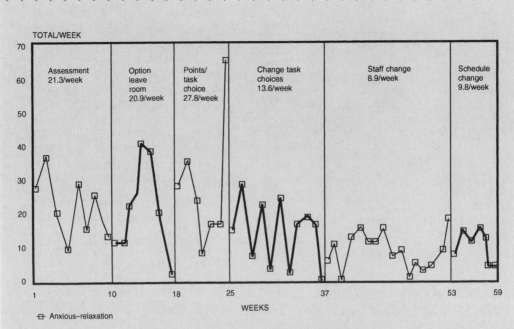

Fig. 7. Relaxation as a function of EDM-directed modifications.

level of crowding, this finding was considered especially significant. Second, aggression appeared to be associated with those times when Oscar worked in the kitchen (Figure 9). As lunch, a high-aggression activity was also a high-crowding activity; the decision was made to address crowding as the primary correlate to aggression and kitchen activities as a secondary correlate. (It bears noting that this outcome was contrary to staff predictions. Prior to assessment, staff perceptions were that kitchen tasks were the primary correlate to aggression. Crowding, although viewed as possibly related, was not predicted as a primary correlate. This highlights the importance of a data-based assessment in determining the function of a behavior.)

As a result of this initial analysis, functional escape training was initiated to address Oscar's difficulty with crowds. Functional escape training consisted of prompting Oscar to request to leave the room when there were more than 10 people in his environment. The option to escape was also offered in place of relaxation if staff perceived the overall level of activity in the environment as potentially disturbing to Oscar.

Functional escape training was introduced in Week 10, resulting in a 66% reduction in the frequency of aggression with, oddly, no related reduction in anxious behavior (Figure 6 and Figure 7). Of particular interest is that Oscar only once accepted the opportunity to leave the situation. It seems possible that he perceived leaving the situation as a form of punishment and, therefore, less desirable than remaining in the stressful, crowded situation.

CURRICULAR CONSIDERATIONS

At this point, the continuation of the applied functional analysis procedure throughout functional-escape training provided clearer support for kitchen-associated activities (i.e., lunch prep and lunch cleanup) as now being the primary correlates of aggression. A review of the ongoing data in accordance with the elements of Component III suggested two possible explanations for kitchen activities precipitating aggression. According to the A-B-C log, on a number of occasions across programs, Oscar had declined to chose a reinforcer to work as part of his token system. Apparently his reinforcement menu was no longer functionally defined. Second, although all problematic kitchen activities were previously documented as within Oscar's repertoire, they simply appeared to be nonpreferred (boring?) activities.

Working on these data-based assumptions, two complementary strategies were introduced at this point in addition to continuing to offer Oscar the opportunity to escape crowded situations. Oscar's token program was modified in such a way that he would earn points for each task completed. The longer, or more complex the task, the greater its point value. In conjunction, a reinforcer assessment was used to identify a broader array of functional secondary reinforcers for which Oscar could cash in points. Second, to address the potential boredom, task-choice options were introduced into all kitchen-related activities. This allowed Oscar to choose his kitchen activity from a variety of tasks, each of which was assigned a specific point value.

In Week 18, the point-earn system and task-choice procedure were implemented. Aggression returned to levels equal to those obtained during the initial assessment, with no change in the frequency of anxious behaviors (Figures 8 and 9). Initially, a return to the previous token system and a suspension of the task-choice procedure was considered in an attempt to reduce the frequency of aggression. However, the decision was made to continue with the changes while additional data were collected. The intent was to effectively modify either or both procedures in such a way as to reduce both aggression and anxious behaviors.

In Week 25, based on information obtained from the continued A-B-C log, the choice-making procedure was modified such that a greater array of shorter tasks was made available, and the nature of some of the task choices was modified (e.g., prepare chili or sandwiches). With the introduction of

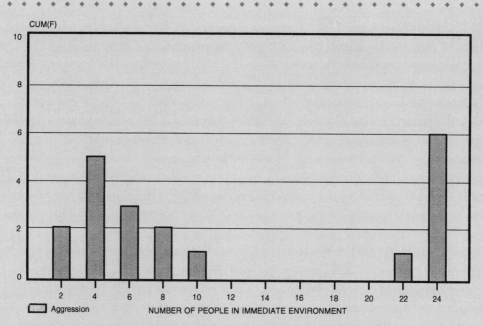

Fig. 8. Aggression as a function of crowding.

this change, the frequency of aggression was reduced such that there were only four episodes over the next 12 weeks. In addition, for the first time, a drop in the frequency of anxious behaviors was evidenced, indicating a general lowering of Oscar's overall level of anxiety (Figures 8 and 9).

Two additional changes, not related to the EDM or ongoing assessment, are noted on the graph and deserve attention. First, in Week 37 Oscar's teacher-job coach left, resulting in higher rates of aggression during the training and transition of new staff. Although higher than during the previous 12 weeks, aggression continued to be lower than during assessment. Additionally, despite the increase in aggression, anxious behaviors were maintained at the previously obtained lower rates indicating continued overall reductions in anxiety. Within 3 months, rates of aggression were back at near-zero levels. Second, in Week 53, as a result of some changes in program structure, a change was made in Oscar's daily schedule. This change resulted in a single aggression, followed with a rapid return to zero rates of aggression (Figures 8 and 9).

DISCUSSION

The case of Oscar is provided as a relatively straightforward example of the use of the EDM in the development of an applied functional analysis and related intervention strategies. This case serves to highlight the

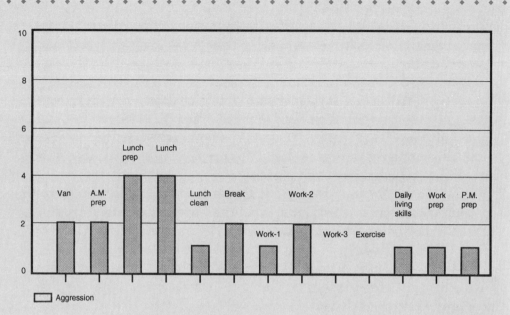

Fig. 9. Aggression as a function of work task.

benefits of the use of the EDM in addressing a severely problematic behavior; that of a high-intensity aggression of relatively low-frequency
(that is, in terms of data collection for assessment purposes). First, by
reviewing the separate components of the EDM, an applied functional
analysis or assessment process may be developed that addresses a variety
of stimulus conditions that may be associated with the defined behavior.
In Oscar's case, this resulted in the elimination of possible medical causation, the identification of possible environmental factors associated with
the behavior (crowding), and the identification of the curricular conditions
under which the behavior most frequently occurred (kitchen tasks).

Second, the EDM provides for the integration of separate strategies
into one, comprehensive treatment package. In the case of Oscar, this
resulted in a final package of strategies that included functional escape
training, training in the use of tasks choices, continued emphasis on
alternate response training (relaxation), and a functionally defined reinforcement system. In Oscar's case, differential reinforcement alone was
not considered an appropriate option due to the intensity of aggression
and the potential for harm. As previously noted, this required a potentially aversive component (restraint) being in effect throughout the EDM
process. However, given the lack of any reductive effect of restraint, it
could not be considered a functional aversive. Restraint, in the case, could

more accurately be described as a crisis-management procedure that allowed for the EDM process to continue while ensuring the safety of Oscar and others.

Third, the EDM allows for (indeed, requires) direct line-staff input at all levels of assessment. Involvement of this type can have many advantages, including a sense of professional validation for observations and perceptions used as a basis for the assessment process and increased staff compliance (as a result of a degree of "ownership" in the process) in the data collection and assessment process.

Last, the ongoing nature of the EDM assessment process allows for the continuing assessment of stimulus conditions over extended periods of time. This may be extremely important in cases where the behavior is of relatively low frequency, and stable data may only be obtained over extended periods of assessment. Additionally, continuing assessment allows for the identification of secondary or changing stimulus conditions that may precipitate the behavior.

Some cautions, however, are in order regarding the use of the EDM assessment process. The EDM, as discussed here, is presented solely as a set of general guidelines. Utilization of this model is not presented as a total or sufficient condition for the implementation of any decelerative behavioral procedure. Programmatic options presented with each component are only examples and are not intended to represent the totality of treatment options available.

Further, the EDM does not stand alone. In the development of intervention strategies, consideration must be given to the individual for whom a strategy is being considered in terms of his/her past history with behavior contingencies, his/her possible response to any procedures, individual likes and dislikes, and the nature of the behavior itself. Concerns for the protection of an individual's right to effective treatment and to live and work in an environment free of abuse and neglect must also be an active component of the decision-making process. Aversive treatment strategies are to be chosen from a hierarchy of intrusiveness so as to select the least intrusive option that is likely to be effective. Behavior management and human rights peer-review committees must be knowledgeably staffed and actively maintained. Informed consent, meeting the three requirements of competence, knowledge, and volition (DiLorenzo and Ollendick, 1986), must be obtained and may be withdrawn at any time. Finally, staff training and supervision must promote the development of the highest level of technical expertise and ethical behavior among all concerned (Lovaas & Favell, 1987).

Professionals in the human service field face a variety of challenges as they endeavor to make habilitative and educational decisions with and for clients. In no area are these decisions so potentially controversial as they are in the area of behavior reduction. One active step toward reducing this potential for controversy is the careful and individualized use of the applied functional analysis process. The EDM is one way of accomplishing this, in a manner that is feasible, effective, and easily adaptable for ongoing assessment and monitoring in the applied program setting.

The authors would like to acknowledge the following individuals who contributed to both the development of the Eden Decision Model and this manuscript: Carol Markowitz, Anne S. Holmes, David Roussell, James Ball, Micheal Alessandri, and the staff of Eden W.E.R.C.s. The authors would like to thank Andy Bondy and Michael Powers for their insightful comments on an earlier version of this manuscript. Last, but by no means least, we would like to express our sincere gratitude, appreciation, and respect to the Eden Family of Services' participants and their families.

8

Structure &

· · · · · ·

Curriculum of Services:

· · · · · · · · · · ·

From Birth to Age

· · · · · · · ·

Twenty-One

· · · · ·

Thanks his chapter describes the services Eden offers to children from
birth until the age of twenty-one,[1] and explains what is unique
about the services Eden provides. Eden offers a program for infants and toddlers,
four main programs for school-aged children, and several outreach and support
programs. The curriculum of each program is defined as a structured set, but one
flexible enough to meet the needs of each student.

Infants and toddlers are served through the Outreach Services Division by
the Wawa House program, one of the fastest growing programs at Eden. Wawa
House provides crucial early intervention to very young children with disorders
on the autistic spectrum. Teachers in Wawa House use a child-initiated, therapist-
directed approach to behavioral treatment. They connect with a child through his
own interests, however limited, and then expand those interests to other areas of

---

[1] The following chapter presents Eden's services for adults, particularly its residential (ACREs) and
employment (WERCs) programs.

the child's environment. The child is exposed to a broader range of experience, and is taught to interact more effectively with the world around him.

From age three until twenty-one, students are served through the Eden Institute's Day School. It offers Early Childhood, Middle Childhood, Transition, and Vocational Programs. Eden also offers several outreach services and support services. These programs extend the school year for students who cannot take the summer months off from treatment, and they provide help to the families of the children in Eden Institute's Day School through respite and training programs. The Outreach and Support Divisions also offer behavior technology workshops, a consultation and evaluation service, and help in integrating students into less restrictive settings.

The curriculum developed at Eden Institute is designed to be functional for students; it is readily tailored to each student's abilities. And, it is functional in the type of skills taught. The curriculum guides teachers toward enabling the student to be a participating member of society. As with the individualization of behavior management programs described earlier, teachers are able to mold the curriculum to suit students' individual needs. The curriculum emphasizes the importance of communication training and adaptive physical education in teaching people with autism, as well as the generally accepted practices associated with the development of pragmatic educational skills.

WAWA HOUSE: EARLY INTERVENTION FOR INFANTS AND TODDLERS

◆ ◆ ◆ ◆ ◆ ◆ ◆ ◆ ◆ ◆ ◆ ◆ ◆ ◆ ◆ ◆ ◆ ◆ ◆

Over the past several years, an increasing number of children under the age of three have been referred to Eden who either met the diagnostic criteria for autism developed by the American Psychiatric Association in 1994 (DSM-IV), or appeared to be at risk for developing autism. Too young to be eligible for an educational program, but already showing measurable developmental delays, these children faced limited or no options. Parents did not have the proper guidance to help them overcome their delays, but generally were doing the best they could. A few facilities offered care to the child, but they were mainly day-care facilities, and did not offer the necessary specialized programming to enable the children to catch up to their typically developing peers.

> There are now some programs that are beginning to appear that focus on early intervention for children with autism. But at the time Wawa House began, there were no such programs. Parents could not find programs for their children.
>
> —Andy Armstrong, Director of Development

To meet the needs of these children, Eden's Outreach Division, in partnership with Wawa, Inc., created Wawa House, an early intervention program for infants, toddlers, and their families. Through Wawa House, children under three who are experiencing delays in communicative, social, cognitive, physical, or behavior development receive individualized therapy to build critical skill areas.

There are two components to Wawa House. The formal program serves eighteen children on an intensive, one-to-one basis with a multidisciplinary team with backgrounds in special education, sensory-

The research is already indicating a much brighter prognosis for young children with disabilities who attend early intervention programs. We see that in Wawa House. Many children with autism do not develop verbal language, but a number of the children who were nonverbal when they began the Wawa House program are now talking. Also, the children who leave Wawa House, even if they go into a specialized preschool setting, already have a foundation for learning. For instance, two three-year-olds from the program joined the Eden Institute's Day School. They did not have to begin the curriculum with sitting, eye contact, and attending because those skills were already established. The children could get on to more complex tasks.

—**Anne S. Holmes, Director of Outreach Services**

motor integration, and speech-language pathology. It provides in-home intervention, clinic-based therapy, and parent training, support, and advocacy services, all developed under an Individualized Family Service Plan (IFSP) for each child. Wawa House also offers supplemental services which are less intensive that are designed to serve a greater number of families, but still provide many of the same services, like speech therapy, sensory-motor education, behavior therapy in the home or clinic, in-home programming, and consultation. The supplemental program averages fifty students, but is growing. The average age of children at Wawa House is between one and a half to two years, but children as young as eight months have been served.

Early intervention programs like Wawa House for children with autism or who are at risk of developing autism are becoming increasingly important. Research indicates that early diagnosis and intervention can have a significant impact on the prognosis of children with autism (Anderson, Avery, DiPietro, Edwards & Christian, 1987), (Alessandri, Bomba, Holmes, Van Driesen & Holmes, in prep.). Anne S. Holmes, Director of Outreach Services:

> *There is a big difference in outcome when children come to us at younger ages. With a three year old, it is relatively easy to work through tantrums and redirect behaviors. With a child who is already five or seven, it gets more difficult. At a later age the child is not only bigger, but has practiced behaviors for years. The behaviors are more ingrained. For example, if a three year old is just getting destructive, we can curtail it with a very mild intervention. It may take much more intensive programming to stop an older child from being destructive.*

One of the most successful reports of early intervention is described by Ivar Lovaas (1987). In his study, 47 percent of the children treated were able to enter regular education programs and achieve average or above average scores on standardized intelligence tests. Lovaas used an intense applied behavior analysis approach in treatment called discrete trial training.

TREATMENT APPROACH

The strategy Eden's teachers have found most effective in working with infants and toddlers in Wawa House is applied behavior analysis with a combination of child-initiated and teacher/therapist-directed approaches to treatment. Infants

and toddlers normally learn about their world and what impact they have on it by carrying out their own "experiments," such as dropping objects from their high chairs, scribbling on paper, and building towers with blocks (Schickendanz, 1990). Jean Piaget (1963) referred to this stage of development as the "sensorimotor period" because infants and toddlers build their intelligence by discovering the interrelationships between their actions, senses, and what goes on around them.

The child-directed approach to learning, often taken by programs that serve typically developing children, lets the child direct interactions with the teacher. It supports the active exploration of the environment by the child. The exploration and manipulation skills critical to this approach, however, are generally lacking in children with autism and other pervasive developmental disorders. They typically have extremely limited interests, and would not explore their environment if left on their own. They need to be taught how to explore in order to close the gap between them and their typically developing peers.

A therapist-directed approach alone would be similarly ineffective with the children served in Wawa House. The discrete trial teaching method made successful by Lovaas, used with students in Eden Institute, is a therapist-directed approach. The teacher, or therapist, actively teaches the student a preselected skill. The student and teacher go through many trials until the student learns how to perform the skill. Discrete trial training alone, however, is not conducive to helping infants and toddlers learn because it cannot teach them how to experiment, explore, and manipulate their environment. They must be guided to do that on their own.

Wawa House has found that a combination of child-initiated and therapist directed therapy works best. Becoming less afraid of and in turn interested in their environment is critical for children with autism and other developmental delays because it gives them motivation to experiment and participate in activities. Without interest in their environment, children run the risk of relying on artificial guidance (prompts). They also become fearful of experimentation. For example, Stan took virtually no initiative in his environment. His mother even had to prompt him to take a bite of food. Stan seemed perpetually frightened:

> *When Stan first came into Wawa House, we could hardly glimpse his face, as he clung to his mother, afraid to look around. When we tried to touch Stan, he cried inconsolably. He did not speak any intelligible words. He could not explore his world and so therefore could not respond to people other than his mother and father. (Leslie S. Weitzner in* Blueprint, *1992).*

To get children interested in their environment and teach them skills, teachers at Wawa House use a combination of child-directed and therapist-directed teaching approaches. Therapy starts with any initiations made by the child, even a glance or gesture toward a toy, which the therapist then develops into a learning experience. So, the approach begins more child-initiated, and evolves toward being therapist-directed as needed.

Diane Van Driesen, Assistant Director for Clinical Services:

> *Children coming into Wawa House are not usually too interested in their environment. If they show any interest, it is mostly in their parents, and do not like to separate from them or engage with anybody else. So the key is getting them interested in what is around them, like toys, people, and common objects. We have set up an environment in the program which is colorful, comfortable, and playful. It already sets the stage for children to become less apprehensive and a bit more interested in what goes on around them.*
>
> *We let a child explore the environment on his own first. Then we start to very subtly intervene and get him interested in something, or get him to tolerate a toy for a few seconds, even if he is crying and screaming. We just want a very short interaction at first. We use applied behavior analysis techniques to reinforce him all along, and then teach the parents to do the same.*
>
> *Once the child has explored a bit on his own and can tolerate minimal interactions, we begin*

> *to introduce a language task, a cognitive task, or a gross or fine motor task into that interaction. As the child begins to accept more interaction, we begin therapist-initiated tasks, so the child becomes more flexible and is able to both explore on his own and accept therapist-directed exploration.*

By consistently following through and elaborating on a child's initiations, the teacher reinforces the child's ability to successfully interact with his environment. As therapy progresses and the child becomes more capable of and interested in manipulating his environment, the teacher then controls the environment from which the child makes choices to optimize learning experiences. Anne S. Holmes:

> *We started to interact with Stan by having his mother simply orient him toward the environment, and away from her. We then very slowly brought toys over to him, so he did not have to actually explore the environment on his own. We brought the environment to him. Once he became accepting of those things, he was all of a sudden getting up off his mother's lap, walking around, and exploring curiously on his own. Once he started exploring more, we saw a rapid decline in his glaringly unfocused behavior. However, when we started to place learning demands on him, we got tantrums that lasted fifty minutes to an hour and a half. We worked through them, all the while working to increase his language because he was not speaking when he first came. Now he is talking in sentences and having a successful time fully mainstreamed in a regular preschool. It is quite remarkable progress.*

Despite promising indications, however, many basic issues remain unresolved in the relatively unexplored field of early intervention for children with autism or other pervasive developmental disorders. Important questions need to be answered about the frequency and intensity of therapy (Parette, Hendricks & Rock, 1991), the identification of children for services, the implementation of programs, and the efficacy of treatment models (Murray, 1992).

The majority of the literature on early intervention programs remains at the level of program description (Autism Society of America, 1995). Little empirical evidence has been provided to support the efficacy of treatment (Anderson, Avery, DiPietro, Edwards & Christian, 1987). Although Eden is currently engaged in quantifying its treatment outcomes (Alessandri, Bomba, Holmes, Van Driesen & Holmes, in prep.), and although Ivar Lovaas has made numerous claims of success with early intervention, few formal studies have been conducted to assess which specific components may have the most impact (Black, 1991).

Much support, however, can be found for the ideas behind a child-initiated, therapist-directed approach to treatment. In a 1992 study, Koegel, Koegel, and Surratt looked at a teaching approach very much like the approach used at Wawa House. They compared the frequency of disruptive behaviors in preschool children under either a "analog" or "natural language" teaching approach. Under the analog approach, the teaching was directed by the teacher, and followed the discrete trial teaching method. Under the natural language approach, teachers reinforced the children's attempts at a targeted behavior with reinforcers the children themselves chose. Children were also allowed to choose, to a large extent, their own stimulus materials. This group of children was therefore taught under a more child-initiated approach, but was guided by the teacher's behavior modification techniques. The study found that the children's disruptive behavior decreased, and their skill acquisition increased, more under the natural language approach than under the analog approach. Koegel's study suggests that young children do better when they are given partial control over the teaching interaction. It suggests that young children need to be able to direct the teaching interaction to things they themselves are curious about.

> We formalize things pretty quickly with the children in Wawa House. We may start out more with incidental teaching to get the children to tolerate their environment, but we quickly put behavioral parameters on their activities. For example, we work first on the floor, but as the teaching interaction gets tighter, we quickly get them sitting in a chair and attending.
>
> We do not have children in early intervention for a long period of time. They are already almost preschool-aged. We want to effect as much progress as possible as quickly as possible.
>
> —Diane Van Driesen, Assistant Director for Clinical Services

The effectiveness of the natural language approach in their study can be explained by an increase in the children's motivation to participate in interactions with the teacher. This motivation would presumably arise from the children's ability to decide for themselves which tasks and reinforcers they would like. It would also arise from their ability to guide the interaction to things they wanted to explore or learn. A motivation to interact would account for the increase in skill acquisition that the children exhibited.

This explanation would also account for the decrease in disruptive behavior. Much of the current literature suggests that disruptive behavior is often exhibited by people with autism to escape from difficult teaching tasks (Carr & Durand, 1987; Carr & Durand, 1985). The children's greater motivation to respond during the teaching activities of Koegel's natural language approach could correlate with a reduced desire to escape.

> Spike's parents have a hard time getting him to eat a variety of foods. However, if he is given a choice between foods, he will eat more easily. For example, Spike doesn't really like broccoli, but he likes it better than corn. If he has to choose between eating broccoli and corn, he will eat broccoli more easily. He has fewer tantrums about eating, and seems to accept his choice. If he were simply given broccoli, the meal would be a real battle.
>
> —Denise Burns-Jennings, Coordinating Teacher, Early Childhood

Research with older children and adults presents a similar picture. Studies have shown that giving school-aged children and adults more opportunities to make choices in their environment has greatly reduced social avoidance behavior  (Koegel, Dyer & Bell, 1987), increased spontaneous communication (Dyer, 1989; Peck, 1985), and improved task performance (Mithaug & Mar, 1980; Parsons, Reid, Reynolds & Bumgarner, 1990). However, the best approach for older children and adults seems to be a combination of the child-initiated approach and a more structured, rule-governed environment like that provided through applied behavior analysis.

Although Koegel et al.'s study was with preschool children, it is highly unlikely that the best teaching environment for children changes dramatically on entering preschool. The implications of the study could reasonably be extended to infants and toddlers under age three.

ASSESSMENT PROCEDURES

To make sure that the child-initiated, therapist-directed approach to therapy works, and to monitor the progress in both skill acquisition and behavior reduction of the children in Wawa House, several assessment procedures are used. Before therapy is begun, each child is given a battery of tests to see how his development compares with that of his typically-developing peers across the major developmental domains. Four standardized tests are used: the Developmental Profile II (Alpern, Boll & Shearer, 1986), the Vineland Adaptive Behavior Scales - Interview Edition (Sparrow, Balla & Cicchetti, 1984), the Preschool Language Scale (Zimmerman, Steiner & Pond, 1979), and the Early Learning Accomplishment Profile (Glover, Preminger & Sanford, 1988).

Standardized tests are used for several reasons. Because children pass through so many developmental stages during the first three years of their lives, standardized testing makes it easier to determine whether signs of delay are symptoms of a developmental disability or just characteristic of an individual child's slower, but still normal, timetable. Standardized tests are used with the young children at Wawa House because the developmental gap between them and their typical peers is much smaller than that of older children. For example, a common gap for children at Wawa House is ten months. For older children, a gap of fifty months is more common. The younger children have a very real possibility of "catching up." Gaining three or four months' development is a substantial increase for young children, but would be only moderate or negligible for an older child. Standardized testing is the most effective way to document these gains in young children.

Standardized tests are also administered to children in Wawa House as part of a long term research project being conducted at Eden (Alessandri, Bomba, Holmes, Van Driesen & Holmes, in prep). The study is designed to measure how well young children with autism are able to catch up to their typically developing peers when given highly specialized early intervention services. The study will also assess how well the children at Wawa House are able to keep up with their peers when they enter the school-age years. Preliminary results are beginning to indicate substantial increases in the communication, appropriate behavior, and social skills of children exiting the program. This may indicate that Wawa House serves children during a crucial "window" or period of their development, before they lose much of their ability to adapt. Final analysis of the study is expected in the near future.

Of the standardized tests given to children, the first two, the Developmental Profile II (DP II) and the Vineland Adaptive Behavior Scales (VABS), are administered as an interview with a person well acquainted with the child, usually the parents. These two tests assess the child's development in gross and fine motor skills, self-help skills, social and emotional level of functioning, cognitive and academic functioning, and communication. They tell the evaluator how the child is functioning in his environment by identifying skills that are emerging or fully established in the child's repertoire. Since the tests are administered as interviews with the child present, they tend to give the evaluator a more complete picture of the child's behavior. The evaluator collects information from the parents, and is able to obtain information on behaviors unlikely to occur in a struc-

◆ ◆

According to their scores on the Vineland Scales of Adaptive Behavior (Interview Edition):

- ◆ 67% of infants and toddlers at Wawa House are below the third percentile in their communication skills. 100% of the infants and toddlers fall below the 15th percentile.
- ◆ 67% of infants and toddlers at Wawa House fall below the 10th percentile in their daily living skills. 100% fall below the 25th percentile.
- ◆ 67% of infants and toddlers at Wawa House fall below the 5th percentile in socialization skills. 100% fall below the 35th percentile.
- ◆ 50% of infants and toddlers at Wawa House fall below the 10th percentile in motor skills. 67% fall below the 25th percentile, while 100% fall below the 50th percentile.
- ◆ 67% of infants and toddlers at Wawa House fall below the 5th percentile in adaptive behavior. 100% fall below the 35th percentile.

◆ ◆

tured testing situation, such as how the child interacts with his peers and how independently the child can toilet himself.

The remaining two tests, the Preschool Language Scale (PLS) and the Early Learning Accomplishment Profile (ELAP), are administered directly to the child in a structured testing environment. The PLS assesses the child's expressive and receptive language skills, and the ELAP provides another assessment of the child's development across the major domains. The ELAP assesses the child in the same

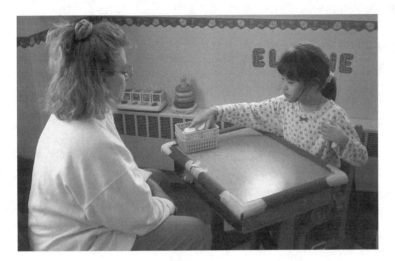

areas as the DP II and VABS administered by parents, but often enables the evaluator to see behavior the parents may not have identified. The ELAP is used to provide a more complete profile of the child's strengths and deficits.

The initial battery of tests given to children entering Wawa House gives a basic picture of the child's development. This picture provides a baseline from which the child's Individualized Family Service plan (IFSP) is developed. The IFSP is like the Individualized Education Plan, or IEP, developed for school-aged children. Because the ELAP is a developmentally based assessment, teachers use the areas it assesses as an outline for developing age-appropriate goals for each child. Once a child masters the skills typical of his age level, he moves on to the next set of skills defined in the ELAP as appropriate for his age. Goals, however, are functional and individualized for each child. For example, if a child shows a particular deficit in fine motor coordination, teachers will develop a program for him to improve his coordination, and will add this to other programs developed for him from the ELAP. Common goals included in the IFSPs of children entering Wawa House include appropriate sitting and eye contact, as well as gross motor, and verbal imitation. Most students also work on developing gestures, pointing appropriately, and complying with directions. All students are incidentally reinforced for playing appropriately and performing tasks (Wolfberg, 1995).

Each child's progress is measured daily through trial-by-trial data as well as data on the number and type of prompts teachers used. Because the teaching approach is not strictly based on the discrete trial method, trial-by-trial data alone is insufficient to properly record children's progress. Data on the number and type of prompts used in unstructured teaching sessions are also required as well as anecdotal data collected from written reports and video; each child's therapy session is monitored on video.

Teachers meet weekly to discuss each student's progress, and implement troubleshooting procedures if a problem is found. In addition, staff meetings are held on each child each month, and regular reports of his progress are made. A report is made after a child's first month at Wawa House, and then once every three months. During troubleshooting, meetings are held more frequently.

PARENT TRAINING

The final component of Wawa House, and one of the most important, is parent training. Parents' confidence in being able to effectively help their child is one of the strongest predictors of the child's progress (Bruey, 1989; Rosenberg, 1977). Parents' confidence is especially important for the children in Wawa House because the children can make substantial gains in a short period of time with a partnership of trained parents and professionals working in harmony. With parents and professionals working collectively with the child, unacceptable patterns of behavior are less likely to become permanent. Further, there is evidence to suggest that children are more "neurally plastic," or flexible (Levy, Amir & Shalev, 1992; Ramey, Lee & Burchinal, 1989). They are easier to influence than adolescents or adults. To take advantage of this neural flexibility, parents and professionals can effectively mold the child's behavior toward adaptive responses rather than allowing maladaptive responses to take hold.

The parent training offered through Wawa House is similar to that offered to parents of children entering Eden Institute's Day School, but is geared to the unique learning opportunities available when working with younger children.[2] The same techniques are taught, and so the content is the same, but parents of children in Wawa House are taught how to encourage more social and play skills, and to take advantage of more incidental teaching opportunities, thereby reducing the development of maladaptive behavior. The parents of children who are school age, on the other hand, are taught how to encourage more independence, how to control the teaching environment, and how to reduce or eliminate maladaptive behavior.

Along with the school, residential, and employment programs, Wawa House enables Eden to provide lifespan services to children with autism from birth through adulthood. Although taking part in Wawa House does not necessarily mean that a child will need to continue on to Eden Institute's School program, several children have done so, and so fulfill Eden's goal to extend its services to provide continuing, effective programming to as many children as it can.

The most recent expansion in the services Eden offers is Wawa CARES (Comprehensive Autism Referral and Education Services), a mobile autism services unit. Wawa CARES consists of a specially-equipped van staffed by professionals from the Eden Family of Services through which consultation, diagnostic, referral, evaluation, and community education services are offered to a broad geographic

---

[2] See Chapter 10 for a detailed description of the training offered to parents of children at Eden Institute.

region. Equipped with video, telecommunications, fax capability, and meeting space, the primary function of Wawa CARES is to provide on-site diagnostic, resource, and referral services to families, schools, hospitals, and other agencies. The concept of bringing the services to those who need them is of particular value to those families and agencies who remain unable to access other means of information and support. In addition, Wawa CARES serves as an important community education tool, and has participated in local health fairs and community programs.

SCHOOL AGE PROGRAMS

When a student is of school age and enters Eden Institute's Day School, he is placed in one of five programs: the Early Childhood, Middle Childhood, Transition, Prevocational, or Vocational Preparation program. Each of these programs is described in the next section. Students are generally placed according to age, but age is not the only factor in placement.[3] A student's general cognitive and behavioral functioning are also considerations, as well as his ability to attend and

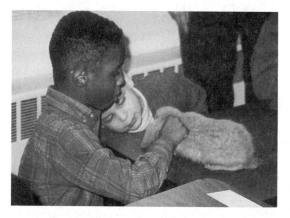

work in a group. The program which best suits a student's needs is determined through these variables, through curriculum-based assessments, and, when appropriate, standardized tests.[4]

Students in each program meet in groups for some activities, such as listening to a story or doing simple assembly. However, most of the students at Eden Institute's Day School, especially those in the Early Childhood Program, find it difficult to attend to an activity for long periods of time while in a group. Some students can pay attention for only ten minutes, so short group times are scheduled for them. Other students are gradually able to participate in group activities for up to thirty minutes at a time as they progress in both age and their ability to pay attention. A student can move between various groups even if he primarily remains in the educational program for students of his age.

Student-to-teacher ratios are also varied to suit students' learning needs. At first, most students need intensive, highly structured teaching situations. They receive instruction in a one-to-one or two-to-one setting. Once students have built up a basic repertoire of skills, they are generally required to transi-

---

[3]   The programs are designed to meet the average needs of students in a particular age group, and so are tailored to provide slightly different types of services.

[4]   See Chapter 4 for a description of the admissions process to Eden Institute.

tion to a three-, four-, or even six-to-one group for the development of socialization and language skills. However, the small group setting is maintained for teaching skills the student finds particularly challenging.

Teachers try to move a student into a larger group as soon as he is ready because larger groups encourage social skills such as peer modelling, waiting turns, and generalization. Students are exposed to other students who have similar, but different, abilities, and students can see the rewards other students receive for completing a skill correctly, and can learn from the successes and failures of others.

If students require a more challenging curriculum or more socially and academically challenging peers than those in their program, they are able to attend other programs within Eden. For example, a student in the Early Childhood Program may attend both the Middle Childhood and Transition Programs for several sessions each day to improve his academic, socialization, and language skills. If he does well in those programs, he may attend them on a full-time basis, and leave the Early Childhood Program entirely, or move directly to a regular public school program.

THE EARLY CHILDHOOD PROGRAM

The Early Childhood Program serves children from ages three through seven, a crucial period of development. About eleven children are in the Early Childhood Program. Children from ages three to five participate in the program's preschool portion.[5] From five to seven, children are in the regular Early Childhood Program. Most of the instruction in Early Childhood is initially on a one-to-one basis. Teachers focus on skills which prepare young students for independence in learning, through training in such areas as learning readiness, basic self care, communication, and academic readiness. At the conclusion of the Early Childhood Program, the child will either enter the public school system or the Middle Childhood or Transition Program.

A general picture of the level of ability in students entering Eden Institute can be gathered from the assessments of children entering the Early Childhood Program. Over the last five years, only one student has come to Eden (from Wawa

---

[5] By law, children with age differences of over four years cannot be in the same educational program. Although the Early Childhood program was designed for children ages three to seven, the program is occasionally the most appropriate place for eight-year-olds. Eden has, therefore, created a separate preschool portion for the youngest children.

House) with fully established learning readiness skills. Most begin by needing instruction in all four areas of learning readiness: eye contact on command, appropriate sitting, gross motor imitation, and simple one-step commands. Over the 1994-1995 school year, five students entered the Early Childhood Program. All five students required instruction in each area of learning readiness. Over the 1993-1994 school year, four new students entered the Early Childhood. Two worked on all four learning readiness programs. One student worked on two of the programs, and one student had established learning readiness skills. He had learned them through the Wawa House program. In 1992-1993, only one new student entered Early Childhood. He worked on all four skill programs. In 1991-1992, two students came to Early Childhood. Both worked on all learning readiness programs. In 1990-1991, Early Childhood had three new students, all of whom worked on at least one learning readiness program.

THE MIDDLE CHILDHOOD PROGRAM

The Middle Childhood Program is designed for students from ages seven to twelve. Eleven children are in the program. Children are instructed primarily in communication, academics, and social skills, with an emphasis on impulse control and socially appropriate behavior. Groups are usually small, with a three-to-one ratio of students to teacher. In Middle Childhood greater emphasis is placed on learning to respond in a group rather than requiring individual direction. From Middle Childhood students occasionally enter the regular education system, but most often continue into the Transition or Prevocational and Vocational Preparation Programs.

THE TRANSITION PROGRAM

Students who demonstrate the social and academic potential for entering a more typical classroom environment are placed in the Transition Program. The program is designed to accommodate about six students, who generally range from age seven to twelve. Students enter the Transition Program either directly from the Early Childhood Program, or during their years in the Middle Childhood Program. In the Transition Program, independent work is stressed through small group instruction in academic and interactive language and social skills. Students who excel in the Transition Program may attend public school classes and eventually return to their local school district or to other less specialized educational environments.

THE PREVOCATIONAL AND VOCATIONAL PREPARATION PROGRAMS

The Prevocational and Vocational Preparation Programs are for thirteen- to twenty-one-year-old students. There are an average of ten students in the Prevocational Program, and another fifteen in the Vocational Preparation Program. The programs provide continued instruction in self-care and social skills. However, academics are not emphasized as students are introduced to the world of work. The programs provide, in larger group settings of three- or five-to-one, job-related communication skills, daily living and pre-employment skills, as well as general employment skills culminating in community-based work-study programs. The goal of vocational education is to provide students with employable skills, and to enable them eventually to enter vocational technical programs, the competitive work force, or Eden's employment program for adults, Eden WERCs.

OPPORTUNITIES FOR ENRICHMENT AND MAKING TRANSITIONS

Students at Eden Institute's Day School regularly participate in many community activities to help them generalize the skills they learn there to more typical settings, and to become more socially responsible. Students often go grocery shopping, to the movies, to restaurants, bowling, to amusement parks, and on day trips. Students also participate in overnight trips every year, including camping trips, visits to Eden's Wawa Education and Retreat Center in Connecticut, overnight stops at Eden's seashore house, and to places like

> Jill attends a music group at a local school. She loves it. Although she has learned some about music, the most important part of the experience for her is the interaction she gets with children in the group. They are all about her age, and she knows them by name. She has a couple of friends there, and has even learned some of their sayings, like "See you later, alligator."
>
> —**Cheryl Bomba, Assistant Director for Technical Support**

Disney World, ski areas, and cities with specific points of interest to faculty and students. One student in Middle Childhood went to Washington, D.C. to meet the President. He was the students' representative when Eden received the Blue Ribbon National School of Excellence Award in 1992. Recently, students from Eden Institute become involved in New Jersey's "Adopt a Road Program" and are responsible for helping to keep clean a section of a local road, all in the spirit of community involvement.

When appropriate, students make transitions to regular educational classrooms. Transitioning students into regular classrooms enables them to interact with their nondisabled peers in a structured, positive way. It provides students from Eden Institute's Day School with additional peer models, and gives them the opportunity to practice the skills they have learned. For example, if a student has learned how to raise his hand to get the teacher's attention, he will be able to do this in a setting where raising one's hand is expected. He will be able to practice his skill in the environment where it often occurs. This type of interaction is particularly important for students with mild or moderate disabilities. Their skills are often advanced enough for success in a part-time regular school program, but not yet refined enough to interact appropriately in a full-time setting. Teachers at Eden Institute's Day School have developed a network of local placement opportunities to provide students with transition opportunities.

Many students at Eden spend time during the week in either regular educational placements or work placements. Over the last several years, the number of students spending time outside of Eden has grown from only two students in 1989-1990 to fourteen students in 1993-1994. This number continues to grow as teachers individualize the benefits of community services, and find appropriate placements for students. The chart below is a summary of placement opportunities students have taken advantage of over the last several years.

OUTSIDE PLACEMENTS FOR THE **1994-1995** SCHOOL YEAR—TOTAL: **9**

In Early Childhood:
1 student in a less specialized educational program 12.5 hours per week.
1 student in a less specialized preschool program 12.5 hours per week.

In the Vocational Preparation Program:
3 students spend 7.5 hours per week working at a local convenience store.
2 students spend 1 hour per week doing assembly for a local company.
2 students spend 1 hour per week doing clerical work for a local company.

OUTSIDE PLACEMENTS FOR THE **1993-1994** SCHOOL YEAR—TOTAL: **14**

In Early Childhood:
2 students in regular preschool 9 hours per week.

In the Transition Program:
1 student has a music class 2 hours per week.
1 student attends regular classes for 4 hours per week.

In the Prevocational and Vocational programs:
4 students spend 2 hours per week doing assembly for a local company.
1 student spends 3 hours per week doing assembly for a local company.
1 student spends 4 hours per week doing assembly for a local company.
2 students spend 7 hours per week working at a local convenience store.
2 students spend 12 hours per week working at a local convenience store.

OUTSIDE PLACEMENTS FOR THE **1992-1993** SCHOOL YEAR—TOTAL: **11**

In Early Childhood:
1 student attends a local regular preschool for 15 hours per week.
1 student attends a local regular preschool for one-half hour per week.

In the Transition Program:
1 student attends regular classes for 5 hours per week.

In the Prevocational and Vocational programs:
1 student spends 2 hours per week doing assembly for a local company.
2 students spend 4 hours per week doing assembly for a local company.
1 student spends 6 hours per week working at a local convenience store.
2 students spend 7 hours per week working at a local convenience store.
1 student spends 7.5 hours per week working at a local convenience store.
1 student spends 10.5 hours per week working at a local convenience store.

OUTSIDE PLACEMENTS FOR THE 1991-1992 SCHOOL YEAR—TOTAL: 6

In Early Childhood:
1 student spends 1 hour per week at a local preschool.

In the Prevocational and Vocational programs:
2 students spend 1 hour per week doing assembly for a local company.
2 students spend 2 hours per week doing assembly for a local company.
1 student spends 6 hours per week working at a local convenience store.

OUTSIDE PLACEMENTS FOR THE 1990-1991 SCHOOL YEAR—TOTAL: 2

In Early Childhood:
1 student attends a preschool part-time.

In the Transition Program:
1 student attends regular education classes locally half time.

OUTSIDE PLACEMENTS FOR THE 1989-1990 SCHOOL YEAR—TOTAL: 2

In the Transition Program:
1 student spends 5 hours per week in local regular education classes.

In the Prevocational and Vocational programs:
1 student works part-time at a local convenience store.

If a student's teachers feel he would benefit from a regular educational placement, they call together a team composed of the student's Coordinating Teacher, his primary teacher at Eden Institute's Day School, his speech pathologist, and the Director of Educational Services. This team examines the student's language, behavior, social skills, and academic functioning. The team looks at the student's IEP and progress reports to determine whether he will likely be able to generalize skills acquired into a less structured classroom. After careful observation and evaluation by both the coordinating teacher and speech pathologist, a regular educational site is chosen. Communication is then established with the cooperating school, and a formal plan for the student's transition is created (Holmes, 1976).

The student is at first accompanied by at least one teacher from Eden. Depending on the age of the student, parents may also come to the new school. The teacher from Eden Institute's Day School initially acts as the student's teacher in the new setting, while also serving as a consultant to the new teachers.[6] The teacher helps the new teachers understand the student and his individual learning style. In part-time placements, the Eden teacher usually remains with the student for the entire experience. If the student is placed full-time in another setting, a schedule for fading his original teacher from the new setting is established.

The development of goals, assessment, and monitoring of students who spend part or most of their time in regular educational settings are the same as for students remaining full-time at Eden Institute. Students who are placed fully into other educational settings are monitored for at least three years. During the early

> It's critical that Archie's teacher Denise go with him when he goes to the regular nursery school. He needs that. They work on things at Eden that help Archie handle being there. With Denise's help, Archie can do so much more in the regular school than he could do last year. He can sit in group time, he can answer questions, and he can play with other children. For example, the school does a group activity where each child gets to pick two other children, a girl and a boy, to play with. The teacher said to Archie "Okay, Archie, you pick a girl and a boy. Who do you want to play with?" Archie pointed to two children, a boy and a girl, but the funny part is that the children got up to go play, and Archie just sat there. They came back and said "Archie!" Then he ran off with them. He learns a lot from the children there. They encourage him.
>
> —**Nancy Cantor and Steve Brechin**

---

[6] The Support Division assists the process of making a transition to a regular educational classroom by providing training to teachers in the regular classroom setting. Support makes sure that regular education teachers feel comfortable with having a child from Eden in their classrooms. The teachers are given information about autism, training in how to handle the child with autism who is coming into their classroom, and what to do if behavior issues occur.

period of their transition, these students are treated just as other students at Eden. Once they have established themselves in the new setting, Eden continues to monitor their progress, but is not as involved in their programming.

More students tend to access regular educational placement opportunities during their early years, especially during preschool. The demands placed on a student in regular education at this age are less rigid, and students from Eden can often keep pace. From grade school to high school, the curriculum becomes more challenging and rigid academically. Students from Eden do not often do well in these classes. However, during their later high school years, many students from Eden return to regular educational settings for the vocational training opportunities they offer.

Currently, about 20 percent of students in the Early Childhood Program spend time in regular educational classes. In the Middle Childhood and Transition Programs, the number drops to 10 percent. About 50 percent of Prevocational and Vocational students currently have some type of work placement, and several students receive vocational training at their local school.

The five school age programs of Eden Institute's Day School—Early Childhood, Middle Childhood, Transition, Prevocational, and Vocational Preparation—are unified by a common curriculum. The specific skills taught through the curriculum may be similar to those taught in other programs serving children with autism, but Eden's curriculum is a clearly written compendium of skills to be learned, and focuses strongly on the functionality of the skills taught.

EDEN INSTITUTE'S CURRICULUM

The curriculum of Eden Institute's Day School is functional in two basic ways. It is functional for students first because it works within their needs and abilities. Second, the skills themselves are functional because they are task analyzed, developmentally sequenced, and designed to prepare students to take care of themselves and to gain and maintain employment as adults.

Eden Institute's curriculum is functional in the supportive but challenging environment established for the student.[7] Martin Kozloff (1994), who has writ-

---

[7] See Chapter 3 on the prosthetic environment created for students and adults at Eden.

ten several books on designing a functional curriculum for students with disabilities, and whose work has greatly influenced Eden, describes the importance of such an environment:

> A child's behavior develops in a productive direction within any . . . environment only if the environment fits (is congruent with) the child's current needs, preferences, competencies, and capacities.

An environment which "fits" a student will be the most productive place for him to learn, and will enable him to learn the greatest number of skills. Like a well-tailored suit, the environment will be comfortable, but not cozy, and will make the business of work more enjoyable.

For such an environment to be established for each student, the curriculum must be somewhat flexible. It must have established parameters, but must also be able to adapt itself to the ever changing needs of each student, rather than mold students to fit its parameters. The curriculum must be individualized in much the same way that behavior modification programs are individualized. Just as behaviors are carefully assessed to design effective reduction strategies,[8] each student must be assessed individually to create a learning program, or IEP, tailored specifically for him. Mary A. Falvey, author of *Community-Based Curriculum: Instructional Strategies for Students with Severe Handicaps* (Paul H. Brookes Publishing Co.,1989), supports this notion. She states:

> [T]he age of the student, present levels of ability, communication and/ or language ability, preferred learning modality, and functionality of the academic content should all be examined when determining which [academic curricular] approach is best for the individual student.

Students at Eden are assessed regularly throughout the year to ensure that the skills described in their IEP remain functional and challenging.[9]

Eden Institute's curriculum provides guidelines for each student's progress, but is flexible enough to be shaped to each student. Students are able to transition to larger groups and sessions that are longer in duration, and even to different educational programs within Eden Institute. When a student makes such a transition, his IEP is re-evaluated to reflect the change. The skill acquisition programs in his IEP will likely be modified so that he can take advantage of the changes in his environment. For example, a student in the Middle Childhood Program had mastered in a one-to-one setting how to take turns in a game. His teachers felt he was ready for more group activities, and so moved him into a two-to-one setting. His IEP was changed to include listening to a story, raising his hand, and taking turns with another student, all of which require being a member of the group in a shared activity.

---

[8] See Chapter 6.

[9] These assessments are described in the section below on progress monitoring.

Defining particular points in the curriculum which are flexible is difficult because the entire teaching process is flexible. Nowhere is the curriculum set in stone; it is designed with general parameters as every teaching interaction must address students' particular needs. The flexibility of the curriculum reflects the ability of Eden's services as a whole to adapt, yet not become chaotic. For example, Eden's Respite Services are able to provide care and a temporary home for a student if parents are overwhelmed by the challenges he presents, or are otherwise incapacitated. Respite then provides training and coping strategies so the parents feel better able to work with their child. Eden also has a Primary Intervention

History of the Primary Intervention Program

Although the Primary Intervention Program is used today mainly to teach vocational skills, it was originally started for a young woman who had very few skills at all.

Nicole came to Eden at age five, but had to leave when she was eight because her family moved away. She found a program near her new home, but it did not provide services specialized to her needs. The program served people with a variety of disabilities.

When Nicole was fifteen, her family moved back into the area, and she came back to Eden. Her teachers were distressed to find that Nicole had learned virtually no new skills, and the skills she left Eden with had deteriorated badly. Nicole had problems even feeding herself and using the bathroom. She had to be taught the type of skills children in the Early Childhood Program worked on, but was too old to be taught alongside them. She needed an entirely different approach to Eden's curriculum than any other student at Eden Institute.

Nicole's teachers developed a specialized program for her, titled Primary Intervention. The program included intense, one-on-one teaching, and followed an accelerated skill schedule to help her catch up to the other students in her program. However, the school district did not want to fund a program designed just for Nicole. So, Nicole's family took the district to court. The family won.

Nicole continued in the Primary Intervention Program for about five years. She relearned the skills she had lost, then began working on new skills that would help her get employment. She now does subcontract work at Eden WERCs and is a resident at Eden ACREs.

Program for students entering its educational programs whose skills are far behind their age-matched peers' capabilities. The Primary Intervention Program provides one-on-one intensive training which is designed to give them a jump start on learning. The Primary Intervention Program is usually used for older students entering Eden who have had little earlier training. It teaches them the necessary learning readiness skills they will need to develop productive work skills required for employment and living in the community.

The flexibility of Eden's curriculum ensures a student's environment is as functional for him as possible. Eden Institute's curriculum, however, is functional in another way as well. It focuses on functional skills. These skills enable the student to be more independent, and increase the degree to which he can be integrated into society. Martin Kozloff:

> [H]umans need to develop competence at tasks that are biologically important and socially expected of "persons" and "members in good standing" in the culture; that is, functional tasks.[10]

Students at Eden Institute's Day School are taught primarily self-care, communication, social, and vocational skills. Teachers introduce academics when they are tied to a vocational agenda, or when a student is able to be considered for regular educational classes.

The skills in Eden Institute's curriculum are divided into three separate but equally important domains: General Special Education, Communication, and Adaptive Physical Education.[11] Eden's curriculum is organized into three domains for a specific reason. People with autism most often have severe learning difficulties (Handleman, 1992) and profound communication deficits (Rutter et al., 1971; Schopler & Mesibov, 1985). They also tend to have extremely disruptive behavior or withdrawal which often can be traced to sensorimotor adaptation difficulties (Ayres, 1979) which in turn severely inhibit their ability to function independently. To emphasize the importance of communication and adaptive physical education in teaching people with autism, Eden has grouped these skill programs separately, yet included with more general education skills taught in its specialized setting.

Skill acquisition programs in all three curricular domains are taught in each of the educational programs in Eden Institute's Day School: Early Childhood, Middle Childhood, Transition, and Prevocational and Vocational Preparation Pro-

---

[10] Functional skill development has been supported legally by two cases: *Wyatt v. Stickney*, 344 F. Supp. 387 (M.D. Ala. 1972), *aff'd sub. nom. Wyatt v. Aderholt*, 503 F.2d 1305 (5th Cir. 1974) and *Armstrong v. Kline*, 476 F. Supp. 583 (E.D. Pa., 1979), *aff'd*, CA 78-0172 (Third Cir. July 15, 1980). *Wyatt v. Stickney* ruled that a student's education should be one that "assists the individual to acquire those life skills which enable him to cope more effectively with the demands of his own person and of his environment and to raise the level of his physical, mental, and social efficiency." These skills are by definition functional. *Armstrong v. Kline* determined that the goal of a student's education should be "within the limits of his/ her handicap, to become self-sufficient." In becoming self-sufficient, the student must gradually reduce his reliance on others, which means learning for himself those things which others had done for him.

[11] The skill acquisition programs in each domain of the curriculum are described in Appendix A.

grams. Skills in each domain are taught through the techniques described in Chapter 6 to increase behavior, especially through applied behavior analysis emphasizing the discrete trial teaching method.

PROGRESS MONITORING

To ensure that students at Eden have learned as many skills as possible by age twenty-one, when they enter adult services, teachers have set up strict procedures to assess and report students' progress.

Even so Eden rarely administers standardized tests[12] to assess students' performance. The use of standardized testing for assessing students with severe disabilities has been widely criticized (Sigafoos, Cole & McQuarter, 1987; Garner, 1985). Few, if any, of these tests include students with severe disabilities in their norms, and the presence of specific disabilities, such as a lack of verbal language, may adversely affect the students' ability to respond to test items. In addition, the skills assessed by most standardized tests are not the most functional for students with severe disabilities. For example, one standardized test looks at whether or not a child can stand on one leg in order to assess his motor skills, balance, ability to imitate, and cognitive ability to understand directions. The test makes sense for typically developing children. Children with autism, on the other hand, would have to be specifically taught how to stand on one leg. That is not a functional skill for them and, therefore, although capable, they will not respond to requests to perform such a task. It makes more sense to teach them how to wash their hands and tie their shoes, far more functional skills that may not be measured in standardized tests.[13]

Standardized tests that are designed specifically for groups of students with disabilities are similarly problematic. Obtaining norms for low-incidence, heterogeneous groups of students with severe disabilities is difficult at best, and of questionable validity (Sigafoos et al., 1987; Garner, 1985; Sommers, 1989). Although there are a few tests to determine degrees of autism (Krug, Arick & Almond, 1980; Schopler, Reichler & Rochen Renner, 1990), these tests do not offer guidelines for curriculum development and have limited applicability in the educational setting.

---

[12] Standardized tests compare students' performance to that of nondisabled students of the same age.

[13] Standardized tests are, however, used in the Wawa House Program. See earlier for an explanation of why they are used for younger children.

Instead of standardized tests, teachers at Eden Institute's Day School use criterion referenced tests, which measure the student only on what he individually is capable of demonstrating. Eden's tests are based on the curriculum and IEP for each student. These tests are conducted several times a year as part of an overall monitoring of each student's progress. An assessment for each student is completed at the beginning of every school year. This assessment provides the basis from which teachers develop a student's IEP. When students first return to Eden in the fall, teachers have a preliminary IEP for each child until assessments and a current IEP are developed. The preliminary IEP is based on how well students were doing at the end of the regular school year program, or on how well they did during summer programming.

Students who are new to Eden also begin the year with a preliminary IEP. Teachers base the preliminary IEP for a new student on the student's previous records, reports from earlier teachers, and intake assessments done at Eden. During the first month or two, teachers interview the student's parents, administer tests to the new student, and generally get to know him. When they feel comfortable in their assessment, they create a formal IEP for him. Once the school year is under way, data are collected daily for both new and returning students.

During the school year, several assessments of students' progress are made. These are:

> **A weekly review** of the daily data collected for students within each program of Eden Institute. The teachers and coordinating teacher of the program meet to discuss each student's progress, and teachers identify potential problem areas. The weekly faculty meeting gives teachers a chance to receive feedback on teaching practices and ideas for developing programs. The weekly meeting also enables teachers to coordinate their efforts, and make sure that each student is being treated as consistently as possible.

> **Progress reports** are issued four times a calendar year for each student. The reports are based on the data assembled from weekly faculty meetings. One additional report is issued for students attending summer programs. Progress reports are compiled and reviewed by the student's primary teacher, language and adaptive physical education teachers, and coordinating teacher. Completed progress reports are circulated to everyone working with the student, including the coordinating teacher, Director of Educational Services, the student's parents, his Child Study Team (CST), and the Executive Director.

> **Staffings** are held a minimum of twice a year to review a student's progress and determine a unified approach to addressing areas of difficulty. The student's primary teacher, language and

A progress report was completed for Kevin, age 3 years, 1 month, at the end of his summer session. Teachers compared his performance on curriculum-based assessments at the beginning of the session, and at the end of the session. They then summarized his performance and made recommendations for his fall programming. These are given below. Similar progress reports are completed for each student at Eden.

Summary and Recommendations for Kevin, August, 1993:

(Approved by his Coordinating Teacher, Primary Teacher, Speech Therapist, Adaptive Physical Education Teacher, the Director of Educational Services, and the Executive Director of Eden.)

Kevin enjoys social interaction with his teachers. He communicates through signs and verbal approximations, as well as by bringing a person to a desired object and pushing away a nondesired item. Kevin knows the signs for "computer," "book," and "more." He produces these signs spontaneously to request desired items. He also approximates the sign for "bathroom."

Effective reinforcers for Kevin include Cheerios, juice, Teddy Grahams, books, tickles, hugs, "peek-a-boo" games, songs (especially "John Jacob" and "Head, Shoulders, Knees, and Toes"), and his typewriter toy. Kevin particularly likes the computer and enjoys the "First Verbs" and "First Words" programs.

Kevin is currently working on learning readiness skills such as eye contact, appropriate sitting, object manipulation, and gross motor imitation. He has adjusted well to the Early Childhood Program at Eden and has shown a steady progression in all of his programs. Kevin is also working on self-care skills (particularly putting on his pants and shirt), in which he has also shown progress. Kevin responds well to faded physical and gestural prompting. He is currently on a 25 minute toileting schedule.

Kevin's aggressive behavior has been most effectively managed by using extinction. His tantrums are most effectively managed by working through them, due to the fact that they usually function as an escape or avoidance tactic. Kevin's hand flapping behavior has decreased significantly since he started at Eden. He usually only requires a very faded physical or gestural prompt to discontinue the behavior.

Recommendations for Kevin include continued one-to-one instruction in learning readiness and self-care skills. Kevin has more difficulty transferring between teachers than he does between activities. Therefore, it is recommended that Kevin be put on a formal picture schedule, and that all mastered skills be generalized to different teachers to help him transfer from teacher to teacher more easily. Kevin should be encouraged to verbalize, as well as sign, as much as possible. It is strongly recommended that Kevin's aggressions remain on extinction since they tend to increase when given any attention. Kevin's hand flapping, visual self-stimulatory behavior (with lights), and tantrums should continue to be redirected.

adaptive physical education teachers, and coordinating teacher are again involved, as well as the Director of Educational Services and other faculty members with specific clinical expertise or previous experience with the student.

IEP meetings are held for each student at the beginning and end of the school year to develop the IEP, and then assess what gains the student has made over the year. The student's parents and Child Study Team, as well as several teachers and administrators from Eden, develop the IEP together, and discuss changes that need to be made for the following school year based on the student's progress reports.

Each meeting and each report measures a student's progress against his larger goals, so teachers are fully aware of why skill programs are being taught, and where the student is headed. Keeping a student's larger goals in mind helps teachers avoid getting caught up in the details of teaching a skill acquisition program. In other words, it keeps the student's programming from "drifting" away from his larger goals. For example, in teaching toothbrushing, students need to be taught how to put the cap back on the tube of toothpaste. One student learned the program well, but had extreme difficulty putting the cap back on. After many different caps were tried, over several weeks of training, the student still had difficulties. His teachers established a goal of being able to get himself ready for school in the morning, which meant not only brushing his teeth, but getting dressed, combing his hair, picking up his lunch box, and walking to the bus stop. Because they had these larger objectives in mind, his teachers were able to move on to the next self-care skill, and not get "stuck" on a less important objective. They allowed him to not put the cap back on the toothpaste, and began teaching him to comb his hair.

The general progress students at Eden Institute's Day School have made over the past several years can be seen in the figure. The students' inconsistent learning style and varied levels of disability cause some scatter in the data.[14] However, the figure provides a general picture of how well students do in the different programs of the Eden Institute's Day School.

---

[14] There are several factors in the data which create a scattered picture of progress. There were very few students in some programs, which made it impossible to obtain a meaningful average for the program. For example, scores in the Middle Childhood Program for the 1989-90 year were skewed upward by two students who achieved 100 percent of their reading objectives. In 1988, only one student in the Transition Program worked on prevocational goals, and he mastered 100 percent of his objectives. (This student moved into the Vocational Preparation program the following year.) In addition, between 1989 and 1991, the skill level of students in the Transition Program changed significantly. Three older students, with strong vocational skills, graduated to the Vocational Preparation Program, and three new students, who still needed to build their prevocational skills, entered the program. The scatter in the Speech and Language area is due to the extreme language deficits of most children with autism. Long-term goals, therefore, often take several years to attain.

TROUBLESHOOTING

If a student is not progressing with a skill acquisition program, or seems to be having difficulty with a program, teachers begin to troubleshoot the program. Troubleshooting can be initiated by the student's teacher or parents, by faculty at the weekly monitoring meetings, in the reviews of a student's progress reports, or

Eden Institute
Percentage of Instructional Objective Mastered
Blue Ribbon Schools Program, October 1991

Data submitted to the U.S. Department of Education for 1991-1992

CURRICULAR AREA	EARLY CHILDHOOD			MIDDLE CHILDHOOD			TRANSITION		
	88-89	89-90	90-91	88-89	89-90	90-91	88-89	89-90	90-91
Learning Readiness	67%	86%	96%	69%	—	86%	—	—	—
Preacademic	70%	79%	92%	50%	68%	78%	—	—	—
Academic	75%	63%	79%	74%	96%	84%	65%	88%	92%
Prevocational	57%	66%	87%	67%	70%	84%	100%	94%	88%
Self-Care	45%	69%	89%	57%	77%	88%	—	—	—
Domestic	—	44%	67%	47%	74%	76%	83%	82%	82%
Speech/Language	88%	93%	77%	91%	85%	89%	96%	93%	86%
Adaptive Phys. Ed.	25%	47%	60%	32%	44%	54%	48%	78%	58%
Average Objectives Mastered	61%	68%	81%	61%	73%	80%	78%	87%	81%

—— = No student worked on any objective in this area.

during the regular IEP meetings. The Troubleshooting Process is similar to the steps and procedures of the Eden Decision Model and Accountability Process presented in Chapter 7, but where these primarily address developing and refining behavior reduction programs, the Troubleshooting Process is used more often in skill acquisition programs.

In order to begin troubleshooting, the student must have shown limited progress with a program over ten therapy sessions, or two weeks of school. Teachers think about what might be causing a student's lack of progress from the moment they notice a problem, but they must wait two weeks before initiating formal troubleshooting. This gives a student a chance to assimilate the different as-

Percentage of Instructional Objective Mastered

Updated Statistics, 1995-1996

CURRICULAR AREAS	EARLY CHILDHOOD 1995-96	MIDDLE CHILDHOOD 1995-96	TRANSITION 1995-96	PRE-VOCATIONAL 1995-96	VOCATIONAL 1995-96
Learning Readiness	80%	50%	—	—	—
Preacademic	62%	59%	—	—	—
Academic	71%	87%	92%	78%	***
Prevocational	—	71%	90%	70%	80%
Self-Care	72%	66%	***	20%	***
Domestics	—	63%	92%	78%	87%
Speech/ Language	63%	64%	54%	38%	18%
Adaptive Phys. Ed.	26%	79%	66%	42%	67%
Social Skills	60%	49%	85%	***	***
Average Obj. Mastered	62%	65%	80%	54%	63%

—— = No student worked on any objective in this area.
*** = Instructional objectives worked on incidentally.

pects of a new skill acquisition program, and overcome any minor illnesses or temporary distractions that may affect his attention to skill development programs. Waiting before attempting to troubleshoot a program allows for natural "lulls" in students' learning, and enables teachers to make more careful decisions about programming.

The Troubleshooting Process provides a step-by-step analysis of the teaching environment. These steps take the form of questions to be asked about the data, the student's attention and motivation, any prompting techniques used, and the skill acquisition program itself. The steps of the process are:

First, analyze the data.
1. Is the data actually measuring performance of the targeted skill?
2. Does the data truly reflect the rate at which the student is learning the skill?
3. How does the rate of skill acquisition compare with the student's rates in other skill programs?
4. How frequently is the skill program implemented?
5. Is data recorded accurately and reliably by faculty members?

Second, evaluate the student's attention and motivation.
1. Is the room and furniture set up appropriately?
2. Are there too many distractions?
3. Is the reinforcer varied sufficiently?
4. Is the reinforcer given too slowly?
5. Has the student become satiated with the reinforcer?

Third, examine prompting techniques.
1. Are prompts effective? In other words, there should be no incorrect prompted trials.
2. Have prompts been faded too quickly?
3. Are prompts offered unintentionally when they should be completely faded?

Finally, analyze the program.
1. Does the student have the necessary prerequisite skills to learn the program?
2. Are the steps of the program clear and specific?

Throughout the Troubleshooting Process, teachers also take into account the length of time a student has worked on a particular program, and whether the program remains functional and appropriate for him. A student may have worked on a program long enough to become bored with it, for example, which would account for his lack of progress. Or, a student may have difficulty with a shoe-tying program because he is now wearing loafers instead of tennis shoes, so he has

Troubleshooting

A student in Early Childhood was having a particularly difficult time mastering learning readiness skills. Because these skills are the foundation of all later learning, and because this student was getting ready to move into the Middle Childhood program, it was crucial that he master them. For this student, the troubleshooting process began with a team assessment of his: 1) strengths and inconsistencies, 2) educational and behavioral history, 3) learning style, and 4) motivation. The review of his strengths revealed that self-care was a successful and functional area for this student, so programs from this domain were incorporated into his IEP. His primary inconsistencies lay in the area of learning readiness, again, critical skills for progress. Since this student was not acquiring learning readiness skills through the traditional programs, new programs were written to better fit his strengths and learning style. Because motivation and skill acquisition are closely related, a review of his past reinforcers was conducted and a highly individualized menu and schedule were developed. Additionally, a review of his educational data indicated that 80 percent correct responding would be a more effective criteria for him; although he could reach between 80 and 85 percent correct responding fairly consistently, he seemed to lose interest in his programming before reaching 90 percent. In addition to these straightforward strategies, the troubleshooting process yielded some creative strategies as well, such as having his teacher wear neutrally-colored clothes and no jewelry to help with his distractibility. A one-year plan was developed that outlined these strategies and defined "checkpoints" at which the troubleshooting strategies would be assessed for effectiveness.

The results of these efforts are listed below.

BASELINE AND FINAL RATES, 1990 - 1991 SCHOOL YEAR

Program	Baseline Rate, 9/90	Final Rate, 6/91
Eye Contact on Command	Step 3, 75%	Program mastered 11/90
Appropriate Sitting	Step 2, 0%	Program mastered 5/91
One-Step Commands	Step 1, 0%	Program mastered, 6/91
Motor Imitation	Step 2, 50%	Program mastered, 5/91
Toilet Training	30 minute schedule; no independent toileting	1 hour schedule; 25% independent toileting
Sorting	Step 1, 0%	Step 1, 100%
Single Object Assembly	Step 1, 0%	Steps 1-6, 100%
Dressing: Pants	Step 2, 0%	Program mastered, 6/91
Simultaneous Communication	Step 2, 0%	Steps 1-4, 100%

no chance to practice tying. The length of time a program has been worked on and the functionality of a program are not assessed formally during the Troubleshooting Process, but are informal questions teachers ask when troubleshooting.

Once teachers arrive at a consensus about what programmatic changes would be most likely to encourage the student to progress, those changes are implemented, and the student's progress is again monitored. As with the EDM and Accountability Process, the Troubleshooting Process is continued until all faculty are satisfied with the student's progress. The Troubleshooting Process is designed to modify skill acquisition programs that are already in place. Occasionally, however, existing skill programs are influenced by decisions made through the EDM.

HOW THE EDM IS USED IN CURRICULUM DECISIONS

The behavior reduction programs developed through the EDM and Accountability Process can alter the way skill acquisition programs are taught, or even which skill programs are taught. Donna Vicidomini, Assistant Director for Education and Retreat Support Services:

> *If we realize through the EDM that a student does something unacceptable as a way to get our attention, such as pull on our pants leg, we will write a program to teach him other, more appropriate ways of getting attention. For example, we would teach him how to tap someone on the shoulder, or say our name. If we learn that a behavior is occurring to escape from a task, we may need a program to teach him how to make decisions, so he can choose an alternate to the task. All these teaching programs need to be included in his IEP and become part of his curriculum.*

The EDM usually influences curricular programs when a student needs to be taught a skill to replace problematic behavior. These skill programs most often take the form of communication training because so much of the unacceptable behavior students exhibit comes from frustration or a misunderstanding (Carr & Durand, 1985).

ADDITIONAL PROGRAMS OFFERED BY EDEN INSTITUTE

◆ ◆ ◆ ◆ ◆ ◆ ◆ ◆ ◆ ◆ ◆ ◆ ◆ ◆ ◆ ◆ ◆

Eden Institute's programs described above—the Early Childhood, Middle Childhood, Transition, and Prevocational and Vocational Preparation Programs—are the core programs of its Day School. They are the primary means by which Eden educates its students. However, there are also several additional programs offered. These provide extended programming for students both in the home and over the summer months. They also help families teach their son or daughter with autism

Eden's summer residential program offers students a summer camp-like environment where they can practice their educational, independent living, leisure, and recreational skills. The Wawa Education and Retreat Center gives the children the opportunity to grow physically, emotionally, and in independence. This fosters a sense of self-confidence and self-worth. I'll always remember the day Sasha learned to swim for the first time. It happened during the last day of the summer program, just before he was about to go home. When he came out of the water, his face beamed with pride. Events like these continually remind me how the program impacts on the lives of our students.

—**Donna Vicidomini, Assistant Director for Education and Retreat Support Services**

◆ ◆ ◆ ◆ ◆

When we first drove Sasha to camp, he was a little bit nervous and unhappy, but only for the first day. That's a normal reaction. All of us were this way when we were children. Now when we pick him up, he sometimes doesn't want to come home. He really enjoys it, and he knows all his teachers there. He mixes well with the other children. He's gone hiking, went on weekend excursions, spent the night at a motel, and had all sorts of excursions. He even learned to swim last summer. That was really exciting for him. It's good for him to have to adjust to another place.

—**Sasha and Dasha Polyakov**

◆ ◆ ◆ ◆ ◆

When Geoffrey went to camp, it was the first time we had any time off from him. At first, we didn't know what to do. We felt confident leaving him there, because he had been at Eden for three years and a former teacher of his was the director of the camp, but it was still difficult. For the first few days after Geoffrey left, we kept forgetting he was gone. We had forgotten how to relax. We kept trying to fit him into our plans until it dawned on us that we could do whatever we felt like doing.

—**Charles and Nancy Richardson, parents of Geoffrey**

at home and in the community. Several programs offered through Eden's Outreach and Support Divisions offer people with autism, their families, and other agencies support from the professional staff of Eden Institute in designing and implementing effective programming.

EXTENDED SCHOOL YEAR PROGRAMS

Eden offers two programs to extend students' education over the summer months: the summer day program and a residential education camp.[15] Both pro-

---

[15] The camp, located in Chaplin, Connecticut, is reserved for children over the summer, and becomes a retreat center for children and adults throughout the rest of the year. Adults are given summer vacations at a shore house, so they do not share the camp with the children.

grams focus on maintaining and expanding the preacademic, academic, speech, social, motor development, and vocational skills taught during the school year. In the day program, the schedule and grouping of students is the same as during the school year, and swimming lessons and community experiences unique to the summer are also provided.

The residential education camp provides one to eight week programs for students, depending on their age and level of ability. By design, the "camp" is fairly small, forty-five acres, with cottages, recreational facilities, and a large New England style lodge. The camp provides opportunities for swimming, hiking, field trips, and art and music activities. At two to one, the student to teacher ratio is smaller than in the day program. This is because students need assistance around the clock. They do not return home at the end of the day.

Students are supervised at all times, but are given training in becoming responsible for caring for themselves. They are taught not to rely on others doing things for them. They have to dress in the morning, brush their teeth, comb their hair, and be ready for breakfast.

The summer programs help students expand upon what they learn over the school year, but more importantly, they help prevent regression. Data at Eden show that students who do not take part in summer programming lose as much as three months' worth of gains. In other words, it takes three months to get students back to where they were when they left Eden for the summer. When added to the time that could have been spent over the summer working on skills, those three months become five months of lost treatment time. Five months loss in the life of a child with autism can be a phenomenal loss. For this reason, teachers strongly encourage schools and families to continue their child's education over the summer.

RESPITE PROGRAM

The Respite Program is designed to give families a much needed break from the rigors of raising their child, and to teach the child skills he needs at home, but which cannot easily be taught in school. During respite sessions, teachers from Eden Institute go into the family's home for up to forty hours a month and teach the student how to better follow the rules of his family and the community. Jamie Klim, Coordinator of the Respite Program:

> *When we come into a home, we can be sensitive to what a particular family wants, and can tailor our teaching programs to suit that family. Many families have rules about how children have to behave at*

dinner time. They may need to stay at the table until everyone is done, or may need to ask permission to leave the table. We can teach those rules to a child at home, but cannot in school.

Dinner time is stressful for many families. Their child with autism often cannot attend to a task for long periods, so by the time all the dinner gets on the table, he is up walking around the house. Someone, usually mom, then has to go get him, sit him down, and help him pay attention to eating. Mom then cannot eat dinner herself because she has to help her child sit in his chair and eat. That causes a lot of tension. As a solution, families often make shifts for eating, even though they would much rather all eat together. When we come into the home, we can work with the child and help him stay at the dinner table, so the family can all eat together.

Respite services can be crucial to maintaining a consistent environment for students. Through Respite, teachers are able to create in the home the type of environment students receive in school. This helps teachers work on problems that may occur at home, but never in school. For example, a student may have mastered toileting skills at school, but still have accidents at home, or he could be quite well behaved in the classroom but have regular tantrums at home. Through Respite, teachers are able to address these inconsistencies.

It's easy to think of respite as just a professional baby-sitting service. But in order to be successful, it needs to be more. The more involvement we have in the home environment, and the more parent training and communication that goes on, the more self-sufficient the student will become. We ask parents to talk to us, and tell us why, for example, Mom can't have a few minutes a day to relax. If that's important to the family, we may have to teach the student some leisure activities so he won't bother Mom for a while. If we don't have that communication with the student's family, we're going to be a lot less effective in improving the family's home situation.

—**Carol Markowitz, Director of Educational Services**

Respite services are provided mainly to families within Eden, but since the Respite Program is funded by New Jersey's Divisions of Youth and Family Services and Developmental Disabilities, it is also able to provide respite services to a small number of families outside of Eden. Approximately 10 percent of the respite care goes to families outside of Eden's services.

HOME CONSULTANT PROGRAM

The Home Consultant Program is similar to Respite in that teachers from Eden Institute come in to a family's home to work with the child and his family.

But in the Home Consultant Program, the focus is not on the child, but on the parents. Through this program, the student's consultant visits the family's home on a regular basis (weekly, if necessary) to help the family prioritize and design programs to change the student's behavior or teach the student particular skills. The consultant then trains the family to implement these programs. Parents, Nancy Cantor and Steve Brechin:

> During home training, we sit down with the parents and ask them what they would like their child to work on. We then help set up programs for them and give them ideas on how to deal with problematic behaviors. When we go into the home, we can give parents the tools they need to make their home life better, and can give them feedback right then and there about how they deal with their child.
>
> —**Cindy Bregenzer, Coordinating Teacher, Middle Childhood**

> *We have had a series of behavior problems at home, mainly with noncompliance and tantrums. Archie does not want to do things our way, and so throws fits. We were trying to change Archie's behavior in a lot of different ways, and had gotten some of our signals crossed. Our home trainer helped us clarify what we wanted to do in given situations, and what exactly we wanted to work on. With home training, we have been able to separate out issues of aggression, general behavior issues, and what to reinforce.*
>
> *If Archie is feeling unhappy or frustrated, as he often gets, we want to redirect his mood. We want to make him feel better. It is hard to effectively do that when the behavior itself needs controlling. That is the most difficult aspect for us. We are used to dealing with people's moods and emotions, and using language in a way we cannot with Archie. Our home trainer has helped us focus on the idea that we are not trying to redirect his mood. We are trying to redirect his behavior.*

The Home Consultant Program is an intensive program usually used by the families of newly-admitted students. In conjunction with other components (parent training, home visits, and classroom visits; see Chapter 10 for a more detailed description), the Home Consultant Program offers families comprehensive training in dealing with their child most effectively. As with each service Eden offers its families, the goal of the Home Consultant Program is for parents to integrate behavioral techniques into their natural parenting styles and family values and, as a result, feel more confident in their abilities and require less and less support from the consultant.

AFTER-SCHOOL PROGRAM

Since its inception, Eden has offered various after-school programs. These programs extend the students' day in order for them to enjoy activities not usually available to them at home. Teachers enable students to be involved in many community outings as well as arts and crafts and other leisure activities. Eden's After School Program is also a vehicle for involving student teachers from various colleges and universities in helping children with autism. Involving student teachers gives them an opportunity to be exposed to the needs of children with autism and effective remedial practices.

OUTREACH AND SUPPORT SERVICES

The Outreach and Support Divisions are actively engaged in conducting diagnostic and programmatic evaluations, professional consultations, training, and research with the goal of improving the general quality and quantity of services for people with autism. Although the two divisions are closely allied, the services offered through Outreach focus on families and agencies outside Eden, while Support Services provide multiple services as well as internal oversight and continual training to programs, parents, and staff within Eden. Together, the Outreach and Support Divisions offer several programs, each of which is described below. Some programs are offered under both divisions jointly, such as parent training and the Behavior Technology Workshop; others are offered singularly, such as Consultative and Evaluative Services (Outreach), Internal Oversight (Support), Continuing Education (Support), Research (Support), Eden Press (Support), Retreat Services (Support), Princeton Lecture Series (Outreach), Web Site (Support), Eden Florida (Outreach), and Eden Connecticut (Outreach).

Outreach Services

Consultation and Evaluation Services—Services available to parents, professionals, and public and private agencies dedicated to providing effective services for individuals with autism. Tailored to the unique needs of the individual, these services can include: diagnostic; speech-language and learning evaluations; home programming; educational, residential, and employment program consultation; assistance with transition to other settings; and program development.

Princeton Lecture Series—Held in conjunction with Princeton University, Eden's annual lecture serves as a catalyst for leading researchers and practitioners in service delivery, cell biology, and related disciplines to share theories and influence the autism research agenda.

Eden Connecticut—Training, consultation, evaluation, and programmatic services for individuals with autism, their families, professionals, and public and private agencies at the Wawa Education and Retreat Center in Chaplin, Connecticut.

Eden Florida—A full range of outreach services including training, consultation, evaluation, and clinical services available through Eden's newest facility in South Fort Myers, Florida.

Support Services

Internal Oversight—Provides a comprehensive and objective evaluation of each program on a semi-yearly basis. Oversight areas include technical skills, programmatics, data and documentation, staff interactions, as well as parent and staff feedback.

Continuing Education—Mandatory participation in a minimum of four inservice presentations is required of all full-time staff. Presentations focus on a variety of topics relevant to autism and professional skill development and are given by both Eden trainers and outside presenters.

Retreat Services—Offers a variety of recreational and educational opportunities for Eden students, participants, their families, faculty and staff at the Wawa Education and Retreat Center in Chaplin, Connecticut.

Research—Includes both internal research, presenting Eden's teaching and treatment methods to the professional arena through journal publications and conference presentations, and external research, during which Eden assists outside investigators with pertinent research projects.

Eden Press—A comprehensive collection of resources to assist parents, professionals, and agencies to provide effective services to individuals with autism. Publications include curricula for educational, residential, and employment programming, behavior technology guides, and proceedings from Eden's Princeton Lecture Series.

On-line Services—Eden is an active presence on the Internet and World Wide Web, using the information superhighway to communicate with parents and professionals interested in effective treatment for individuals with autism.

PARENT TRAINING PROGRAM

Research has shown that one of the strongest predictors of a child's progress is the parents' conviction that they can be effective in facilitating their child's development (Bruey, 1989; Rosenberg, 1977). Teaching parents effective ways to deal with their child can only strengthen that confidence. Through parent training, parents are taught the techniques used by their child's teacher. These techniques enable parents to capitalize on their child's interest in daily events, build

Archie has recently joined Eden. We're getting a sense of the educational processes and techniques used, but it's a lot to take in at first. Archie's behaviors are always changing, so we have to figure out how to change ourselves. He's a moving target, and we're now just beginning to catch up to speed.

We can think about techniques in the abstract, but when we're trying to live life, with the phone ringing, making dinner, dealing with another child, and trying to get something done at work, it's very hard to translate the abstract, theoretical ideas into something pragmatic. The situations become very complex and ambiguous. The parent training program has helped us figure out what techniques to use in different situations, and how to work on one behavior at a time.

—**Nancy Cantor and Steve Brechin**

necessary skills, and handle difficult situations (Bruey, 1989). With parent training, interactions within the family have also been shown to improve. Training also bolsters the family's psychological health, as family members learn to engage the child with autism effectively (Bruey, 1989).

Parents of students first entering Eden Institute as well as parents outside of Eden are provided training through the Parent Training Program.[16] The program equips parents with the necessary techniques and skills to teach, reduce, or modify their child's behavior. The initial training provided to parents is continued through the Home Consultant Program, home visits, and classroom visits.

◆ ◆

Parent Training Series, 1994-1995

SESSION 1
Teaching and Reinforcement*

SESSION 2
Reducing Behavior*

SESSION 3
Communicating With Your Child

SESSION 4
Respite and Recreation

SESSION 5
Problem Solving at Home

* To ensure families have all the information they need right away, these basic topics are presented in an intensive, two-night format as soon as their children begin the program.

◆ ◆

BEHAVIOR TECHNOLOGY WORKSHOP

Behavior Technology Workshops are an extension of the training staff members receive when they first join Eden. Workshops encompass a wide range of topics in the field of special education, but focus on the design, implementation, and assessment of educational and behavioral programs for people with autism. Workshops are offered every other month,[17] and have covered topics such as new ideas for teaching behavior, dealing with problematic behaviors in the community,

---

[16] The training offered to parents is similar in content to that given to staff members when they first join Eden. See Chapter 11 for a description of the entire training process.

[17] The Outreach Division also puts together a yearly conference which is targeted to staff in other service agencies, but is open to Eden's staff members as well.

how to manage the community's perception of people with autism, and recent studies on effective behavior modification. Workshops are led by professionals from both Eden and other agencies.

Although designed for teachers at Eden, workshops are available to any one with an interest in behavior modification techniques and diagnostic teaching procedures. The workshops form part of a training institute at Eden for future professionals. Undergraduate and graduate students who study psychology, special education, speech therapy, and nursing often take part in the workshops. Students from surrounding colleges and universities have been particularly involved. Princeton University offers a course at Eden, and after the course, its students have often volunteered. From The College of New Jersey and Rutgers University, Eden receives practicum students and student teachers. These students help teachers in the classroom, assist administrators, and obtain general direct care experience and training.[18]

CONSULTATION AND EVALUATION SERVICE

The consultation and evaluation services are the fastest growing services at Eden. They are used by members of the general public, private and public schools, and state and private agencies in the United States and internationally.

One component of consultation and evaluation services is an information service on treatments for autism and other developmental disabilities. Through the information service, Eden's staff and teachers have collected a library of information about autism and different treatment methodologies. They give presentations about autism to local schools and hospitals, and provide daily information over the phone to scores of people. The information service is Eden's primary link to other agencies and people concerned with services for people with autism. Marlene Cohen, Director of Support Services:

> W e try not to turn anyone away from Outreach. If a family doesn't have money, for example, and can't afford the therapy offered through the Wawa House Program, we will help them somehow. We may help by giving the family training and advice, free phone consultations, or by consulting with the program their child is in.
>
> **—Anne S. Holmes, Director of Outreach Services**

> *So many people telephone asking for advice or an opinion. Parents and professionals call and say, "As a program for people with autism, we would be interested in your opinion about facilitated communication, or auditory training, or dolphin therapy." They ask us for information on what we think of new therapies, and if we have done any research on particular topics.*

---

[18]   See Chapter 11 for more on how Eden helps students in special education.

The consultation and evaluation service also offers diagnostic and prescriptive reporting services through consultations with families of children with au-

tism. Anne S. Holmes, Director of Outreach Services, consulted with a family that needed a program for their child.

We helped Daniel's mother find a private school for him. She had a very good program for him at the time, but he was becoming too old to stay there. She wanted a place that fit Daniel's learning style and abilities, and asked us to help.

We conducted an evaluation of Daniel, offered her advice, and visited the places she was considering. She had asked for advice from the program Daniel was in as well, but did not rely solely on them. She used us too because she knew we would be objective. She also knew that once Daniel did change schools, we would still be there to help and offer advice.

Marlene Cohen describes another consultation, done with a family whose child was in the Wawa House Program at Eden:

We did a consultation with a family whose child was just old enough to be covered by the Department of Education. The family wanted help in approaching their child study team. We assisted them by explaining to the child study team the kinds of services that the child would need. We also watched together an actual session with the child at Wawa House, and we were able to point out to the child study team some of the child's specific learning characteristics. The child study team decided to support the child in a summer program, but if our meeting had not happened, those services would probably not have been made available.

Outreach also provides numerous program evaluations and program development recommendations. At least one of these, done for a local school district that needed specialized services for preschool children, has resulted in a proliferation of services at the state level for children with autism. Anne S. Holmes:

A few years ago Eden had two slots open for preschool children, but there were forty children applying who were appropriate for those slots. That is an indication of how few services were around for them. The local school districts decided to develop more services, and asked Eden to help them get started. We have now helped fifteen districts set up specialized preschool classes in the public school system. What is most interesting, however, is that the specialized classes are following the children through the school system. When the children age out of their specialized preschool class, some school districts are setting up specialized classes in the first grade, second grade, and so on. The districts are beginning to see how important specialization is for children with autism.

The number of services for people with autism is expanding not only at the preschool level, but at all ages, and generally in all parts of the United States (Schopler & Van Bourgondien, 1990). As this happens, the questions about autism and how to serve people with autism will most likely also increase. Eden expects to help meet these questions by further expanding its outreach services.

RESEARCH ACTIVITIES

Because Eden's mission is to provide lifespan services to people with autism, research is not a first priority. Nevertheless it recognizes the important role that research plays in improving the understanding of autism. With this in mind, Eden has been involved in numerous research projects both of its own design and in cooperation with outside researchers. Coordination of outside projects and the design of in-house projects is done through the Support Division.

The data-based nature of applied behavior analysis makes it relatively easy for research activities to be conducted in-house. For each of the behavior and skill acquisition programs in place for students, data is recorded daily and charted. Researchers can use these raw data as the basis for study. At Eden Institute, research has been conducted on, among other topics, the marital satisfaction of parents receiving respite services (Alessandri et al., 1993), the efficacy of facilitated communication (Bomba et al., 1996), and the impact of early intervention services on developmentally delayed children's educational progress (Alessandri, Bomba, Holmes, Van Driesen & Holmes, in prep.). Addi-

One of our students is really bright and together. He will probably attend regular school at some point, but he's a Jekyll and Hyde. At school he's fine, but at home, he has total control. His parents are at the end of their rope. They are so ready and willing to try to help him, but don't know what to do. So, we decided to bring them into school to work with their son here, where we have control over his behavior.

As an experiment, we decided to take some satisfaction data before and after we try this, to see if there's any difference in how they feel. There's a real potential in their situation to determine whether this model of treatment—bringing the family into the controlled school environment—works. It's a small study, but along with other internal studies we do, it provides information that helps people with autism in general.

—Anne S. Holmes, Director of Outreach Services

tionally, Eden has worked with other researchers on topics ranging from the molecular genetics of autism (Darras & Mannheim, in prep.) to the development of "theory of mind" (Leslie, in prep.).

Outside researchers have conducted studies at Eden as well. Eden lends professional support, technical assistance, and research participants with autism for study by agencies engaged in basic research on the causes and treatments of autism. These studies have examined topics such as the emotional adjustment in families that have a child with autism, and biogenetic markers for people with severe autism.

Chapter **9**

Adults

· · · · ·

with

· · · · · · ·

Autism

· · · · ·

Only recently have children or adolescents with autism grown up to be called adults with autism. Prior to 1943, the year Leo Kanner identified the syndrome, people with autism tended to be labeled schizophrenic or mentally retarded (Holmes, 1989). There were services available for children and adults who were either schizophrenic or mentally retarded, but none specifically for those with autism. People with autism were placed in whatever services were available, even though those services were not designed to meet their needs and generally proved ineffective.

This trend is gradually changing for children as advocates procure more services designed specifically for people with autism. In the state of New Jersey, for example, a decade of parent and professional advocacy resulted in "autism" becoming a separate educational category in 1990. Since that time, the number of educational programs specifically designed to serve students with autism increased from four schools to fourteen, with additional classrooms being developed each year (COSAC, 1996). Many of these classrooms are located in public schools, expanding the continuum of services available to students with autism by allowing appropriate students to take advantage of the peer models available in their neighborhood schools.

Once students reach age twenty-one, however, services again become scarce. Although the Individuals with Disabilities Education Act (IDEA) ensures that all students with autism receive a free appropriate public education, no such law ensures free and appropriate services for adults (Gerhardt & Holmes, 1997). Currently, the parent and professional advocacy that brought services to children with autism is working toward securing services for adults. Due process cases in New Jersey are setting precedents that begin to ensure services for adults. For example, in 1992, the Superior Court of New Jersey determined that the Division of Developmental Disabilities failed to ensure a "fair execution of [its] statutory mandate" when it recommended a program for a severely disabled thirty-five-year-old woman that was "idealized, but non-existent" (Superior Court of New Jersey Appellate Division, A-3793-90TI, 1992). The precedent set in this case places the burden of obtaining or developing an appropriate placement on the governmental agency, not on the parents or the individual. Further, in 1995, the Supreme Court of New Jersey rejected the Division of Developmental Disabilities' suggestion that budgetary problems compelled the agency to place an individual in a service that would likely cause him to regress and ruled that B.F., a twenty-one-year-old man with autism, could not be transferred from an out-of-state autism center until an appropriate, adult placement became available.[1] In this important decision, the court again placed the burden of obtaining an appropriate placement on the agency, and stated that if an agency's decision was "manifestly mistaken," the court would not hesitate to "shed its traditional deference" to the agency and reverse the decision.

THE ADULT LIFE OF A PERSON WITH AUTISM

As the services available to adults with autism expand, the needs of adults are being discovered in more detail. Adults with autism are emerging as people who very often require a continuation of the intensive training they received in childhood and adolescence into their "educational" years. Adults are able to retain skills they have acquired over their educational years, and are able to learn new skills when specialized services follow them into adulthood.

As a result of improving services, adults with autism appear to have normal life spans (Edwards & Bristol, 1991). During adolescence, 20 to 40 percent of people with autism develop epilepsy (Olsson, Steffengurg & Gillberg, 1988), but past adolescence, having autism does not seem to predispose people to any disorders that do not affect mainstream adult society.

Of course, no one can predict precisely how a child with autism will present himself as he enters adulthood. The progress made during the adult years depends on a person's earlier services, his capacity for learning and his intelligence, health, and work and life skills. Research shows that children with autism are not

---

[1] *P.F. v. New Jersey Division of Developmental Disabilities,* 139 N.J. 522 (1995).

Without such a continuation of intensive services, however, many adults with autism will regress terribly. Claire's story provides one such illustration. After her graduation from Eden Institute at age 21, no appropriate program was available for Claire. Shortly, Claire's self-injurious behavior—hitting herself in the face or chest when frustrated—returned, and according to her mother, she became depressed. She would enter an unlit room and sit passively in the dark. Mornings, instead of getting up at 6:00AM as she had done during her school years, she lay in bed until noon. "When grown children live at home, they tend to do it for economic reasons," Claire's mother said. "They usually have cars and dates and hobbies. That's not the case with Claire. She's home all day with a single parent who arrives drained from work. It's just not right. In a group home experience, there are other people their own age, planned activities, recreation and new staff coming in every so often...I feel as if we've been derailed and can't get back on track....

—Adapted from "Dream of Life In Specialized Home is Denied to Autistic Woman"
by Mary Jo Patterson, Star Ledger, January 31, 1994

likely to acquire new behavior challenges after adolescence, but they probably will retain many of their undesirable behaviors and demands of their childhood years that have not been remediated, such as having tantrums or demanding no alterations to a rather rigid life style (American Psychiatric Association, 1994; Schopler & Mesibov, 1983). As children and adolescents with autism become adults, many of their needs do remain the same, but many change. The rest of this chapter section describes how the needs of adults are both similar to and different from their needs as children and adolescents.

NURTURING INDEPENDENCE

Like younger people with autism, adults with autism need help in acquiring skills that will ensure greater independence (Baumgart et al., 1982; Brown et al., 1979). They need a supportive environment at home and at work in order to maintain skills, and learn new skills. Like children, adults can do many things on their own, but they need others to monitor their physical and mental health, and to teach them appropriate social behavior. Like children, adults

Robert came to Eden at age twenty-one. He has learned to communicate much better, but still doesn't talk, although he wants to very much. He has learned to sign to let us know what he wants. He has also learned many independent skills, like showering and dressing himself, and uses them when he comes home. He can work in the community, and really tries to interact. However, there are some things he can't do by himself. He needs the help he receives in the group home and his employment position.

—Mike Walsh, Parent

We have visited group homes or day programs where not much is going on. When we've asked why, the staff at the home says "Well, they don't want to do anything. It's their choice."

We too have free choice in leisure activities, but we read a book, ride a bicycle, or do something other than just sit. If I did nothing else but stay in my chair 24 hours a day, I wouldn't be able to support myself or my family. Most people don't live that way.

Most of the participants at Eden are cognitively unable to make such independent decisions in all their daily activities. We work on giving them that ability by training them to make decisions. They don't always have to do something they do not want to do, but they have to do something. If they appear to not want to do a particular task, we respond by saying "Okay, you don't have to do this task, but you have to do one of these tasks." Sometimes they can choose to do nothing, but this is not a frequent option.

—**Dave Roussell, Director of Residential Services**

need individualized programming, and need to be treated "as if" they are capable of accomplishing the goal of being a fully included member of adult society.

Adults with autism must be treated with respect and dignity, and must not be made to perform tasks they are unprepared to perform, but must be held responsible for their actions and for ever-increasing adaptability to adult life. To treat someone with respect and dignity is to expect that they will be productive members of society, and will participate as much as they can, utilizing and developing the skills they need for independence (Baumgart et al., 1982).

However, not all programs for adults require that they participate in their own self-care. Care-giving is unfortunately more common in programs for adults than for children because no laws yet guarantee appropriate residential or work placements. The adults who come to Eden from institutional or care-giving settings, where generally care is given at the expense of training, have fewer skills and more behavior challenges than adults coming from programs like the Eden Institute, where training is emphasized. Jamie Klim:

> There is a big difference between the people we have had at Eden since age six or seven, and the adults that come to us from institutions. One man came to Eden from the lock-up ward of an institution. He was very aggressive. He was used to eating, getting locked up, and sleeping, because that was all he did there. When he came to the group home, he was not sure how to make choices, or how to do things for himself. It was a while before he understood that alarms would not go off every time he left his bedroom. Another man who came to us from an institution did a lot of food hoarding, covering up his meal, and eating very fast. He had several rigid behaviors, like the ritual he went through every morning, and also did not know how to occupy himself appropriately. He did not understand much, and had poor communi-

cation skills. What little speech he had he could not use functionally. The adaptive difficulties that these two men had were in areas that students at Eden Institute work on overcoming from day one, so we do not tend to see these types of problems in people coming straight from Eden Institute or other appropriate services.

DIFFERENT TEACHING PHILOSOPHY

Although the approach to teaching adults should be the same as that for children, adults have some needs that differ from those of children or adolescents. The IEP of a student's school years is replaced with the Individualized Habilitation Plan, or IHP. This change reflects a shift of focus from teaching general educational skills,

which range from learning readiness training to academics, to teaching those skills that most directly enable adults to function independently. These are predominantly life skills and domestics, such as washing and cooking, as well as recreation, communication, behavior management, and employment skills.[2] IEPs and IHPs may both contain programs to teach the same skills, but those skills taught in the IHP must be strictly functional for the person with autism. In other words, the skills he learns must have a direct relation to his home and work activities.[3] Although the focus of skills taught changes when a student enters adult services, staff members at Eden continue to use Eden's EDM and Accountability Process to modify behavior and its troubleshooting process for skill acquisition programs.

SPECIAL NEEDS OF ADULTS

Adults require some skills that children and most adolescents do not yet need. Adults need to be able to generalize their skills across a wider variety of environments because they often both live and work in the community. Adults also need to be prepared for the changes their body goes through as they mature. For example, they need to be taught how to control their diet, or how to take care of menstruation. Adults also need to be taught to engage in differing age-appropriate activities, such as taking a walk or jogging instead of playing on a slide or swing.

---

[2] See the previous chapter for a description of what skills are taught in each of these areas and how the skills are sequenced.

[3] Only functional academics are taught to adults. The academic concepts which are taught to adults are work related. For example, an adult might be taught liquid and solid measuring in order to obtain a job filling salad cartons.

The most important functional needs adults with autism have, however, focus on residential services in the community and support in finding and carrying out employment. Residential and employment services are necessary for adults with autism because these services enable adults to have the same experiences as their nondisabled peers: living apart from one's family and supporting and taking care of one's self, having social contacts, and working for monetary rewards, as well as gaining a sense of accomplishment, pride, and self-esteem.

The main types of appropriate residential programs for adults with autism are community group homes, supervised apartments, skill development homes, and natural or surrogate family homes. Group homes usually house up to six to eight residents and several staff members. They are located in typical neighborhoods in the community. Supervised apartments house fewer people in general and people who are more able to take care of themselves. In supervised apartments, a supervisor or staff member regularly checks up on the residents, but may not live in the apartment. Skill development homes are typical family homes in which a person with autism can live. The families have been trained in teaching people with autism, and take the person into their home as another member of the family. An adult's natural family, of course, is also an appropriate option, but is not as secure an option as the programs mentioned above. It is very important for parents to secure quality community based services while they are able. To wait until they can no longer serve their adult child will result in less than appropriate services for him.

Residential placements for adults with autism should be no different than any other residence except that they are more highly structured. The residence should become the new base for learning in the adult's life, and so must serve functions formerly addressed by the family and school or currently addressed by his employment services. Life skills, recreation, community experiences, and com-

> Joelle moved into our newest group home. She can be very violent, and so had been in a lock-up unit at an institution before coming to Eden. However, she's relatively high functioning. She writes me letters when I'm not at the home about her parents and asks when I'll next visit her. She also writes her own schedule every day. Before coming to Eden's group home, she was part of a work program at Eden WERCs, and so had active services planned during the day, but when she went home to the institution at night, she would have nothing to do.
>
> The day she was coming to the group home, we went and picked her up. As we were leaving, I remember she took her key off her neck. She then turned around and handed it to the institution staff, saying "No more keys for me." I said "That's right Joelle, no more keys for you." She still asks when she's going back to the hospital, and if she'll go there if she's bad. That's what had always happened to her.
>
> —**Jamie Klim, Coordinator of Respite Services**

munication and socialization skills must all be taught in the residence. The only skills the residence does not need to focus on are work skills. These should be taught in the work place or at an employment training center.

Work placements must have similar attributes to residential placements. The jobs generally held by people with autism require consistency, and follow a set schedule (Gerhardt & Holmes, 1997). Because people with autism thrive in structured environments (Schopler, Brehm, Kinsbourne & Reichler, 1971; Comer, 1995), many of them seem to find work highly satisfying and very therapeutic. Norm and Barbara Greenberg's son works at a Wawa, Inc. convenience store:

> *Steven's job is making salads. The job requires good cutting skills, eye-hand coordination, and weighing skills. It also takes good organizational skills, because he has to put all parts of the salad together, and then label and stack them.*
>
> *Steven lives for structure, and his job is a structured, organized, scheduled activity. He goes to work at the same time three days a week. His peers at Wawa love him because he is a working machine. He would work more if he could. If he is needed for an extra day, he loves it. His eyes light up when he goes to work. Work is very positive for him.*

Some people with autism are able to work as independently as Steven, but others require more support. Employment programs must provide varied levels of independence in the work place to suit each person. For adults who require a great deal of support, employment should be provided in secure work settings. In secure work programs individuals are taught adaptive work and life skills, and contracted work is brought in for completion. Adults work in a highly specialized environment and are carefully supervised by trained staff members.

For those who can sustain more independent employment, a supported work placement should be provided. In supported employment, adults usually work with a job coach in the community. For people who can work virtually independently without specialized supervision, competitive employment placements should be obtained. These jobs are competitive. Steven's job making salads is competitive because he was considered for the job along with nondisabled people. He had to be able to do the job as well as or better than a typical worker in order to be hired. Working as a grounds keeper, a data entry clerk, and packing goods for shipment all without specialized supervision are examples of other competitive employment placements.

EDEN ACRES (A COMMUNITY RESIDENTIAL EXPERIENCE)

◆ ◆ ◆ ◆ ◆ ◆ ◆ ◆ ◆ ◆ ◆ ◆ ◆ ◆ ◆ ◆

In the summer of 1975, responding to an urgent need for respite on the part of parents, an eight-week summer group home was established at Eden for some of its participants. This program, housed in the Bonnell family summer residence, was home to eight young men and women and four full-time staff (2:1 participant to staff ratio). During the five years this program was in place, Eden's staff developed the structure and schedule it would use in later group homes.

This summer program came to a close when the first twelve-month group home was opened in 1980. This home housed six participants and six staff working on 2 shifts of three staff each (2:1 participant to staff ratio). Staff members in the summer program found that eight participants in a home made it a bit crowded. It was difficult to bring everybody together for mealtimes and community outings. The first twelve-month group home, Winsten House, was home to only men. As Eden is concerned about male staff members living with female participants, it does not offer co-educational group homes. Although male staff members treat female participants with the utmost discretion, the home was in the community, and everyone involved wanted to ensure the participants were being welcomed by their neighbors by managing potentially wrong impressions. So, the first home, as well as the next five homes,[4] was opened only for men. Plans were drawn up for a group home for women as there were finally enough female participants to complete the capacity of a home. This home (Farley House), opened in 1992, was only the second in the nation exclusively for women with autism.[5] Since then, Eden has contracted with the State of New Jersey to develop an eighth group home, Dempsey House, scheduled to open in the summer of 1997. Additionally, two supported apartments will be operated by Eden ACREs and will open during the summer and fall of 1997. Dempsey House will be Eden's first attempt at a co-educational home. Although the concerns mentioned above still exist, with experience and safeguards, they will be minimized.

Every group home attempts to offer typical experiences for each participant. During the summer, participants vacation at the seashore and, with the establishment in 1995 of an education and retreat center in Chaplin, Connecticut, participants are now able to vacation year-round in Eden managed facilities. This does

---

[4]   These are Sobolevitch House (1982), Bonnell House (1988), Blaxill House (1987), Lombardi House (1983), and most recently Farrell House (1994).

[5]   The first was opened in 1985 by New Horizons, an organization also in New Jersey.

not preclude, however, vacation opportunities to many other destinations. Group home participants have vacationed in places like Florida's Disney World, the Poconos, Washington, D.C., and Oregon.

As mentioned above, Eden ACREs currently operates seven group homes located throughout the central counties of New Jersey. Each home has six participants. In general, participants are not independent enough to live in supervised apartments or skill development homes. However, plans are being developed for some of the more skilled adolescents and adults to live in supervised apartments in the next 5 years.

PARTICIPANTS

Six variables are assessed when considering a participant for a home: gender, age, physical size, degree of independence, degree of behavior disturbance, and general physical health. These variables determine which home would best suit the participant. Staff members try to keep an equal ratio of more dependent and independent participants in a home,

> Our goal is to have every one of our participants live successfully in the community. This could mean a natural home, a group home, a supervised apartment, or even living by oneself. It all depends on the individual's needs and wishes.
>
> **—Michelle Brooks, Coordinator of Group Home Operations**

and an equal ratio of participants with severe and mild behavior problems, so the make-up of homes is generally consistent.[6] This enables staff members to move from home to home as needed, and makes it easier to bring all participants together for gatherings and outings.

Approximately 50 percent of participants have received training at Eden Institute before entering ACREs. The remaining participants come from state institutions or private programs, and are referred to Eden by the state.

STAFF

All staff members are trained through Eden's comprehensive training program,[7] and further are knowledgeable in crisis intervention, first aid procedures, and CPR. Each group home is supervised by two rotating shifts of three staff members. A low participant-to-staff ratio makes it easier to handle problems. It also enables staff members to be both house companions and intensive teachers. With a

---

[6] Although Eden attempts to keep homes uniform, differences develop based on attrition. For example, some of the newer group homes house younger participants than the more established homes. The newer homes were simply available when the younger participants needed a residential service. This has created an age difference in the homes, but has not affected the types of services being offered. As the age discrepancy between homes grows as more homes are established, staff members plan to tailor services to the age of the homes' participants. In fact, plans for a home tailored to the needs of elderly participants have already begun.

[7] The training given to staff in ACREs is the same as that for staff at Eden Institute. This training is described in Chapter 11.

A Home, a Job, and a Dream
Adam Bloomberg, an adult with autism, happily has all three

Lessons begin at 10:00 a.m. every Saturday at the Triple F farm in Jobstown. Adam Bloomberg saddles his horse and heads out to the practice ring.

His coach, Sue Harrigfeld, guides him through practice. She is currently helping him improve his diagonals, which will make him ride with the motion of the horse instead of against it. He is currently preparing for a show in October.

Mr. Bloomberg is a regular on the Special Olympics circuit, Ms. Harrigfeld said, and placing high at the October show will better his chances of being selected for the 1994 International Special Olympics in Spain. It is his dream to be there.

Mr. Bloomberg, 25, is an adult with autism, but he does not let that hinder his riding success. He rides in the STRIDE (Springfield Therapeutic Riding Instruction for Development of the Exceptional) program at the Triple F farm and has been riding for almost 10 years. He is one of the most experienced riders, said Ms. Harrigfeld, and it is not uncommon for him to place high in a horse show. Her hope is that someday Mr. Bloomberg will be able to join in open competition.

He was one of the two New Jersey representatives at the 1991 International Special Olympics in Minnesota, where he placed fourth in the world. To be selected, Mr. Bloomberg had to place in the top three in Special Olympics qualifying rounds, said Ms. Harrigfeld. Then, it was on to a series of other tests and competitions before final selection.

Mr. Bloomberg's specialty is equestrian, in which he must demonstrate walking, trotting, and cantering. Judges look for improvement every year, said Ms. Harrigfeld, and getting his diagonals down will vastly improve Mr. Bloomberg's form.

After his hour-long session, Mr. Bloomberg cools his horse down and removes his tack. He can ride any horse in the barn, said Ms. Harrigfeld, but is well suited to one named Sissy. If time permits, he might also brush or hose the horse down. From there, it's back to his home and another week of work.

Mr. Bloomberg lives in Robbinsville in Sobolevitch House, one of six group homes run by the Eden Family of Services in Princeton, which provides services for people with autism and autistic-like behavior. He has been living there with five other male roommates since 1988 and does his part with the housework, grocery shopping, and cooking.

"Sometimes it is hard because they are all older than me," he said of his roommates. His relationship with them is brotherly, but his closest friends live elsewhere.

Sobolevitch House and his roommates are just a small part of the history between Mr. Bloomberg and Eden.

"My mother noticed sometime between the ages of 1 and 2 that Adam was different," explained his brother, Eric Bloomberg, 32. It was through word of mouth that Mrs. Bloomberg found Eden. She wanted an appropriate educational placement, he explained, and approached the hunt as many parents do a college search. Mr. Bloomberg began in Eden's school when he was around 8 and has been part of the program ever since.

He recently got a job through Eden's WERCs program. Meaning "Work, Education and Resource Center," the program places adults with autism and autistic-like behavior in competitive jobs. Mr. Bloomberg works a five-day, 40-hour week as a dishwasher at Clancy's Place in the Princeton Shopping Center.

"It's pretty cool," he said with a grin. "I like the employees most because they are funny people my own age. They are very cool."

Mr. Bloomberg has been at Clancy's for a little over seven months. Shortly after he began, he had to face another unexpected transition. He had to cope with the sudden loss of his mother.

Marge Bloomberg was a very important part of her son's life. She made sure he had many interests and encouraged him to learn to ride. She went to the Special Olympics with him, went to all his horse shows, spent weekends with him and firmly supported Eden and all its programs. Sometimes it is hard for him to ride knowing his mother isn't there. He misses her being at his shows, he said.

"God said it was time to go," Mr. Bloomberg said with acceptance. He was there when she died. "She was a great mom."

"Adam's family is the most important thing to him which made it more difficult to lose his mother," said Pam Hileman, coordinator of group home operations at Eden. "It came as a shock to all of the Sobolevitch House parents," she said. The parents of the Sobolevitch residents are now making arrangements to plant a tree at the house in her honor.

Mr. Bloomberg's father died in 1982 and the death of his mother makes him the first participant at Eden to be without parents. Because of this and the admiration shared by many for his family, Mr. Bloomberg is often visited and taken out by other families and volunteers in the program.

Mr. Bloomberg's family life now consists of his brother, sister-in-law Camille, and 11-month-old niece. They spend some weekends, holidays, and special occasions together and work to keep life as normal as possible.

(continued)

The brothers talk on the phone every day, go to baseball games, to the movies, or out to eat. "Adam will do anything. He does the same activities that other people do," said his older brother.

One of Mr. Bloomberg's favorite parts of his family life is spending time with his niece. "She is so funny," he said. He is currently working with the "Hooked on Phonics" system so he can fulfill one of his main goals—to read her a book.

The two brothers are very close, but Mr. Bloomberg's older brother cites more than the death of their mother as the binding element. "As Adam matures, we become closer. We are two normal brothers."

As for his friends, Mr. Bloomberg tries to keep in touch with them on the phone or by visiting. For Ms. Hileman, he tries to make his rigatoni whenever she visits. She has known Adam since she arrived at Eden six-and-a-half years ago to work as a physical education teacher.

"He made it easy for me to assimilate into the school because he had been here since he was very young," she said. "Adam is interested in people and wants to be part of what's going on."

Perhaps it is his interest in people and activities that makes Mr. Bloomberg so welcoming to strangers and new ideas. It is what makes him look to the future and the direction he will take next.

"I'm tired of people doing drugs," he said, and is unable to accept any reason for doing them. He would like to work with drug addicts and help them change their lives. He is also interested in working in a nursery school or helping abused children. Whatever career his future holds, it will most likely involve helping people. People keep him going. "I don't want to be a dishwasher forever," he said.

He also has hopes of living on his own one day, maybe on a farm where he can have a horse. Although plans to stay at Sobolevitch are indefinite, Ms. Hileman said that Eden hopes to one day have Adam live on his own in a supervised apartment complex. Eden does not run such a complex currently, but plans are being made to have one in the future.

For now, Mr. Bloomberg is content with his life. He likes his job, friends and family and home. But off in the distance, the dream of Spain hangs. Perhaps one day you will see him, gold medal hanging proudly, standing on the Olympic platform.*

—by Jennifer Lobley, Special Writer
The Princeton Packet, Tuesday, August 24, 1993

* At press, Adam is living in his own supported apartment. This apartment is one of two that Eden ACREs was awarded a grant by the State of New Jersey to develop.

two-to-one participant to staff ratio, staff members can spend time with individual participants or organize group activities.

Of the six staff positions in each house, four live in the house, with at least two staff members on duty each night. Giving staff members living quarters in the homes makes the staff an integral part of participants' lives. It also makes the neighbors feel more secure and comfortable in interacting with the participants in the home because the staff become familiar to them.

> **S**taff members have to be twenty-four hour teachers, but they really do a lot more. Their goal is to teach, but sometimes they have to be mommy and daddy, or brother, sister, or chauffeur.
>
> —**Annette Cavallaro, Assistant Director of Residential Services**

RESIDENTIAL SCHEDULE

The schedule of activities for participants is designed to simulate as much as possible the experiences of participants' typical peers. However, free time and unscheduled events which are typical of most people usually cause confusion for people with autism. So, staff members at ACREs provide these activities within a structured framework. Staff members plan excursions such as eating lunch or dinner at a restaurant, going to a movie, and even taking a vacation. Participants gain experi-

◆ ◆

This is a typical weekly schedule for participants in Eden's ACREs.

Saturday & Sunday		Monday through Friday	
am	8:00 Rise	7:00	Rise
	8-8:30 Preparation	7:30	Preparation
	8:30-9:30 Breakfast	7:30-8:30	Breakfast and clean up
	9:30-10 Clean up	8:30-9	Travel to work or school
	10-10:30 Language development	9:00	Day services program
	10:30-11:30 Morning activities	11:30-12:30	Lunch
pm	12:30-1 Clean up	3:00	End of day services
	1-2 Rest and relaxation	3:00-3:30	Travel to home
	2-4:30 Afternoon activity	3:30-4:30	Afternoon activity
	4:30-5:30 Dinner	4:30-5:30	Dinner
	5:30-6 Clean up	5:30-6	Clean up
	6-6:30 Preparation for evening activity	6-6:30	Preparation for evening activity
	6:30-8 Evening activity	6:30-8	Evening activity
	8-8:30 Snack	8-8:30	Snack
	8:30-9:30 Evening activity	8:30-9:30	Evening activity
	9:30-10 Prepare for bed	9:30-10	Prepare for bed
	10:00 Lights out	10:00	Lights out

◆ ◆

Participants work hard all day. They need a break when they get home. We try to be sensitive to that. We make their leisure time flexible and easy going, but still within a teaching atmosphere.

To have a good break, they have to know how to spend their break appropriately, so we teach them leisure skills. They might sit in a rocking chair and rock back and forth for half an hour, or go into their room for ten or fifteen minutes to look at magazines, write a letter, or just relax. The learning atmosphere in the homes is pretty intense, so their break is important.

—**Michelle Brooks, Coordinator of Group Home Operations**

ences they would not generally seek themselves, but which are important elements in a typical adult's life.

Participants' days are scheduled from morning to bedtime. Appropriate weekend activities and special events are planned around holidays and vacation times to provide scheduled breaks in the regular routine.

COMMUNITY INVOLVEMENT

In many ways, living in a group home is itself a normalizing experience for participants. Participants live apart from their family, take care of themselves, and are responsible for contributing to their upkeep. Also, the staff members in group homes are often the same age as participants, and so serve as typical peer models. Because group homes are located in the community, participants are able to take part in several activities typical of their nondisabled peers, such as bowling, attending church, roller skating, going to the movies, food and clothing shopping, swimming, going to dances and socials, and attending "canteens" organized by other local service organizations to provide people with disabilities the opportunity to interact socially.

As fully participating members of the community, volunteering to make the community a better place to live is also a responsibility of each participant. Participants give back to the community through several community service organizations. Annette Cavallaro:

> We have participated in walkathons, bikeathons, and several March of Dimes activities. We are also involved in the Adopt-a-Highway, Adopt-a-Beach, and Adopt-a-County-Road programs in New Jersey. We walk the dog of an older man who does not get out much. Because we live and work in the community, we are involved daily in all sorts of activities. We go to the mall, the barbershop and the supermarket. Around the holidays, we bake cookies for our neighbors, and visit the local senior citizen center and nursing home. We try to give as much as we can to the community, to return the support people in the community give us and just to be good neighbors.

It is important that group homes become involved in their communities. Being involved in the community not only gives participants experiences outside the home, but also educates the community about the home, its participants, and what the home has to offer.

Unfortunately, many communities do not tend to immediately welcome the idea of having a group home in their neighborhood. They do not know enough about autism or what the home does. Dave Roussell, Director of Residential Services:

> *People often have fear and anger about having a group home near them. That is understandable. Most people do not know what autism is. Several have been afraid that a group home would lower the value of their property. When discussing a group home with members of the community, we try to alleviate these concerns. We offer to meet with the communities in which group homes are planned, and try to educate people about what having a group home in their neighborhood means.*
>
> *With the last group home we opened, I went door-to-door inviting people in the proposed neighborhood to come see a home that had been established for years. I collected testimonials from the neighbors of our existing homes. They said "Oh, you are wonderful. You cut your grass better than my other neighbors. You have been no trouble at all." We*

Just because a group home is in the community does not mean its participants are community members. Below is EDEN ACREs' Community Experience Participation Summary, designed to ensure that each participant is accessing the community to the extent beneficial to him or her.

Community Experience Participation Summary
Dates: from June 1, 1996 to June 30, 1996

Week of		1-7	8-14	15-21	22-28	29-end	Cum. Total
Community Experience	1-Month Target	Number per Week/Cumulative Total					
Purchase of Goods	8 Times 4 Individual	2	4	3	2	1	12
Community Give	1 Time	0	0	1	0	0	1
Recreation Outdoor	4 Times	1	2	2	2	1	8
Recreation Cultural/Social	1-2 Times	1	0	0	0	0	1
Recreation Indoor	4-8 Times	1	1	2	1	0	5
Other							

Community Involvement

Mary Smith has been involved in the following community involvement activities this month.

1. New Jersey Aquarium
2. Superfresh Supermarket
3. Bowling
4. Library
5. Howell Living Farm
6. Quakerbridge Mall
7. Golden China Restaurant
8. Swimming and Barbecue at Winsten House
9. Mercer County Park
10. Adopt - A- Spot
11. Boston Market
12. Movies
13. Great Adventure
14. Washington Crossing Park
15. New Hope—shopping
16. Eden Shore House - 5 days
17. Dairy Queen
18. Bay Village Water Park
19. LBI miniature Golf
20. LBI Arcade
21. Library
22. Bowling
23. Movies
24. McDonalds

showed members in the proposed community video tapes about people with autism and how Eden teaches them. We showed them how Eden helps people with autism hold a job, and we took them on tours of our homes. Most people understood what we wanted to do and were supportive, but there were still people who had reservations about the development of the home.

There seem to be a few people near each of our homes who remain uncomfortable with our presence. To reassure them, and to maintain the respect of the rest of the community, we are careful to keep our houses well groomed. We regularly have landscapers come in to cut the lawns, trim the bushes, put mulch around the flowers, change the flowers throughout the year, and make sure that our homes are positive additions to the appearance of the neighborhood.

Our efforts have changed the opinion of many doubters. For example, after we had gotten settled in our last group home, we had an open house for the community. One of the neighbors who had been the most vocal advocate against the development of the home came and said "You know, it has been a year now, and things have been fine. You keep your house very nice. You are welcome."

The home would not have gotten her support if Eden did not care about its place in the community and work with the community in mind in running the home.

CURRICULUM, ASSESSMENT, AND MONITORING

When participants first enter a group home, they undergo a battery of tests to determine their initial goals and to develop an IHP. Although the IHP for a participant in ACREs is officially separate from the IHP developed for participants in WERCs, both contain consistent and similar programs and goals. All of the participants in ACREs are also part of WERCs, and so staff members from both programs come together with parents to develop IHPs and to monitor their implementation. This ensures that staff members in both programs work consistently with participants, and work toward compatible goals.

Overall monitoring of the group homes takes many different forms, and occurs throughout the year.[8] Eden's Support Division performs semi-annual evaluations of each home. During these evaluations, the general condition of the home is reviewed as well as the quality of life for each participant. IHPs are reviewed and their implementation is studied. Each staff member is evaluated on his or her expertise in the use of applied behavior analysis as well as his or her interpersonal relationship with each participant. Families are interviewed to get a "consumer" perspective on how their child is doing and how the group home is doing. Each evaluation is followed by an action plan that precisely details how the staff will make improvements in areas of deficit.

The Eden ACREs Operating Committee also performs an annual program evaluation that is less broad in scope than Eden's Support Division but allows for intense probing into home operations that are both extensive in scope and intensive in nature. Finally, each participant's progress is monitored on a daily and weekly basis through data analysis and weekly staff evaluations of progress on the participant's IEP goals and objectives. With all of this monitoring, there is greater security in quality of life matters as well as dynamism in the learning process in each of ACREs' homes.

---

[8] See section on "Quality Control" in Chapter 11 for a more in-depth discussion of Eden's monitoring system.

The ACREs Curriculum (Holmes et al., 1994) is the road map for remedial programming in the group homes. It relates directly to the Eden Institute Curriculum (Holmes et al., 1991) and the WERCs Curriculum (Holmes et al., 1994). The primary emphasis of the curriculum is residential skills with training in the areas of self-care, domestics, recreations, and leisure skills. Each training unit clearly analyzes the skills to be addressed. For example, the skill in the following box of "making frozen juice" describes the steps necessary to become proficient in making orange, grapefruit, or other juices from frozen concentrate.

Making Frozen Juice

THE TARGET BEHAVIOR
Given the *Sd* "make juice," the individual will independently make frozen juice.

PREREQUISITES FOR THE PROGRAM
1. Appropriate sitting and eye contact
2. The ability to attend to a task for at least five minutes

THE CRITERION
No prompts for each step for 2 consecutive days.

THE MEASUREMENT
Number and type of prompts needed for each trial.

THE PROCEDURE
1. Individual will retrieve juice mix.
2. Individual will retrieve pitcher and spoon.
3. Individual will use can opener or pull tab to open juice.
4. Individual will pour contents of juice container into pitcher.
5. Individual will turn on cold tap water.
6. Individual will fill juice container with water and pour into the pitcher.
7. Individual will repeat step 6 as needed.
8. Individual will stir juice.
9. Individual will clean up area.

PROMPTING TECHNIQUES
1. Full physical prompt—staff member takes the individual's hand and assists him or her to complete the activity.
2. Faded physical prompt—staff member moves the individual's hands or body to begin the activity and the individual finishes.
3. Gestural prompt—staff member points to indicate the correct response.
4. Above procedures are gradually faded until no prompts are necessary.

◆ ◆

Joelle is a 31-year-old woman who has been a participant in ACREs since 1992. She has been with WERCs since 1986. She is verbal and is able to express her wants, desires, and needs, but much of her language is obsessive in nature. She requires frequent redirection from staff members. She is able to follow an independent daily schedule with minimal supervision, and is independent in most of her self-care skills.

This is a summary of her level of performance at her six month progress report for ACREs in 1994. Each of these programs was initiated in 1992.

Progress Report

MEAL PREPARATION

Joelle can read a recipe and identify a meal (step 1), and retrieve ingredients for a main course (step 2) with gestural prompts. Her goal is to master steps 1 through 5.

KITCHEN CLEANING

With gestural prompts, Joelle can ensure that the dishwasher is completely loaded (step 1), turn on the warm water and add soap (step 2), and wash and rinse the pots and pans (step 3). Her goal is to master all 9 steps of the program.

BEDROOM CLEANING AND LAUNDRY WASHING

Joelle can go to her bedroom, retrieve her laundry basket, and strip her bed of sheets (step 1). She can also take the laundry to the laundry room and start the first load (step 2). She initially needed gestural prompts to complete these tasks, but can now do them with only verbal prompts. Her goal is to master steps 1 through 8.

FIRE ALARM

Joelle needs gestural prompts to complete step 1, leaving the house through the nearest exit when given the command "Get out of the house." Her goal is to master all 5 steps.

PURCHASING ITEMS

Joelle can enter the store (step 1), pick out items (step 2), and wait in the check out line (step 3) when given both gestural and verbal prompts. Her goal is to learn the final three steps in the program.

HOUSEKEEPING

Joelle can complete all steps of the housekeeping program independently. She can clean the refrigerator (step 1), clean the bathroom (step 2), mop any floor (step 3), and sweep any floor (step 4). No prompts are necessary.

(continued)

FOLLOWING A SCHEDULE

With physical, gestural, and verbal prompts, Joelle can complete the first three steps of the program. She can go to the office and locate her schedule. She can locate the correct task on the schedule, and she can identify an activity for herself or the group. Her goal is to master all 7 steps.

TAKING MEDICATION

Joelle takes two 20 mg tablets of Prozac twice a day. With gestural prompts, she can complete the first 5 steps of the program. She can go to take her medication at the appropriate time. She can get a glass of water and go to the medicine cabinet. She can locate her medication box and remove the correct dosage, and check the bottle for her name. She can also retrieve the medication log and initial in the appropriate area. Her goal is to master the next and final step, putting the medication and log away.

COMMUNITY INVOLVEMENT

In addition to working on the above skill areas, Joelle will participate in three of the following activities each week:

Bowling	Grocery Shopping	Visit NJ State Museum
Movies	Out to dinner	Shopping
Visit Franklin Institute	Canteen events	Visit Philadelphia Zoo
YWCA swimming	Ice skating	Roller skating
Attend local concerts	Go out for ice cream	Go to church
Visit library	Go to the shore	Visit historic New Hope
Play local sports	Visit arcades	Go to a park

Progress reports are based on the IHP's goals and objectives and are produced on a monthly basis. Each participant's program is reported across skill acquisition, behavior reduction, and social and recreational domains. Community involvement is measured by frequency counts.

EDEN WERCS (WORK, EDUCATION, AND RESOURCE CENTERS)

In the early 1980s, the state of New Jersey tried to serve graduates of the Eden Institute in a general work program for people with disabilities, but found their programs ill-equipped to deal with the behavior challenges and special needs of the adults with autism coming from Eden. The story of one graduate of Eden,

Scott, was told previously. Scott was particularly challenging to the state providers. Within his first three weeks at a generic employment center, he had engaged in a number of behaviors that endangered his safety and the safety of others.

The state agreed that the adults needed a work program designed especially for their needs, and helped Eden found Eden WERCs in 1983. WERCs began by providing six participants with secure, supported, and competitive employment opportunities. Since then, it has expanded to serve fifty-six participants in numerous community jobs and three employment centers.[9] Forty-two participants are also ACREs residents. Most of the remaining participants live at home with their parents or have housing through other agencies. The state refers and funds all participants.

> **W**e have always hoped for as much independence for Steven as possible, and we knew that if he couldn't work, he wouldn't stand a chance of being independent.
>
> **—Norm and Barbara Greenberg**

In a 1991 survey of the parents of Eden Institute's fifty-three former students, 38 percent attended WERCs, and 21 percent entered some residential programs. Twenty-three percent transitioned to less specialized settings, and thirteen percent had moved out of the state. One former student was receiving adult services from an agency other than Eden, and one was attending a program for students with cerebral palsy. Over the past several years, most of the students graduating from Eden Institute enter WERCs. In 1992, five students graduated; four attended WERCs, and one attended a non-Eden residential placement. In 1993, three students graduated. One attended WERCs, one entered an adult workshop, and one began work in a family-owned business. In 1994, five students graduated, and all attend WERCs. In 1995, two students graduated and both attend Eden WERCs; in 1996, four students graduated and all attend Eden WERCs.

PARTICIPANTS

There are no more than fifteen to twenty participants at each WERCs center. Staff members at WERCs have found that this number of participants is the maximum number of participants a program can comfortably serve without creating

---

[9] A fourth work center is being planned, and will open once funding has been approved from the Division of Developmental Disabilities. The other three are the Bendas Center (1983), the Briggs Center (1989), and the Dobias Center (1993).

Driven by Ritual

AN AUTISTIC MAN EXPRESSES HIMSELF

With a pile of white paper and a handful of markers, Mark Driver Johnson can design vivid representations of ideas, people and animals.

But his is a world in which everyday things come a little harder than for others. Mr. Driver Johnson is autistic.

Mr. Driver Johnson, 32, is a participant in the Eden WERCs program, one of the many services offered by the Eden Family of Services in Princeton. When he is not out working at his job at Riviera Finance in the Princeton Corporate Center, he can be found either at the Eden's Bendas Center on Burnt Hill Road or at his home, where he lives with his parents.

Mr. Driver Johnson graduated from school at the Eden Institute in his early 20s, then went to another facility to find employment, explained Peter Gerhardt, director of employment services for Eden. When that did not work out, he returned to Eden to participate in the WERCs (Work, Education and Resource Center) program.

While he has been a part of the WERCs program, Mr. Driver Johnson has also held another role at Eden—that of resident artist. He does everything from scenes to portraits to animals, said Mr. Gerhardt, and only works with markers or pen and ink. His work has been used to illustrate thank you notes and holiday greeting cards for Eden. Recently, a collection of his work was made into a calendar.

Drawing is what he chooses to devote his spare time to. Some of his drawing is done at Bendas Center, said Mr. Driver Johnson but he also works at home.

"His work is a mix between Keith Haring and Andy Warhol," said Mr. Gerhardt. Mr. Driver Johnson, who has no formal artistic training, has developed a distinctive style. His pieces are bold and use a variety of color and labels. Give him a box of 100 markers and he'd use every color, Mr. Gerhardt added.

As people without autism have special skills and abilities, so too do autistic people, explained Steve Foltiny, a teacher and job coach with the WERCs. It just happens that Mr. Driver Johnson's interests and abilities lean toward the arts.

Mr. Driver Johnson, one of approximately 55 participants in the WERCs program, is employed at Riviera Finance through the WERCs program. His job involves sorting through invoices and stamping them as Riviera accounts. Other WERCs participants perform janitorial work and restaurant and convenience store duties.

"You have to find the right job for the right person," explained Mr. Gerhardt. For Mr. Driver Johnson, Mr. Gerhardt had to find a job where he was comfortable and at ease. "It took a while to find the Riviera job, but Mark has been there for over four years and is happy there," he said. "Mark is one of the most professional people at Riviera," said Mr. Foltiny, who used to work at Bendas Center and spent time with Mr. Driver Johnson, transporting him to and from his job. "He loves to work."

He works three half-days a week and then returns to Bendas Center for the afternoon. At the center he and other Eden participants either leave from there to work outside the facility or do a variety of in-house subcontract work, such as the Princeton Chamber of Commerce mailing they are now working on.

Autism is a communication and social skills problem, explained Mr. Gerhardt. Mr. Driver Johnson can read, write and do math, he said, but the autism presents limitations and makes things that we take for granted harder for him.

"His reactions to situations are more immediate. Mark can't put up the social disguises we can to cover our discomfort," said Mr. Gerhardt. He explained that when people are uncomfortable, they can usually smile and get through the difficult situation. In Mr. Driver Johnson's case, such disguises of feeling are nearly impossible.

For the staff at Eden, the task was to develop a support system for Mr. Driver Johnson that would teach him social skills and how to manage in the workplace.

People take such social skills as saying hello for granted, explained Mr. Gerhardt. Mr. Driver Johnson needed to learn that you don't say "Hey buddy, how are you doing?" every time you see someone, as in an office where the same people pass by you two and three times an hour.

A system of prompts was used to teach these skills. A check list was used at first so Mr. Driver Johnson could check off who he said hello to and when. Then he could look at his list and know that he had already done it, said Mr. Gerhardt.

Mr. Driver Johnson also had to be taught about time. He had to be shown how to use his watch and to be aware of when he had a break at work and how long he had to be there and when he needed to return to his office.

In his artwork, the same rituals are found. He has a series of birds that he draws, said Mr. Gerhardt, and he will draw them in order and start again, never deviating from this order. Now, the staff is trying to get him to expand his bird repertoire.

Presidents have also been part of his subject matter, said Mr. Gerhardt. He is interested in the presidents and reads everything he can about them. If Mr. Driver Johnson goes out to buy a book on the presidents he doesn't come back with some light reading, said Mr. Gerhardt. He'll come back with an in-depth study of a president.

He likes to draw those who have inspired him. A recent portrait of Martin Luther King, Jr. is one that Mr. Driver Johnson was quick to mention when asked about his work.

Other interests include music, especially Motown music, said Mr. Gerhardt. One other drawing included in the calendar depicted Sly and the Family Stone.

When not working at Bendas Center, he does a lot of drawing at home, said Mr. Gerhardt. There he has all the art equipment he needs. He is very protective of his work and won't let it out of his sight if he can help it.

"It is just a matter of finding things he likes to do," said Mr. Gerhardt. "Sometimes you have to push him to try something new" to break him out of his routine.

—Jennifer Lobley, Staff Writer,
The Princeton Packet, January 17, 1995, 9A, 12A

I think my son Craig is one of the highest wage earners in Eden's programs. He was working for the township raking leaves, and made a lot of money. The last financial statement he sent me showed that he was making over a hundred dollars a week. I thought of asking him for a little loan.

—Al Scocco

unnecessary distractions. In addition, employment centers are kept small because people with autism do not generally work well in large groups. As in ACREs, having small groups also helps maintain a close connection between participants and staff members.

There is about a one-to-five ratio of women to men in the centers. All participants reside either in an ACREs group home, with another service delivery agency, or with families in the community. Participants enter WERCs from the Eden Institute and other programs both within and outside the state of New Jersey.

The placement of participants in centers is determined by availability of space, and, as in ACREs, participants with a range of abilities are placed in each WERCs program. This provides participants who have fewer skills with opportunities for positive peer modelling, and allows more able participants to have extra responsibilities around the center, such as making lunch for the rest of the participants, or writing up a daily schedule for events at the center.

Peer modelling doesn't generally occur naturally with participants, but it's a good way to learn, so we try to teach it. We do a lot with peer-led groups. At one center, a participant leads an exercise group on a regular basis. He calls and models all the movements. At another center, we have social interaction activities, like baking a cake, with one chosen leader to guide the activity. The leader is in charge of asking someone else to, for example, get the eggs and milk, and work with everybody cooperatively. They have only minimal supervision from a teacher or job coach.

—Peter Gerhardt, Director of Employment Services

STAFF

There is a general ratio of one staff member for every three participants across Eden WERCs, but that ratio varies for different types of employment opportunities. Some participants require one-on-one assistance to complete work. Others, in supported employment placements, may have a four-to-one ratio with staff. And in competitive work placements, almost no assistance from staff members is needed.

EMPLOYMENT OPTIONS

As mentioned above, Eden WERCs offers three levels of employment: secure, supported, and competitive. At the most basic level, participants work in a secure employment environment, which means they perform jobs or receive job training in the employment center with close supervision. Participants in secure employment have done many jobs, including manufacturing items from raw materials, and creating crafts, ceramics, wood-shop products, and other simple goods. Much of the work is subcontract work from local companies, but some of it comes from larger companies, such as Johnson and Johnson, Sunrise Professional Service, United Distillers, and IBM. Participants are taught product completion and quality control, and are encouraged to increase the amount of time they can attend to tasks.

> **P**articipants who don't have outside employment all make money in the center. And they are out in the community at least one day a week doing food shopping, eating lunch out, or taking part in other community activities. On some days, the employment centers are empty because everybody is out.
>
> Every participant who doesn't have outside employment could conceivably get a job. We just have to work on coming up with the proper supports. Only about five people present a real challenge to us in figuring out what supports are necessary, and what the right job match is. But that's what we do.
>
> —Peter Gerhardt, Director of Employment Services

Participants who are able to complete secure employment jobs well and have successfully developed skills in daily living are placed in supported employment settings. In supported employment, one to four participants work at a job location with a full-time job coach as a supervisor. The job coach instructs participants, reinforces appropriate work skills, and deals with any unacceptable behavior that participants may exhibit. Participants perform assembly jobs for several companies, clean offices and apartments, price and stock items at food markets, do mass mailings, package goods for shipment, and perform data entry services.

Participants who no longer require immediate specialized supervision are moved to competitive employment settings. Competitive employment is an extension of the supported employment option. Participants perform similar jobs, but without the support or instruction of a job coach. Participants in competitive employment have over the years been employed in food markets, hospitals, in local corporations as janitorial staff, and as dishwashers and busboys in restaurants and country clubs.

Currently 66 percent of participants at WERCs are involved in some type of community job placements. Although only a few participants are currently able to hold a competitive job placement, ap-

> **H**aving participants in the community educates the community about what people with disabilities can do. National figures show that 90 percent of people with severe disabilities don't have any job at all. Currently, two thirds of our participants are involved in some type of community job placement, so we feel pretty successful. One participant works thirty-five hours a week, and another works twenty-five to thirty hours a week. They don't have job coaches, but do have natural support systems in place to help them be successful. Many other participants work between five and twenty hours in the community each week.
>
> —Noreen Miele, Assistant Director of Employment Services

proximately 65 percent have supported employment placements while 35 percent work in secure employment placements. The number of participants in each type of job placement fluctuates a little as participants move to more challenging placements, or fall back on more supportive placements because of behavior or other problems. This "safety net" effect ensures that no one at WERCs is ever without work. Eden expects the general number of participants in each type of employment setting to grow as WERCs grows to serve more graduates from Eden Institute and other adults with autism who require services.

FINDING JOBS AND MAKING A MATCH

Staff members at WERCs solicit jobs for participants by networking with local companies and by marketing participants' employable skills. Peter Gerhardt, Director of Employment Services:

> To solicit work, we go through a networking process. We make contacts with some businesses, and they in turn make other contacts. Most of our secure employment jobs are obtained through word of mouth. For example, people at a local company had a mailing done, and liked the quality of the work, so they referred another company to us. We also visit businesses to advertise what participants can do. We developed a Business Advisory Council comprised of local business leaders to let local companies know how they could benefit from hiring our participants. Now that the Americans with Disabilities Act is in effect, it really behooves companies to consider working with us. We are well versed in the requirements of the ADA, and can help companies meet them.
>
> However, getting an opening for a job is a long process. It may take two or three visits, with four or five phone calls before companies agree in principle to try something. This is especially true of bigger companies that are less willing to change the way they have done things. Small companies, with under twenty employees, are much more willing to listen to us.

Noreen Miele, Assistant Director of Employment Services, does a lot of networking for WERCs. She explains how she approaches companies:

> When I approach businesses that have jobs our participants can do, I do not stress participants' disabilities. I do not want a participant to

*get a job because someone feels sorry for him. I want him to get a job
because he has good skills, and does good work. That is what I sell. I
show businesses what participants can do, and show them our past
records. I give them references from other companies in which participants have worked. These references attest to the quality of participants' work.*

When companies offer employment opportunities to WERCs, a process begins to match the job with a participant, or several participants if the job requires
a group. The first step in determining a job match is to figure out exactly which
skills the job requires. The employer outlines the basic skills needed on the job,
and the staff at WERCs fill in the specific details of the job. Peter Gerhardt:

*When finding the right job match for a participant, we look at many of
the same things anybody looks at in a job. We look at how enjoyable
the job is, what sort of support an employee would receive, what the
pay is, and whether the job has opportunities for growth. Next, we
assess participants in need of jobs, and whether they would be able to
meet the demands of the job.*

*Before we think about who would best fit in a job, we do the job
ourselves. We have to know the details of the job. If it is a cleaning
crew, for example, we would learn how many rags are used, where
they are kept, and when things have to be cleaned. When we then
bring a participant into the job, we have a better idea of what all the
job demands are, and can offer more effective support.*

After talking with the employer, and assessing the skills the job requires, staff
members at WERCs consider who would be best suited to the job. Peter Gerhardt:

*In one job, an employer wanted someone who could be there at 9:00 in
the morning. That is pretty easy for most of the participants. But the
employer also wanted someone to work until 3:00. That narrowed
down the pool. Most participants do not initially stay motivated that
long. The job required collating and sorting skills, and was in a*

*somewhat noisy environment. That
reduced the pool a little more.*

*When we got a pool of potential
candidates, we asked the employer if we
could bring several of them in and
assess them working in the actual
environment. That was a challenge for
the employer, because she was obligated
to pay them during the assessment
period, but she also wanted the most
qualified worker for the job.*

We also did a regular job interview, but our participants are generally nonverbal, so the interview did not provide the type of information the employer wanted to know. She wanted to know how quickly the person works, how cooperative he is, and what type of supervision he would need. Trying the participants out in the job was like a hands on job interview. Seeing the person at work gave the employer the sort of information she wanted, and made sure the best person for the job was chosen.

Jobs are usually solicited from companies for WERCs participants in general, but they can also be solicited for specific participants. Peter Gerhardt:

Adam is one of the most able participants at WERCs. But he also has some very challenging behavior, mostly related to staying focused on his work, and had been fired from jobs in the past. One of Adam's first jobs was working in a convenience store. But in the busy store environment, Adam's desire to socialize with the other employees interfered with everyone's productivity. Additionally, when directed back to work, Adam would often lose his temper. After being released from the store, we placed Adam in the kitchen of a restaurant where his primary responsibility was washing dishes. Although Adam still had the opportunity to socialize with his co-workers, in the quieter, less public environment, this was not a problem. This job match worked out so well that Adam remained with the restaurant until it eventually closed.

When a participant begins a job, especially a job in the community, staff members at WERCs continue to assess the participant's skills and the demands of the job. Continual assessments ensure that the match remains a good one for both the participant and the employer. Assessments also help resolve the minor difficulties participants tend to have when first starting a job in the community. As Peter Gerhardt explains:

We can teach mail sorting, filing, packaging, and collating. But it is difficult to teach all the associated job skills, such as greeting appropriately, knowing what to do in an emergency or if work runs out, how to take a break appropriately, what to do if the soda machine does not work, and what to do if somebody bumps into you accidentally as they are passing by and knocks the work off your work station. These are all little things, but we have to design effective strategies to enable the participant to deal with these situations. That is why we have continual day-to-day assessment of the participants on the job.

These daily assessments are part of a broader schedule to assess and monitor participants' progress.

After we've made an initial job match, we have to do constant assessments because job matches change. The job demand may change, or people the participant identified with, and came to work well with, may move on. The participant himself may be ready to move on. We all move on. I worked in a college admissions office and in a clothing store, but I never intended for that to be a career. We try to give the people here opportunities to move on too.

One participant, however, has been working at Wawa for over eleven years. It's not usual that someone stays with them for that long. We could argue that he should have other job opportunities presented to him, but all signs indicate that he still enjoys his job. He looks forward to going there, he interacts well with the people, and he makes over twice the minimum wage. If another job opportunity came up that we thought was a spectacular job match for him, we might consider offering it to him because we don't want to deny him an opportunity, but we're not actively seeking to change his job.

—**Tyffini Dodge, Coordinator of WERCs Operations, Briggs Center**

CURRICULUM, ASSESSMENT, AND MONITORING

Regular assessments are conducted for participants to keep their skill profiles up to date, and address any problem areas. Assessments include a standardized vocational assessment, an assessment of general and specific vocational or task related skills, a communication skills assessment, and a social skills assessment. Although many of the assessments are geared toward vocational skills, they are generally conducted at both WERCs and ACREs for those participants who are members of both. Staff members from the two programs jointly assess participants' abilities in order to develop consistent, comprehensive IHPs for both programs.

Standardized Assessment

The Vocational Adaptation Rating Scales (VARS) (Towner et al., 1989), a standardized assessment measure, is completed for each participant entering WERCs. The VARS provides both a frequency and severity rating on 133 individual work-related items which are then grouped into several categories: verbal manners, communication skills, attendance and punctuality, interpersonal behavior, respect for property, knowledge of rules and regulations, and grooming and personal hygiene.

After entering WERCs, a VARS assessment is collected for

The assessments we do are like checklists so we can say "Okay, a participant is really lacking in this area, and doesn't have these skills at all. These he displays in certain situations, and these he can generalize to other situations. Let's start by working on this skill, and let's work on it in a way that will help him get this job."

—**Michelle Newman, Supervisor, Bendas Center**

each participant approximately every six months, and is part of a progress report. The progress report documents gains made by a participant and indicates areas in which he may have problems, or need additional training.

The VARS assessment does have some disadvantages. The normative group on which it is based consists primarily of individuals in the mild to moderate range of mental retardation, and it excludes people with other disabilities or different degrees of ability. However, the VARS was chosen for its ease of implementation and the broad scope of its assessment. It is designed to be completed by direct care staff with a minimum of seventy hours of direct contact with a participant, and it provides a reliable tool for the ongoing assessment of a variety of general work-related behaviors for adults with autism. However, because it is not an ideal measure of abilities, the VARS assessment is not used to determine the types of employment most appropriate for a participant. It is used mainly to identify areas in which participants need more training. Skill based assessments are employed utilizing the WERCs Curriculum as a foundation.

Skill Based Assessments

The WERCs Curriculum format enables participants to be assessed on their ability to perform certain skills that are often required in their jobs. These include collating, sorting, filing, sealing, labeling, stamping, and a variety of assembly and packaging skills.

Participants' employability skills are also assessed. These are skills which do not directly relate to completing a job task, but are needed to increase independence across a variety of work environments. Employability skills include the ability to remain on task without supervision, the ability to identify, gather, and maintain an adequate supply of work materials, the ability to monitor and maintain an acceptable level of quality control, the ability to monitor and respond to time and production cues in the environment, and, if appropriate, work-associated physical skills such as mobility and fine motor coordination.

A comprehensive battery of skill based and employability assessments is done when a participant enters WERCs and once a year from then on. However, staff members conduct abbreviated assessments on an ongoing basis and compile these into three additional assessment reports each year.

Communication Skills Assessment

Staff members at WERCs conduct several assessments of each participant's communicative ability. On entering WERCs, participants are given the Eden Services' Speech and Language Assessment (Holmes & Holmes, 1985) and the Eden Services' Functional Communication Questionnaire (Weitzner & Holmes, 1990). These are skill based assessments that reflect Eden's Communication Curriculum and test skills such as identifying objects, making appropriate eye contact, answering *wh* questions, and communicating simple messages. These assessments enable staff members to design speech and language programs and goals for participants' IHPs. After entering WERCs, communication skills assessments are conducted monthly.

> **I**f we want to work on saying "excuse me," we will begin by setting up an artificial situation. We might have the participant interrupt a conversation two teachers are having, and practice saying "excuse me."
>
> Then we would make "excuse me" a functional communicative tool. We might have the participant say "excuse me" at their job during the day. If he collects trash from offices, he would have to say "excuse me" each time he reached for the trash can, or he may need to say "excuse me" each time he knocks on a door.
>
> —**John Gennuso, Supervisor, Dobias Center**

Less formal communication assessments are performed during the process of analyzing a job before a participant begins work. There are three steps in assessing

communication skills on a potential job. In the first step, a speech therapist identifies the receptive and expressive communicative requirements of a job. In most cases, this is done by directly observing the job being completed by a worker without a disability. In the second step, the potential employer prioritizes the requirements identified by the speech therapist. In the final step, potential employees are assessed according to their ability to meet the communication requirements of the job. Their abilities are assessed according to data collected during a trial period. During the trial period, the participant works at the job site under the supervision of both staff from WERCs and the potential employer.

An inability to meet the communication requirements of a job does not necessarily disqualify a participant from placement consideration. The speech therapist, job coach, employer, and co-workers are often able to develop specific on-the-job training programs designed to improve the participant's skill.

Specific Social Skills Assessment

A social skills checklist is completed for participants entering WERCs. The checklist assesses a participant's ability to wait in line, knock on closed doors and wait before entering, use appropriate greetings and responses, purchase lunch or break items, eat appropriately, respond to emergency situations, and attend to personal appearance and hygiene. Social skills are assessed annually for participants after entering WERCs. However, if a participant holds any type of community based job, social skills are assessed much more often. In some cases, weekly assessments are done. In community employment, having the appropriate job related social skills is often more important in obtaining a job than having the actual production skills to do the job. Peter Gerhardt:

> *A participant can have great production skills, but inappropriate social skills, and he will lose a job much more quickly than someone who has appropriate social skills and inferior production skills. For example, Mark has been a competitive worker at a local finance office for about two years. We had taught him to say "Hi" when he sees*

> *someone walk by. His work environment, however, is fairly busy, and people were walking by his desk two or three times in five minutes. He was saying "Hi, buddy, how are you doing" every time a person walked by. We had taught him to do that without realizing how it would affect the other workers.*
>
> *He was going to lose his job because of the disruptive impact this had on the office; he was annoying everyone. People were walking far out of their way to avoid his desk, which significantly restricted the benefits he could reap by working in the community and being a part of their social environment. Despite this, he was producing goods at 110% of what they expected of a typical worker, and had 100% quality control. We went in and worked with him again to identify when to say hello. We developed a chart system which he used quietly to check off when he greeted someone. That worked well for a while.*
>
> *When his hours increased, another problem came up. He would greet someone at the beginning of the day, and then not say another word to them. At his review period, the employer was again concerned that the job might not be right for him, because he did not talk to anybody, and did not seem happy. So, we again went in and developed a much more flexible and appropriate schedule for him to identify when and how to greet people. It worked.*
>
> *Staff members at WERCs did finally find the right supports for Mark, but a very simple social skill of greeting almost lost him his job, independent of the fact that he was working better than any worker ever had at the job. That is why social skills are so important in maintaining employment.*

As with ACREs, WERCs has a curriculum (Holmes et al., 1994) based on remedial programming like the curriculum of Eden Institute. The WERCs curriculum focuses on the skill domains of introductory work skills, manufacturing

Clerical Collating I

THE TARGET BEHAVIOR
Given the *Sd,* "Collate," the individual will independently complete, with 100% accuracy, a predetermined number of sets.

PREREQUISITES FOR THE PROGRAM
1. Attending skills
2. Introductory work skills

THE CRITERION
No prompts for each step for 3 consecutive days.

THE MEASUREMENT
Number and type of prompts needed for each trial.

THE MATERIALS
Collator, pages to be collated, rubber bands, and baskets.

THE PROCEDURE
1. Individual will retrieve work materials.
2. Individual will collate last page of set into collator.
3. Individual will collate next to last page of set into collator.
4. Individual will repeat step until all pages are in collator.
5. Individual will retrieve rubber band and place around collated set.
6. Individual will place banded set into "finished" bin.
7-12. Individual will continue working for 1, 3, 5, 15, 30, 60 minutes.
13. At end of session, individual will return: a) collator, b) basket, and c) rubber bands.
14. Individual will report amount of completed work to staff.
15. Individual will record amount of completed work in subcontract ledger.

PROMPTING TECHNIQUES
1. Full physical prompt—staff member takes the individual's hands and assists him or her to complete the activity.
2. Faded physical prompt—staff member moves the individual's hands or body to begin the activity and the individual finishes.
3. Gestural prompt—staff member points to indicate the correct response.
4. Above procedures are gradually faded until no prompts are necessary.

skills, subcontract skills, and community skills. Each of these domains has task analyzed programs that address necessary skills for being a proficient employee in the work force. (See the box above for an example.)

The VARS, skill based assessments, communicative skills assessments, and social skills assessments for each participant are compiled every three months into a progress report. The progress report measures how well a participant has achieved the goals of his IHP and helps staff members determine if changes need to be made. If a participant is having trouble with a particular program, staff members will meet to troubleshoot the problem. A participant's progress is measured against baseline measures taken when he first entered the program. Progress is also measured against data from the participant's IHP of the previous year.

The IHP forms the basis of each participant's progress report. IHPs are developed once a year through the collective efforts of the family or guardian, staff members at ACREs and WERCs, and the state Case Manager.[10] Developing IHPs across both ACREs and WERCs ensures consistency in the two services. To maintain this consistency, daily logs are shared among the services and the participant's family if he lives at home.

Initial drafts of IHPs are compiled by a participant's teacher or job coach, along with the participant's speech therapist. The supervisor of the center and the group home manager then review the report and pass it on to the assistant director of the program, the director of the program, and finally the Executive Director of Eden. The family and case manager also review the IHP and suggest changes or modifications. The goals developed for a participant in his IHP guide his programming throughout the year.

---

[10] Although a participant's progress is measured in depth once a year during the development of IHPs for the ensuing year, staff members at both WERCs and ACREs are given monthly opportunities to suggest alterations in a participant's IHP.

◆ ◆

This is a summary of goals for Paul as presented in his WERCs IHP for 1994. The goals reflect Paul's progress to date, and provide a synopsis of his formal WERCs IHP. The goals give a picture of the type of skills on which participants in WERCs focus.

Goals Summary

CLEANING BATHROOM MIRROR
Goal: Independent completion of all steps of the program, from retrieving to returning the spray glass cleaner and paper towels from a carrier. Emphasis on quality control.

TRASH COLLECTION
Goal: Independent completion of steps 2, 3, 4b, and 5b (locate full trash can, open trash bag, pick up and empty trash into bag, and return can to proper place). Completion of step 10 (returning the trash can to its proper place) with one gestural prompt. Completion of step 11 (proceed to next full trash can) independently. Color codes for prompts will be used when on a cleaning crew.

VACUUMING
Goal: Chaining of steps 10 and 11 (move various pieces of furniture and return them to their proper location) with two or fewer gestural prompts. Note: Use the same vacuum every time in order to give Paul a consistent method by which to turn on the vacuum.

TABLE SETTING
Goal: Independent completion of the entire program, but for one table only.

TABLE CLEARING
Goal: Independent completion up to step 5 (carry own plate to the cleaning area).

MEAL PREPARATION
Goal: Completion of step 6 (making of main dish) with two or fewer gestural prompts.

LOADING DISHWASHER
Goal: Chaining of steps 21 and 22 (locate detergent and place it in the dishwasher).

(Continued)

DUSTING

Goal: Chaining of steps 1 through 5 (gather materials, go to first area to be dusted, use social courtesies such as "excuse me" if needed, dust flat, open surfaces, and lift and dust under objects) with three or fewer gestural prompts.

CERAMICS, POURING MOLDS

Goal: Independent chaining of steps 14 through 18 (stir slip, retrieve pitcher and ladle, fill pitcher, and pour mold). Emphasis on motivation and attention to the task.

CERAMICS, BISQUE

Goal: Completion of steps 4 through 11 (including retrieving cleaning supplies, filling bowl with water, sponging off the piece of bisque, emptying bowl, selecting paint or glaze color, and retrieving appropriate paint or glaze) with two or fewer gestural prompts.

SUBCONTRACT WORK SKILLS

Goal: Paul will double rubber band newsletter in post office format with two or fewer prompts per tray. He will also independently request more materials as his supply is depleted.

WOODSHOP SANDING

Goals: Completion of step 7 (sand flat surface for one minute). Use of chalk prompt to indicate that the project is finished.

FIRE ALARM

Goals: Consistent compliance leaving the building with one gestural prompt upon hearing the fire alarm.

◆ ◆

Chapter 10

Families

· · · · · ·

Our second responsibility is to the families of individuals with autism. We must help them understand autism and how they can help their children reach their full potential. We must be ever cognizant of the stresses a family with an individual with autism encounters and must be diligent in our efforts to support the family members.

—**Eden Credo, 1991**

It does not take many overnight experiences with a child or adult who has autism for a member of Eden's staff to gain a deep respect for the challenges that families face, especially parents. Families are an integral part of the services offered at Eden. Families are the primary decision makers regarding their child's programming, and they are an indispensable element of his therapy. They are central to the design of new programs, and they are the most powerful advocates for services for people with autism. This chapter discusses the essential role of families in the treatment of their child at Eden.

Parents often get together and help out around the school, which gives us a sense of family, of belonging. It's hard having a child with autism, and having to explain his disability to people all the time. We have our own way of talking to our son, and people look at us as if we were crazy. For example, we say "Hands quiet." Who speaks that way? I have to deal with problems that no one I know has had to deal with. I usually think I can deal with the challenges I face alone, but I know that with Osi I don't have to bear the burden all by myself. That makes a big difference. I know that there are people here who care and who will help when I need them.

—**Meme Omogbai**

In the group homes, parents are still very involved in their son or daughter's life. They come in and spend some time, take their son or daughter home for the weekend, and spend vacations together. Parents also support their child's group home in a variety of ways. They come to gatherings and parties, help with the housecleaning, and sometimes invite the group over for a picnic. Also, in every group home, there is a parent who coordinates parent donations to the home in order to make it a more comfortable place for the participants. Parents' involvement with participants in the group homes creates a collaborative and supportive environment. We work together.

—Annette Cavallaro, Assistant Director of Residential Services

PARENTS AS PARTNERS

Eden Institute was founded through the collaborative effort of both professionals and families. Parents are treated as colleagues. They are often as well trained as staff members, and know their child better than anyone else. Parents serve as members of Eden's Board of Trustees, they serve on committees, and they are part of the decision making teams that develop IEPs, IHPs, and behavior management procedures.

Eden gave us the confidence of knowing that we could handle Steven. We also knew that if there was a problem, somebody would help us handle it. His teachers are more than just teachers. Some of them have known Steven for over fifteen years. He's a part of their lives, and they are a part of our family.

—Norm and Barbara Greenberg

Treating parents as colleagues provides them support, and it highlights their importance as agents of change in their child's life. The support Eden offers parents gives them confidence in helping their child. This enables parents to create a more secure and consistent home environment, which translates into greater progress for their child.

PLACEMENT AGREEMENT

When a child is being considered for placement at Eden, the child's family is given a comprehensive introduction to the services Eden offers and the support they can expect from Eden. Parents are presented with Eden's philosophy of treatment, and are briefed in the behavior management procedures Eden employs.[1] This introduction is one part of the "placement agreement" between Eden and the parents of the student or participant Eden serves.

---

[1] In order for their child to be accepted, parents must sign a Treatment Policy Statement indicating their approval of the behavioral procedures used at Eden. A copy of this form appears on the next page.

EDEN FAMILY OF SERVICES
Treatment Policy Statement

It is important that every parent/guardian of a student/participant enrolled in the Eden Family of Services understand methods of treatment utilized as part of our service. Eden employs a full range of options in behavioral technology. This includes strategies for both accelerating and decelerating behavior. The purpose of this statement is to ensure that Eden's treatment techniques for modifying behavior are understood.

Behavior accelerating techniques are categorized as follows:
Discrete Trial Theory Utilizing
◆ Positive Reinforcement
◆ Prompt/Fade Techniques
◆ Shaping Procedures
◆ Chaining Procedures
◆ Negative Reinforcement (for increasing response time, compliance, and adaptive behavior)
◆ Generalization
◆ Selected Reinforcement Schedules
◆ Incidental Teaching

Behavior decelerating techniques are categorized as follows:
◆ Extinction
◆ Selected Reinforcement Schedules
◆ Aversive Conditioning
◆ Time-out
◆ Contingent Exercise
◆ Overcorrection
◆ Flooding
◆ Negative Reinforcement (for decreasing response time, noncompliance, and maladaptive behavior)
◆ Physical Restraint
◆ Chemical Restraint

It is important for parents/guardians to be familiar with Eden's accountability process and how behavior decelerating programs are developed. Parents/guardians are included in the development of any and all behavior reduction programs designed for their child. No procedure can be used without consent from parent/guardian as well as our behavioral oversight committees (Behavior Management Committee, Human Rights Committee). Parental consent must be free and informed.

I/we have read the foregoing **Treatment Policy Statement** and support its spirit and intent.

_____   _____
Parent or Guardian   Date

_____   _____
Parent or Guardian   Date

The other important part of the agreement outlines expectations Eden holds for the parents' involvement in their child's life at Eden. Parents are expected to take part in the training Eden provides, visit their child's classroom, group home, or employment center, help out around Eden's facilities, and possibly become involved at some level with the Board of Trustees. The placement agreement also emphasizes the open and frequent communication expected between parents and teachers, and the priority Eden places on mutual respect. The placement agreement clarifies from the start what Eden expects of families, and what families can expect from Eden. It makes clear that Eden needs the family's support in treating their child as much as the family needs Eden's services and support.

FAMILY TRAINING

Many people with autism need support 24 hours a day, 365 days a year. However, trained professionals are not always available. Giving training to families enables them to extend the therapy their son or daughter receives from professionals. With training, families at Eden are expected to continue skill acquisition or behavior reduction programs in the home as much as they can.

> Without the training I've received and the parent support group here, I don't know if I would be able to cope with Osi. I would be lying if I said I've come to terms with all the implications of his disability. It's nice to have someone to talk to about Osi, and about how I feel in dealing with him. It also helps to know that other people have the same problems, and that there are many ways to deal with the problems we have.
>
> —Meme Omogbai

Family training is begun soon after a child is placed at Eden.[2] The training provided to parents is the same as that given to Eden's staff, and lasts four to six weeks. The training sessions consist of lectures, video tapes, and readings about autism, teaching techniques, behavior reduction techniques, and applied behavior analysis theory. "Homework," or the application of the techniques learned in the classroom setting to their child at home, is a major part of the training. "Homework reports" are reviewed at the next training session with other families in the class and with senior staff members at Eden.

Most families find training extremely helpful in handling the challenges their son or daughter presents. Parents, Barbara and Norm Greenberg:

> *The parent training we received taught us how to handle difficult behavior situations with Steven. We are not afraid to take him with us anymore because we know techniques to help him stay under control. For example, we had a difficult instance years ago during a really rough time we were*

---

[2] Although parents are required to take part in the training, any member of the extended family is welcome to the sessions as well.

When Michael and Patrick came to Eden, we understood how people could institutionalize their children. They were so disruptive that we knew we couldn't continue that way. One of the main things we learned was that everything was at an equal level of disruption for us. Michael and Patrick do a lot of heavy breathing, but quite honestly, who cares? It's not appropriate, but knocking over lamps is a lot less appropriate.

The parent training taught us basic behavior modification techniques, but first they told us to decide what the biggest problem was. Then we decided what an appropriate contingency would be, and learned to be consistent. One of the first things we addressed was Michael's aggression. I had switched to contacts because Michael would hit my glasses off my face. I had adapted to suit him, but there was no pressure on him to change. That was indicative of how he and Patrick ran the house. We started a program to press his arms at his side when he hit and say firmly, but not in anger, "No hitting." He rarely hits anymore. It took a long time, because aggression was one of his favorite things, but it worked. There are many similar techniques we learned through the training.

—Judy Farrell

having with Steven. We were in the supermarket, and had gotten to the check-out counter with no problem. Then, for no reason whatsoever, he started to punch Barbara's arm. She had a winter jacket on, but still ended up black and blue. We got out of there quickly and immediately called the school. They went over some of the behavior management techniques they use, and taught us a special hand squeeze that really got Steven's attention and interrupted whatever he was doing. It worked every time. We never had an incident like that again.

Cheryl Bomba explains how important it is for families to be involved in their child's treatment:

Michelle's mother Donna is a single parent with no living parents of her own, and so had very little support. But she wanted her daughter to learn to take care of herself. Michelle had several problems. She was resistant, nonverbal, aggressive, and self-injurious. Donna studied the techniques teachers at Eden use to teach skills, and started using them in the home. She has been very successful with them. For example, when Donna decided that Michelle needed to learn to sleep through the night, she took all Michelle's toys out of her room and set them up in the garage, so Michelle only had a bed and dresser. When Donna then put Michelle to bed, Donna slept right outside her door, so she could tuck Michelle back in every time she got out of bed. It took several months, but Michelle learned, and now sleeps through the night. That was a big relief for Donna.

> *Donna has also taught Michelle to toilet herself, eat with a fork, knife, and spoon, shower herself, and dress herself. At age 14, Michelle is now completely independent in the home. She is responsible for her own schedule, goes to bed when tired, does not have behavior management problems, buys her own clothes with money she gets by doing chores around the house, collects videos, and has joined several clubs. The only thing Donna cannot do is leave Michelle home alone.*
>
> *Donna can now relax about Michelle's future. She put in six or seven years of hard, exhausting work, but now it is mostly over. Donna has her own life, her own activities, and can enjoy her daughter. She takes her to the ballet, they play tennis together, and go shopping. Michelle is now in the Transition Program. She is going into the Vocational Preparation Program, and is headed toward a good job. Her mother was instrumental in making that possible.*

ONGOING INVOLVEMENT

After participating in training sessions, families begin visiting their child in the classroom, taking advantage of home visits from teachers, and utilizing Eden's after school or respite care services. Parents' use of these services is discussed below.[3] After training, families also begin actively participating in the design and implementation of programming for their child. The family's involvement in providing and determining services for their child is in keeping with Eden's support of family choice.

FAMILY CHOICE CONCEPT

Most national advocacy organizations recognize the important role parents play in choosing services for their children with special needs. The Council for Exceptional Children (1994), the Autism Society of America (Torisky, 1990), and the National Association of Private Schools for Exceptional Children (Holmes, 1991) all support the idea that each decision in a student's programming should be a cooperative venture involving educators, parents, and when appropriate, students. In addition, the education reform proposals of the Bush and Clinton administrations, *America 2000*, focus attention on parents as key players in education reform. The proposal states: "It will take America's parents in their schools, their communities, their homes, as helpers, as examples, as teachers, as leaders, as demanding shareholders of our schools to make America 2000 education strategy work." And the National Governor's Association, in a report on the

---

[3] The services themselves are described in Chapter 8.

Parents come to IEP meetings to let us know what they foresee their child doing, and what they would like him to do. They are an extremely good source of information for us. They have some great ideas for new programs. They have come in and said "Do you have a program to teach —?" And we have said "No, but that's a really good idea. We could use something like that." For example, at one meeting, a parent said "I'm trying to teach Jon how to get undressed, and I can't seem to teach him how to do it. How do you teach it?" We discovered that we didn't have an undressing program. We had a dressing program, but didn't teach undressing. So I said, "Well, we'll work out a program to teach him." It's through that sort of communication with parents that a large number of our programs have developed.

—**Nina Marcus, Coordinating Teacher, Prevocational Program**

status of American education (1988), states that parental choice is essential for education's success.

At Eden, parents make a wide range of decisions about their child's programming. They help to choose what skill programs their child will learn, and they develop IEPs and IHPs along with their child's teachers. They are also involved in day-to-day decisions that affect their child's schooling.

As important as parents' role in developing their child's programming is their role in making decisions about programs Eden will offer in the future is even more important. Eden frequently asks parents what services they perceive their child will need as he gets older. These services become the focus of group discussions between parents and staff and administration at Eden. Once defined and clearly articulated, these services become part of Eden's strategic plan for future service delivery.[4]

A large number of Eden's programs have been developed from parents' suggestions. Perhaps most dramatic are Eden's residential services. The staff and administration at Eden at first were a bit overwhelmed by the idea of providing residential services to those it served. Residential services were a big responsibility, and a big challenge, requiring teachers 24 hours a day, 365 days a year. However, it was obvious families needed residential services. So, working together, families and the teachers at Eden were first able to establish a summer group home to house students over the summer months and then to establish Eden ACRES.

---

[4] The following chapter explains Eden's strategic plan in more detail.

Parent Involvement Summary, 1995-1996

Service	Number of Families	Student's Age
Parent Training	5	3 - 12
Classroom Visits	50	3 - 21
Home Visits	49	3 - 21
Home Consultant Program	13	3 - 12
Parent Support Group	7	4 - 15
Respite Services	36	7 - adult
Emergency Family Support	13	3 - adult

Regularly consulting with parents about the service needs of their child is one way in which Eden is able to develop services proactively. Another way in which Eden is able to plan for services before they are actually needed is by including parents in policy decisions as members of the Board of Trustees. In order to ensure that families had a say in Eden's future direction, By-Laws were developed at Eden's founding which state in part:

> *A bare majority of the Trustees (more than half of the total number, but no more than half the total number plus one) shall be parents or guardians of autistic individuals or individuals with autistic-like communication/behavior disorders enrolled in one of the programs of the Eden Family of Services (Article 8, Section 1).*

Having parents, the representative consumers of Eden's Services, on the Board of Trustees keeps Eden's mission in focus and helps direct the overall governance of Eden's services.

HOME VISITS

Home visits are an extension of the training initially offered to parents. During home visits, teachers from Eden come into the family's home to work with them on effectively modifying their son or daughter's behavior. Teachers offer advice, and help families analyze their child's behavior. Many families find home visits helpful in sorting out the motivations behind their child's behavior, and what parents may be doing to reinforce the problem. Parents, Nancy Cantor and Steve Brechin:

> *Archie has been engaging in some behavior problems at home that we really have to get control of. We are especially concerned about his tantrums. For example, he is really into straightening things. Everything has to be in order, and in its place, or he has a tantrum. He tantrums even if a door is open, a bowl is not in the right place, or if the rug is askew. Nancy Guggenheim, our home therapist, has spent time with us to figure out some of the ways in which we are reinforcing the negative behavior unintentionally, and how to try to work through it. She has been really helpful in getting us to say to him "No, that door is going to be open now." She has also helped us learn to not pay as much attention to his outbursts.*

Archie's school teacher, Denise Burns-Jennings, describes how home visits helped Nancy and Steve modify their approach toward Archie:

> *Nancy and Steve were firm in some areas, but more lenient in others, and so were not being consistent with Archie. For example, Archie has tantrums over not wanting to do things. If he is playing, or otherwise occupied, and Nancy and Steve want to go to Grandma's, he will have a tantrum. They were saying "Okay, we will wait until you are done playing." But that was letting things be set only on Archie's terms, not on their own. With any other child, they would have said "Sorry, it is time to go now." Having a teacher come into their home and work with them and Archie helped them see this.*

Sasha and Dasha Polyakov have also found home visits helpful:

> *We continually get advice through home visits on how to work through problems with Sasha. The practical advice we get is perhaps the most important. For example, Sasha began having tantrums every morning because he did not want to go to school. We asked his teachers for advice. They suggested that we introduce a system of tokens he could get if he behaved well. They then helped us figure out how we could implement this system in our home. It worked amazingly well. We were surprised, because we had been promising him anything to get him to go to school, and these small wooden tokens did it very quickly.*

RESPITE SERVICES
• • • • • • • • • • • • • • • • •

Respite services are another way in which teachers help ease problems families have in the home. Respite services were originally designed to give families a chance to spend some time away from their son or daughter with autism, while teachers worked with the child on behavior management and skill acquisition programs in the home. Respite services have evolved over the years to involve families more. During respite time, families often watch the respite teacher work with their child. They observe the techniques the teacher uses, and discuss questions they may have. Visits from respite teachers are similar to parents' visits to their child's classroom. But respite visits take place in the home environment, and so are more directly related to the family's everyday needs.

> Every family needs a break from their child at some point, but in order to make the home environment functional for the long term, we need everybody to get involved in respite visits. Parents understand that, and they want to learn how to manage their child's behavior themselves.
>
> —Cindy Bregenzer, Coordinating Teacher, Middle Childhood

CLASSROOM VISITS
• • • • • • • • • • • • • • •

Parents are expected to make regular visits to their child's classroom, and have at least two conferences a year with their child's teacher. During visits, they observe their child's program and occasionally engage in role reversal, when they teach their child and the teacher observes. The teachers give immediate feedback regarding progress on skill acquisition and behavior reduction procedures. Donna Vicidomini:

> *Parents sign a contract at the beginning of the year outlining what they are committing to. The contract includes how many school visits they will make, how many home visits they would like, and various services they expect to be able to do for Eden. Although parents are required to come in to the classroom at least twice a year, they are welcome at any time; the door is open. Parents first come in and observe their child in different settings: language therapy, adaptive physical education, and play. Then they sit down with their child and work on a particular task, with the teacher prompting the parents on how to teach their child. That is really a nice activity, because the children are often distracted by their parents watching them. But when we bring the parents in to sit down and work with their child, the child learns, and the parents receive immediate feedback from the teacher on how they interact with*

> *their child. It gives the parents the confidence that they can work with their child, and helps them realize that if they can do it in the classroom, they can carry it over into the home.*

Parents, Eric and Erica Lofgren:

> *The contract we sign each year is our agreement to come into Spike's classroom a certain number of times. When we come in, we watch Spike working, and we work with him. It really does give us perspective. We learn how to deal with Spike at home by learning how he is taught in the classroom. It was especially helpful when Spike was very young to see how the teacher got him interested, kept his interest, and moved him through a situation. After a while, those techniques became second nature to us. We find that they have been useful for us even in dealing with our other children.*

In addition to classroom visits, teachers communicate with parents through daily logs which are kept on each child's progress. These are sent home for parents' information and to receive their comments. Donna Vicidomini:

> *We are in communication with parents every day. We write home telling them what their child did during the day, what progress they made, what they had for lunch, maybe that their child did not eat so well at lunch, and so might be hungry when he gets home. We try to give parents as much information as possible. They often call or write us in addition, so we find out about problems at home right away. We try to get parents involved as much as possible. That gives the children the most consistent environment possible. When teachers and parents are working toward common goals, it gives us both more strength.*

FAMILY COUNSELING

Much of the anxiety, guilt, panic, and other negative emotions parents have are often the results of raising a child with autism without having the proper tools to combat the child's behavior challenges. Eden's first priority is therefore to teach families about autism and equip them with the techniques they need to help overcome their child's learning challenges. If, once parents have been taught to be effective teachers of their

> When Geoffrey first came to Eden, the school put on a Christmas program. He and his classmates were sitting in a row dressed as elves. It was so cute, so moving, and so gratifying to see their hard work pay off in a holiday program just like any other school's holiday program. For the older students, Eden has a prom, and a graduation ceremony with caps and gowns. That may not mean much to the students, but it does mean a lot to us.
>
> **—Charles and Nancy Richardson**

> **W**e went through some rough times with Chris. There were times when we had him on medication for being abusive. We needed to have a lot of communication with his teachers. We needed to be able to put our heads together and say let's try this, or try that. We needed to feel we had some place to go, and weren't just hitting our heads against a wall.
>
> —**Don and Nancy Briggs**

child, they continue to demonstrate symptoms of guilt or despair, Eden offers them counseling. Counseling helps families sort out the negative feelings or frustrations they may still have.

The emotional struggle families endure in raising a child with autism can be highly charged and complicated. Several authors have addressed the impact a child with autism has on the family. See, for example, S.L. Harris, *Families of the Developmentally Disabled: A Guide to Behavioral Intervention* (Pergamon Press, 1983), H. Featherstone, *A Difference in the Family: Life with a Disabled Child* (Basic Books, 1980) about one family's experience raising a child with severe disabilities, C.C. Park, *The Siege: The First Eight Years of an Autistic Child with an Epilogue, Fifteen Years Later* (Atlantic Monthly Press, 1982) which is one of the best personal accounts of raising a child with autism, and for a good discussion of sibling issues, T.H. Powell and P.A. Ogle, *Brothers & Sisters: A Special Part of Exceptional Families* (Paul H. Brookes, 1985), as well as S.L. Harris, *Siblings of Children with Autism: A Guide for Families* (Woodbine House, 1994). See also C.T. Bruey, *Daily Life With Your Child,* in M.D. Powers, ed. *Children with Autism: A Parents' Guide* (Woodbine House, 1989).

The counseling Eden offers is open to all members of the family: parents, siblings, and even grandparents. Although grandparents do not typically take advantage of the counseling services offered at Eden, they play an important role in the lives of families. Grandparents can make the job of parenting much easier through their support and encouragement.

Involving the whole family in counseling results in the best possible environment for the family's child. It also helps keep the family together. Having a child with autism can cause families to split into different parts. For example, the family may not be able to eat

> **T**he kinds of problems that came up in these group sessions over the months—in-laws, sibling rivalry, the responses of strangers to their handicapped child, what would happen to the children when they grew up—were topics that touched a responsive note for most parents in the group.... The process of sharing with other people how difficult life can be with a handicapped child was comforting in itself.
>
> —**S.L. Harris, Families of the Developmentally Disabled: A Guide to Behavioral Intervention**

dinner together, or may not be able to vacation together because of the behavior of their child with autism. The family may develop "roles" or shifts to take care of their child with autism. For example, the mother may spend her evenings preparing their child with autism for bed, while the father helps the other children with their

homework, cleans up dinner, and reads bedtime stories. In families of more than one child, siblings are often treated differently than the child with autism. The demands of the child with autism may cause him to be the center of attention, the ruler of the house. Other siblings cannot have the same privilege.

To bring the family together, Eden counsels each member of the family about the importance of keeping their perspective about their child with autism. He should simply be a part of the family, not its exception, and not its dictator. Eric and Erica Lofgren, parents of Spike:

> *Parents of a child with autism have to have a very pragmatic attitude toward family life. They cannot neglect the whole for the part. They have to deal with the whole family as a unit. That is what will make the family successful.*

BALANCING PARENTS' NEEDS WITH THEIR CHILD'S NEEDS

One of the most common subjects of counseling with parents is their conflict between wanting to protect their son or daughter, and their desire to let him or her lead as independent a life as possible. This conflict tends to become most pronounced when students graduate from Eden Institute's Day School, and are ready to enter residential services. Annette Cavallaro, Assistant Director of Residential Services:

> *It is really hard for parents to leave their children at a group home. They know it is the best thing for their child, and that their child is going to a good place, but there is still a tremendous amount of guilt involved. We try to be as sensitive as we can. Before their child comes to us, we have parents meet at the group home and talk through what the transition means for both them and their child. We make it clear that once their child is with us, they are free to visit or call whenever they like, and even have their child home for visits, vacations, and on holidays.*
>
> *I think parents of a child with autism have a more difficult time letting their child live away from home than parents of typical children, because their child has been so much more dependent on them, and very vulnerable. When parents first bring their children to us, it can be very emotional. When they go home, they call every day. However, once parents see their child get settled in the group home, and can be more independent, they feel more comfortable with their decision. The transition is complete when the group home becomes "home," and not the parent's house, and their child is content and secure.*

Even at a young age, however, parents can have a hard time suppressing their desire to protect their child. Norm and Barbara Greenberg:

> *Ever since Steven was four years old, he has gone to Eden's summer program. That was not an easy thing for us to do at first. He was so young. But it has turned out to be very important for us. It gives us a break from his behavior challenges, and he maintains the skills he has learned. And he loves camp. Letting him go to camp helps us get through the year. It also gives us a chance to do some things alone and with our other son, Paul. While Steven is off at camp, we have gone to Wyoming, Japan, and Hawaii. We could never make these trips with Steven. The time difference alone would be too much for him.*

Although difficult, balancing parents' needs and the needs of their child is crucial to enabling their child to live as independently as possible and for the parents to remain healthy and energized as the child's primary advocates.

SIBLINGS

◆ ◆ ◆ ◆ ◆ ◆ ◆ ◆ ◆ ◆ ◆ ◆ ◆ ◆ ◆ ◆ ◆

Siblings of a child with autism can confront many significant issues. They can feel ignored by parents because of the heavy demands their brother or sister places on the parents' attention. They can feel burdened by the expectation that they help raise their brother or sister. They can feel socially isolated or embarrassed by the nature of their brother or sister's behavior.

> **O**si's younger sister can get him to do things that even I can't, and he's three times her size. She thinks she can make a difference, and tries very hard to do that. Sometimes I worry that it's too much of a burden for a child her age to want to do so much.
>
> **—Meme Omogbai**

Teachers at Eden work closely with siblings, offering them counseling and support groups, as well as the opportunity to be involved in teaching their brother or sister. To this end, siblings can be involved in formal training programs if they wish, but often pick up on the behavior management techniques that their parents use in the home. Parents, Nancy Cantor and Steve Brechin:

> *Archie's sister has picked up on many of the things we have learned with Archie. For example, one night at dinner, Archie began screaming. We had decided with our home therapist that we were going to try to extinguish his tantrums by not attending to them. But it is hard to actually do that when he is screaming. Our daughter Maddy started to tell Archie not to scream, and we told her we were going to try to just let him scream, and not pay attention to it. She said "Yea, that's right, because whenever I tell him to stop, it just makes him to do it more." She wants to figure out how to help Archie too.*

Siblings are included in the services for their brother or sister through activities such as "Sibling Day," when brothers and sisters visit Eden and see, first hand, what goes on. Coming to Sibling Day is difficult for some siblings. Nancy Cantor and Steve Brechin:

> *When Maddy came to Sibling Day, it was very hard for her. It scared her. When she got home, she spent about four hours in her room by herself. She saw behavior she does not yet associate with Archie. Archie is her brother. She can deal with his behavior. It is another thing altogether to be surrounded by a world of people who have problems like Archie's.*

Although having a sibling with autism can be frustrating and disappointing at times, as Harris (1994) says, ". . . most children learn to cope effectively with their sibling's special needs." Eric and Erica Lofgren:

> *We were sitting in a movie theater waiting for a movie to start, and we asked our two daughters how many children they would like to have. The first one said "I'd like three: two girls and an autistic boy." The second one wanted five children: "three girls, a regular boy, and an autistic boy." So clearly, not only is it okay with them to have a brother with autism, it feels like the right thing to do. The younger one especially feels fine with Spike. Recently, she, Erica, and Spike were in the supermarket. Spike had a horrible tantrum, and our youngest daughter Dinah went off and sat on her own until Spike had calmed down. Erica assumed she just wanted to get away from it, but when we asked her later why she left, she said "Because I was so mad at those people staring."*

There are many new books that either focus on the perspective of a sibling or child with autism or are directed at the young reader to sensitize him or her to the unique qualities of the child with autism. We have found the following books to be useful for siblings and/or the young reader:

> Nancy Dalrymple, 1989. *Learning Together.* Available from: Indiana Resource Center for Autism, Institute for the Study of Developmental Disabilities, Indiana University, Bloomington, Indiana.

> Ann M. Martin, 1990. *The Babysitters' Club: Kristy and the Secret of Susan.* New York, NY: Scholastic Books.

Ann M. Martin, 1984. *Inside Out.* New York, NY: Holiday.

Mary Thompson, 1996. *Andy and His Yellow Frisbee.* Bethesda, MD: Woodbine House.

Esther Watson, 1996. *Talking to Angels.* New York, NY: Harcourt Brace & Company.

DETERMINING NEEDS AND WANTS

Parents play many important roles in their child's life: mother, father, teacher, friend. Parents of a child with autism, however, take on an additional role: advocate. Although parents of a typically developing child are also advocates, there comes a time in their child's development when their advocacy is no longer needed.

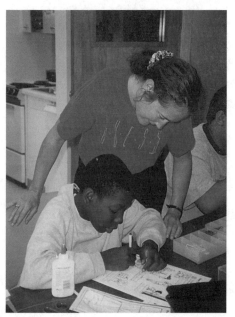

As an independent adult, he assumes that role himself. For the majority of children with autism, however, the parents' role of advocate is continuous. Parents must guide their child's future, both in envisioning the type of services they want for their child and demanding that those services exist.

In offering guidance to parents as they advocate for their child, it has become apparent that there are important similarities between what people with autism need and what typical people want. "Needs" are usually associated with basic biological drives. Every human being needs shelter, food, water, stimulation, and sleep. People with autism have these needs, but they also have a neurologic dysfunction that affects these basic needs. For example, a person with autism could stand in a rainstorm without understanding that he is cold and damp. Others would not, if left on their own, eat enough food to survive. People with autism need stimulation, but the self-stimulation they often engage in may actually be physically harmful. Thus, although the needs of people with autism are basic, the fulfillment of these needs is challenging.

In order to fill these needs, people with autism require additional services. These services would fall into the category of "wants" for people without disabilities, because "wants" are generally considered to be choices one makes above basic needs. For example, people need shelter, but they want residences tailored to their particular liking. People with autism do not, in the same sense, want specialized residences with full time teachers, planned activities, and someone to sched-

ule their day; they do, however, need that sort of residence. And they need employment services, twelve month educational programs, crisis intervention, specialized transportation, recreation programs, and, eventually, geriatric care. These are not optional services for people with autism. Without them, the basic needs of people with autism are not met.

People with autism also have wants, but their wants are, again, different from the wants of typical people. Most people have wants that are driven by social values and mores. They want a better car, a good job, and a happy family. People with autism, on the other hand, most often have wants that are driven by their condition. For example, they may want to twiddle their fingers before their eyes, rock back and forth for hours, or eat french fries at every meal. These are not "wants" in the typical sense. It is difficult to compare the wants of typical people and those of people with autism because for people with autism, their wants are not driven by societal values and mores.

Being aware of the full range of needs people with autism have, and understanding how their wants differ from the norm, makes parents better advocates for their child. They are better able to describe their child's needs, and can therefore better lobby for those needs.

PARENTS AS REPRESENTATIVE CONSUMERS

Throughout history salesmen of dubious moral character have taken advantage of people in need, selling products that do not live up to their advertised qualities. In the nineteenth and early twentieth centuries, many were called "snake oil salesmen." The various potions and lotions they sold were touted as cures to problems that could not be cured through the medicine of the time.

Some of the "breakthroughs" in the treatment of autism seem to parallel snake oil sales. To a certain extent, the media's budding interest in autism is the cause of the sensationalization of treatment methodologies. For example, the news media has promoted the preliminary stages of research with the drug Naltrexone (Maugh, 1991) as a major breakthrough in treating people with autism. However, the research is only in the early stages of evaluating the drug's effectiveness. Not too long ago, the *New England Journal of Medicine* touted fenfluramine, a derivative of a diet pill, as another major breakthrough (Geller et al., 1982). However, after millions of dollars in sales and ensuing research, it was determined that the drug did not have the global effects originally ascribed to it.

Although there are some "snake oil salesmen" in the field of treatment for autism, most techniques and products arise from the eagerness of both parents and researchers to "ameliorate" or "cure" some of the devastating effects of autism. Unfortunately, though, many such "breakthroughs" cause more harm than good. They raise expectations that cannot be fulfilled, they distract researchers from furthering more established methods of treatment, and most importantly, they disrupt the consistent application of proven techniques. Keeping calm in the face of exciting new discoveries may be difficult, but it is absolutely crucial to providing the best treatment to people with autism.

Parents are consumers, representing their child's interests. And as consumers, they must remember *caveat emptor:* let the buyer beware. They must be cautious as they purchase services or products, to ensure that these have demonstrated valid, quantifiable results in treating people with autism.[5]

PARENT ADVOCACY

Parents are their child's best advocate. They know what their child needs. Nobody knows the child better than mom and dad.

—Beth Thomas, Clinical Support Specialist

Many people with autism cannot really speak for themselves, so people have to speak for them who know them really well. Of course, the parent knows them best. And who has the child's interests at heart more than the parent?

—Nancy and Charles Richardson, parents of Geoffrey

For the first twelve years of Robert's life, my father gave me the money to help pay for services for him. Everything Robert got we, his family, paid for. The Division of Youth and Family Services would not help Robert at all. They gave all sorts of reasons why they should not support him, until one day I just lost my temper. I started banging my shoe on the table. That got their attention. From that day on, we have had financial support for Robert. I simply could not give Robert appropriate services without that financial support.

—Mike Walsh, father of Robert

I never want to find myself in a crisis over services for my son. I do not want to be in a situation where I'm so desperate for services that I feel something has to be done right away. The whole idea is to figure out what the level of needed services is and create it ahead of time.

—Helen Hoens

---

[5] See Chapter 5 for Eden's guidelines for new theories and practices.

Parents must be involved in securing services for their child with autism because they alone have the greatest power to cause change. Parents are more effective advocates for their child than state and federal governments, service professionals, or advocacy professionals because they know their child best and have nothing to lose.

Primarily through the advocacy efforts of parents, Public Law 94–142, The Education for All Handicapped Children Act (now The Individuals with Disabilities Education Act), was enacted in 1975. Public Law 94–142 ensures that every child, typical or disabled, receives an appropriate education. More recently, in 1986, Public Law 99–457 (enacted in 1986), which ensures educational services for children from birth to age three, came about in large part due to the advocacy of parents.

Two parents from Eden, Kathy and John Watts, were among those who advocated for Public Law 99–457. Along with their daughter Wendy, they testified before a congressional hearing on the importance of early intervention for children with autism. They informed the Senate Education Committee that early intervention saved their child's life. Without such services, their daughter would have been vegetating at home and unable to acquire life skills. Throughout their testimony, they made reference to Wendy in the audience. Congress listened to them and other parents who testified, and unanimously passed the bill.

There have been services for people with autism established over the past few decades, but many more services are still urgently needed. How-

> **W**e worked with our school district to get Wendy into Eden's preschool service. The district did not recognize autism as a distinct classification, so she was classified as emotionally disturbed, or mentally retarded. We really did not care what classification she was given, as long as the services were appropriate. We knew Eden was an appropriate place for her, and insisted on bringing her here. We had to go to court, and it took over a year, but we won. More importantly, Wendy won. She is still the only child from her school district at Eden.
>
> —**John and Kathy Watts**

ever, for those services to continue growing, parents have to be involved in advocacy efforts. Their involvement includes contacting local advocacy agencies, writing letters to their local members of congress and state representatives, talking about their child and what he needs, and working with people in the field of special education to design and develop the services that their child needs today, and which will be essential in his future. Eden has an unwritten rule that each parent works to the best of his or her ability for the good of every child. If all parents advocate for services, parents who have been "in the trenches" can be relieved by parents freshly in the fight.

Parents, however, also need an advocate. One of Eden's primary responsibilities as an organization is to advocate for parents. How is it that an organization can advocate effectively in the face of limited resources? The next chapter describes fully Eden's model for running a lifespan service organization for children and adults with autism and their families.

I woke up one morning and realized that if I did not get out there and work to get my son services, nobody else would. Some people are better equipped than others to deal with the challenges of life, but I cannot expect anybody else to deal with them for me. I have to do something about them. Advocacy really works. Senior citizens have a large number of programs because they are organized, and they advocate. They spend a lot of time pressing for the things they feel they are entitled to. The disabilities community needs to be just as organized. If parents do not get themselves motivated, down the road they will be looking for a group home placement that is just not there.

—Helen Hoens, mother

Chapter 11

Eden's Model
for
Running a
Service Delivery
Organization

There are many elements crucial to the successful running of a service delivery organization (Drucker, 1990; Stanton, 1989). The organization must have clearly defined lines of responsibility and communication, but retain a collegial atmosphere in which all members of the organization feel a sense of ownership. The organization must carefully select and train the staff members delivering service. It must have a clear administrative structure and a detailed plan for the future. At the same time, the organization must be careful to avoid the risks that come from growing in unintended directions, or not at all. To keep its members focused on its mission, an organization must control the direction as well as the quality of its services through regular evaluations. A service delivery organization must also secure stable yet diversified funding sources, which is especially difficult for organizations that rely on state initiatives. Finally, a service delivery organization must be a responsible member of the community in which it provides services.

This chapter reviews each of the elements required in a service delivery organization. The organization of Eden, including the Eden Institute, Eden WERCs, Eden ACREs, and the Eden Institute Foundation, is used as a model for discussing these elements.

LEADERS, MANAGERS, AND STAFF MEMBERS

Leaders, managers, and staff members are the people who make a service delivery organization run. Leaders establish the culture of the organization. They set the guidelines for the organization's activity, and they plan for its future. Leaders have a vision for the organization, establish the organization's mission, and make sure that managers and staff members remain focused on that mission. Leaders are responsible for the organization's fulfillment of its long term goals, and for the resources required to realize those goals. Leaders expand resources and exemplify the values of the organization. Leaders also take the necessary risks to protect those values.

> Don't confuse management with leadership. You can manage a business, but you lead people.
>
> —General Norman Schwarzkopf,
> *Take Charge*, 1992

Managers are responsible for the daily operations of the organization. They delegate staff members to carry out the organization's activities, and make sure they do so efficiently and effectively. Managers are responsible for the best pos-

> Where there is excitement and enthusiasm there also is usually some kind of vision. People don't get excited about jobs, they get excited about possibilities. Vision is the articulation of possibilities.
>
> Vision keeps things from being boring. Vision is seeing beyond what is there and what we are doing to what we can and should be doing. Vision is what adds excitement to what might otherwise be considered a mundane or routine job.... Organizations with highly-focused individuals are what we call (at least in the short-term) productive organizations. So, the more focused the activities of individual organizational members are, the more productive the organization becomes.
>
> Having vision is to have a purpose. Vision creates a focal point, which in turn creates the driving force within each person. When people have a purpose, they work hard because they are accomplishing something that's worthwhile and meaningful to them.
>
> —From *Championship Management: An Action Model for High Performance* by James A. Belohlav (1990). (Productivity Press, Inc., P.O. Box 13390, Portland, OR 97213-0390; (800) 394-6868). Reprinted by permission.

sible use of the organization's resources. By focusing on the daily, efficient running of the organization, managers provide a balance, or counterpoint, to the leaders' visionary role.

Staff members are entrusted with the business of the organization. They are the providers of services. Because a service delivery organization's purpose is to provide service, staff members are its most important resources. Efficient hiring and training of a quality staff is, therefore, critical.

HIRING STAFF MEMBERS

There are many types of people. Eden hires professionals who look for reasons to become involved in the world around them, and have a "why not" attitude. Conversely, there are some who find reasons not to get involved, saying "Yes, but...." Those who embrace opportunities, and seek out positive change, saying "Why not!" are the type of people a service delivery organization needs. Staff members should also be dedicated, empathetic, young of mind and heart, energized, quick learners, responsible, and trustworthy.

Eden seeks out energetic, "make a difference" staff members through a variety of approaches. First, Eden instituted the Ann M. Martin Scholarship Program (described later in this chapter) to identify the best and brightest high school seniors and stimulate their interest in autism by extending a scholarship for advanced studies in special education or related disciplines. Next, Eden purposely stimulates interest in employment by presenting the challenge of autism and the Eden model at colleges and universities, to address the "change-the-world" attitude of many college students.

> Our third responsibility is to the men and women who work for the Eden Family of Services. They must feel professionally stimulated and challenged. They must be trained to offer the highest quality of program possible. They must have a sense of security in their jobs. Compensation must be fair and adequate. Working conditions must be clean, orderly, and safe.
>
> **—Eden Credo, 1991**

Additionally, Eden attends job fairs with an exciting video and program display to spark interest in serving children and adults with autism. Eden has also found that the extended network of Eden staff is a viable way to attract a quality pool of job applicants; as an incentive, staff members whose referral is hired and passes a ninety-day probationary period receive a $100 "finder's fee."

Eden also uses more mainstream approaches such as advertising in newspapers and posting employment opportunities in high-visibility locations. For senior positions, Eden has used "head hunter" services, but this is rare due to the organization's policy of promoting instead of hiring.

Eden does not discourage hiring family members of staff, but does have a "conflict of interest" policy which calls for the full disclosure of such practices. If the family member is an energetic person, committed to Eden's mission and the relationship is fully disclosed, nepotism has not occurred.

Eden Family of Services' Full Disclosure Policy

It is the policy of the Eden Family of Services that full disclosure will be made to the Executive Director and/or the Chairman of the Board of Trustees when there is a conflict of interest or the appearance of a conflict of interest between the private interests and official responsibilities of an employee or Trustee. Specifically, full disclosure shall be made by the party involved to the Executive Director for employees and to the Chairman of the Board of Trustees for trustees in all potential conflicts of interest including, but not limited to, the following:

- a staff person is related to another staff person.
- a Trustee is related to another Trustee.
- a staff person or Trustee is related to an Eden student or participant.
- a staff person is related to a Trustee.
- a staff person in a supervisory capacity is related to or has a personal relationship with another staff person he/she supervises.
- a staff person or Trustee, or relative or friend of a staff person or Trustee, receives payment from the Eden Services for any subcontract, goods, or services.
- a staff person or Trustee is a member of the governing body of a contributor.

Following full disclosure of a potential conflict of interest or any condition listed above, the Executive Director and/or Chairman of the Board of Trustees shall determine whether a conflict exists and a determination will be made to authorize or reject the condition or transaction, and inform all interested parties of the decision.

Failure to comply with the terms and conditions of full disclosure as outlined above may be grounds for dismissal from employment or the Board of Trustees.

NOTE: Under no circumstances may a parent of a student or participant be employed by any member agency of the Eden Services.

Eden Family of Services' Orientation Period

New staff will function in an orientation status for not less than 3 months nor more than 4 months. During the orientation period, benefits will be limited to salary, state unemployment and disability insurance, and social security. No paid sick days or paid personal days will be allowed.

Upon the conclusion of the 3 month orientation period, the staff member will be evaluated by his/her supervisor as to attendance, punctuality, and all elements of job performance. (Teaching staff will also be evaluated by the Support Services division.) A determination will be made at this point to: offer a full-time position, terminate, or extend the orientation status for an additional month.

If the staff member receives a satisfactory evaluation (B or better rating) by the supervisor (and Support division for teaching staff), the staff member will receive full-time status and benefits will begin. Medical/dental, life insurance, and long term disability benefits will begin the first of the month following the end of the orientation (3 month) period. Additionally, paid sick and personal days will become available per Eden's policies.

If the staff member fails to receive a satisfactory evaluation (B or better rating) upon completion of the 3 month orientation period, the staff member may be offered an additional month of orientation status or may be terminated. If an additional month of orientation is offered, benefits will not begin until the first of the month following the successful completion of the extended orientation period. (See above.)

NOTE: If the results of a background investigation, reference check, or medical examination indicate that a new staff member is not suited for employment with Eden, the staff member will be terminated.

NOTE: Successful completion of the orientation period will result in enhanced benefits; however, employment will continue "at will" and the staff member may be discharged at any time for any reason. Successful completion of the orientation period should not be construed as creating a contract or as guaranteeing employment for any specific duration, or as establishing a "just cause" termination standard.

Difficult Challenges

Because autism is a lifelong disability with often times very challenging behavior, it is especially important that Eden's staff members be committed to providing services, no matter what the obstacles. They must garner rewards from the

often small improvements people with autism make in learning skills and behavior. They must be very self-assured and secure in their ability to make a difference in the lives of those entrusted to them. Above all, they must be completely committed to the mission of the organization.

However, even the most dedicated staff members require reinforcing feedback to let them know that their efforts are having a positive impact. Eden addresses this phenomenon through its highly specific, data-based discrete trial methods.[1] With these procedures, staff members see, graphically, even the smallest gains students and participants make. Improvements in the most challenged children may only be detected through longitudinal graphs of a student's or participant's skill acquisition. The graphs provide tangible reinforcement to staff members, and in turn make them more committed and more refined "detectives" in troubleshooting programs.[2] The discrete trial method gives staff members the confidence to take their teaching skills to any learning environment, and work with people of any level of ability. These are good attributes of staff who implement the kind of services Eden is committed to offering.

Asking For Help

If students or participants at Eden fail to progress, staff members must be comfortable asking others for help. They must understand that failure to progress is not the person's fault. It simply means that the right "keys" have not yet been found to help him learn. Cindy Bregenzer:

> I do not have the right answers every time, but that does not mean that I am ineffective. If something I am doing with a student is not working, I turn to other people at Eden to figure out how to make it work. We come together regularly to discuss students' learning problems, and what might be done to improve particular situations. I have to accept that I cannot know everything, and that it takes a joint effort, with a lot of communication, to find the best solutions.

---

[1] See Chapter 6 for a description of the discrete trial method.

[2] See Chapter 8 for a description of Eden's Troubleshooting Process.

TRAINING STAFF MEMBERS

Hiring dedicated, optimistic staff members is crucial to a service delivery organization's success. But equally important is the training and support the organization gives its new staff members. Training should give them the tools they need to effectively fulfill the organization's mission. Training should enable staff members to feel confident in their efforts and should eventually prepare them to have supervisory responsibility over other staff members.

Once hired, new staff members receive rigorous training. The first component of their training is Orientation Training. This interactive video series introduces new staff members to the continuum of lifespan services provided by Eden, provides an overview of autism and the learning and behavioral challenges associated with the developmental disability, and presents the highly specialized teaching and behavior reduction techniques used at Eden, along with the rationale for their use.

A trainer from Eden's Support Division guides new staff through the video series, gives a written test and concludes the training with a practicum

> It's difficult to teach people with autism because they often take a long time to learn something. Teaching them is exciting too, though, because I have to try many different ways to get them to learn. If the first time I try something it doesn't work, that doesn't mean it's not going to work. It just means that I have to keep trying and be creative.
>
> —**Edha Majumdar, Coordinating Teacher, Transition Program**

session, where the new staff person practices the techniques learned during training with one of Eden's participants. This process is followed so that the trainer can be sure that the staff person understands the techniques both in theory and in application. Within two weeks of Orientation Training, the trainer visits the staff person at work and evaluates his ability to integrate the techniques into the programming of students or participants.

The second component of Eden's training process is Entry Level Training. This intensive, three day training is held bimonthly for all staff newly hired since the previous training. Conducted by senior Eden staff, Entry Level Training covers the learning characteristics of individuals with autism, speech and language characteristics, teaching techniques, behavior reduction techniques, and topics related to professionalism, all in greater detail than the exposure to Eden and autism in the Orientation Training. Lectures are supplemented with written material, video tapes, group exercises, and discussion. Like Orientation Training, Entry Level Training also includes a written test and a practicum, which staff are required to pass with a grade of at least a B to maintain their employment status.

Finally, all staff members are required to participate in continuing professional education opportunities throughout their employment with Eden. Behavior Technology Workshops, mentioned in Chapter 8, cover popular issues surrounding autism and methods of treatment for people with autism. Different workshops are given for entry level and experienced staff members. New staff members are required to attend Entry Level Training twice to ensure they have a solid foundation in the principles of applied behavior analysis and the instructional strategies derived from them.

Eden Family of Services Continuing Education Schedule 1996 - 1997

FALL SERIES
Topics in Behavior Technology
Workshop 1: Maximizing the Eden Decision Model
Workshop 2: How to Evaluate a Behavior Modification Program
(Clinical and Applied Settings)
Workshop 3: Autism: The Diagnostic Process
Workshop 4: Behavior Jeopardy (Test Your Knowledge)

WINTER SERIES
Human Relations: How Effective Are You?
Workshop 1: Defining Your Problem Solving Style
Workshop 2: The Art of Good Listening
Workshop 3: Handling Issues in the Community

SPRING SERIES
Health and Safety Topics
Workshop 1: Current First Aid Practices
Workshop 2: Managing Stress on the Job
Workshop 3: Basic Nutrition Facts

ONGOING TEAM BUILDING SERIES
A Series of Team Building Exercises
Workshop 1: Jigsaw Exercise
Workshop 2: We Need You!
Workshop 3: Toxic Waste Dump
Workshop 4: The Joy of Six

ONGOING EDUCATIONAL SERIES
CPR/First Aid Certification
Curriculum Development
Research

For staff members who have been with Eden for two years, more advanced training opportunities are available. Based on areas of need and interest identified by both supervisory and direct-care staff, several workshop series and ongoing education opportunities are designed each year. The workshop series allows staff to receive comprehensive training in a particular area, such as effective communication, advanced treatment methodologies, and theories surrounding the causes of autism. Although staff are required to attend a minimum of four trainings per year, many go beyond this minimum requirement. In fact, in 1996 staff attended an average of seven trainings, with some attending as many as eighteen.

In addition to workshops, staff members undergo ongoing training once they begin working with students and participants. Through teacher quality assessments, supervisors regularly assess staff members' knowledge

> We had a workshop on working through and troubleshooting disruptive behaviors in the community. We discussed how to deal with the behavior, what the community's comfort levels are, and what we need to do to make the community more comfortable. Continuing workshops are important because they keep ideas flowing. They keep our work from getting routine. They remind us of new developments in the field. Just as medical doctors need to keep learning to update the information they received in school, we need to keep in touch with what's new in the field of autism. In the workshops, we can also share ideas with new staff. We can tell them about experiences we've had, and talk about experiences they're having as a new staff member.
>
> **—Beth Thomas, Clinical Support Specialist**

of technical skills, and their application of those skills. The technical feedback staff members receive assesses their ability to: 1) understand remedial techniques, 2) troubleshoot programs, 3) assimilate previous feedback, and 4) develop new programs. The feedback they receive on their application of technical skills focuses on their consistent and appropriate application of behavioral techniques, as well as their professional demeanor and compliance with Eden's policies. Through teacher quality assessments, staff members are able to "fine tune" their skills and to improve their effectiveness as service providers.[3]

As staff members become more competent in their application of applied behavior analysis and demonstrate increasing professionalism, they are given supervisory responsibility. They first become mentors to new staff members, and then become involved in their ongoing training. Giving staff members supervisory responsibilities at the most basic level engenders ownership in the services Eden provides. Early supervisory responsibility is an expectation Eden holds for all its staff members. Just as participants are treated "as if" they are capable of

---

[3] Eden also enables staff members to continue their academic training. Staff members receive reimbursement for college courses taken during their employment.

being functioning, productive members of society, staff members are treated as if they are competent and responsible providers of high quality professional services and capable of becoming leaders at Eden.

As staff members' competence increases, they are given more substantial supervisory responsibilities, and the supports they are offered are gradually reduced. Staff members can find this difficult. For example, if a participant in a group home becomes ill at 3:00 a.m., the staff members in the home are expected to ensure his well-being. They may need to find an open pharmacy, or call a doctor for advice. They can certainly call their supervisor for advice, but the responsibility for dealing with the situation falls primarily on their shoulders. The less they access supervisor help under such circumstances, the more resourceful they become, which has a powerful positive effect on Eden's services.

In addition to regular supervision, ongoing training, and regular teacher quality assessments, staff members are evaluated twice a year by Eden's Support Services Division. These evaluations are designed to be a more independent assessment of their program supervision and training process. During the Support Services evaluation, a time sample of a staff member's performance is taken, and, like the teacher quality assessment process, the staff member's every teaching interaction and use of discrete trial and behavior management techniques is noted.

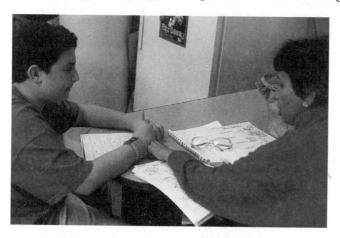

Throughout the year, these evaluations and those of the teacher quality assessments are compiled into a cumulative evaluation by the staff member's immediate supervisors. From the cumulative evaluation, a report on the staff member's overall performance is made. Evaluations are used to determine promotions, as well as areas in which staff members need improvement. The evaluation process ensures that staff members remain highly qualified and continually challenged to improve the quality of services they provide.

WORK ATMOSPHERE

A major challenge to organizations like Eden is engendering collegiality among its staff. This challenge stems from the dynamics of their working environment, which is highly specialized, emotionally charged, and very stressful. In order to maintain a healthy, cooperative work atmosphere, organizations like Eden need to make a conscientious effort to support and encourage benevolence amongst staff members.

Collegiality is fostered at Eden through staff members' reliance on each other individually and collectively. In groups, staff members review programs, conduct evaluations, develop program parameters, and discuss topics of concern, such as a student's challenging behaviors, the failure of a student to progress, or proposed changes in a student's programming. Much of the work is team work.

In a healthy work atmosphere, staff members should also feel a strong sense of ownership in the

> I am not just a person who walks in the door to come to work. This is my program, and these are my students. I am responsible for them. I really am part of the decision making and planning that goes on here. I am not told what to do. Instead, I have a lot of say in what goes on. I help analyze what we need, and how to meet those needs.
>
> —**Donna Vicidomini, Assistant Director for Education and Retreat Support Services**

organization's services. Staff members should feel personally responsible for the services they provide. Ownership at Eden is engendered in a number of ways. Staff members are involved in every decision made about a student's or participant's programming. They help develop programs and track progress on the program through daily data collection. They also make the initial decisions regarding behavior management programs.[4]

Staff members are also responsible for most of the communication Eden has with its families. Staff members meet with students' and participants' families on a regular basis throughout the year to exchange ideas and to coach parents on effective teaching and behavior management techniques they can use with their child. In addition, staff members play an important role in Eden's internal oversight. Along with senior staff, staff members perform internal program evaluations through "peer monitoring." That is, they monitor one another, and then suggest areas in programs that need improvement and ways in which to improve them. Staff members are then responsible for implementing changes to continually improve programs.

Staff members are also actively involved in developing Eden's curriculum. At Eden, the Curriculum Committee, composed of staff members and supervisors, reviews and revises the educational curricula regularly. This holds true in Eden WERCs and ACREs, where staff members and supervisors meet regularly to write and modify curricular programs. Staff members are also involved in planning workshops to improve and update their knowledge of autism and treatment methodologies for autism. At the outset of each year, each staff member is asked for suggestions of topics they would like covered. These topics are then addressed in continuing workshops or one-time seminars offered by guest lecturers or senior staff. Eden's long range strategic plan and its development of policies and procedures for day-to-day operations also include staff members. They are asked for feedback prior to their final ratification by the Board of Trustees.

---

[4] See Chapter 7 for a complete description of the role staff members play in developing behavior management programs.

> **W**hen people are committed, then quality, productivity, and innovation become common events. The impact of commitment can be seen in three distinct areas. First, people use their discretionary time, time that they could be using for other things, working for the organization. Why? Because they are motivated to do so, and they also receive satisfaction from doing their job and satisfaction from being associated with the organization.... With commitment, what we accomplish is ownership which in turn is a function of individual and organizational persistence and consistency. This does not represent simple endurance or stamina but determination and perseverance, or what might be best described as relentless persistence. Organizations and the people in these organizations follow what they believe with tenacity. If it is not working, they fix it as best and as fast as they can.
>
> —From *Championship Management: An Action Model for High Performance*, James A. Belohlav. Portland, OR: Productivity Press, Inc. P.O. Box 13390, Portland, OR 97213-0390 (800/393-6868). Reprinted by permission.

To strengthen the sense of ownership among staff members, and to reinforce a collegial work atmosphere, Eden celebrates staff members' accomplishments. Each year Eden gives staff members awards for their length of service to children and adults with autism. Some staff members have been with Eden since its inception in 1975. Eden has given awards for five, ten, and fifteen years of service, and in 1995 extended 20th anniversary awards to some of its staff. Eden engenders such longevity in the face of tremendous adversity by challenging staff to meet the lifespan service needs of Eden's students and participants and equipping them to meet that challenge. Eden trains, mentors, and provides necessary resources so that staff feel a sense of pride in making a difference in the lives of so many and a recognition that, without their efforts, many lives would be entirely unfulfilled.

PROMOTING VERSUS HIRING

A key component in Eden's employment practices is its principle of promoting competent people to greater levels of authority and responsibility rather than hiring from outside sources. There are three core messages expressed to staff members by promoting instead of hiring. First, staff members are recognized as highly qualified and well trained. Secondly, because of the high regard Eden has for its staff members, it works to keep them challenged with additional responsibility. Finally, by promoting staff who are committed to Eden's mission, Eden demonstrates that it, in turn, is committed to its staff.

Promoting rather than hiring aids in controlling for "burn out" in staff members. Burn out can come from being overworked; more often, however, it comes from being underchallenged. The intrinsic rewards staff members get from working arise from the challenges the work itself presents. Promoting staff members presents them with new professional challenges. As they expand their knowledge learning how to meet the demands of a more senior position, they become more dynamic, influencing the entire organization.

◆ ◆

Eden's turnover rate for 1994-1995 was 18%, compared to the reported range of 30% to 70% in other human services organizations (Braddock & Mitchell, 1992). The number of services awards given to Eden staff since 1991 are listed below.*

Eden Staff Service Awards

YEAR	5 YEARS	10 YEARS	15 YEARS	20 YEARS
1991	6	3	0	0
1992	8	4	0	0
1993	5	3	1	0
1994	4	3	0	0
1995	6	5	3	1
1996	16	4	2	0
1997	8	5	4	0

*These figures do not reflect the number of staff who fall between the five-year ranges.

◆ ◆

There are always staff members who need some change in their work, but for whom promotion is not a timely option. When this occurs, they are given additional responsibilities within their existing position or they are given the opportunity to pursue a different position within Eden. For example, a staff member who no longer feels challenged as a teacher at Eden Institute's Day School might find a more challenging position at Eden WERCs as a job coach. Providing staff members with a "change of atmosphere" keeps them in the organization, thereby preserving the time and investment Eden has made in its staff members. This protects an important resource for the organization.

Providing staff members with a new position or a change of atmosphere creates an employment "safety net" as well. The safety net is much like that provided to Eden's students and participants. The safety net for students and participants ensures that they remain challenged by their programming and never have gaps in services. If they feel too challenged, or are not able to sustain the level of independence asked of them, they are given additional support, or "safety netted." Similarly, the employment safety net for staff members ensures that they remain challenged by their work and suited to the demands of their job. However, if they feel dissatisfied with their work, feel uncomfortable with the level of responsibility given to them, or find that they are unable to satisfy the demands of their position, they can discuss their concerns with their supervisor, and receive counseling, advice, or further training to better prepare them for their job's demands or an alternate position within Eden.

I worked in the adult program for nine years, and had been a supervisor for the last five or six years. I knew my job so well that when I came to work in the morning, I knew exactly what I needed to do. After a while, though, I began to feel that I knew my job too well. Professionally, my supervisor kept patting me on the back, but I needed to give more in order to feel sufficiently reinforced by my work. So, I spoke with my supervisor and other administrators, and found a position in the Middle Childhood Program. They were very flexible. Because of the training I received, they felt comfortable placing me in a different position. I'm now working with children, as opposed to adults, and am working more with families. It has given me a new perspective on Eden's programs, and has expanded my own abilities. I feel refreshed.

—**Cindy Bregenzer, Coordinating Teacher, Middle Childhood Program**

MANAGEMENT BY OBJECTIVES

"Management by objectives" is the managerial system under which Eden operates. Management by objectives has been utilized as an administrative organization system by corporate America for many years. Thomas Walker, Esq., a member of the Board of Trustees and the Foundation Operating Committee, has seen the management by objectives approach used in many businesses with positive results. He explains the basic concepts behind management by objectives:

> *The management by objectives approach means establishing a specific group of objectives, and then measuring progress regularly against those objectives. And it means being serious about accomplishing those objectives. Those objectives are designed specifically with the client group in mind, which often means that companies have to specialize what they do, and do only those things they are particularly good at. In time, as the client's needs change, the mode of delivery, and therefore the company's objectives, ought to change. Companies should not be confined to historical ways of doing business.*
>
> *The management by objectives approach is particularly important in an organization like Eden because of the specific nature of the goals set. It is easier for the corporate community to get behind an organization with very specific goals, and a track record of accomplishing them. Eden is good at setting concrete goals and then accomplishing them. I think that is one reason they receive as much support from the corporate community. It also helps attract individual support. It is much easier to feel a sense of accomplishment and purpose when there are specific objectives.*

The Board of Trustees defines general goals for Eden. At the outset of every fiscal year, each Standing Committee of the Board sets goals and objectives for its year of operation. These goals and objectives reflecting Eden's Strategic Plan are validated by the Board of Trustees, and are evaluated again in the middle of the year, with a final evaluation at the end of the fiscal year. The evaluation process ensures that the Board stays focused on the fulfillment of Eden's mission, and uses its strategic plan as its map.

On a more basic level, staff members also create goals for themselves at the beginning of each fiscal year. Every staff member outlines a series of goals, and intermediate objectives to fulfill those goals, for professional activities as well as for personal growth and development. The staff member's immediate supervisor reviews these goals and objectives in light of the staff member's job parameters and professional growth, as well as in light of Eden's expectations for growth reflected in the Strategic Plan. Once approved, each staff member undertakes a semi-annual progress report on their goals and objectives, followed by a year-end self-evaluation and an overall evaluation by the supervisor.

Having staff members develop their own annual goals and objectives for progress enables them to measure their own progress against their goals, which gives them ownership in their own progress and reduces the need for immediate direction by supervisors. It supports staff members' ability to establish appropriate directions for themselves, while inadvertently enhancing their supervisory skills. It keeps staff members focused on their jobs and enables them to be more creative about professional and personal growth. It also promotes maturity, independence, commitment, and personal responsibility.

ADMINISTRATIVE CLARITY
◆ ◆ ◆ ◆ ◆ ◆ ◆ ◆ ◆ ◆ ◆ ◆ ◆ ◆ ◆ ◆ ◆ ◆

Having a clearly articulated administrative structure is crucial to the efficient running of a service delivery organization (Overton, 1993). A service delivery organization should also have an organizational chart that graphically describes its administrative structure, thereby defining lines of communication and responsibility. The chart should make each employee's job responsibilities clear, and the lines of authority should indicate where each staff member, manager, and leader fits in the general profile of the organization.[5]

---

[5] See next page for the organizational chart of Eden.

The Eden Family of Services Organizational Chart

| Eden Institute, Inc. Board of Trustees | | Eden A.C.R.E.s, Inc. Board of Trustees |

| Eden Florida Steering Committee | | President and Executive Director |

Sr. Vice President and Director of Educational Services (Eden Institute)	Sr. Vice President and Director of Residential Services (Eden A.C.R.E.s)	Vice President and Director of Employment Services (Eden W.E.R.C.s)	Sr. Vice President and Director of Outreach Services (Eden Connecticut) (Eden Florida) (Wawa House)
			Associate Director of Outreach Services
	Assistant Director of Residential Services		Assistant Director for Clinic Services
Coordinators Certified Teachers Speech Therapists Adaptive P.E. Teaching Assistants Respite Workers Recreation Aides	Coordinators of Group Home Operations Managers Assistant Managers Teaching Parents Maintenance	Coordinator of W.E.R.C.s Operations Center Supervisors Coordinator of Supported Employment Teacher/Job Coaches Aides	Supervisor of Clinical Services Outreach Program Specialist Behavioral Therapists Speech Therapists
Consultants	Consultants	Consultants	Consultants

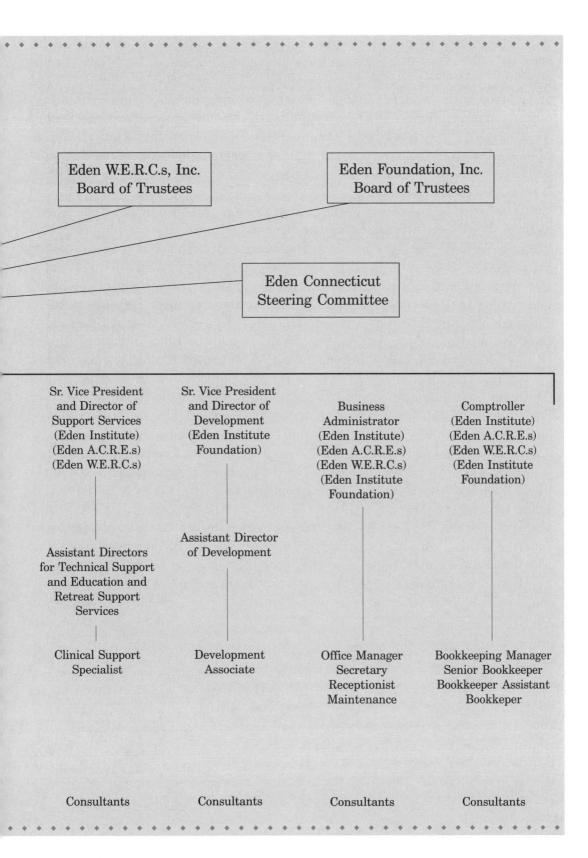

Eden W.E.R.C.s, Inc.
Board of Trustees

Eden Foundation, Inc.
Board of Trustees

Eden Connecticut
Steering Committee

Sr. Vice President
and Director of
Support Services
(Eden Institute)
(Eden A.C.R.E.s)
(Eden W.E.R.C.s)

Sr. Vice President
and Director of
Development
(Eden Institute
Foundation)

Business
Administrator
(Eden Institute)
(Eden A.C.R.E.s)
(Eden W.E.R.C.s)
(Eden Institute
Foundation)

Comptroller
(Eden Institute)
(Eden A.C.R.E.s)
(Eden W.E.R.C.s)
(Eden Institute
Foundation)

Assistant Directors
for Technical Support
and Education and
Retreat Support
Services

Assistant Director
of Development

Clinical Support
Specialist

Development
Associate

Office Manager
Secretary
Receptionist
Maintenance

Bookkeeping Manager
Senior Bookkeeper
Bookkeeper Assistant
Bookkeper

Consultants

Consultants

Consultants

Consultants

The overall organizational parameters must also be discretely ordered. Its services, offices, and programs must be clearly delineated, with distinct parameters. The organization must have a well structured and clearly delimited Board of Trustees, with standards that clearly state the responsibility of all committees, officers, and members. The organization must also have a specific strategic plan for the future. Every facet of the administration of an organization must be interconnected, with a single purpose: to fulfill the organization's mission.

STRUCTURE OF BOARDS

The Board of Trustees is legally and practically responsible for all operations at Eden. The Board of Trustees has the ultimate authority and fiduciary responsibility for the Eden Family of Services. The Board sets forth policy, makes plans for Eden's future, and secures the fiscal requirements of the organization. The twenty-two member board is comprised of parents of students and participants at Eden, members of the community, and the President and Executive Director of Eden. Although officially Eden has a Board of Trustees for each of its major services— the Eden Institute, Eden ACREs, Eden WERCs, and the Eden Institute Foundation—each Board is legally independent, but is comprised of the same members.

The practical functions of Eden's Boards are fulfilled through its officers—the Chairman, Vice Chairman, Secretary, Treasurer—and its Standing Committees. Eden has developed a Board manual which describes the responsibility of each of its officers and standing committees. The Board manual also reflects the by-laws of Eden, which are the legal rules and regulations for its operation as a not-for-profit organization.

Eden's Board members are elected by the membership, comprised of the families of Eden and come from the Board committee structure. Eden has found that it is best for a potential Board member to serve on a standing committee for at least a year. This enables the Board to determine whether the individual is committed to Eden's mission. Committee membership also enables the individual to determine whether Board membership is something to which he or she would like to aspire.

Standing Committees are subordinate to the Board as a whole. They take on the Board's duties, which are broken down into several specialized areas, each assigned to a particular Standing Committee and defined in Eden's Board Manual. The Committees then provide the Board with quarterly reports comprised of information and suggestions related to their particular areas of oversight.

The President and Executive Director's ultimate responsibility is to make cer-

Eden is the first organization in which I have been involved where I am directly confronted with the people who receive the benefit of my help. At the annual "Eden Dreams" event, Eden's largest fund-raiser, one parent came up to me and said "I don't know why you're working so hard on behalf of Eden, but I just want to tell you that you've made a difference in my life and my child's life." That was a powerful experience for me. They let me know that I had directly affected their life. I don't usually get that kind of feedback.

—PJ Dempsey, Community Member, Board of Trustees

The Board's responsibilities are covered by 14 separate Standing Committees described below.

Standing Committees

OPERATING COMMITTEES—responsible for the oversight of the operations of their respective corporations

PLANNING COMMITTEE—responsible for preparing, maintaining, and revising Eden's long-range Ten Year Plan (Strategic Plan)

FINANCE COMMITTEE—responsible for maintaining the fiscal integrity of Eden Human Resources Committee and responsible for developing and maintaining a pool of parent and community members suitable as candidates for positions as Trustees

LEGAL COMMITTEE—responsible for the oversight of all contractual and litigation matters that pertain to Eden

FAMILY ACTIVITIES COMMITTEE—responsible for establishing opportunities for the families of Eden to show their support of Eden (e.g., the Annual Awards Dinner) and to simply "get together" (e.g., the annual Family Picnic)

FACILITIES & GROUNDS COMMITTEE—responsible for the oversight of all facilities and properties owned by Eden

COMMUNITY RELATIONS COMMITTEE—responsible for the general direction of public relations and public education as it relates to Eden

CAPITAL GIVING COMMITTEE—responsible for the development and oversight of all capital giving campaigns (i.e., campaigns which focus on a one-time major purchase)

ANNUAL GIVING COMMITTEE—responsible for the general oversight of the annual giving campaign established by Eden

ENDOWMENT COMMITTEE—responsible for the development and oversight of all endowments of Eden

tain that Eden operates in response to the goals set forth by the Board of Trustees. The President and Executive Director is responsible for the day-to-day operation of Eden's services. The role of Eden's President and Executive Director is clear; the role of the Board is clear. Both work harmoniously, deferring to each other's area of authority and responsibility. This is very important for a human service organization, or any other organization, to run smoothly.

STRATEGIC PLANNING: EDEN'S TEN YEAR PLAN

Setting down clear parameters for the organization's direction is one of the most important roles the Board of Trustees plays. Eden's strategic plan covers development over the next ten years. Initially, however, it covered only the first three years because of the newness of Eden's services, and the rapid growth they would make. The current plan is revisited and updated every three years to ensure that it remains a valid projection for Eden's progress.

Eden's strategic plan addresses the resources Eden needs to fulfill its mission of lifespan services. The Plan outlines the facilities Eden will need as it expands to meet the evolving needs of children and adults, the funds Eden will need to support the growth of services, the projections for staff and administration as Eden grows, and how new services and facilities will integrate into those currently in existence at Eden. The Plan also provides a timeline for the development of services and facilities. It does not collect dust; the Strategic Plan is the foundation of Eden's course during the next ten years.

> The ten year plan does not just set direction. It sets very specific goals. The goals outlined in the ten year plan are then prioritized and become objectives for different years. One of our objectives was to accomplish eighty percent of establishing an education and retreat center in Connecticut. That goal came from the ten year plan. We accomplished that, and have moved on to the objectives for this year.
>
> —**William Noonan, Community Member, Board of Trustees**

GROWTH

◆ ◆ ◆ ◆ ◆ ◆ ◆ ◆ ◆ ◆ ◆ ◆ ◆ ◆ ◆ ◆ ◆ ◆ ◆

> *The scope of the services Eden provides and the number of families, children, and adults that Eden touches have probably trebled in the last three or four years.*
>
> —**Andy Armstrong, Director of Development**

Eden's growth has indeed been tremendous. In a recent fiscal year alone, Eden opened its Wawa Education and Retreat Center in Connecticut, ACREs opened its seventh group home, Eden again surpassed its annual fund goal, a separate facility for the Eden Institute Foundation was acquired, Eden's Outreach Division served more than 400 individuals, families, and agencies, and Eden established Wawa CARES (Comprehensive Autism Referral and Education Services), its mobile outreach unit to provide referral and education services throughout New Jersey, Delaware, and Pennsylvania.

Given the great need for services among people with autism, the growth of service organizations like Eden is positive. However, there are risks that accompany growth. Service delivery organizations must be aware of these risks, and take steps to control them. Unplanned or too rapid growth can cause an organization to lose its sense of mission. Organizations can become distracted by the proliferation of their services, and lose their focus. Organizations can

> Eden ACREs simply cannot stop growing. As long as Eden Institute takes students in, ACREs has to grow. We don't have a choice. Sometimes it is scary to think of having to provide that much service, and maintain the individualized care people in ACREs need. But we will, because we have made a commitment to provide lifespan services.
>
> **—Dave Roussell, Director of Residential Services, Eden ACREs**

control for this by establishing comprehensive evaluation procedures. The evaluation procedures at Eden, described on the next page, help monitor growth at Eden and facilitate careful, deliberate strides along its mission.

With growth, service delivery organizations also risk burying staff members' intuition and feelings under policies. If organizations create an insulated administration, they can become bogged down in bureaucratic "red tape." As a result, staff members' spontaneity can become compromised. Their behavior can become dictated more by policy than by their judgment of what is best for those they serve. One of their greatest strengths, their creativity in helping people with autism, can become encumbered. Eden tries to manage regulation to avoid this risk by only developing regulations that are necessary for safe and legal operations. Staff members are sufficiently well trained that Eden can often allow them greater independence in regulating their delivery of services. Eden does, however, have an Employee Policy Manual in order that staff understand what is required of them and, in turn, what they can expect from Eden.

Quality Control

In order to maintain consistently good services, a service delivery organization must have methods to control the quality of the services it provides. A regular evaluation of services is the best method by which to measure service quality. Evaluations should cover services from the most minute level to the most general. Every aspect of the organization, from individual teaching programs to the functions of the Board, should be examined.

Regular evaluations keep the focus of services from "drifting." Program "drift" refers to the gradual, unintentional change of focus, or direction, that can occur in services over time. For example, if a preschool program were developed to serve children with autism from age three to five, but was having difficulty dealing with the learning and behavioral challenges of the children, it could find itself gradually extending its services to children who had some features of autism but fewer behavioral challenges, then to children who had just minor developmental delays. The focus of the program would have changed and felt successful, but would no longer serve the children it set out to serve. The program would have allowed itself to "drift" into providing those services. Regular evaluations and reflecting on their mission and strategic plan would have enabled the service providers to look at the subtle trends in their service population, and so help them avoid unintended changes in their direction. Unintended changes are controlled at Eden by constant and consistent adherence to our mission and through regular evaluations.

Eden regularly conducts several evaluations. The Board of Trustees, administration, and staff members, and each program at Eden undergoes an extensive evaluation process. The Board is evaluated semi-annually through an examination of its

Synopsis of the Eden Family of Services

	1975-1976	1996-1997
Budget		
Total Revenue	$85,300	$8,330,150
Total Expenditure	$83,300	$8,190,953
Children & Adults Served	20	1000+
Facilities Rented or Owned	2 0	1 17
Staff (Clinical)	10	250+ (full-time, part-time, and volunteer
Vehicles	0	40 owned
Administrative Staff	1	13.5
Fund Raising & Special Events	Garage Sale	Eden Dreams All-Star Dinner Show Eden Raffle Eden Invitational & Eden Challenge Golf Tourneys Eden Evening on the Town Eden Appreciation Reception Eden Awards Dinner Eden's Princeton Lecture Series

annual goals and objectives. Because objectives are clearly defined for each year and are based on Eden's Strategic Plan, the Board's progress on achieving its objectives is the best means of evaluating its accomplishments and controlling program drift.

The achievement of goals and objectives established through a process similar to that of the Board's is also the means by which administration and staff members are evaluated. Each staff member and each member of the administration sets goals and objective for themselves each year. These goals are the basis of their semi-annual evaluation. Administration and staff members' evaluation also reflects their responsibilities as set forth in their job descriptions.

	1975-1976	1996-1997
Total Services	10-month Day Program	10-month Day Program
	Cape Cod Summer Res.	Summer Day & Residential
	Parent Training	Parent Training, Lectures,
		& Parent Support Groups
	Home Program	Sibling Support Groups
	Extended Day Program	Home Program
		Extended Day Program
		Work Study
		Group Home Services
		Adult Employment Services
		Faculty Training Services
		Infant & Toddler Services
		Supplemental Clinic Services
		Diagnosis/Evaluations
		Education/Retreat Services
		Eden Connecticut
		Eden Florida
		Accountability-Behavior Mgmt.
		Continuing Education
		Conferences
		Program Evaluations
		Research/Publications
		Fund Raising/Marketing
		Community Relations
		Outreach Consultations
		Emergency Family Support
		Respite Services
		Information & Referral
		Case Management
		Medical Services
		Recreational Services
		Advocacy/Expert Testimony
		Video Conferencing

The majority of evaluations at Eden are on the programs and services it provides. Programs undergo several evaluations annually. They are evaluated by the Board of Trustees' Standing Committees, through an internal self-evaluation process, through Eden's Support Division, by parents, through peer reviews, and by local and state officials.

Each of the agencies within Eden—Eden Institute, ACREs, and WERCs— have their own internal self-evaluation process. Supervisors of one program, along with one or two staff members from that program, visit another program. They study data from the program, and observe its daily operations. They then give a report on the program offer suggestions, and discuss any concerns they may have. For example, staff of the Middle Childhood Program at Eden Institute might evaluate the Early Childhood Program. And staff of one group home or employment center would evaluate another home or center.

Each program is also evaluated semi-annually by Eden's Support Division. The Support Division's evaluation is much like that done internally in the programs. But

the Support Division's evaluation is used by the executive director to ensure that each program remains focused on the philosophy, mission, and credo of Eden, and is demonstrating progress in fulfilling Eden's Strategic Plan.

Every few years, Eden invites professionals of national prominence to perform a peer review of its services. This process is an extensive, on-site evaluation of programs. The process typically results in a written report analyzing and offering a critical analysis of Eden's services.

Finally, the State of New Jersey has licensing authority over Eden's services. Eden operates as a means of enabling the State to fulfill its legal responsibility to educate and offer support to children and adults with autism and developmental disabilities. With the State's responsibility to extend services comes their responsibility to ensure that those services are performed well. The Department of Education evaluates the Eden Institute's Day School on an annual basis. Eden ACREs is evaluated by the Division of Developmental Disabilities (under the Department of Human Services) also on an annual basis. Eden WERCs is audited by the Department of Labor on an annual basis. WERCs is also audited by the federal government under its Medicaid Community Care Waiver provision, which looks at service providers to determine whether the Division of Developmental Disabilities is in compliance with its regulations. Representatives from the state analyze the full operation of each of Eden's services, including the IEP or IHP of each student and participant, and prepare a written report based on their review.

Self-monitoring by the Board, by the Support Division, by parents, by peers, by leaders in the field of service delivery, and by the State means that Eden's services receive a high level of exposure. Several times a month, a variety of Eden services are analyzed through one of the evaluation processes described above. This helps Eden maintain the quality of its services, and keeps its programs focused on fulfilling their goals and objectives, and ultimately its mission.

FUNDING

Funding can be one of the most difficult parts of running a service delivery organization. Funding is often dependent on factors the organization cannot control, such as the economy, the willingness of people and businesses in the community to contribute to the organization and to create partnerships. What organizations can and should do to secure funding is to determine from their state regulatory agencies what corporate status offers the most opportunities. For example, should you incorporate as a for-profit or not-for-profit corporation?

WORKING WITH THE STATE

Eden has found that a not-for-profit status is the best organizational strategy for securing needed funding from the state (Oleck, 1988). In order to establish a not-for-profit corporation, or a "501(c)(3) organization" under the federal Charities Registration Act, Eden submitted a Charter to the Secretary of State. The Charter reflects Eden's philosophy and mission statement, and describes Eden's reasons for wanting to be a not-for-profit organization. The Charter also establishes Eden's "inherent public goodness" in order to realize its tax exempt status.

The state requires that the Charter be supported by a set of by-laws in order to ensure Eden operates under New Jersey statutes controlling the operation of not-for-profit organizations (NJS - Title 15A). The by-laws establish the rules under which Eden conducts business as a not-for-profit organization.

In working with the state, Eden has secured funds in payment for services needed. States have a fiduciary responsibility to secure the well-being of their citizens. To this end, states will often contract with private providers of services. Eden receives payment for services from the state in this way.

The term "state funded" is often used to describe the cooperative relationship between the state and private agencies. Although this relationship can give the impression of state control over the private agency, the relationship should be viewed as one of mutual respect and reliance. At Eden, the State of New Jersey's responsibility is to serve children and adults with autism. Eden has a precisely articulated contract, primarily through each student's or participant's IEP or IHP, with the state's Departments of Education and Human Services to enable the state to fulfill its responsibility. This contract enables New Jersey and Eden to work together, while maintaining Eden as an independent private agency.

For activities outside the realm of its contract with the state, and to ensure Eden remains independent and responsive to the needs of people with autism, it must engage in fund raising. To this end, Eden developed a foundation.

HAVING A FOUNDATION

In order to stabilize and secure funding, service delivery organizations should also establish a foundation (Berendt & Taft, 1984). A foundation manages the private funds an organization receives, and is able to manage those funds in ways that increase their value over time. For example, a foundation could increase operating funds through an annual giving program as well as careful market and real estate investments, or with capital funds in an endowment building program, or through other planned giving activities. Having a foundation gives a strictly business side to an organization, and so makes it easier for the organization to interact with the community. From a purely business standpoint, a foundation also makes it easier for the organization to approach other businesses in the community for funding, support, or employment opportunities for those the organization serves.

Eden's Foundation is responsible for securing the funding Eden needs to maintain its current services, as well as to provide for the programs Eden envisions for the future. The Foundation has a small endowment and a minor market investment plan. The majority of Eden's equity lies in real estate and facilities. The financial resources the Foundation has been able to secure for Eden have grown substantially over the past several years. Andy Armstrong, Director of Development:

> *Twelve years ago, Eden was raising about fifty or sixty thousand dollars a year, primarily through a single annual fund raiser, a raffle, and some spontaneous gifts from local organizations, such as the local rotary club and a parent's church. Eden also had a modest, infrequent, direct mail campaign.*

Eden receives the majority of its revenue from the state through the Departments of Education and Human Services. That's both good and bad news. It's important money that we need, but at the same time there are often many strings attached. Our goal is to slowly wean ourselves from dependence on the State through fund raising and, in particular, through building our endowment. That will free us up to be able to do things as we need to do them, without having to wait for the State's largess. For example, we have felt constrained in the past few years in developing new group homes and employment centers because there has been a freeze in state funds. It has also been very difficult to secure sufficient funding for transportation. The fund raising we do helps bridge the gap between what we receive and what we need, and it ensures that we'll at least be able to continue providing the level of services and quality we currently have. Relying more on our own funds also allows us to expand in a deliberate and controlled fashion. For example, we have planned an education and retreat center for several years, and have now built one in Connecticut. We have been able to do that through fund raising and community support.

—Andy Armstrong, Director of Development

A not-for-profit organization, especially one that derives much of its funding from discrete grants that follow a current group of students and clients, does not have the ability to set aside cash resources, or to create a large endowment for the future. So Eden tries as much as possible to accumulate real estate and other physical resources that it can use, but which also provide a stable and valuable economic base for the future.

—Todd Martin, Community Member, Board of Trustees

In contrast, during the 1996 fiscal year, Eden raised over one million dollars in cash contributions, plus another one hundred thousand in gifts in kind. Eden now has, in addition to the raffle, five or six major annual fund raisers. These include three golf outings, a major black-tie gala, an elegant gourmet dinner party, and an annual dinner show that Frankie Avalon and several Bandstand-era entertainers do as a benefit. Eden now has a fairly sophisticated direct mail campaign, and applies for corporate and foundation grants. Eden is also instigating a planned giving program.

Although the Eden Foundation has greatly increased the funding Eden is able to raise, Eden is not financially independent. Eden needs the support of the State. Eden also needs the support of its parents to advocate for services for their children. Parents have been essential partners in securing additional services and funds from the state. This has been especially true regarding residential services for adults. Because adults with disabilities are not yet automatically entitled to state-sponsored residential services, the support the state does offer has been due largely to parents' advocating for their own child. In addition to state funding, the greatest support the Foundation has garnered for Eden has come from businesses and corporations in the community. Corporate partnerships have become essential to Eden's service delivery.

CORPORATE PARTNERSHIPS

Corporations can be strong allies of service delivery organizations. Corporate partnerships however do not benefit only the service delivery organization. Corporations benefit from the advertising and cause-related marketing opportunities of the partnership through an improved community image. In addition, employees feel a sense of goodness that their company is helping others. Corporate partnerships are truly win-win relationships.

Corporations benefit from supporting service delivery organizations in a

The Wall Street community has been exceptionally generous in its support of Eden over the years—the men and women who participate in the Eden Invitational represent many of Wall Street's leading financial firms. In the third week of May each year, their support of Eden's cause is combined with a premier golf outing and a wondrous day of sociability.

—Frank Basile, Eden parent and trustee, and member of the steering committee for the Eden Invitational golf and tennis outing

Being a Do-Gooder Can Be Profitable

Corporations that once gave just out of the goodness of their hearts are now starting to tout their deeds, realizing consumers of the '90s want them to be socially responsible and will reward them (with loyalty and increased sales) if they are....

The benefits of using CRM [cause-related marketing] are clear: deeper, long-lasting relationships with customers, enhanced corporate image, differentiation from competitors, increased sales. When used as part of a corporate mission, CRM has an even bigger impact on customers, employees and the corporation as a whole.

—From: "Being a Do-Gooder Can Be Profitable." (1996, July 18). John Naisbitt's *Trend Letter*, 15(15). 1-3.

more subtle way, as well. Christopher Tarr, Esq., a community member of Eden's Board of Trustees and a long-time corporate supporter of Eden:

Autism is not a high profile condition, but it does unfortunately affect a large number of people. If businesses in the community looked at their employee population, they would most likely find that there are several people whose lives have been affected by autism. Businesses often do not realize just how great a contribution human service agencies provide toward enabling them to have a highly skilled and stable work force as well as a support system for their employees who have children with autism and other disabilities.

As mentioned above, Eden has found corporate support invaluable to providing services. Without corporate support, it would have taken many more years before Eden could provide many of its services. Perhaps the greatest instance of corporate support at Eden is the development of Wawa House, Wawa CARES, and the Wawa Education and Retreat Center in cooperation with Wawa, Inc. Irene Farley, Chairman of the Eden Institute Foundation:

> We realized a number of years ago that we were not meeting the needs of people at the beginning of their lifespan, in early intervention services for children under the age of three. There was no state funding available for a program like that, so we had to not only create the program, but somehow find the funding for it. We came up with a rather creative approach, which modeled the Ronald McDonald House concept, and used one of our primary corporate supporters, Wawa, Inc. Wawa had been employing our students and participants in stores, and they had done fund raising for us over the years for smaller scope projects.

Eden gets extraordinary support from the business community, both in cash contributions and in kind support. My own company donates raffle prizes and provides facilities for telephoning and printing. We make available business equipment that we no longer use, such as office furniture and computers.

—Thomas Walker, Community Member, Board of Trustees and Senior Vice President, American Re-Insurance

> *We approached Wawa, Inc. with the concept of using their network of stores to raise the funds for a house which would provide a pioneering new early intervention service for infants and toddlers. The customers, the stores, the store personnel, and corporate Wawa could all be involved in supporting the program. At the same time, we would be able to establish the service, and maybe give the public information about autism at the same time. We said that if we could have their commitment, we would accordingly name the new program Wawa House.*
>
> *They agreed, and over two hundred and thirty stores throughout New Jersey, Connecticut, and eastern Pennsylvania have participated for the last several years in raising funds. They have used coin canisters, bowlathons, golf tournaments, and other fund-raising campaigns to raise over 600 thousand dollars. They helped us purchase and renovate the building now known as Wawa House, and they continue to raise funds to help in expanding our services. Most recently, they have enabled us to develop a mobile outreach unit, Wawa CARES, and the Wawa Education and Retreat Center.*

Many other corporations (see box on the next page) have extended valuable resources to Eden in the form of "loaned" executives, furniture, supplies, multimedia presentation equipment, advice on corporate operation strategies, and funds to bolster Eden's services.

COMMUNITY INVOLVEMENT

> *Our fourth responsibility is to the community at large. We must be good neighbors to those in whose community we offer services. We must continue to educate the community about autism. We must offer community members opportunities to fulfill their spirit of volunteerism. We must also advocate for the community of families that have children with autism. We must offer them: research into the causes and treatment of autism, consultation services, and support of government policies that encourage the development of services to families and their children with autism.*
>
> **—Eden Credo, 1991**

A final, but crucial, element of any service delivery organization is their commitment to the communities in which they are located. Service delivery organizations, especially those like Eden, utilize community resources daily. Eden's students and participants, for example, regularly visit parks, libraries, and shopping outlets. Because of their use of community resources, service delivery organizations must be responsible members of their community. That means not only tak-

Corporate and Foundation Donors

A-1 Limousine Inc.
Abrams Foundation
Alma Offset Printing
American Cyanamid
American Re-Insurance Company
American Speedy Printing Centers
Bell Atlantic—New Jersey
Beneficial Management Corp.
Bohren's United Van Line
Bristol-Myers Squibb Company
Buchanan Ingersoll
Cantor Fitzgerald & Company
Carter-Wallace
Chase Manhattan Bank
Ciba Geigy Corporation
Collier Foundation
Commodities Corporation LLC
Consolidated Drake Press
CoreStates Bank
Creative Marketing Alliance
Datastudy, Inc.
Ecolab
Ellsworth's
Enchanted Unicorn Enterprises
Ernst & Young LLP
Ethicon
First Union Bank
Fleet Bank
Forest Jewelers
The Forrestal at Princeton
Frigidaire
GE American Communications
Linus R. Gilbert Foundation
Hill Wallack, Attorneys at Law
Howard Design Group
Hyatt Regency, Princeton
Hyde & Watson Foundation
Janssen Pharmaceutica

KPMG Peat Marwick, LLP
Kresge Foundation
Lehman Brothers
Leigh Photographic Group
Makrancy's Garden & Floral Shop
Ann M. Martin Foundation
Mason, Taylor & Colicchio
Curtis W. McGraw Foundation
McMaster Carr Supply Co.
McNamara Trading Company
Merrick's
Merrill Lynch & Co., Inc
Morgan Mercedes Human Res. Group
Nassau Club
National Starch & Chemical
Parker, Remsen & Sullivan
Price Waterhouse LLP
Princeton Area Community Foundation
Princeton Flower Shop
Princeton Marriott
Princeton University
The Prudential
Public Service Electric & Gas Company
Refine Design Inc.
Rhone-PoulencInc.
RJR Nabisco
Rotary Club of Princeton Corridor
 Foundation
Lee H. Sager Jr., Inc.
Sarnoff Corporation
Smith, Stratton, Wise, Heher
 & Brennan
Souffle
Summit Bancorp
Troster Singer
Turrell Fund
Wawa, Inc.
Wheat, First, Butcher & Singer

◆ ◆

Eden WERCs Business Advisory Council

A-1 Limousine Steven B. Pitel	Bohren's United Van Lines Louise Froehlich Sharp
Cooper Pest Control Philip Cooper	Corestates NJ National Kathleen Dauer
Leigh Photographic Group Peter Dawson	Polychrome Bill Schenck
Trenton Janitorial Supply Mitchell Saifer	Wawa Food Markets, Inc. Scott Kent

◆ ◆

ing, but giving back the support the community offers the organization. Service delivery organizations are in fact community businesses, and so must contribute to their community just as their business neighbors do.

Eden gives back to the community in many ways. During its annual awards dinner, Eden presents awards to leaders in the community who have helped Eden. Eden also has an Eden Appreciation reception each year when people in the community

> I have now been honored by a large, firmly established organization with a remarkably effective array of services....I well remember that a key factor in deciding to help Eden was the scope of the services, the number helped, and the determination to assist autistic children through the long years of their need. No organization of the hundreds I have gotten to know has exceeded by so much the hopes we had for their life and growth.
> —Dr. Carl Fjellman, former Executive Director of the Turrell Fund

are recognized by the students and participants of Eden. Community members receive various crafts and baked goods made by students and participants as well as a plaque signifying their support of Eden.

In addition, Eden's staff volunteer on community boards and perform civic duties throughout the communities in which Eden's services are found. Eden's Outreach Division provides information to the community about autism, about services for people with autism, and about the role of government agencies in providing services to people with autism. Eden supports the community in many other ways as well. Judy Farrell, parent and Chairman of the Board of Trustees:

> *The responsibility we feel toward the community is part of our Credo.*
> *It is a priority for us to educate the community about autism, and to*

provide opportunities for them to volunteer and become involved with Eden. However, it is important that we not just be a not-for-profit organization asking for help, but that we also give back and help the community in any way we can. We make a strong effort to get involved in community activities and fund raisers. Students and participants have ridden in bikeathons to support juvenile diabetes, we have participated in walkathons, and a few years ago we participated in Hands Across America. Several of our group homes are involved in the Department of Transportation's Adopt-a-Highway Program, and a couple of our group homes are walking the dog of an elderly man who cannot get out much. In a modest way, the Eden Institute Foundation financially supports other similar agencies or programs to encourage them to become involved in their communities. It also supports fire and rescue squads in the communities where our group homes are located.

In addition, we have the Ann M. Martin Scholarship Program[6] which provides a $1000 scholarship to qualified high school seniors who have made a commitment to pursue special education and related disciplines in college. We give one scholarship out for each facility we operate in a given community. So, for example, in West Windsor we have three facilities, so provide three $1000 scholarships to students in the West Windsor-Plainsboro area. Last year, we gave out a total of twelve scholarships, including one in Connecticut where our education and retreat center is located. At the end of their four years of college, the Eden scholar who has best demonstrated a focus on autism receives an additional $1000 award. In addition, we offer, through the Autism Society of America, a scholarship to a student with autism who is going on to college or trade school. The scholarships are our way of giving back to the community while at the same time supporting and encouraging interest in special education.

> The community knows Eden well, and Eden has made itself known to the many corporate enterprises in the area. Having participated in fund raising for many different organizations, I would say that Eden is the region's favorite charity. But it is so because of its own efforts to reach out to the community and make itself known.
>
> —**Irene Farley, Community Member and Chairman of the Eden Institute Foundation**

Eden has also recently established the Eden Prize, awarded to an individual or group that shows a strong commitment to studying autism or improving the lives of people with autism. The Eden Prize is given to people working at all levels

---

6   The Ann M. Martin Scholarship program is named after a former teacher at Eden, who is now a successful author of children's books.

of service and research, from determining the causes of autism to developing effective treatment or services for individuals with autism and their families. The 1995 recipients of the Eden Prize were Dr. Bernard Rimland for research and Dr. Eric Schopler for services. The prize includes a monetary award of up to $5000 and is accompanied by a lecture series during which recipients discuss their work and disseminate their findings.[7]

On a larger scale, Eden is involved in the state and national community of people concerned with services for people with autism. Eden's staff members are participating members of the Autism Society of America, the American Psychological Association, the American Speech and Hearing Association, the Council for Exceptional Children, the Association for the Advancement of Behavior Therapy, the Association of Behavior Analysis, the National Association of Private Schools for Exceptional Children, and the National Commission of Accreditation of Special Education Services. Members have served as chairmen and trustees of many of these and other state and national organizations.

Eden itself is a member of organizations such as the Autism Society of America, the National Association of Private Schools for Exceptional Children, the Association of Schools and Agencies for the Handicapped, the State Services Provider's Association, the Center for Outreach and Services for the Autism Community, and the Center for Non-Profit Corporations. State and national involvement has given Eden a high level of visibility and has positioned it to proactively influence the services state and federal governments provide people with autism.

By being responsible members of the community, whether local or national, Eden gives back a portion of it resources in order to help others. This benefits people with autism because, as Eden is perceived, so are the people with autism it represents.

Our final responsibility is to those who support the Eden Family of Services. Eden is steadfast in its focus on its mission. This is often a challenge; often, service organizations find themselves focusing their energies on appeasing funders who may want control over how their money is spent. The service agency, worried over losing support, may relinguish control over its fiscal or programmatic direction to the funder under the notion of saving the agency. This does not work in the long run and compromises the agency's mission. Ultimately, if funders and supporters are genuinely interested in the service the agency provides, they will be gratified that it has not diminished its zeal to accomplish its mission. If the agency sticks to its mission, funders will receive the greatest satisfaction possible, that of knowing that their support was merited.

---

[7] Proceedings from the 1995 Eden Institute Foundation Princeton Lecture Series on Autism, "Affecting the Research and Service Agenda," are available by contacting Eden.

Medical Student Teaches a Valuable Lesson

by Kate McCartin

When Betty Wu was a student at Princeton University, she spent Friday mornings volunteering at the Eden Institute, a school for autistic children in West Windsor. The tangible rewards were few, Wu said. She worked with only one child during her time there, but the toddler's disability was so severe it was impossible to say if he remembered her from week to week. She never got a smile of recognition, or a hug or a hello. The progress they made was painfully slow.

But still, that experience at Eden helped shape Wu's life, she said. And in turn, her dedication to children and her commitment to volunteerism helped change the way doctors are trained at New Jersey's largest medical school.

"Working with the children [at Eden] was completely and utterly frustrating— probably the most frustrating thing I've ever done—but I just enjoyed working with those kids and I really respected the people who worked with them every day," said Wu.

Actually as of this week, that's Dr. Wu. The dynamic 25-year-old Piscataway resident graduated yesterday from the Robert Wood Johnson Medical School and plans to start a pediatrics residency in Portland, Maine, at the end of June.

Although she's leaving Piscataway, Wu has left an imprint on her alma mater. Based on her experience with Eden, Wu broke away from the books and singlehandedly set up a program to match medical student volunteers with the Laurie Neurodevelopmental Institute, a center for disabled children in New Brunswick.

The partnership is now part of the standard curriculum for first year students at RWJMS, said Dr. Susan Rosenthal, assistant dean for student affairs.

"Betty is a very unusual young woman. She's bright and extremely energetic, and came to us very committed to continuing with the kinds of volunteer activities she had started at Princeton," Rosenthal said. "She found she enjoyed the challenge of working with developmentally disabled children even though she stayed realistic about her expectations. She's a neat person, very interesting, and I think she's going to make a fantastic doctor."

Young children with developmental disabilities—that's kids with all sorts of problems ranging from mental retardation and autism to cerebral palsy and perceptual difficulties—need all kinds of help, Wu said. Some need speech therapy, or physical therapy, or special help with learning. And the earlier they get that special training, the more successful it is likely to be.

Doctors and other specialists at the Laurie Developmental Institute evaluate such children and design special therapy packages for each one. They then train the parents to provide many of the exercises at home. But raising a developmentally disabled child is often a 24 hour a day job, Wu said, and parents can get exhausted and discouraged.

So Wu's idea was this—to get a team of medical students who could spend one day a week at the children's homes, helping to provide the needed therapy and giving the parents a temporary respite. The volunteer students liked the program so much, the medical school decided to incorporate it into the curriculum, Rosenthal said.

"It's nice for the students because they learn about the pediatric patient in the context of the home and the family; they have a much better idea of the whole picture," Rosenthal said. "And the families also have been very positive about it. They like to have the students there, and especially, they like teaching the students the things they wish other doctors were aware of."

And that, really, was the whole point for Wu, she said. Medical students traditionally spend all of their time on academic pursuits and they lose something of themselves in the process, she said.

"For me, it was very hard at first. I found I was not staying in touch with the reason I wanted to go into medicine in the first place, which was to work with people," Wu said. "It's very upsetting to me that medical school is run that way. It's easy to lose yourself in the books—students don't go to the gym, they don't go outside, they don't do anything fun. But I think if they could just break out from time to time, they would actually be more efficient, and more caring for their patients."

Medical schools used to take pride in pushing their students to the edge of endurance, but Wu's opinions on this matter are not considered blasphemous any more. The latest movement in medicine is to train a new breed of physicians, to turn out doctors who are friendlier, more accessible to their patients, less remote and authoritarian. Enlightened hospitals now encourage residents, the post-graduate doctors who work long, grinding hours with little sleep, to save some time for themselves, to continue old hobbies and get away from the wards.

Rosenthal credited Wu's "exceptionally mature outlook on medicine" in part to the young woman's experiences at Princeton.

The University may not be known as a hotbed of activism, but still about 700 students are members of the Student Volunteers Council, an organization which matches undergraduates with worthy causes, said university spokeswoman Mary Caffrey. They shovel snow for elderly townspeople, mentor local elementary school children, and help out with social programs in Princeton and Trenton, just to name a few of the dozens of alliances, she said.

Wu did some volunteer work in high school, mostly running little fund-raisers for local organizations, but she said her real commitment developed when she got involved with Eden, with a Trenton day care center for abused children run by the state Division of Youth and Family Services, and several other volunteer projects through friends at SVC.

In medical school she kept just as busy, not only setting up the Laurie program but also dressing up like Woodsy the Owl, teaching high school students about AIDS, and helping with a project for abused women.

And although Wu admits her drive to start new projects is unusual, she denies her desire to participate in the community is anything special.

"I was amazed at how much interest everybody showed when I finally came up with this program," Wu said. "There hadn't been enough available for students in medical school before, but they were all very eager to sign up once the opportunity was there."

Trenton Times, May 23, 1996
Section E, 1-2

A Summary

· · · · · ·

# of Skill Acquisition

· · · · · · · ·

Programs Taught at

· · · · · · · ·

Eden Insitute

· · · · · · ·

THE SPECIAL EDUCATION DOMAIN

The special education domain of Eden's curriculum is comprised of its Core Curriculum, designed to build a foundation for future learning, its Classroom Orientation Curriculum, which primarily teaches academic skills, and its Vocational Education Curriculum, which prepares students for employment.[1]

The Core, Classroom Orientation, and Vocational Educational Curriculum together correspond to the age progression of a student through Eden Institute. In general, a student begins in the Early Childhood Program by focusing on basic skills taught through the Core Curriculum. If the student progresses to the Middle Childhood Program, he focuses more on the academic, domestic, and social skills

---

[1] The complete curriculum at Eden is available as a five volume set. Contact Eden's Support Services Division for details.

taught in the Classroom Orientation Curriculum. The Transition Program focuses on the same skills, but with a heavier emphasis on academics. When the student enters the Prevocational or Vocational Education Programs, his focus of study centers on acquiring the more work-oriented skills of the Vocational Education Curriculum.

The process of skill acquisition for any given student, however, rarely progresses straight from the Core to the Classroom Orientation, and on to the Vocational Educational Curriculum. Most often, a student will be working on skill acquisition programs in all three areas at one time. As he grows, the focus of his programming will gradually shift from the basic skill acquisition programs in the Core Curriculum to the more advanced skill acquisition programs in the Classroom Orientation and Vocational Curriculum. It is much more important that skill acquisition programs be appropriate for a student than that the student progresses "cleanly" from one area of the General Education Curriculum to another.

The skill acquisition programs taught through the General Education Curriculum for Eden Institute's Day School are described below. Because skill programs in a student's IEP are generally devoid of the Core, Classroom Orientation, and Vocational Education Curriculum framework, the description of skill programs below is also devoid of this framework. Instead, skill programs are divided into several categories: learning readiness, self-care, preacademic, social/play, academic, prevocational, vocational, and life skills. These specific categories more closely follow the temporal progression of students through Eden Institute's Day School.

LEARNING READINESS SKILLS

This is the first and most crucial area of skills to be taught. The ability to attend to a task, imitate, and follow directions is necessary for all students. They absolutely have to be able to sit in a chair quietly and attend to a teacher before learning any task. Because of the importance of these critical readiness skills, a significant percentage of a student's day is focused on mastering them. To ensure that students learn these skills, teachers need to be especially creative in their in-

We can't get very far without teaching a child how to sit appropriately in a chair and look at us. Teaching the child to look at us is teaching him not to look at something else distracting in the room, so it helps him focus and pay attention. When we say "Look at me" we expect direct eye contact, and a focus on what we're doing. When children first come to Eden Institute, we do many different things to get them to look at us. For example, one child likes peanuts, so I held a peanut right up to my nose and said "Look at me." What he was really looking at was probably the peanut, but we wanted to train that up, then fade the peanut away so "Look at me" would become something he understood. He now does understand it, and will look at us without any prompting at all.

—Denise Burns-Jennings, Coordinating Teacher, Early Childhood

The following is an example of a standard skill acquisition program for teaching a student appropriate sitting behavior. This program is modified, if necessary, and personalized for each student who needs to learn to sit appropriately.

Standard Skill Acquisition Program

TARGET BEHAVIOR

Within one second of the *Sd* "Sit quiet," the student will sit motionless with hands flat on lap or table, and feet on floor for at least ten seconds.

PREREQUISITE SKILLS

None.

CRITERION

The criterion for mastery of any skill is 90% correct responding for the target behavior over three days; for each step, the criterion is 90% accuracy for one day.

MEASUREMENT

Trial by trial data.

PROCEDURE

1. Teacher presents *Sd* "Sit quiet" with student seated on a chair in front of him or her. Reinforce for 2-3 seconds of correct sitting with primary reinforcers.
2. Present *Sd*, reinforce for 4-6 seconds of correct sitting.
3. Present *Sd*, reinforce all correct trials for 6-10 seconds of correct sitting.
4. Child is required to respond to *Sd* correctly for all trials in individual sessions and while performing tasks.
5. Child is required to respond to *Sd* while engaging in various activities, such as speech and music.

PROMPTING PROCEDURE

1. Full physical prompt—teacher holds student in chair.
2. Partial physical prompt—teacher places student in correct position (not actually holding him down in the chair).
3. Faded physical prompt/Gestural prompt—teacher points to body part, such as a leg, which is in an incorrect position.
4. Probe—no prompt is offered.

structional strategies. In the case of one student, teachers found that the best teaching strategy was one in which they were not even present. He would not imitate the actions of his teacher, but was extremely motivated to imitate the actions he saw on a videotape. So, his teachers prepared a series of instructional tapes for him to teach learning readiness, play, and language skills. The tapes have worked well. He learned several skills through the tapes and, through a prompt fading procedure, is now beginning to learn to imitate the live actions of his teachers and parents.

Once a student is able to reliably sit in a chair quietly and pay attention to a teacher, as indicated by performing these skills with ninety percent accuracy across three days of trials, the skills are incorporated into other areas. In general, this is done by ensuring appropriate eye contact and sitting behavior before beginning any teaching session. Incorporating these skills into other areas maintains them and helps students generalize them across learning environments.

With these skills established and generalized, students are taught to respond to basic one-step commands, such as "Come here," or "Stand up." These commands form the basis of a student's interactive vocabulary. When basic readiness skills are mastered, students are also able to begin imitating simple gross motor movements, such as clapping hands. Mastering gross motor imitation skills is essential for students. Gross motor imitation skills provide the framework for modelling more complex behaviors, such as washing hands or brushing teeth.

Basic self-care skills are taught once learning readiness skills have been established. Toilet training is the first in the sequence of self-care skills and is one of the student's first steps toward independence. Without this skill, access to community environments is severely restricted. Other age-appropriate skills such as dressing and hand washing are also part of the student's program. Most self-care skills represent fairly complex behaviors, and, through task analysis, are broken down and taught in small, sequential steps.

Self-Care Skills

Toilet Training (Urination)	Toilet Training (Bowel)
Dressing (Pants)	Dressing (Pullover Shirt)
Dressing (Socks)	Dressing (Shoes)
Snapping	Buttoning
Zipping (Connected)	Zipping (Unconnected)
Shoe Tying	Hand Washing
Face Washing	Bathing
Toothbrushing	Sanitary Napkin
Hair Brushing	Nail Clipping
Shaving	

The standard skill acquisition program below is used at Eden Institute to teach students how to tie their shoes. Tying shoes is a self-care skill that many students have learned. It is generally taught after the student has gotten dressed, when the student would typically need to put on and tie his shoes.

Standard Skill Acquisition Program

TARGET BEHAVIOR
Given the *Sd* "Tie your shoes," student will do so without help.

PREREQUISITE SKILLS
1. Learning readiness
2. Buttoning
3. Snapping
4. Zipping
5. Most dressing skills mastered.

CRITERION
No prompts for each step for three consecutive days.

MEASUREMENT
Number and type of prompts needed for each trial.

PROCEDURE (BACKWARDS CHAINING)
With student seated in front of a tying board (a board with laces in it):
1. Student pulls loop tight.
2. Step 1 plus pulls left lace through to form a second loop.
3. Steps 1-2 plus crosses left lace around the right loop.
4. Steps 1-3 plus makes right loop.
5. Steps 1-4 plus makes knot that precedes loop making.
6. Steps 1-5 plus crosses the laces.
7. Student independently ties a bow.
8. Have student tie shoes off the body.
9. Have student tie shoes on feet.

PROMPTING TECHNIQUES:
1. Full physical prompt—teacher takes student's hands and helps student perform activity.
2. Faded physical prompt—teacher moves student's hands to begin activity and student finishes.
3. Gestural prompt—teacher points to indicate correct placement of student's hands.
4. Above procedures are faded until no prompts are necessary.

Self-care skills are usually needed in specific environments and situations. To help students be aware of these, self-care skills are taught in functional "packages." While working on a step in a student's toilet training program, for example, the student would be taught how to communicate his need to use the bathroom. Similarly, hand-washing is taught after toileting, and tooth-brushing is practiced after lunch. Teaching skills in appropriate settings and at the appropriate times helps students understand the role and purpose of a skill, and also helps them learn more quickly how to correctly use a skill.

PREACADEMIC SKILLS

Like self-care skills, preacademic skills are begun as soon as learning readiness skills have been established. Most preacademic skills are learned naturally by students without disabilities, but must be taught specifically to students with autism because of the difficulty they have in focusing on relevant cues in the environment. For example, a typical student would follow a teacher's pointer across a blackboard because the student knows that the pointer indicates something he needs to pay attention to. A student with autism, on the other hand, might pay attention to the teacher's shiny necklace instead, and so would miss entirely what the teacher was saying. A student with autism would have to be taught that the pointer is the most important indicator in the room, not the teacher's necklace or any other cue in the environment. Teaching such basic skills gives the student with autism the building blocks he is missing, but needs for learning academic skills.

Preacademic skills begin with visual motor development, which focuses on matching, visual discrimination, and identification of the shape, color, and size of letters or numbers. Fine motor development skills are then taught which include visual tracking, tactile discrimination, proprioception, and motor planning. Finally, some simple occupational skills are taught, such as bead stringing, using a pegboard, completing puzzles or patterns, and sorting. These skills provide students with a basis from which they can begin functional academic or prevocational programs.

SOCIAL AND PLAY SKILLS

Social and play skills help students take part in more typical, less specialized, settings. For example, understanding the social concept of taking a turn allows a student to take part in group games. It is a more typical turn-taking situation than sitting one-on-one with a teacher taking turns. In the General Special Education Domain of Eden Institute Day School's curriculum, social and play skill programs focus on teaching appropriate leisure and recreational skills. Formal social skills, such as requesting a break from an activity, tend to be taught through the Communication Domain.

Social skills are taught in small groups of four to six students. Small groups encourage students to socialize. Students work on a variety of activities, but the focus is on teaching appropriate social skills. The focus of an art session, for

CURRICULUM FLOW CHART FOR PREACADEMIC SKILLS

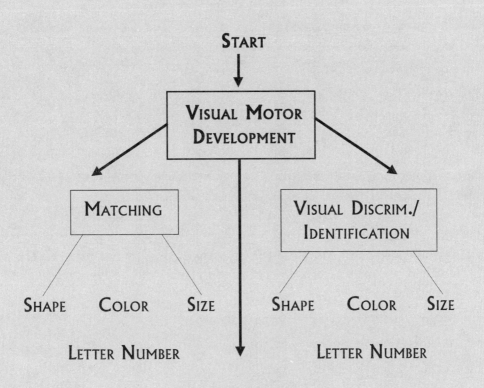

START

VISUAL MOTOR DEVELOPMENT

MATCHING

VISUAL DISCRIM./ IDENTIFICATION

SHAPE   COLOR   SIZE   SHAPE   COLOR   SIZE

LETTER NUMBER   LETTER NUMBER

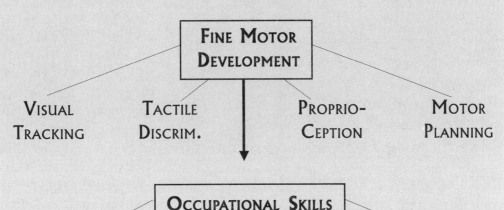

FINE MOTOR DEVELOPMENT

VISUAL TRACKING   TACTILE DISCRIM.   PROPRIO-CEPTION   MOTOR PLANNING

OCCUPATIONAL SKILLS

PEGBOARD/ BEAD STRINGING   PUZZLE/PATTERN COMPLETION   SORTING

Many of the students at Eden Institute don't know how to play appropriately. But if we can teach a student how to play, then he can take that skill home and play with his brother or sister, or other children in the neighborhood. That's normal play. Playing is one of the few ways siblings can interact with their brother or sister.

Brothers and sisters of students at Eden Institute come in on Sibling Day to play, have lunch, or go on a field trip with us. On one Sibling Day, Jill, a nine-year-old student here, was playing with the sister of another student. The sibling was playing with a doll house, and Jill started playing with her. They had a whole play scene going. They said "Oh, let's get the dog," and played with the figures. Jill had the male doll and said "What is daddy doing? Do you think he's going to work?" and she walked him around. We thought it was great. Jill was really interacting with someone. She got a lot of feedback from the little girl, which probably kept the whole interaction going, but the comments and the type of play were typical for her age, and were totally appropriate for the two of them, so the other girl played along.

—**Sue Williamson, Teacher, Middle Childhood**

example, would not be to complete the art project, but rather to teach the students to attend to group directions, share materials, and actively participate in the project at hand.

Archie has made enormous progress in his first six months at Eden. He's a lot more in our world. The most striking thing is that he has learned to play. He can even have a play scheme. He says "The train is going to New York," or takes a shopping cart around. He plays in stereotyped and repetitive ways, but at least he plays. He never used to do that at all. He was really in his own world for much of the day. He would sit for hours drawing circles in the sand, or arranging things in patterns. Recently, he went bowling with his class at Eden, and when he came home he said "I'm going to go play bowling." He didn't actually do it, but he set up the pins and got his ball out. That was good.

—**Nancy Cantor and Steve Brechin**

Play skills are equally important, especially for younger students. Students are taught to play alone and in small groups. Students learn isolated toy play first, then move on to parallel toy play, which leads to cooperative toy play, and simple games, which lead to more competitive games.

Social and play skills, like preacademic skills, are learned easily by children without disabilities. Teaching these skills to children with autism is quite a challenge, but nevertheless crucial. Social and play skills enable children with autism to interact with their peers in less specialized environments.

ACADEMICS

Because students with autism require a highly pragmatic curriculum, academics are addressed in a functional way, with the goal of increasing independent living skills. Before a decision is made to teach academics to a particular student, teachers assess whether the student needs academic skills in order to learn vocational, employment, or independence skills. Based on the student's current abilities, teachers also assess the student's possible use of academic skills in the future. For example, if a student, age fourteen, showed good assembly skills, but had trouble counting the parts he had put together, an academic program to enhance his counting skills would be appropriate. If the same student had difficulty with writing the letters of the alphabet, and had not gotten them in a year of practice, that academic program would be dropped from his IEP. Although it would be nice for him to be able to write, and would undoubtedly increase his employment skills, taking the time it would require from his daily schedule to teach him to write would compromise his learning skills for which he shows more promise. Learning writing skills simply would not be the best use of his time.

> We have always taught varying levels of academics to our students. Occasionally, people from outside Eden have questioned whether we really should be doing that. We know, however, that functional academic training is important. For example, we have one student who's working at Wawa. He was hired because he had the math skills to do the weighing by ounces that they required for a salad maker. He learned those skills through the academic curriculum.
>
> —Ken Dorfman, Coordinating Teacher, Vocational Preparation Program

Academic programs that are part of students' IEP are incorporated as much as possible into daily activities and are taught as little as possible in isolated instructional settings. The reading curriculum, for example, focuses on reading written directions, menus, shopping lists, and recipes. Math skills such as number identification and counting are part of stock requisition, assembly, and collating skills. Money concepts are generalized to the purchase of a soda from a vending machine or lunch at a fast food restaurant, and liquid and solid measurements are used daily in lunch preparation.

Academic skills are grouped by subject and are arranged by level of difficulty to accommo-

> Eden Institute's curriculum is extremely well defined. Other schools usually have a more global curriculum, with goals such as "Child will spell name." Well, how does the child learn to spell his name? The handwriting program alone here has fifteen beginning steps, and eight additional steps to teach a child how to write his name. We know through task analysis what step each child is working on, and so can teach them step by step.
>
> —Edha Majumdar, Coordinating Teacher, Transition Program

◆ ◆

This is the basic skill acquisition program for teaching a student to read sight words. Note that the words to be taught through the program are chosen by the student's teacher, often with help from the student's parents.

Standard Skill Acquisition Program

TARGET BEHAVIOR
The student will receptively and expressively identify sight words and demonstrate comprehension.

PREREQUISITE SKILLS
1. Receptive and expressive picture ID or object ID.
2. Completion of preacademic skills.

CRITERION
Criterion is 90% correct responding for each step over three consecutive days.

MEASUREMENT
Trial by trial data.

PROCEDURE
1. Present word card in isolation and *Sd* "Touch __."
2. Present word card with 1 distractor and *Sd* "Touch __."
3. Present word card with corresponding picture or object and *Sd* "Match."
4. Present word card with 2 distractor picture/objects and *Sd* "Match."
5. Present word card with 2 distractor words and one picture/object and *Sd* "Match."
6. Present word card in isolation and *Sd* "Read."
7. Randomize steps 4-6.
8. Introduce second word as in steps 1-7.
9. Randomize first and second word as in step 7.
10. Continue to introduce new words using above steps.

PROMPTING TECHNIQUES
For matching and receptive identification:
1. Full physical prompt—manipulate student's hand to perform correct response.
2. Faded physical prompt—manipulate student's hand to begin correct response and student completes response.
3. Gestural prompt—teacher points to correct response.
4. Probe—no prompt offered.

(Continued)

Prompting techniques

For expressive identification:
1. Full verbal prompt—teacher says full response and student repeats.
2. Faded verbal prompt—teacher says initial sound(s) of response and student provides full response.
3. Probe—no prompt offered.

Materials

picture cards, sight word flash cards.

Note

Use sight words which will be functional for the student to read.

◆ ◆

date students' differing levels of ability. Writing, reading, and mathematics comprise the bulk of academic skill programs.

The cognitive and motor difficulties of some students make writing impossible, but for students who show some ability, writing programs are begun with imitation. Students copy lines, shapes, and then letters. From there, students are taught to print their names and addresses, and ultimately words. At the highest level, students are taught to complete forms, write complete sentences, and do simple composition.

Students studying reading begin with receptive and expressive letter identification and the recognition of sight words, especially safety words such as *exit*, *danger*, and *stop*. Students are then taught to follow written directions and match sentences to pictures. Phonics, spelling, and reading comprehension for sentences and paragraphs are then addressed. Students who read on or near grade level are given textbooks from their local education agency, but most functional reading materials are made by teachers.

Several programs at Eden address mathematics. Math skills are useful in most employment opportunities open to Eden's graduates. For example, assembly, light office work like collating and counting mailings, and restocking shelves all require basic math skills. For this reason, most of the students at Eden work on mathematics.

Students begin learning mathematics by matching and identifying numbers and quantities (more/less), then move on to counting, addition, subtraction, money concepts such as coin identification and making change, time and calendar concepts, liquid and solid measurement, and linear measurement. Again, for the most advanced students, additional materials are garnered from textbooks.

OTHER ACADEMICS

Several areas which are routine in a regular academic curriculum are not addressed directly with students at Eden. These areas are history, science, and geography. Teaching these subjects would not meet the functional needs of Eden's students. These subjects are addressed instead in more practical terms.

Students receive basic history information on an informal basis through annual holidays. For Early and Middle Childhood students, emphasis is placed on the actual events of each celebration, but students in the Transition Program are taught some information and background about each holiday. They have language discussion groups around the holiday and do related activities, such as preparing a Thanksgiving dinner and crafting holiday decorations and gifts. In addition, teachers tell students about local historical events. The New Jersey State Museum in Trenton, the Franklin Institute in Philadelphia, the Mule Barge ride in New Hope, Washington Crossing State Park, and the Howell Living History Farm are a few places students have learned about and visited.

Some students at Eden access history materials from textbooks and the library, but they must meet several criteria first. They must have mastered the academic skills of number sequencing and time and calendar concepts, and they must have sufficient language skills to be able to use the past verb tense, relate to past events, and comprehend who, what, where, when, and why questions. Science instruction is absent from the Early and Middle Childhood programs, but some students in the Transition Program are able to work on basic science concepts. These usually overlap with mathematical skills and include programs for using liquid, solid, and linear measurements, and understanding basic weather concepts.

For students who have a limited awareness of their environment, the most important geographic goal is to maneuver through familiar surroundings. Students must be taught to find their classrooms, the bathroom, and how to get around independently at home. Again, students in the Transition Program may work on more traditional geography skills using materials from textbooks.

PREVOCATIONAL SKILLS

When a student leaves the Early Childhood Program and enters either the Transition or Middle Childhood Program (ages 8 - 13), teachers and parents begin determining realizable goals for adulthood. Vocational skills training is an impor-

We think Sasha is happy with his life. He has learned how to entertain himself, and has found many interesting occupations. We want to keep him happy as he gets older. It's quite clear now that he will be able to have a simple job. At home he does chores perfectly, and he likes them. It's important for all of us to feel like we do something useful, and so it's important to him to be able to do things successfully, and to be proud of what he's doing.

—**Sasha and Dasha Polyakov**

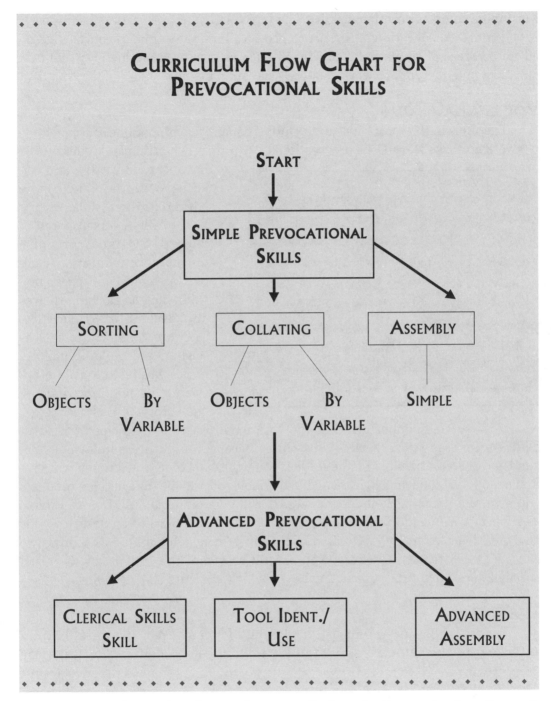

Curriculum Flow Chart for Prevocational Skills

START

SIMPLE PREVOCATIONAL SKILLS

SORTING

COLLATING

ASSEMBLY

OBJECTS

BY VARIABLE

OBJECTS

BY VARIABLE

SIMPLE

ADVANCED PREVOCATIONAL SKILLS

CLERICAL SKILLS SKILL

TOOL IDENT./ USE

ADVANCED ASSEMBLY

tant step toward ensuring that students can find productive work when they exit the educational system, whether they continue at Eden or are able to make the transition to regular placements.

Skill acquisition programs in the prevocational curriculum encompass a variety of production and clerical areas, including sorting, collating, and assembly. Mastery of these skills provides students with the basic knowledge they need in order to learn more complex vocational skills. The introduction of prevocational skills early in the student's educational experience provides him more time to concentrate on advanced areas of vocational competence, such as increased productivity and task duration, and appropriate work-related social and language skills.

VOCATIONAL SKILLS

The skills in the vocational curriculum are mainly combinations of simpler one or two step tasks learned in prevocational programs. For example, students who have learned sorting and collating would be taught more advanced clerical skills, such as how to file a mixed batch of papers. Students are also taught stock requisition, complex assembly and packaging skills such as stocking shelves and assembling furniture. They are taught crafts, such as sewing, and building maintenance skills like sweeping, vacuuming, washing windows, and emptying wastebaskets.

> We begin vocational training with simple assembly tasks, like putting travel toothbrushes together. Then we do more complicated assembly, such as putting school boxes together with rulers and pencils. Gradually, students will be able to recognize the objects and follow a diagram. Some of the more advanced students can incorporate their reading skills to follow a written inventory sheet. Those students who have reading skills do filing in the administration office.
>
> —Ken Dorfman, Coordinating Teacher, Vocational Preparation Program

It is especially important that the vocational programs developed for a student are tailored to his particular abilities because his future employment depends on the vocational skills he learns. Knowing how to sign his name will give him a degree of independence, but knowing how to assemble marketable products will give him much more independence. It will give him a job. As Denise Elkins, Teacher of Vocational Preparation, put it, "Because we offer lifespan services, our goal is to teach as many job related skills and provide job training as soon as we can." For this reason, teachers keep careful record of the skills students learn through vocational programs and areas in which students show promise.

LIFE SKILLS

The life skills curriculum is for older students at Eden Institute. It is an extension of the self-care skills taught to younger students. The skills are renamed to reflect a shift of focus toward developing self-sufficiency in adulthood. Emphasis is placed on combining isolated skill areas, and on using skills as they are needed in daily activities.

> Parents of young children at Eden often ask what they can do to help their child be independent. I always say "Teach him living skills. Have him set the table. Have him make a sandwich. Teach him how to do his laundry and make his bed." Adults coming into the group home who don't know how to do these things are far less independent than those who do.
>
> —Dave Roussell, Director of Residential Services

If we want to teach someone to make his own breakfast, much of what goes into the development of a program for him is going to depend on his skill levels. We need to know if he can read, if he has adequate receptive language skills, and if he can attend to a task for relatively long periods of time. Let's say a student has a very short attention span, tends to wander around, and has limited receptive language. With him, we are probably going to have to stand next to him and provide gestural, verbal, and maybe an occasional physical prompt. Food could be extremely reinforcing to him, so making his own breakfast would be immediately gratifying. We would fade our prompts to the point he could prepare breakfast independently. We would then chain that into a larger program to start off his day in the morning, with skills like getting up, shaving, showering, brushing his teeth, making his breakfast, and getting ready for work.

—**Annette Cavallaro, Assistant Director of Residential Service**

For example, washing and drying dishes are chained together to make a general clean-up program. Laundry washing, drying, and folding are also combined into one program.

The few isolated skill programs in the life skills curriculum address the needs of older students. These include programs for shaving, showering, and using sanitary napkins. Once mastered, they too are be chained to fit into a daily personal hygiene routine. The life skills curriculum also contains programs that address the developing sexuality and social awareness of students, and programs giving information on personal needs and bodily awareness.

THE COMMUNICATION DOMAIN

The goal of the communication curriculum is to develop an individualized, pragmatic communication system for each student. This system should incorporate any means of communication the student can use effectively, including speech, gestures, simultaneous communication (pairing verbalization with sign), and communication boards or other augmentative communication systems. Each of these systems has been shown to be functional for people

With Sean we recently added "Take a break" and "Go for a walk" to his computer system. We're training him to understand the pictures by prompting him to touch them, then giving him a break in the middle of a work session, or letting him go for a walk. Our hope is that rather than hit his head to escape or avoid the situation, he will touch the picture to leave work for a while. He is beginning to pick up on it. He has learned what the pictures mean, and his self-injurious behavior is beginning to decrease.

—**Lyn O'Donnell, Coordinator of Clinical Services**

with autism (Carr et al., 1978; Mirenda & Schuler, 1988; Mirenda & Mathy-Laikko, 1989). A wide variety of communication options is necessary because many people with autism who cannot speak can use other methods to generate language (Kirk & Gallagher, 1989). Among those who can speak, many need additional prompts, such as visual cues, in order to speak (Batshaw & Perret, 1992). As Lyn O'Donnell, Coordinator of Clinical Services, says, the important thing is to get them to communicate:

> *Many children take a long time to develop a functional system of communication. What they settle on is often a multi-modal approach. They may use a word or two, a couple of signs, and their picture board. We let them. Any way they want to communicate in an appropriate fashion is fine with us, as long as they communicate.*

At Eden 44 percent of students use speech as their primary communication system. Twenty-four percent use primarily sign language, and 32 percent use augmentative devices as their primary means of communication.

The communication curriculum at Eden is divided into four areas: learning readiness (which is basically the same as that under the Special Education Curriculum), receptive language training, verbal language and expressive language training, and pragmatic skills to incorporate what the student learns into his environment. All communication skills are taught in one-to-one sessions with a speech and language pathologist, and are generalized throughout the day by the student's teachers and parents.

RECEPTIVE LANGUAGE TRAINING

Once learning readiness skills have been established, and a speech and language assessment has been completed, students are introduced to beginning language training. This starts with receptive language training. All skills in the training are nonverbal, requiring only the internal processing of information coupled with motor expression to demonstrate understanding. Lyn O'Donnell explains:

> *The receptive comprehension of people with autism is usually quite impaired. Receptive language training helps them begin to understand the spoken word. With several students we pair signs with the spoken word to give them a more concrete way of understanding what we say. We also utilize telegraphic speech, and we use words repetitiously so they have many opportunities to understand. We see their comprehension of what we are doing when they use the sign or gesture we have taught them, or when they follow commands. However, we have to be very careful that they do not use only contextual or environmental cues from their environment. We have to separate what they actually understand from what they are being cued or prompted to do by their environment.*

◆ ◆

This is the standard skill acquisition program for teaching students the receptive function of objects.

Standard Skill Acquisition Program

TARGET BEHAVIOR

When presented with an object, two distractors, and the *Sd* "Give me what you ___ (play, eat, etc.) with," the student will respond by handing the appropriate object to the teacher within three seconds.

PREREQUISITE SKILLS

1. Has mastered the Learning Readiness Program.
2. Can receptively identify objects.
3. Can manipulate objects.

CRITERION

Ninety percent correct responding for one session for step 1, and 90 percent correct responding for three consecutive sessions for steps 2-7.

PROCEDURE

1. Teacher presents an object with no distractors and gives the *Sd* "Give me what you ___ with." Student will respond by handing the object to the teacher.
2. Teacher presents the same object with one distractor and gives the *Sd*. Student will respond by handing the appropriate object to the teacher.
3. Teacher presents the same object with two distractors and gives the *Sd*. Student will respond by handing the appropriate object to the teacher.
4. Present a second object function to the student. Use the procedure in the above steps.
5. Randomize the first and second object function taught.
6. Follow the same procedure for all object functions continuing to randomize as more are learned.
7. Generalize all object functions taught to a variety of objects, pictures, and teachers.

PROMPTING TECHNIQUES

1. Physical prompt—place student's hand on the correct object and manipulate the student's hand.
2. Gestural prompt—point to the correct picture.
3. Positional prompt—position the correct object near the student, so the student's first response is to get the object.
4. Probe—no prompt offered.

(Continued)

LIST OF SUGGESTED FUNCTIONS

eat—spoon, fork

cut—knife, scissors, saw

wash—soap

write—pencil

play—toy

pound—hammer

drink—cup

brush—toothbrush, hair brush

dry—towel

color—crayon

sweep—broom

clean—sponge

NOTE

Make sure the objects chosen are age-appropriate.

Receptive language training also incorporates skills such as action identification, understanding gestures, remembering sounds, and comprehension of *wh* questions. Other skills, like object manipulation and permanence, are also introduced. These skills are based on the gross motor imitation skills the student learned through earlier programming.

VERBAL TRAINING

Verbal training begins simultaneously with receptive language training and works on many of the same skills, but includes the production of verbal responses. Teachers first attempt to teach students to communicate verbally, before they teach sign language or offer augmentative communication. Communicating verbally enables a student to more easily interact with people in less specialized settings. Other methods of communication are, for the most part, unfamiliar to people in community or regular educational settings, and so tend to isolate students, rather than enable them to participate.

While the ultimate hope is that an individual will acquire speech for communication, which is the most conventional mode of communication in our culture, ... for many individuals with autism, nonspeech communication may be the most effective and efficient mode.

—Barry Prizant, "Building Bridges Through Communication." *The Advocate.* Vol 21, No. 2, 1989, p15.

Teachers have found that students' progress in receptive language programs and their progress in verbal training programs often follow divergent tracks. Many students are advanced in one program, but have difficulty in the other. Students who do well in verbal training are likely to express themselves well verbally, while those who do better in receptive language programs tend to communicate more effectively through sign or alternative methods. Teachers base expressive language training programs on the tendencies students show during the early stages of speech and language training.

EXPRESSIVE LANGUAGE TRAINING

The cognitive level of each student influences the amount of expressive language he acquires. Some students develop expansive expressive speech. However, teachers must make sure that this speech is functional. That is, they must be sure a student is using speech truly as a mode of communication, and not simply in an imitative way. For example, a student was working on how to ask for a glass of water. He and his teacher worked one-on-one after his exercise group to learn the skill. Later in the day, during group time, he asked for a glass of water. His teacher had to determine whether he was truly thirsty, or whether he was simply producing, or practicing, the response they had been working on. Since he had been learning the skill quickly, and had almost mastered it, his teacher decided that he was in fact asking for a glass of water.

In expressive language training, students are taught more advanced skills. These skills include how to ask questions, use pronouns, speak in past and future tenses, use short phrases, and answer "yes" and "no" appropriately. They are also taught basic syntax and the concept of possession.

ALTERNATIVE AND AUGMENTATIVE COMMUNICATION TRAINING

Children who have a strong desire to communicate tend to get their message across somehow.

—Lyn O'Donnell, Coordinator of Clinical Services

Until recently, communication was viewed as synonymous with speech (Calculator, 1988). In working with people who have autism, however, speech-language pathologists have come to recognize that for many, augmentative or alternative systems of communication, which do not rely on speech, may be the most effective and efficient mode of communication (Prizant, 1989). Research has shown that any type of successful communication for children with autism is correlated with a decrease in many of the aberrant behaviors they exhibit, such as aggression and self-injury (Carr & Carlson, 1993; Carr & Durand, 1987; Carr & Durand, 1985).

If teachers at Eden determine that a student either cannot learn to use verbal expression as a means of communication or that using verbal expression would enable the student to communicate significantly less than would an alternative communication method, other communication strategies are tried. The decision to teach an alternative or augmentative method of communication is based on data from the student's speech and language therapy sessions.

> In choosing a system of communication for a student, we first need to get to know the student and what he responds well to. Then we try different systems to see what works best. We first try to teach speech, but sometimes we have no other choice for a student than to go with a very basic system, like a picture board, because the student needs a functional method of communication as soon as possible.
>
> **—Sandra Sersen, Speech Therapist**

If an alternative or augmentative system is used, the age of the student, his therapeutic history, motor coordination, receptive functioning, visual acuity, cognitive level, behavior, and motivation levels must all be taken into account in developing the new system. This means that the alternative or augmentative system must be specifically designed for the student to make sure that the new system has the best chance of providing him with an effective means of communicating.

If teachers decide on an alternative or augmentative approach, the student must be taught the same skills in the same sequence as students being taught to communicate orally. Simply because a student does not find oral communication feasible does not mean he is any less capable, or less cognitively aware. The same developmental sequence of skills must therefore be followed for nonverbal students as for verbal students.

If teachers decide that oral communication is not the best means of communication for a student, their next choice is usually sign language, followed by augmentative communication devices.

Manual Sign Language

In sign language, a person uses his arms and face, but mainly his hands to communicate words or ideas. Originally developed for people with hearing impairments, manual sign language was first used by researchers in autism in the late 1970s to provide mute children with a way to communicate (Bonvillian & Nelson, 1976; Creedon, 1973). Since that time, manual sign language has become a common and effective means of communication for people with autism (Bonvillian & Blackburn, 1991).

There are various forms of sign language. In the United States, the most frequently used systems are American Sign Language (ASL) (Wilbur, 1976) and Signed Exact English (SEE) (Mayberry, 1976). Because ASL has a grammar that is separate and distinct from spoken English, Pidgin Signed English, a system that incorporates ASL signs with English word order and grammar, is most frequently used with students at Eden.

People with autism who have been trained to use sign language have learned to label and request food, toys, and activities (Carr, 1979), and some are able to use sign language to express abstract concepts (Creedon, 1973). Although abstraction is not a skill most of the people have at Eden, occasionally someone does use sign language abstractly. Lyn O'Donnell:

> Most of the children use sign only to make requests, and for very functional communication. Scotty, for instance, will only use it to ask about events that are coming up, especially holidays, but he does not really understand the concept of future. It is more of a preoccupation, and a need to keep a schedule. Children with greater cognitive abilities, however, can tell us things that have happened, and sometimes they make up signs. I can have a conversation with Jimmy and, through his verbal approximation and sign, figure out what he did over the week-

end. He once told me about an entire episode of a television show from start to finish. He signed woman, and swimming, and help. The show was about a woman who was drowning and needed help.

Reports have also indicated that sign language can be used to improve receptive language skills (Dores & Carr, 1979) and facilitate the acquisition of verbal skills in people with autism (Schaeffer, Kolinzas, Musil & McDowell, 1977).

Sign language is a valuable alternative means of communicating for students who are nonverbal but have good fine motor skills. Sign language also tends to be easier to learn than speech. Lyn O'Donnell:

The kinesthetic feedback, or actual feeling, the students get from signing makes it easier as a means of communication. When we take their hand and form it into the shape of a sign, it helps them learn it. We cannot do that with the oral area to make them produce sounds, but with the hand we can form signs. It is more concrete.

Not all students who require a nonspeech communication system will be able to use sign language, however. For those students who are unable to use sign, augmentative communication devices such as picture boards and voice output computers can be used.

Some children will show an ability to sign, but then will bottom out, and not learn any more signs. Or they will learn three signs, and, once they learn the fourth, will forget the first three. Sign is probably not going to be a good system of communication for these children. Once that becomes clear, we start working on another means of communication, and maintain sign only as a secondary means of communicating.

—**Betty Edwards, Speech Therapist**

Picture-Based Systems

Picture-based communication systems are typically boards covered with pictures that a student points to in order to communicate basic requests, such as "eat" and "bathroom." Frequently used by people with cerebral palsy, picture-based systems are appropriate for people with autism who lack the cognitive ability to understand abstractions (Coots & Falvey, 1989), or who do not have the motor skills to produce clearly differentiated manual signs. It is also helpful for those who appear to have difficulty retrieving correct signs from memory.

Picture-based systems have several advantages: 1) they can be created by teachers working with the student, with minimal time and effort, 2) they can be highly individualized, and 3) They are easy to expand as the student's communicative ability grows (Bondy & Frost, 1992).

* *

This is a program to teach Jaime in Middle Childhood how to use different pictures on his computer. As usual, the criterion is 90% correct responding for each step over three consecutive sessions, and data is measured trial by trial.

Standard Skill Acquisition Program

TARGET BEHAVIOR

Jaime will respond to varied stimuli (specifically, a picture indicating a request for music, another for a drink, and the third for a tickle) using his augmentative communication system, the Wolf™ computer.

PROCEDURE

1. Teacher presents Jaime with his computer.
2. Teacher instructs Jaime to "Turn it on." Jaime activates the computer with a toggle switch.
3. Teacher presents Jaime with the stimulus material. Jaime depresses or activates the appropriate square on his computer pane.

[The standard program for teaching a student the meaning of pictures on his computer includes a fourth step: "The number of stimulus questions asked is increased by one after criterion is met for each." Jaime is not yet working on this step.]

PROMPTING TECHNIQUES

1. Physical prompt—the teacher prompts Jaime hand over hand.
2. Faded physical prompt—the teacher prompts Jaime hand over hand to begin his response, and he completes it.
3. Gestural prompt—the teacher points to indicate the correct response.
4. Probe—no prompt offered.

OBJECTIVE FOR JAIME

Step 1 through step 3, then on to step 4 if possible.

BASELINE, SEPTEMBER 1993

On step 3, Jaime requests music with 70% accuracy, a drink with 70% accuracy, and a tickle with 0% accuracy.

FINAL RATE, JUNE 1994

On step 3, Jaime requests music with 90% accuracy, a drink with 80-90% accuracy, and a tickle with 60% accuracy.

* *

Computerized Systems

Like picture-based systems, many computerized devices are relatively straightforward, and are used with people who have a variety of disabilities. They are designed to take in programmed information, store the information, and reproduce the information on demand (Exceptional Parent, 1983). A student's vocabulary is represented by pictures or symbols, which are "spoken" by the computer when touched.

Because students receive immediate feedback from a computer, these systems are often highly motivating to students, especially if the computer's "voice" is that of a person familiar to the student, such as a parent or teacher. Computerized systems can also increase the student's receptive language skills, because visual images are constantly paired with verbalizations.

Computerized systems and picture boards, however, are teachers' last choice of communicative systems for students because they do not encourage abstract thought. Students do not have to independently retrieve a word or sign from memory, and then employ their motor skills to produce them. Rather, they simply need to press one of several buttons in order to communicate complete thoughts.

Still, computerized systems are proving to be efficient and highly motivating alternatives to speech for several students at Eden. Teachers use the Wolf™ and IntroTalker™ devices to introduce computerization to students. More advanced devices, with greater storage capacity and the ability to produce sequences of thoughts and ideas, such as the Vois 136™, Vois 160™, and Zygo Macaw™, are available for students who "outgrow" the basic systems. For students who have literacy skills, the Canon Communicator™ is available. It allows them to type messages and receive a printed output of their communication.

Sean has some severe aggression and self-injury. We determined through the EDM that these behaviors were related to his inability to communicate and his desire to escape from situations. When he was younger he had verbal language. But Sean has Landau-Kleffner Syndrome, which is a neurological disorder in which language skills deteriorate rapidly, so he has lost all of his language. That has made him very frustrated.

He's resistant to physical prompting and finds signing very difficult. He doesn't have good picture recognition skills, so picture boards aren't optimal for him either. He now has a computer with a digitized voice. When we first gave him the computer, he responded to the voice by trying to repeat what was said. He knew what many of the words meant, so we thought we could slowly teach him what the pictures meant and improve his picture recognition skills. He's still unable to speak anything but an occasional word, but he has learned the meaning of many pictures. And he picks up on the feedback he gets from the computer. For example, if he presses the wrong picture and hears that it's wrong, he'll correct himself.

—**Sandra Sersen, Speech Therapist**

This is the standard skill acquisition program teachers use to teach students how to take turns. It is part of pragmatic language training.

Standard Skill Acquisition Program

TARGET BEHAVIOR
When given an object (e.g., drum and sticks) and the *Sd* "Your turn," the student will engage in proper turn sequence.

PREREQUISITE SKILLS
Program should be taught concurrently with object manipulation and gross motor imitation programs.

CRITERION
90% correct responding for three consecutive sessions for all steps.

MEASUREMENT
Trial by trial data.

PROCEDURE
1. Teacher models desired activity.

The Canon Communicator™, and other similar print-out systems, have been extensively advocated by proponents of facilitated communication as a treatment for autism. Although many programs for people with autism have enthusiastically embraced facilitated communication, Eden has not been able to demonstrate or find empirical evidence of its effectiveness. Facilitated communication is therefore rarely, if ever, used in Eden's programs.[2]

Pragmatic Training

Pragmatic language training helps a student assimilate his communication skills into daily life. From the beginning of language therapy, the speech and language pathologist incorporates a student's language programs into his daily activities to make sure those skills are transferred to a variety of settings and people. For example, speech and language pathologists will help a student produce, in the classroom, skills he has shown in formal speech and language sessions. Community trips are also planned as a way to generalize language skills. Students go to local restaurants, for example, to practice ordering food, and to a bowling alley where they have to request the right size shoes. Pragmatic training programs also include skills such as turn taking, communicating basic needs and desires, increasing the number of requests students can make, and telling stories.

---

[2] See Chapter 5 for a discussion of the controversy surrounding facilitated communication.

2. Teacher models same activity and gives the *Sd* "Your turn." Student will respond appropriately.
3. Use the procedure in steps 1 and 2 for a second activity.
4. Randomize the first and second activities.
5. Use the same procedure for several subsequent activities.
6. Generalize the student's responses to various teachers in various settings.

PROMPTING TECHNIQUES
1. Full physical prompt—manipulate the student's hand through the desired response.
2. Faded physical prompt—touch the student to begin his movement.
3. Gestural prompt—gesture with hands or point to the object.
4. Fade the gestural prompt.

SUGGESTED ACTIVITIES

Ball—passing back and forth	Jack-in-the-box
Banging on a drum with two drumsticks	Stacking rings
Putting pegs in a board	"Slap me five"
Turning pages of a book	Taking turns jumping
Sandbox with 1 pail, 2 shovels	Make juice or sandwich

THE ADAPTIVE PHYSICAL EDUCATION DOMAIN

The adaptive physical education domain of Eden Institute's curriculum addresses the difficulty many students have in organizing sensory input and responding to sensory data. Sensory motor integration is enhanced through controlled sensory input, which is provided through gross and fine motor activities. When a student is more able to integrate his sensory stimulation, recreational programs are offered.

SENSORY MOTOR SKILLS

Sensory motor programs concentrate specifically on two sensory systems: the tactile and proprioceptive systems. The tactile, or touch, system monitors how stimuli affect the body. The proprioceptive, or vestibular, system controls the body's balance and the position of the body in space according to Ayers and Tickle

When Jaime goes to sensory integration therapy, he wears a weighted vest. The vest is heavy, but not so heavy that he can't move around. It helps calm him down. After sensory integration therapy, he seems to find it easier to work on skills, and to interact with other people.

—**Nancy Guggenheim, Coordinating Teacher, Adaptive Physical Education**

(1980). The tactile and vestibular systems are two of the most dysfunctional systems in people with autism.

Helping students correctly interpret the sensory stimulation they receive through these systems enables them to respond more appropriately to their sensory environment. Nancy Guggenheim, Coordinating Teacher of Adaptive Physical Education:

> *We give students various activities designed to help them respond better, more quickly, and more naturally. For example, in climbing down a sharp incline, some of the students will try to go down head first. They do not realize that it is dangerous, and that they could easily flip over, so we teach them how to motor plan the activity.*

Sensory motor skill programs are designed to improve balance, tactile discrimination, general awareness of the body, spatial relations, gross motor development and strengthening, and awareness of proprioceptive feedback. The methods used to improve sensory motor skills were influenced by Jean Ayres' Sensory Integration Therapy.[3]

In sensory motor training we do similar activities with students, but for different reasons. For example, some students don't like being up off the ground, so working on the open climber would help them overcome a gravitational insecurity. For other students, it would be a way to learn how to get up and down a ladder. Similarly, some students have a tactile aversion to putting their hands on the floor, so riding a scooter board would have a different purpose for them than it would for a student who doesn't have the ability to stretch his hands out over his head and pull.

Jaime and Spike are both on tactile stimulation programs, but for very different reasons. Jaime actively seeks tactile input, so his program is geared toward moderating his desire, and helping him be happy with a normal level of input. Spike loves to have his feet and legs touched, but is defensive of tactile stimulation on his face and hands. His program helps him tolerate tactile experiences on his upper body by rewarding him with a foot or leg rub.

—**Nancy Guggenheim, Coordinating Teacher, Adaptive Physical Education**

The goal of sensory integration is to incorporate students' dysfunctional sensory responses meaningfully into their general network of sensations. Sensory integration makes students' sensory processing more functional. They become more able to move through their environment and complete skills. Sensory integration training also tends to result in less self-stimulation, more active social interaction, and increased confidence in movement and practical tasks.

---

[3] See Chapter 5 for a description of the therapy developed by Jean Ayres.

◆ ◆

This is a standard sensorimotor program for balance and vestibular processing. There are no prerequisite skills, and the criterion is individualized for each student.

Standard Skill Acquisition Program

TARGET BEHAVIOR
The student will demonstrate appropriate balance reactions.

MEASUREMENT
Anecdotal data will be taken each session by the teacher.

PROCEDURE
1. The student rocks back and forth while lying on a vestibular ball.
2. The student rocks from side to side while lying on a vestibular ball.
3. The student rocks back and forth while sitting on the vestibular ball.
4. The student climbs up and down the climber.
5. The student performs segmented (step-by-step) log rolls.
6. The student performs somersaults.
7. The student tolerates spinning on a platform swing for one minute.
8. The student maintains balance while bouncing on a gymnastic ball.
9. The student rides the Hoppity-Hop.

PROMPTING TECHNIQUES
1. Full physical prompt—the teacher places the student's body, hand, or finger in the correct position.
2. Faded physical prompt—the teacher moves the student's body or hand in the direction of the correct position.
3. Gestural prompt—the teacher points to the body part or where the hand should go.

MATERIALS
Vestibular ball, barrel, platform swing, climber, floor mats, gymnastic ball, and Hoppity-Hop.

◆ ◆

RECREATION
Recreational programs get students to move their bodies and maintain their general physical fitness. Recreational programs are divided into two areas: cardiovascular fitness and sports skills. The cardiovascular fitness program is modified for different groups of students to suit their fitness level and ability to follow a teacher. Individual as well as group exercise classes are held, and students are trained in using Eden Institute's fitness equipment.

Sports skills are taught not only because they help maintain fitness, but also because they give each student the opportunity to develop age appropriate leisure skills. Younger students are taught to use playground equipment, and older students are given choices between swimming, volleyball, basketball, soccer, track and field, and bowling.

Sports often form the basis of community outings for students. For example, they go bowling and swimming regularly, and take part in Special Olympics. Nancy Guggenheim:

> *At Special Olympics, students have participated in bowling, basketball, track and field, and one student is an equestrian. The downhill and cross-country skiing, though, is one of the neatest things we have done. We started by sending only Scott, who had learned to ski with his family. Last year, four downhill and four cross-country skiers went. They learned how to put their skis on and off, fall, and stand at Eden Institute before we got to any snow. But in order to go to the Olympics, they had to pass their time trial, which meant they had to practice. So, we took a few overnight trips to a nearby ski lodge for practice on the slopes.*

Regular sporting events are arranged at Eden Institute as well, so all students get the chance to participate in group fitness activities.

The adaptive physical education curriculum, along with the communication and special education curriculum, comprises the meat of Eden Institute's skill development programs. All students work on skills in these areas through programs which match their evolving level of ability. On graduation, the tripartite nature of Eden Institute's curriculum is carried over into the adult services Eden offers through Eden WERCs and Eden ACREs. The Individualized Habilitation Plan, or IHP, of adults follows a curriculum with skill programs developed for adults that progress naturally from the curriculum offered to students. Like students at Eden Institute, adults at Eden work on a variety of skills, but adults focus even more on the life and employment skills they need to find and maintain gainful employment, and live successfully in the community. Chapter 9 describes the types of skill programs offered to adults.

Eden
A.C.R.E.s
Participant
Report

Participant Report (page 1)

EDEN A.C.R.E.s

One Logan Drive
Princeton, NJ 08540
(609) 987-0099

PARTICIPANT: Mary Smith
DATE OF BIRTH: 11/15/65
HOUSE: Farrell
REFERRAL AGENCY: DDD

DATE OF REPORT: July 1996
CHRONOLOGICAL AGE: 30 years, 8 months
PARENT/GUARDIAN: Tom and Barbara Smith
STARTING DATE OF RESIDENCY: 9/15/88

SUMMARY

Mary has had another great month at Farrell House and has been in high
spirits. She recently had her yearly physical and was given a clean bill of
health. Programmatically, she is doing quite well; she moved up a step on her
bathroom cleaning program and has made significant progress in several
other areas as well. Behaviorally, Mary continues to do well. The frequency of
aggressions and destructive behavior remain well below baseline and the
rates for both programs are down for the third month in a row. Mary has
been very active in the community this month and has enjoyed an array of
exciting activities. Among the highlights were trips to the Aquarium, Howell
Living Farm, Great Adventure, Washington Crossing State Park and shopping in New Hope. Mary's favorite event this month was going to the Eden
shore house for several days where she spent her days swimming in the ocean
and crabbing in the bay followed by dinner at a local restaurant. Afterwards,
Mary would visit the local water park or try her hand at miniature golf. Mary
continues to lead a productive and fulfilling life at Farrell House and is
looking forward to many more exciting activities before the season is over.

AUTHOR OF REPORT: _____

HOUSE MANAGER: _____

COORDINATOR OF HOME OPERATIONS: _____

DIRECTOR OF RESIDENTIAL SERVICES: _____

EXECUTIVE DIRECTOR OF EDEN SERVICES: _____

Participant Report (page 2)

PROFESSIONAL CONTACTS

NAME: Dr. Fine   **DATE:** 6/12/97

REASON FOR VISIT: Yearly physical

TREATMENT: Physical

PRESCRIPTION GIVEN: (List Below) ☐ Yes ■ No

FOLLOW-UP REQUIRED? ☐ Yes ■ No

NAME: **DATE:**

REASON FOR VISIT:

TREATMENT:

PRESCRIPTION GIVEN: (List Below) ☐ Yes ☐ No

FOLLOW-UP REQUIRED? ☐ Yes ☐ No

NAME: **DATE:**

REASON FOR VISIT:

TREATMENT:

PRESCRIPTION GIVEN: (List Below) ☐ Yes ☐ No

FOLLOW-UP REQUIRED? ☐ Yes ☐ No

Participant Report (page 3)

CURRENT MEDICATION

MEDICATION	AMOUNT	DOSAGE
Depakote	250 mg.	1 @ 8 a.m., 2 @ 4 p.m., and 2 @ 8 p.m.

List below any medication changes during the past month.

MEDICATION	AMOUNT	PREVIOUS DOSE	CURRENT DOSE
None.			

Participant Report (page 4)

PROGRAMMATIC DATA

PROGRAM TITLE: Bathroom Cleaning

PREVIOUS MONTH STEP	PREVIOUS MONTH %	CURRENT STEP	CURRENT REPORT STEP	CURRENT STEP %	PROMPTS USED
7	80%	8	Mops floor using a back and forth motion and rinses mop after every three strokes.	75%	GP

PROGRAM TITLE: Dusting

PREVIOUS MONTH STEP	PREVIOUS MONTH %	CURRENT STEP	CURRENT REPORT STEP	CURRENT STEP %	PROMPTS USED
4	90%	4	Sprays furniture polish on area	100%	none

PROGRAM TITLE: Vacuuming

PREVIOUS MONTH STEP	PREVIOUS MONTH %	CURRENT STEP	CURRENT REPORT STEP	CURRENT STEP %	PROMPTS USED
4	50%	4	Turns on vacuum	75%	GP

PROGRAM TITLE: Tablesetting

PREVIOUS MONTH STEP	PREVIOUS MONTH %	CURRENT STEP	CURRENT REPORT STEP	CURRENT STEP %	PROMPTS USED
6	80%	All	All steps—Program mastered this month!	100%	none

PROGRAM TITLE: Loading Dishwasher

PREVIOUS MONTH STEP	PREVIOUS MONTH %	CURRENT STEP	CURRENT REPORT STEP	CURRENT STEP %	PROMPTS USED
3	80%	3	Places all plates in bottom rack of washer	80%	GP

Participant Report (page 5)/Programmatic Data Cont.

PROGRAM TITLE: Washing Laundry

PREVIOUS MONTH STEP	PREVIOUS MONTH %	CURRENT STEP	CURRENT REPORT STEP	CURRENT STEP %	PROMPTS USED
3	40%	3	Sorts laundry into darks and lights	70%	GP, PP

PROGRAM TITLE: Folding Clothes

PREVIOUS MONTH STEP	PREVIOUS MONTH %	CURRENT STEP	CURRENT REPORT STEP	CURRENT STEP %	PROMPTS USED
2	85%	3	Folds shirts in thirds widthwise and in half lengthwise and places aside	N/A new step, no date yet	N/A

PROGRAM TITLE: Game Playing

PREVIOUS MONTH STEP	PREVIOUS MONTH %	CURRENT STEP	CURRENT REPORT STEP	CURRENT STEP %	PROMPTS USED
3	60%	3	Initiates her turn	80%	GP

PROGRAM TITLE: Fire Alarm

PREVIOUS MONTH STEP	PREVIOUS MONTH %	CURRENT STEP	CURRENT REPORT STEP	CURRENT STEP %	PROMPTS USED
5	100%	All	All Steps—Program mastered	N/A	none

PROGRAMMATIC COMMENTS:

Mary is doing beautifully in the area of programmatics! She mastered both her Tablesetting and Fire Drill programs this month. In addition, she moved up a step on her Bathroom Cleaning and Clothes Folding programs. Her percentage of correct responses increased on several other programs. Although she continues to require prompting on her laundry program as sorting is an especially difficult task for her, staff increased the number of sorting trials and her percentage increased by 30%!

Participant Report (page 6)

BEHAVIORAL DATA

DEFINITION: Aggression: Any aggression to include hitting, kicking, grabbing or biting of others or objects in the environment. Also to include attempts.

CONSEQUENCES: Sd, "No, _____" (appropriate to the behavior). A visual screen will be applied and Mary will be prompted to lie on her stomach upon a commercially manufactured gym mat with her hands behind her back for one minute of quiet. Quiet is defined as no vocalizations or tensing of musculature. After one minute of quiet, the visual screen will be removed and Mary will be prompted to return to task.

AVERAGE: .02 / duration: 1 minute
PREVIOUS MONTH: .03 / duration: 1 minute

DEFINITION: Destruction: Any destruction of objects to include ripping books, throwing usable items away in the trash and/or toilet. Also to include attempts.

CONSEQUENCES: Sd, "No, _____" (appropriate to the behavior). Mary will be prompted to remain on the treadmill at a speed of 4 mph for five minutes plus one additional minute of quiet. Quiet is defined as no vocalizations or attempts to remove herself from the treadmill.

AVERAGE: .03 / duration: 5 minutes
PREVIOUS MONTH: .10 / duration: 5 minutes

DEFINITION:

CONSEQUENCES:

Participant Report (page 7)

COMMUMITY EXPERIENCE PARTICIPATION SUMMARY

DATES: FROM: JUNE 1, 1996　　　　　　　　　**TO: JUNE 30, 1996**

WEEK OF		1-7	8-14	15-21	22-28	29-END OF MONTH	CUM. TOTAL
COMM. EXPERIENCE	1-MONTH TARGET	NUMBER PER WEEK/CUMULATIVE TOTAL					
Purchase of goods	8 Times/ 4 indiv.	2	4	3	2	1	12
Community Give	1 Time	0	0	1	0	0	1
Rec: Outdoor	4 Times	1	2	2	2	1	8
Rec: Cultural/ Social	1-2 Times	1	0	0	0	0	1
Rec: Indoor	4-8 Times	1	1	2	1	0	5
Other							

COMMUNITY INVOLVEMENT

Mary Smith has been involved in the following community involvement activities this month:

1. New Jersey Aquarium
2. Bowling
3. Howell Living Farm
4. Golden China Restaurant
5. Mercer County Park
6. Boston Market
7. Great Adventure
8. New Hope—shopping
9. Dairy Queen
10. Long Beach Island miniature golf
11. Superfresh Supermarket
12. Library
13. Quakerbridge Mall
14. Bay Village Water Park
15. Adopt-A-Spot
16. Movies
17. Washington Crossing Park
18. Eden Shore House - 5 days
19. Swimming & Barbecue at Winsten House

Appendix **C**

Eden
• • • • •
W.E.R.C.s
• • • • • • • •
Individual
• • • • • • • •
Habilitation
• • • • • •
Program
• • • •

Program Report (page 1)

EDEN W.E.R.C.s
One Logan Drive
Princeton, NJ 08540
(609) 987-0099

PARTICIPANT: John Smith   **DATE OF REPORT:** March 1996
DATE OF BIRTH: 5/26/61   **CHRONOLOGICAL AGE:** 34 years, 10 months
CENTER: Bendas   **LOCATION:** Skillman
COMMUNITY PLACEMENT: Lombardi House

INDIVIDUAL HABILITATION PROGRAM
GOAL SUMMARY SHEET

PARTICIPANT: John Smith   **DATE GOALS DEVELOPED:** December 1995

CERAMICS—POURING MOLDS
Goal: Independent completion of step 22-23 (retrieves draining rack and places it over bucket).
Progress: John requires gestural prompting in order to complete steps 22-23.
New Goal: Completion of steps 22-23 with one gestural prompt for the sequence.

CERAMICS—PAINTING BISQUEWARE
Goal: Independent completion of steps 32 (applies one coat of glaze).
Progress: John requires gestural and physical prompts in order to complete step 32.
New Goal: Completion of step 32 with gestural prompts.

SUBCONTRACT—WORK SKILLS
Goal: Independent completion of step 19a (works for 20 minutes when provided with ample materials).
Progress: John requires gestural prompting to stay on task for 20 minutes. He also needs gestural prompts to maintain quality control.
No New Goal.

MEAL PREPARATION
Goal: Independent completion of step 7 (makes side dish).
Progress: John requires verbal and gestural prompts to make a side dish. He also needs physical prompting if it requires him to use the stove.
No New Goal.

Program Report (page 2)

LOADING DISHWASHER
Goal: Independent completion of step 11-14 (loads plates in dishwasher).
Progress: John has mastered steps 11-14 (loading plates).
New Goal: Completion of entire program (steps 1-29) with 3 or less gestural prompts.

VACUUMING
Goal: Independent completion of step 10 (moves furniture).
Progress: John requires gestural and physical prompting in order to complete step 10 (moves furniture).
New Goal: Completion of step 10 with 2 or less gestural prompts.

TRASH COLLECTION
Goal: Independent completion of steps 1a, 2,3, 4b, 5b (retrieves large trash bag, locates trash can, opens trash bag and dumps trash into bag). John will collect trash on the second floor of the building.
Progress: John can retrieve trash bags (step 1a) independently. He requires gestural prompts to locate trash cans (step 2). He needs physical prompts to open trash bags (step 3). John can independently pick up trash can and empty it into the large bag (steps 4b & 5b).
New Goal: Completion of steps 2 and 3 with 3 or less gestural prompts.

GROCERY SHOPPING
Goal: Independent completion of step 7a (retrieves 5 items using a written list).
Progress: John requires some gestural prompting and needs positional prompts in order to retrieve 5 items using a written list.
No New Goal.

BANKING
Goal: Independent completion of step 3 (signs check in appropriate place) and step 11 (waits in line appropriately).
Progress: John requires a gestural prompt to endorse his check in the appropriate area. He needs physical prompts to wait in line.
No New Goal.

FIRE ALARM
Goal: Maintenance of independent skill level for entire program.
Progress: John continues to maintain the necessary skills for the entire program.
No New Goal.

Program Report (page 3)

SPEECH AND LANGUAGE

During this report period, John has shown improvement in the use of his expressive language to appropriately initiate, maintain, and terminate interactions with others. The following programs were designed to enhance John's pragmatic use of his language skills.

Enhancing Communication Skills

The Enhancing Communication Skills Program was implemented to enhance John's interactions with others. The goals for this program are to increase John's ability to initiate and maintain conversations with others. John will utilize the phrase "Excuse me" to initiate interactions with 43 percent accuracy. He will spontaneously generate "Excuse me" one time per session. Upon elicitation, John will use the phrase "Excuse me" six times per session. He requires eight prompts to appropriately initiate interactions using the phrase "Excuse me" prior to expressing his primary message.

After John has initiated an interaction, he requires prompts to wait appropriately for a response, before continuing the interaction. John will maintain an interaction by asking questions and responding to others using syntactically correct sentences. He will ask others questions during an interaction with 59 percent accuracy. John will spontaneously generate questions four times per session, and three times per session upon elicitation. He requires four prompts to ask questions to maintain an interaction. John will respond to others using syntactically correct five-to-six word sentence structures with 76 percent accuracy. These sentence structures are produced spontaneously six times per session and two times per session upon elicitation. John requires three prompts to expand his phrases to syntactically correct five and six word sentences.

John will terminate an interaction by utilizing the phrase "Thank you" with 51 percent accuracy. John will spontaneously produce the phrase "Thank you" one time per session and six times upon elicitation. He requires prompts to terminate an interaction with others by saying "Thank you."

John will terminate an interaction by utilizing the phrase "you're welcome" with 72 percent accuracy. He will spontaneously produce the phrase "you're welcome" three times per session. Upon elicitation, he will utilize the phrase "You're welcome" four times per session. John requires three prompts to terminate an interaction with "You're welcome" to others.

Social Interaction (Community Placement)

The Social Interaction (Community Placement) Program was implemented to utilize John's appropriate social courtesies while working in the community. John's targeted goal is to knock on doors before entering an office room and to work quietly during the tasks. He requires a prompt to knock on each door and in a ten minute work session, he needs four prompts to work quietly.

Program Report (page 4)

Increasing Response Repertoire

The Increasing Response Repertoire Program was implemented as an alternative teaching program, for John's behavior reduction program. The targeted phrase for this program was "I want to leave/go"; he will generate this phrase to express his desire to remove himself from an undesirable situation with 30 percent accuracy. John will spontaneously produce this phrase one time per session and three times per session upon elicitation. He requires nine prompts to use this phrase as an appropriate means of escaping undesirable situations.

Nonlinguistic Cues

The Nonlinguistic Cues Program was implemented to enhance John's ability to use nonverbal cues while interacting with others. John's appropriate use of eye contact has been targeted. During a one minute exchange, John requires one prompt to maintain eye contact throughout the entire exchange.

SUBCONTRACT

John has participated in a variety of subcontract jobs including Playmobil USA, MSM and Mercer County PIC. He works an average of eleven hours per week and is paid accordingly per job. His duties range from labeling, collating, sealing, and stuffing to folding, counting, and rubber banding. John requires occasional gestural prompting to remain on task and maintain quality control.

SOCIAL INTERACTION

John participates in a variety of social interactions. He plays ball, partakes in group baking session, plays dominoes, and Jenga. John maintains good eye contact and speaks clearly. He needs prompting to get other's attention and to wait appropriately for a response. John sometimes requires prompting to respond appropriately to a peer's request.

PHYSICAL ACTIVITIES

John partakes in a variety of physical activities. He rides the stationary bike, walks on the treadmill, and jumps on the trampoline. He also partakes in group activities such as nature walks, step aerobics, Twister and horseshoes. Although John participates in many activities, he tends to prefer the stationary bike. He rides for approximately 20 minutes with minimal gestural prompting.

Program Report (page 5)

BEHAVIORAL FUNCTIONING

Definition 1: Screaming: defined as any vocalizations which are not words, including television theme songs, produced at a volume greater than that of normal conversation, with the exception of any response made to a perceived threat to his general health and safety.

OPERATIONAL DEFINITION OF PROPOSED TREATMENT:
At the beginning of each VI DRO period, John is presented with a token board with five tokens attached. John's attention is not to be directed to the token board. For each scream, the *Sd* "John, I want you to work quietly," is presented and a token is removed. If at the end of the period, John retains one or more tokens, he receives a primary reinforcer of his choosing. If he loses all five tokens, the only consequence is that he receives no reinforcement at the end of that period. John starts each period with the full five tokens, independent of his behavior during the previous interval. The length of each interval is to be determined by John's teacher at the beginning of each interval, and John is not to be informed of its length. The length of the DRO interval will be individually predetermined and may change, dependent upon meeting a specific criterion as determined by the Program Director.

BASELINE RATE: 32.4 per day, January 30-February 3, 1989.
CURRENT RATE: See Graph.

Definition 2: Tantrumous Behavior: Defined as any agitated running of fingers through hair, accompanied by screaming and forceful clapping of hands or stomping of feet.

Definition 3: Self-Injurious Behavior: Defined as any audible contact by his hand to his head or face, accompanied by a scream.

Definition 4: Aggression/Destruction: Defined as any audible contact by his hands or other body parts with objects, surfaces, or other individuals in the environment, or any throwing of objects.

OPERATIONAL DEFINITION OF PROPOSED TREATMENT:
A protective device of a boxing headgear with a visual screen attached will be applied and John will be required to sit in a chair for 30 seconds of quiet, defined as no verbalizations, self-injurious behaviors, or attempts at aggression or destruction. Attempts at aggression or destruction are to be briefly interrupted and John

Program Report (page 6)

may be verbally prompted to sit down. All physical prompting is to be held to a minimum.

ADDITIONAL PARAMETERS:
John is currently on a variable interval token earn system. The time parameters of this system are subject to change based on the discretion of the Program Directors. John will lose possession of his token card contingent only upon self-injurious behavior, tantrum, aggression, or destruction. Following 30 seconds of quiet after removal of the visual screen, John is to be presented with a new token and a token period will begin. At this time, he is instructed to choose what reinforcer he will be working for.

BASELINE RATE: Self-Injury: 333 per day, 107min/day, November 1986.
CURRENT RATE: Self-Injury: See Graph.

Definition 5: Leaving of Seat or Area defined as any leaving of seat or area without requesting to do so, including not proceeding directly to a designated area.

OPERATIONAL DEFINITION OF PROPOSED TREATMENT:
Sd "No leaving the area." John will then be prompted back to the area he left and cloth-covered five pound weights will be secured around both of his ankles. John will then be prompted through an overcorrection procedure of walking back and forth from his seat to the area he went, for a period of two to five minutes.

BASELINE RATE: 4.4 per day, November 1994.
CURRENT RATE: See Graph.

CONCLUDING REMARKS
This past term John has shown much progress across the board. His social skills and work skills have been progressively improving. He has been adaptive to going out in the community more frequently. His time on task has been increasing, which is allowing John to be more productive. Overall, John is a pleasure to work with and we are very proud of the progress he has made.

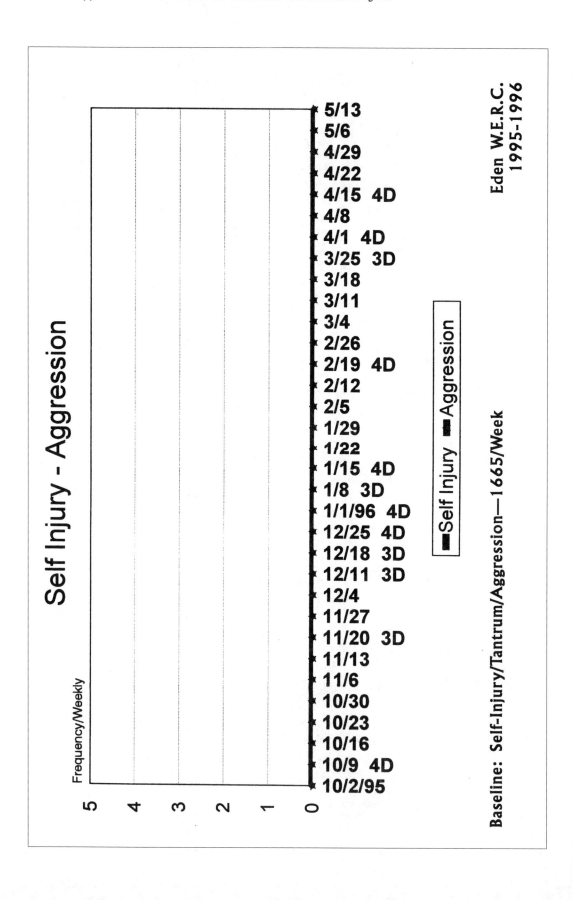

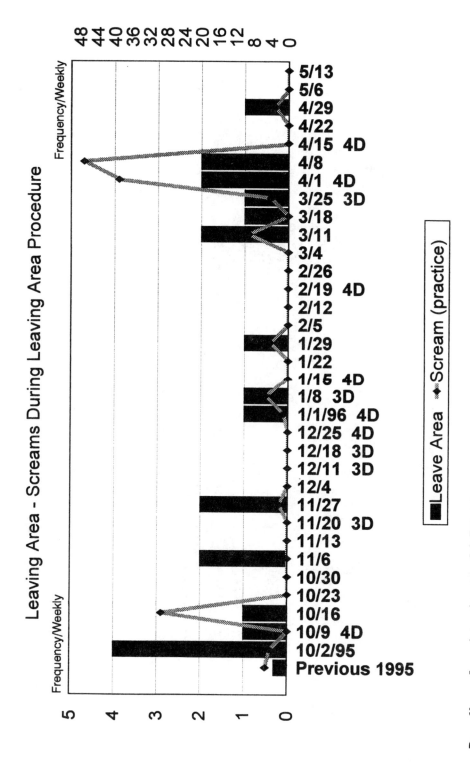

Leaving Area - Screams During Leaving Area Procedure

Eden W.E.R.C.
1995-1996

■ Leave Area ◆ Scream (practice)

Baseline: Leaving Area—22/Week

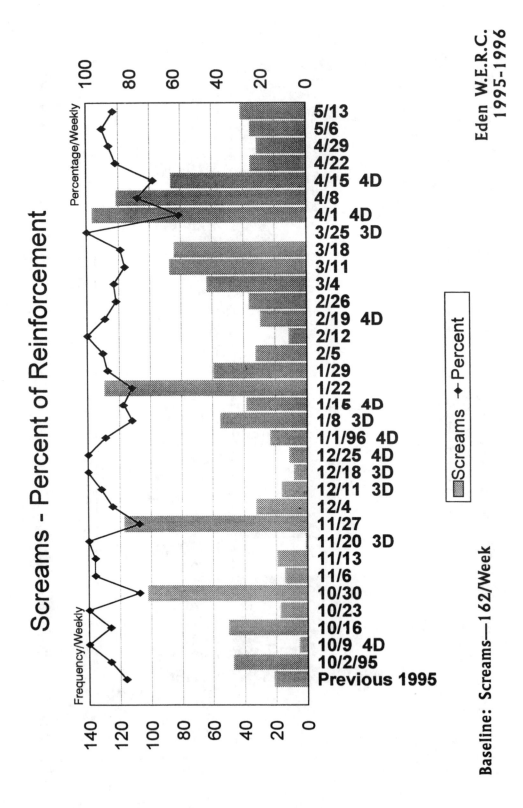

Screams - Percent of Reinforcement

Eden W.E.R.C.
1995-1996

Baseline: Screams—162/Week

Bibliography

Alessandri, M., Bomba, C. & Gonzales, D.L. "The Impact of Respite Care on the Stress Levels and Marital Satisfaction of Mothers and Fathers of Children with Autism." Paper presented at the annual meeting of the Western Psychological Association, Phoenix, AZ, April 1993.

Alessandri, M., Bomba, C., Holmes, A.S., Van Driesen, D. & Holmes, D.L. (in prep.). Changes in Developmental Rates of Learning in Infants and Toddlers with Autism: Preliminary Outcome Data.

Alpern, G., Boll, T. & Shearer, M. *Developmental Profile II, Manual.* Los Angeles, CA: Western Psychological Services, 1986.

American Academy of Pediatrics. The Doman-Delacato Treatment of Neurologically Handicapped Children: A Policy Statement by the American Academy of Pediatrics. *The Exceptional Parent* October 1983, 40-43.

American Association on Mental Retardation. *Position Statement on Aversive Therapy.* Washington, DC: American Association on Mental Retardation, January 1990.

American Psychiatric Association. *Diagnostic and Statistical Manual of Mental Disorders.* 4th ed. Washington, DC: American Psychiatric Association, 1994.

———. *Diagnostic and Statistical Manual of Mental Disorders.* 3rd Rev. ed. Washington, DC: American Psychiatric Association, 1987.

———. *Diagnostic and Statistical Manual of Mental Disorders.* 3rd ed. Washington, DC: American Psychiatric Association, 1980.

Anderson, S.R., Avery, D.L., DiPietro, E.K., Edwards, G.L. & Christian, W.P. "Intensive Home-Based Early Intervention with Autistic Children." *Education and Treatment of Children* 10, no. 4 (1987): 352-366.

Armstrong v. Kline, 476 F. Supp. 583 (E.D. Pa. 1979).

Association for Behavior Analysis. *Position Statement on Clients' Rights to Effective Behavioral Treatment.* Washington, DC: Association for Behavior Analysis, 1989.

Association of Retarded Citizens/United States. *Resolution on Use of Aversives.* Washington, DC: Association of Retarded Citizens/United States, 1985.

Autism Society of America. *Early Intervention.* Bethesda, MD: Autism Society of America, 1995.

Axelrod, S. "ABA and the Mainstreaming Movement." *Journal of Behavioral Education* 2 no. 3 (1992): 219-24.

Axelrod, S. "Doing It Without Arrows: A Review of LaVigna and Donnellan's 'Alternatives to Punishment: Solving Behavior Problems with Nonaversive Strategies.'" *The Behavior Analyst* 10 (1987): 243-51.

Axline, V. *Dibs: In Search of Self.* Boston, MA: Houghton Mifflin, 1964.

Ayres, A.J. *Sensory Integration and the Child.* Los Angeles, CA: Western Psychological Services, 1979.

Ayres, A.J. & Tickle, L. "Hyper-Responsivity to Touch and Vestibular Stimulation as a Predictor of Responsivity to Sensory Integrative Procedures with Autistic Children." *American Journal of Occupational Therapy* 34 (1980): 375-81.

Baldwin, V. "Curriculum." In *Hey Don't Forget About Me!* edited by M.A. Thomas, 64-73. Reston, VA: The Council for Exceptional Children, 1976.

Batshaw, M.L. & Perret, Y.M. *Children with Disabilities: A Medical Primer.* Baltimore, MD: Paul H. Brookes Publishing Co., 1992.

Bauman, M.L. "Microscopic Neuroanatomic Abnormalities in Autism." *Pediatrics* 87 (Supplement 1991): 791-96.

Baumgart, D., Brown, L., Pumpian, I., Nisbet, J., Ford, A., Sweet, M., Messina, R. & Schroeder, J. "Principle of Partial Participation and Individualized Adaptations in Educational Programs for Severely Handicapped Students." *Journal of the Association for Persons with Severe Handicaps* 7 (Summer 1982): 17-27.

"Being a Do-Gooder Can be Profitable." *John Naisbitt's Trend Letter* 15, no. 15 (July 18, 1996): 1-3.

Belohlav, J.A. *Championship Management.* Cambridge, MA: Productivity Press, 1992.

Berard, G. *Audition Egale Comportment.* Sainte-Ruffine: Maisonneuve, 1982.

Berendt, R.F. & Taft, J.R. *How to Rate Your Development Office.* Washington, DC: Taft Corp., 1984.

Bettelheim, B. *The Empty Fortress: Infantile Autism and the Birth of the Self.* NY: Macmillan, 1967.

Bijou, S.W., Peterson, R.F., Harris, F.R., Allen, K.E. & Johnson, M.S. "Methodology for Experimental Studies of Young Children in Natural Settings." *The Psychological Record* 19 (1969): 177-210.

Biklen, D. "Typing to Talk: Facilitated Communication." *American Journal of Speech-Language Pathology* 1, no. 2 (1992): 15-17.

———. "Communication Unbound: Autism and Praxis. *Harvard Educational Review* 60, no. 3 (1990): 291-314.

Bird, F., Doree, P.A., Moniz, D. & Robinson, J. "Reducing Severe Aggressive and Self-Injurious Behaviors with Functional Communication Training." *American Journal on Mental Retardation* 94, no. 1 (1989): 37-48.

Black, M.M. "Early Intervention Services for Infants and Toddlers: A Focus on Families." *Journal of Clinical Child Psychology* 20, no. 1 (1991): 51-57.

Blackman, H.P. "Surmounting the Disability of Isolation." *The School Administrator* 49, no. 2 (1992): 28-29.

Board of Education of the Hendrick Hudson Central School District Bd. of Ed. v. Amy Rowley, 102 S. Ct. 3034 (1982).

Bomba, C., O'Donnell, L., Markowitz, C. & Holmes, D.L. "Evaluating the Impact of Facilitated Communication on the Communicative Competence of Fourteen Students with Autism." *Journal of Autism and Developmental Disorders* 26, no. 1 (1996): 43-58.

Bondy, A.S. & Frost, L.A. *The Picture-Exchange Communication System (PECS).* Newark, DE: Delaware Autistic Program, 1992.

Bonisch, V.E. "Erfahrungen met Pyrithioxin bei Hirngeschadigten Kindern mit Autistischem Syndrom." *Praxis der Kinderpsychologie* 8 (1968): 308-10.

Bonvillian, J.D. & Blackburn, D.W. "Manual Communication and Autism: Factors Relating to Sign Language Acquisition." In *Theoretical Issues in Sign Language Research.* Vol. 2. Psychology. Edited by P. Siple & S.D. Fischer. Chicago, IL: University of Chicago Press, 1991.

Bonvillian, J.D. & Nelson, K.E. "Sign Language Acquisition in a Mute Autistic Boy." *Journal of Speech and Hearing Disorders* 41, no. 3 (1976): 339-47.

Boodman, S. "Intense Therapy Show Signs of Helping Autistic Children." *The Washington Post,* 24 January 1995, p. 10.

Bovee, J.P. "With a Little Help from my Friends." pp. 9-10 in *1996 Autism Society National Conference Proceedings.* Edited by L.A.Tidey & J. Pequet. Bethesda, MD: Autism Society of America, 1996.

Braddock, D. & Mitchell, D. "Review of Research on Compensation and Turnover." In *Residential Services and Developmental Disabilities in the United States.* Edited by D. Braddock & D. Mitchell. Washington, DC: American Association on Mental Retardation, 1992.

Braswell, L. "Integrating Cognitive-Behavioral Training into the Classroom." Paper presented at the New Jersey Department of Education Statewide Conference, Somerset, NJ, April 30, 1993.

Bristol, M. M. "The State of the Science in Autism: Beyond the Silver Bullet." In *Proceedings of the Eden Institute Foundation Princeton Lecture Series on Autism: Affecting the Research and Service Agenda.* Princeton, NJ: Eden Press, 1996.

Brown, A.L., Campione, J.C. & Day, J.D. "Learning to Learn: On Training Students to Learn from Text." *Educational Researcher* 10 (1981): 14-21.

Brown, L., Branston, M.B., Hamre-Nietupski, S., Pumpian, I., Certo, N. & Gruenewald, L. "A Strategy for Developing Chronological-Age-Appropriate and Functional Curricular Content for Severely Handicapped Adolescents and Young Adults." *Journal of Special Education* 13, no. 1 (1979): 81-89.

Bruey, C.T. "Daily Life with Your Child." In *Children with Autism: A Parents' Guide.* Edited by M.D. Powers. Bethesda, MD: Woodbine House, 1989.

Bryson S.E., Smith, Isabel M. & Eastwood, D. "Obstetrical Suboptimality in Autistic Children." *Journal of the American Academy of Child and Adolescent Psychiatry* 27, no. 4 (1988): 418-22.

Calculator, S.N. "Exploring the Language of Adults with Mental Retardation." In *Communication Assessment and Intervention for Adults with Mental Retardation.* pp. 95-106. Edited by S.N. Calculator & J.L. Bedrosian. Boston: College-Hill Press, 1988.

Carr, E.G. "Teaching Autistic Children to Use Sign Language: Some Research Issues." *Journal of Autism and Developmental Disorders* 9, no. 4 (1979): 345-59.

Carr, E.G., Binkoff, J.A., Kologinsky, E. & Eddy, M. "Acquisition of Sign Language by Autistic Children I: Expressive Labelling." *Journal of Applied Behavior Analysis* 11 (1978): 489-501.

Carr, E.G. & Carlson, J.I. "Reduction of Severe Behavior Problems in the Community using a Multicomponent Treatment Approach." *Journal of Applied Behavior Analysis* 26, no. 2 (1993): 157-72.

Carr, E.G. & Durand, V.M. "See Me, Help Me." *Psychology Today* 21, no. 11 (1987): 62-64.

Carr, E.G. & Durand, V.M. "Reducing Behavior Problems through Functional Communication Training." *Journal of Applied Behavior Analysis* 18, no. 2 (1985): 111-26.

Carr, E.G. & Kemp, D.C. "Functional Equivalence of Autistic Leading and Communicative Pointing: Analysis and Treatment." *Journal of Autism and Developmental Disorders* 19, no. 4 (1989): 561-78.

Carr, E.G., Robinson, S., Taylor, J.C. & Carlson, J.I. *Positive Approaches to the Treatment of Severe Behavior Problems in Persons with Developmental Disabilities: A Review and Analysis of Reinforcement and Stimulus Based Procedures*. Seattle, WA: Association for Persons with Severe Handicaps, 1990.

Champagne, J. *Least Restrictive Environment: Decisions in Sequence*. Harrisburg, PA: Pennsylvania Department of Education, 1992.

Chapman, J.W. "Learning Disabilities in New Zealand: Where Kiwis and Kids with LD Can't Fly." *Journal of Learning Disabilities* 25 (1992): 362-70.

Charlop, M.H., Kurtz, P.F. & Milstein, J.P. "Too Much Reinforcement, Too Little Behavior: Assessing Task Interspersal Procedures in Conjunction with Different Reinforcement Schedules with Autistic Children." *Journal of Applied Behavior Analysis* 25, no. 4 (1992): 795-808.

Comer, R. *Abnormal Psychology*. New York: W.H. Freeman & Co., 1995.

Cook, E.H. "Autism: Review of Neurochemical Investigation." *Synapse* 6 (1990): 292-308.

Coots, J. & Falvey, M.A. "Communication Skills." In *Community-Based Curriculum: Instructional Strategies for Students with Severe Handicaps*. (2nd ed., pp. 255-284). Edited by M.A. Falvey. Baltimore, MD: Paul H. Brookes Publishing Co., 1989.

COSAC. *New Jersey Schools and Programs Serving Children with Autism and/or Pervasive Developmental Disorders*. Ewing, NJ: New Jersey Center for Outreach and Services for the Autism Community, 1450 Parkside Avenue, Suite 22, Ewing, NJ 08638, February 1996.

Council for Exceptional Children. *CEC Policies for Delivery of Services to Exceptional Children*. Reston, VA: Council for Exceptional Children, 1994.

Courchesne, E., Yeung-Courchesne, R., Press, G.A., Hesselink, J.R. & Jernigan, T.L. "Hypoplasia of Cerebellar Lobules VI and VII in Autism." *New England Journal of Medicine* 318 (1988): 1349-54.

Creedon, M.P. "Language Development in Nonverbal Autistic Children using a Simultaneous Communication System." Paper presented at the Research in Child Development Meeting, Philadelphia, PA, March 31, 1973.

Crossley, R. "Surprising Success Reported with Facilitated Communication." *Autism Research Review International* 4, no. 4 (1990): 2.

Dalrymple, N. *Learning Together*. Bloomington, IN: Indiana Resource Center for Autism, Institute for the Study of Developmental Disabilities, Indiana University, Bloomington, IN, 1989.

Darras, B.T. & Mannheim, G.B. (in prep.). "Molecular Genetics of Autism." New England Medical Center Hospital, Boston, MA.

Davila, R. "IDEA Does Not Require 'Inclusive Education' for All Children." *Digest of Inquiry*. Washington, DC: U.S. Department of Education, 1991.

Davis, D.E. & Goldberg, R.A. "Aversive Treatment vs. Individual Rights: The Professional's Dilemma." *Polestar* 7 (1979): 7.

Davis, W.E. "The Regular Education Initiative Debate: Its Promises and Problems." *Exceptional Children* 55, no. 5 (1989): 440-46.

Delacato, C. *The Ultimate Stranger*. New York: Doubleday, 1974.

Doman, G. *What To Do about Your Brain-Injured Child*. New York: Doubleday, 1974.

Dores, P. & Carr, E.G. "Teaching Sign Language to Psychotic Children: Assessing Simultaneous Communication." Paper presented at the meeting of the American Psychological Association, New York, September 1979.

Drucker, P. *Managing the Non-Profit Organization*. New York: HarperCollins, 1990.

Durand, V.M. "Functional Communication Training to Reduce Challenging Behavior: Maintenance and Application in New Settings." *Journal of Applied Behavior Analysis* 24 (1991): 251-64.

Durand, V.M. & Carr, E.G. "An Analysis of Maintenance Following Functional Communication Training." *Journal of Applied Behavior Analysis* 25, no. 4 (1992): 777-94.

Dyer, K. "The Effects of Preference on Spontaneous Verbal Requests in Individuals with Autism." *Journal of the Association for Persons with Severe Handicaps* 14, no. 3 (1989): 184-89.

Dyer, K., Dunlap, G. & Winterling, V. "Effects of Choice Making on the Serious Problem Behaviors of Students with Severe Handicaps." *Journal of Applied Behavior Analysis* 23, no. 4 (1990): 515-24.

Edwards, D.R. & Bristol, M.M. "Autism: Early Identification and Management in Family Practice." *American Family Physician* 44, no. 5 (1991): 1755-64.

Evans, I.M. & Meyer, L.H. *An Educative Approach to Behavior Problems: A Practical Decision Model for Interventions with Severely Handicapped Learners.* Baltimore, MD: Paul H. Brookes Publishing Co., 1985.

The Exceptional Parent. "New Voices: Communication through Technology." *The Exceptional Parent* (June 1983): 18-25.

Falvey, M.A., ed. *Community-Based Curriculum: Instructional Strategies for Students with Severe Handicaps.* Baltimore, MD: Paul H. Brookes Publishing Co., 1989.

Favell, J.E., Azrin, N.H., Baumeister, A.A., Carr, E.G., Dorsey, M.F., Forehand, R., Foxx, R.M., Lovaas, O.I., Rincover, A., Risley, T.R., Romanczyk, R.G., Russo, D.C., Schroeder, S.R. & Solnick, J.V. "Association for the Advancement of Behavior Therapy Task Force Report: The Treatment of Self-Injurious Behavior." *Behavior Therapy* 13 (1982): 529-54.

Featherstone, H. *A Difference in the Family: Life with a Disabled Child.* New York: Penguin, 1980.

Fenske, E.C., Zalenski, S., Krantz, P.J. & McClannahan, L.E. "Age at Intervention and Treatment Outcome for Autistic Children in a Comprehensive Intervention Program." *Analysis and Intervention in Developmental Disabilities* 5 (1985): 49-58.

Ferster, C.B. "Positive Reinforcement and Behavioral Deficits in Autistic Children." *Child Development* 32 (1961): 437-58.

Ferster, C.B. & DeMyer, M.K. "The Development of Performances in Autistic Children in an Automatically Controlled Environment." *Journal of Chronic Disease* 13 (1961): 312-45.

Freeman, R.D. "Controversy Over 'Patterning' as a Treatment for Brain Damage in Children." *The Journal of the American Medical Association* 202, no. 5 (1967): 83.

Frith, U. "Autism." *Scientific American* (June 1993): 108-14.

———. *Autism: Explaining the Enigma.* Oxford: Basil Blackwell, 1989.

Fuchs, D. & Fuchs, L.S. "Inclusive Schools Movement and the Radicalization of Special Education Reform." *Exceptional Children* 60, no. 4 (1994): 294-309.

Fuchs, D., Fuchs, L.S. & Fernstrom, P. "A Conservative Approach to Special Education Reform: Mainstreaming through Transenvironmental Programming and Curriculum-Based Measurement." *American Education Research Journal* 30 (1993):149-77.

Garner, J.B. "Intelligence Testing or Testing Intelligently: Implications for Persons Labelled 'Handicapped.'" *School Psychology International* 6, no. 4 (1985): 235-38.

Gartner, A. & Lipsky, D.K. *The Yoke of Special Education: How to Break It.* Rochester, NY: National Center on Education and the Economy, 1989.

Gaylord-Ross, R., ed. *Integration Strategies for Students with Handicaps.* Baltimore, MD: Paul H. Brookes Publishing Co., 1989.

Gelardo, M. "Introduction to the Critical Skills Model of Curriculum Development." Unpublished manuscript, Trenton State College, Trenton, NJ, 1990.

Geller, E., Ritvo, E.R., Freeman, B.J. & Yuwiler, A. "Preliminary Observations on the Effect of Fenfluramine on Blood Serotonin and Symptoms in Three Autistic Boys." *New England Journal of Medicine* 307, no. 3 (1982): 165-69.

Gerhardt, P.F. & Holmes, D.L. "Employment Options and Issues for Adolescents and Adults with Autism." In *Handbook of Autism and Pervasive Developmental Disabilities* (2nd ed.). Edited by F. Volkmar & D. Cohen. New York, NY: Wiley, 1997.

Gerhardt, P.F. & Holmes, D.L. "The Eden Decision Model: A Decision Model with Practical Applications for the Development of Behavior Decelerative Strategies." In *Behavioral Issues in Autism.* Edited by E. Schopler & G.B. Mesibov (pp. 247-76). New York: Plenum Press, 1994.

Gilman, J.T. & Tuchman, R.F. "Autism and Associated Behavioral Disorder: Pharmacotherapeutic Interventions." *The Annals of Pharmacotherapy* 29 (1995): 47-56.

Glover, M.E., Preminger, J.L. & Sanford, A.R. *Early Learning Accomplishment Profile.* Chapel Hill, NC: Chapel Hill Training-Outreach Project, 1988.

Gold, M.W. "Task Analysis of a Complex Assembly Task by the Retarded Blind." *Exceptional Children* 43, no. 2 (1976): 78-84.

Grandin, T. "An Autistic Person's View of Holding Therapy." *Communication* 23, no. 3 (December 1989): 5. From *Autism Research Review International* 4, no. 4 (1990).

———. *Emergence: Labeled Autistic.* Novato, CA: Arena Press, 1985.

Green, G. "The Quality of the Evidence." In *Facilitated Communication: The Clinical and Social Phenomenon*. Edited by H. C. Shane. (pp. 157-226). San Diego, CA: Singular Publishing Group, Inc., 1994.

Greenspan, S.I. "Reconsidering the Diagnosis and Treatment of Very Young Children with Autistic Spectrum or Pervasive Developmental Disorder." *Zero to Three* 13, no. 2 (1992): 1-9.

Groden, G. "A Guide for Conducting a Comprehensive Behavioral Analysis of a Target Behavior." *Journal of Behavior Therapy and Experimental Psychiatry* 20 (1989): 163-69.

Guralnick M., ed. *Early Intervention and the Integration of Handicapped and Nonhandicapped Children*. Baltimore, MD: Paul H. Brookes Publishing Co., 1979.

Handleman, J.S. "Assessment for Curriculum Planning." In *Autism: Identification, Education and Treatment*. Edited by D.E. Berkell. Hillsdale, NJ: Lawrence Erlbaum Assoc., 1992.

Haring, N.G. & Bricker, D. "Overview of Comprehensive Services for the Severely/ Profoundly Handicapped." In *Teaching the Severely Handicapped*. Vol. 1. Edited by N.G. Haring & L.J. Brown (pp. 2-16). New York: Grune & Stratton, 1976.

Harris, K. "Cognitive-Behavior Modification: Application with Exceptional Students." In *Effective Instructional Strategies for Exceptional Learners*. Edited by E.L. Meyen, G.A. Vergason & R.J. Whelan. (pp. 216-42). Denver, CO: Love Publishing Co., 1988.

Harris, S.L. *Siblings of Children with Autism: A Guide for Families*. Bethesda, MD: Woodbine House, 1994.

———. "Your Child's Development." In *Children with Autism: A Parents' Guide*. Edited by M.D. Powers. (pp. 141-67). Bethesda, MD: Woodbine House, 1989.

———. *Families of the Developmentally Disabled: A Guide to Behavioral Intervention*. Elmsford, NY: Pergamon Press, 1983.

Harris, S.L., Boyle, T.D., Fong, P.L., Gill, M.J. & Stranger, C. "Families of Developmentally Disabled Children." In *Advances in Developmental and Behavioral Pediatrics*. Edited by M. Wolraich & D.K. Routh (pp. 44-74). Greenwich, CT: JAI, Press, 1987.

Harris, S.L. & Handleman, J.S. *Educating the Developmentally Disabled: Meeting the Needs of Children and Families*. Boston: College Hill Press, 1986.

Hashimoto, T., Tayama, M., Mori, K., Fujino, K., Miyazaki, M. & Kuroda, Y. "Magnetic Resonance Imaging in Autism: Preliminary Results." *Neuropediatrics* 20, no. 3 (1989): 142-46.

Heeley, A.F. & Roberts, G.E. "Tryptophan Metabolism in Psychotic Children." *Develop. Med. Child Neurology* 7 (1965): 46.

Hinkle, H. "Discussion of Oberti v. Clementon School District." Law Offices of Herbert D. Hinkle, Route 206, 2651 Main Street, Suite A, Lawrenceville, NJ 08648 (1995).

Holmes, A.S. & Holmes, D.L. *The Eden Programs Speech and Language Assessment.* Princeton, NJ: Eden Press, 1985.

Holmes, D.L. "Mainstreaming Exceptional Children." *Journal for Special Educators of the Mentally Retarded* 13, no. 1 (1976): 17-25.

————. "The Years Ahead: Adults with Autism." In *Children with Autism: A Parents' Guide.* Edited by M.D. Powers. (pp.253-76). Bethesda, MD: Woodbine House, 1989.

————. "Inclusive Education: Managing the Impression." National Association of Private Schools for Exceptional Children, 1522 K Street, NW, Suite 1032, Washington, DC 20005 (1991).

————. "Snake Oil or Breakthrough?" *Passages* 2, no. 1 (Spring 1992): 1. Available from the Eden Institute Foundation, One Logan Drive, Princeton, NJ 08540.

Holmes, D.L., Bomba, C., Cohen, M. & Gerhardt, P., eds. *Eden Services Curriculum: Employment Curriculum.* Princeton, NJ: The Eden Press, 1994.

Holmes, D.L., Bomba, C., Cohen, M. & Roussell, D., eds. *Eden Services Curriculum: Residential Curriculum.* Princeton, NJ: The Eden Press, 1994.

Holmes, D.L., Cohen, M., Beck, P. & Sersen, S., eds. *Eden Institute Curriculum Series: Core.* Vol. 1. Princeton, NJ: The Eden Press, 1991.

Holmes, D.L., Cohen, M. & Luckenbill, C., eds. *Eden Institute Curriculum Series: Classroom Orientation.* Vol. 2. Princeton, NJ: The Eden Press, 1991.

Holmes, D.L., Cohen, M. & Dorfman, K., eds. *Eden Institute Curriculum Series: Vocational Education.* Vol. 3. Princeton, NJ: The Eden Press, 1991.

Holmes, D.L., Cohen, M., Holmes, A.S. & Weitzner, L.S., eds. *Eden Institute Curriculum Series: Speech and Language.* Vol. 4. Princeton, NJ: The Eden Press, 1991.

Holmes, D.L., Cohen, M. & Guggenheim, N., eds. *Eden Institute Curriculum Series: Adaptive Physical Education.* Vol. 5. Princeton, NJ: The Eden Press, 1991.

Holmes, D.L. & Holmes, A.S., eds. *Behavioral Technology Guidebook: A Workshop Manual for Educators, Clinicians and Paraprofessionals.* Princeton, NJ: The Eden Press, 1987.

Huebner, R. "Autism: A Neurophysiological Enigma." *American Journal of Occupational Therapy* 46, no. 6 (1992): 487-501.

International Association for the Right to Effective Treatment . "The IARET Statement of Philosophy." *The IARET Newsletter* 6, no. 2 (1994): 9.

"An Interview with Dr. Margaret Bauman." *Advocate* 24, no. 1 (Winter 1992-1993): 13-15.

Jenkins, J., Zigmond, N., Fuchs, L., Fuchs, D. & Deno, S. (in prep.). "Special Education in Restructured Schools: Findings from Three Multi-Year Studies."

Jenkins, J.R. & Heinen, A. "Students' Preferences for Service Delivery: Pull-Out, In-Class, or Integrated Models." *Exceptional Children* 55 (1989): 516-23.

Jenkins, J.R., Jewell, M., Leicester, N., Jenkins, L. & Troutner, N.M. "Development of a School Building Model for Educating Students with Handicaps and At-Risk Students in General Education Classrooms." *Journal of Learning Disabilities* 24 (1991): 311-20.

Kalmanson, B. "Diagnosis and Treatment of Infants and Young Children with Pervasive Developmental Disorders." *Zero to Three* 13, no. 2 (1992): 21-26.

Kanner, L. "Autistic Disturbances of Affective Contact." *The Nervous Child* 2, no. 3 (1943): 216-50.

Kauffman, J.M. "How We Might Achieve the Radical Reform of Special Education." *Exceptional Children* 60, no. 1 (1993): 6-16.

Kearney, C.A. & Durand, V.M. "How Prepared Are Our Teachers for Mainstreamed Classroom Settings? A Survey of Postsecondary Schools of Education in New York State." *Exceptional Children* 59, no. 1 (1992): 6-11.

Kirk, S.A. & Gallagher, J.J. *Educating Exceptional Children*. 6th ed. Boston, MA: Houghton-Mifflin Co., 1989.

Koegel, R.L., Dyer, K. & Bell, L.K. "The Influence of Child-Preferred Activities on Autistic Children's Social Behavior." *Journal of Applied Behavior Analysis* 20, no. 3 (1987): 243-52.

Koegel, R.L., Koegel, L.K. & Surratt, A. "Language Intervention and Disruptive Behavior in Preschool Children with Autism." *Journal of Autism and Developmental Disorders* 22, no. 2 (1992): 141-53.

Kozloff, M.A. *Improving Educational Outcomes for Children with Disabilities: Guidelines and Protocols for Practice*. Baltimore, MD: Paul H. Brookes Publishing Co., 1994.

————. *Improving Educational Outcomes for Children with Disabilities: Principles for Assessment, Program Planning, and Education.* Baltimore, MD: Paul H. Brookes Publishing Co., 1994.

Krug, D.A., Arick, J.R. & Almond, P.J. *Autism Screening Instrument for Educational Planning.* Portland, OR: ASIEP Education Co., 1980.

Lakin, K.C. & Bruininks, R.H. "Social Integration of Developmentally Disabled Persons." In *Strategies for Achieving Community Integration of Developmentally Disabled Citizens.* Edited by K.C. Lakin & R.H. Bruininks, Eds. (pp. 3-26). Baltimore, MD: Paul H. Brookes Publishing Co., 1985.

Lauries, K.R., ed. *Directory of Programs Serving Children and Adults with Autism.* 5th ed. Washington, DC: Autism Society of America, 1985.

LaVigna, G.W. & Donnellan, A.M. *Alternatives to Punishment: Solving Behavior Problems with Nonaversive Strategies.* New York: Irvington, 1986.

Leslie, A.M. (in prep.). "Theory of Mind in Children with Autism." Department of Psychology, Rutgers University, Piscataway, NJ.

Levy, Y., Amir, N. & Shalev, R. "Linguistic Development of a Child with a Congenital Localised L.H. Lesion." *Cognitive Neuropsychology* 9, no. 1 (1992): 1-32.

Lipsky, D.K. & Gartner, A. "Restructuring for Quality." In *The Regular Education Initiative: Alternative Perspectives on Concepts, Issues, and Models.* Edited by J.W. Lloyd, N.N. Singh & A.C. Repp. (pp. 43-57). Sycamore, IL: Sycamore Publishing Co., 1991.

Lipsky, D.K. & Gartner, A. "Capable of Achievement and Worthy of Respect: Education for Handicapped Students as if They Were Full-Fledged Human Beings." *Exceptional Children* 54 (1987): 69-74.

Lobley, J. "Driven by Ritual: An Autistic Man Expresses Himself." *The Princeton Packet,* 17 January 1995, p. 9A.

Lord, C. & O'Neill, P.J. "Language and Communication Needs of Adolescents and Adults with Autism." In *Autism in Adolescents and Adults.* Edited by E. Schopler and G.B. Mesibov. (pp. 57-75). New York, NY: Plenum Press, 1983.

Lord, C., Schopler, E. & Revicki, D. "Sex Differences in Autism." *Journal of Autism and Developmental Disorders* 12, no. 4 (1982): 317-30.

Lotspeich, L. & Ciaranello, R.D. "The Neurobiology and Genetics of Infantile Autism." *International Review of Neurobiology* 35 (1993): 87-129.

Lovaas, O.I. "The Development of a Treatment-Research Project for Developmentally Disabled and Autistic Children." *Journal of Applied Behavior Analysis* 26, no. 4 (1993): 617-30.

———. "Behavioral Treatment and Normal Educational and Intellectual Functioning in Young Autistic Children." *Journal of Consulting and Clinical Psychology* 55, no. 1 (1987): 3-9.

———. *The Me Book: Teaching Developmentally Disabled Children.* Austin, TX: Pro-Ed, 1981.

———. *The Autistic Child: Language Development through Behavior Modification.* New York: Irvington, 1977.

Lovaas, O.I., Berberich, J.P., Perloff, B.F. & Schaeffer, B. "Acquisition of Imitative Speech by Schizophrenic Children." *Science* 151 (1966): 705-07.

Lovaas, O.I. & Favell, J.E. "Protection for Clients Undergoing Aversive/Restrictive Interventions." *Education and Treatment of Children* 10, no. 4 (1987): 311-25.

Lovaas, O.I., Freitag, G., Kinder, M.I., Rubenstein, B.D., Schaeffer, B. & Simmons, J.W. "Establishment of Social Reinforcers in Two Schizophrenic Children on the Basis of Food." *Journal of Experimental Child Psychology* 4 (1966): 109-25.

Lovaas, O.I., Freitag, G., Gold, V.J. & Kassorla, I.C. "Experimental Studies in Childhood Schizophrenia: Analysis of Self-Destructive Behavior." *Journal of Experimental Child Psychology* 2 (1965): 67-84.

Lovaas, O.I., Freitag, G., Nelson, K. & Whalen, C. "The Establishment of Imitation and Its Use for the Development of Complex Behavior in Schizophrenic Children." *Behavior Research and Therapy* 5 (1967): 171-81.

Lovaas, O.I., Koegel, R.L. & Schreibman, L. "Stimulus Overselectivity in Autism: A Review of Research." *Psychological Bulletin* 86, no. 6 (1979): 1236-54.

Lovaas, O.I. & Simmons, J.Q. "Manipulation of Self-Destruction in Three Retarded Children." *Journal of Applied Behavior Analysis* 2 (1969): 143-57.

Lovaas, O.I. & Smith, T. "A Comprehensive Behavioral Theory of Autistic Children: Paradigm for Research and Treatment." *Journal of Behavior Therapy and Experimental Psychiatry* 20, no. 1 (1989): 17-29.

Lundervold, D. & Bourland, G. "Quantitative Analysis of Treatment of Aggression, Self-Injury, and Property Destruction." *Behavior Modification* 12, no. 4 (1988): 590-617.

Mahler, M.S. "On Childhood Psychosis and Schizophrenia: Autistic and Symbiotic Infantile Psychoses." *The Psychoanalytic Study of the Child.* Vol. 7. New York: International Universities Press, 1952.

Martin, A.M. *Inside Out.* New York: Holiday, 1984.

————. *Kristy and the Secret of Susan.* New York: Scholastic Inc., 1990.

Martineau, J., Barthelemy, C., Cheliakine, C. & Lelord, G. "Brief Report: An Open Middle-Term Study of Combined Vitamin B6-Magnesium in a Subgroup of Autistic Children Selected for Their Sensitivity to This Treatment." *Journal of Autism and Developmental Disorders* 18, no. 3 (1988): 435-47.

Martineau, J., Barthelemy, C. & Lelord, G. "Long-Term Effects of Combined Vitamin B6-Magnesium Administration in an Autistic Child." *Biological Psychiatry* 21, no. 5-6 (1986): 511-18.

Mason-Brothers, A., Ritvo, E.R., Pingree, C., et al. "The UCLA-University of Utah Epidemiological Survey of Autism: Prenatal, Perinatal and Postnatal Factors." *Pediatrics* 86 (1990): 514-19.

Maugh, T.H. "Scientists Say Drug Therapy Eases Autism." *Philadelphia Inquirer,* 15 November 1991, pp. 3-a, d.

Mayberry, R. "If a Chimp Can be Taught to Learn Sign Language, Surely My Nonverbal Client Can Too." *ASHA* 18 (1976): 228-33.

McDougle, C., Price, L.H. & Volkmar, F.R. "Recent Advances in the Pharmacotherapy of Autism and Related Disorders." *Child and Adolescent Psychiatry Clinics of North America* 3 (1994): 71-89.

McEachin, J.J., Smith, T. & Lovaas, O.I. "Long-Term Outcome for Children with Autism Who Received Early Intensive Behavioral Interventions." *American Journal on Mental Retardation* 97 (1993): 359-72.

McGee, G.G., Krantz, P.J., Mason, D. & McClannahan, L.E. "A Modified Incidental-Teaching Procedure for Autistic Youth: Acquisition and Generalization of Receptive Object Labels." *Journal of Applied Behavior Analysis* 16, no. 3 (1983): 329-38.

McGee, J.J., Menolascino, F.J., Hobbs, D.C. & Menousek, P.E. *Gentle Teaching: A Non-Aversive Approach to Helping Persons with Mental Retardation.* New York: Human Sciences Press, 1987.

Meichenbaum, D. "Teaching Thinking: A Cognitive-Behavioral Approach." In *Interdisciplinary Voices in Learning Disabilities and Remedial Education.* Austin, TX: Pro-Ed, 1983.

Menage, P., Thibault, G., Barthelemy, C., Lelord, G., et al. "CD4 + CD45RA + T Lymphocyte Deficiency in Autistic Children: Effect of a Pyridoxine-Magnesium Treatment." *Brain Dysfunction* 5, no. 5-6 (1992): 326-33.

Mesibov, G.B. "Current Perspectives and Issues in Autism and Adolescence." In *Autism in Adolescents and Adults*. Edited by E. Schopler & G.B. Mesibov. (pp. 37-53). New York: Plenum Press, 1983.

Meyer, L.H. & Evans, I.M. *Nonaversive Intervention for Behavior Problems: A Manual for Home and Community*. Baltimore, MD: Paul H. Brookes Publishing Co., 1989.

Miller, A. "Cognitive-Developmental Systems Theory in Pervasive Developmental Disorders." *Psychiatric Clinics of North America* 14, no. 1 (1991): 141-63.

Miller, A. & Eller-Miller, E. *From Ritual to Repertoire: A Cognitive-Developmental Systems Approach with Behavior Disordered Children*. New York, NY: Wiley, 1989.

Miller, E., Cradock-Watson, J.E. & Pollock, T.M. "Consequences of Confirmed Maternal Rubella at Successive Stages of Pregnancy." *Lancet* 2 (1982): 781-84.

Mirenda, P. & Mathy-Laikko, P. "Augmentative and Alternative Communication Applications for Persons with Severe Congenital Communication Disorders: An Introduction." *Augmentative and Alternative Communication* 5 (1989): 3-13.

Mirenda, P. & Schuler, A. "Augmenting Communication for Persons with Autism: Issues and Strategies." *Topics in Language Disorders* 9 (1988): 24-43.

Mithaug, D.E. & Mar, D.K. "The Relation Between Choosing and Working Prevocational Tasks in Two Severely Retarded Young Adults." *Journal of Applied Behavior Analysis* 13, no. 1 (1980): 177-82.

Murakami, J.W., Courchesne, E., Press, G.A., Yeung-Courchesne, R., et al. "Reduced Cerebellar Hemisphere Size and Its Relationship to Vermal Hypoplasia in Autism." *Archives of Neurology* 46, no. 6 (1989): 689-94.

Murray, A.D. "Early Intervention Program Evaluation: Numbers or Narrative?" *Infants and Young Children: An Interdisciplinary Journal of Special Care Practices* 4, no. 4 (1992): 77-88.

Mylee, B.S. & Simpson, R.L. "A Clinical/Prescriptive Method for Use with Students with Autism." *Focus on Autistic Behavior* 4, no. 6 (1990): 1-14.

National Institutes of Health. "Treatment of Destructive Behaviors in Persons with Developmental Disabilities." *NIH Consensus Development Conference Statement* 7, no. 9 (1989).

Nelson, K.B. "Prenatal and Perinatal Factors in the Etiology of Autism." *Pediatrics* 87 (1991): 761-66.

Neman, R., et al. "An Experimental Evaluation of Sensorimotor Patterning Used with Mentally Retarded Children." *American Journal of Mental Deficiency* 79 (1975): 372-84.

Nowell, M.A., Hackney, D.B., Muraki, A.S. & Coleman, M. "Varied MR Appearance of Autism: Fifty-Three Pediatric Patients Having the Autistic Syndrome." *Magnetic Resonance Imaging* 8, no. 6 (1990): 811-16.

O'Neill, R.E., Horner, R.H., Albin, R.W., Storey, K. & Sprague, J. *Functional Analysis of Problem Behavior: A Practical Assessment Guide.* Sycamore, IL: Sycamore Publishing Co., 1990.

Oleck, H.L. *Non-profit Corporation Organizations and Associations.* Englewood Cliffs, NJ: Prentice Hall, 1988.

Olsson, I., Steffenburg, S. & Gillberg, C. "Epilepsy in Autism and Autistic-Like Conditions. A Population-Based Study." *Archives of Neurology* 45 (1988): 666-68.

Overton, G.W. *Guidebook for Directors of Non-Profit Corporations.* Chicago, IL: American Bar Association, 1993.

Palfreman, J., producer. "Prisoners of Silence." *Frontline* (19 October 1993). Boston, MA: WGBH.

Parette, H.P., Hendricks, M.D. & Rock, S.L. "Efficacy of Therapeutic Intervention with Infants and Young Children with Cerebral Palsy." *Infants and Young Children* 4, no. 2 (1991): 1-8.

Park, C.C. *The Siege: The First Eight Years of an Autistic Child with an Epilogue Fifteen Years Later.* New York: Atlantic Monthly Press, 1982.

Parrish, J.M., Iwata, B.A., Dorsey, M.F., Bunck, T.J. & Slifer, K.J. "Behavior Analysis, Program Development and Transfer of Control in the Treatment of Self-Injury." *Journal of Behavior Therapy and Experimental Psychiatry* 16 (1985): 159-68.

Parsons, M.B., Reid, D.H., Reynolds, J. & Bumgarner, M. "Effects of Chosen Versus Assigned Jobs on the Work Performance of Persons with Severe Handicaps." *Journal of Applied Behavior Analysis* 23, no. 2 (1990): 253-58.

Peck, C.A. "Increasing Opportunities for Social Control by Children with Autism and Severe Handicaps: Effects on Student Behavior by Perceived Classroom Climate." *Journal of the Association for Persons with Severe Handicaps* 10, no. 4 (1985): 183-93.

Piaget, J. *The Origins of Intelligence in Children.* 1936. Reprint, New York: Norton, 1963.

Pollak, R. *The Creation of Dr. B: A Biography of Bruno Bettelheim.* New York: Simon and Schuster, 1997.

Powell, T.H. & Ogle, P.A. *Brothers & Sisters—A Special Part of Exceptional Families.* Baltimore, MD: Paul H. Brookes Publishing Co., 1985.

Prior, M. & Cummins, R. "Questions about Facilitated Communication and Autism." *Journal of Autism and Developmental Disorders* 22, no. 3 (1992): 331-38.

Prizant, B. "Building Bridges through Communication." *The Advocate* 21, no. 2 (1989): 15-16, 20.

Ramey, C.T., Lee, M.W. & Burchinal, M.R. "Developmental Plasticity and Predictability: Consequences of Ecological Change." In *Stability and Continuity in Mental Development: Behavioral and Biological Perspectives.* Edited by M.H. Bornstein & N.A. Krasnegor. (pp. 217-33). Hillsdale, NJ: Lawrence Erlbaum, 1989.

Repp, A.C. & Singh, N.N., eds. *Perspectives on the Use of Nonaversive and Aversive Interventions for People with Developmental Disabilities.* Sycamore, IL: Sycamore Publishing Co., 1990.

Rimland, B. "Controlled Evaluations of Facilitated Communication." *Autism Research Review International* 7, no. 4 (1993): 7.

———. "Auditory Integration Training (AIT) Update." *Autism Research Review International* 7, no. 3 (1993): 2.

———. "Update III - Auditory Training." *Autism Research Review International* 5, no. 3 (1991): 1.

———. "Controversies in the Treatment of Autistic Children: Vitamin and Drug Therapy." *Journal of Child Neurology* 3 (Supp.) (1988): 68-72.

———. "Vitamin B6 (and Magnesium) in the Treatment of Autism." *Autism Research Review International* 1, no. 4 (1988): 3.

———. "An Orthomolecular Study of Psychotic Children." *Orthomolecular Psychiatry* 3 (1974): 371-77.

———. "High Dosage Levels of Certain Vitamins in the Treatment of Children with Severe Mental Disorders." In *Orthomolecular Psychiatry.* Edited by D.R. Hawkins & L. Pauling. (pp. 513-39). New York, NY: W.H. Freeman, 1973.

———. *Infantile Autism: The Syndrome and Its Implications for a Neural Theory of Behavior.* New York: Appleton-Century-Crofts, 1964.

Risley, T. & Wolf, M.M. "Establishing Functional Speech in Autistic Children." *Behaviour Therapy & Research* 5 (1967): 73-88.

Ritvo, E.R., Mason-Brothers, A., Freeman, B.J., Pingree, C., et al. "The UCLA-University of Utah Epidemiologic Survey of Autism: The Etiologic Role of Rare Diseases." *American Journal of Psychiatry* 147, no. 12 (1990): 1614-21.

Rosenberg, S.A. "Family and Parent Variables Affecting Outcomes of a Parent-Mediated Intervention." Unpublished doctoral dissertation, George Peabody College for Teachers. 1977.

Rubin, D. "Disabled Pose Tough Classroom Problem." *The Times of Trenton,* (23 September 1993). p. A-21.

Rules and Regulations for Implementation of Part B, Education for All Handicapped Children Act (Public Law 94-142), *Federal Register,* August 23, 1977. pp. 42474-42514.

Rutter, M. "Concepts of Autism: A Review of Literature." *Journal of Child Psychology and Psychiatry* 9 (1968): 1-25.

———. "Autism as a Genetic Disorder." In *The New Genetics of Mental Illness.* Edited by P. McGuffin & R. Murray. (pp. 225-44). Stoneham, MA: Butterworth-Heinemann, 1990.

Rutter, M., Bartak, L. & Newman, S. "Autism: A Central Disorder of Cognition and Language." In *Infantile Autism: Concepts, Characteristics and Treatment.* Edited by M. Rutter. London: Churchill, 1971.

Sacks, O. *An Anthropologist on Mars: Seven Paradoxical Tales.* New York: Alfred A. Knopf, 1995.

Sailor, W., Gee, K., Goetz, L. & Graham, N. "Progress in Educating Students with the Most Severe Disabilities: Is There Any?" *Journal of the Association for Persons with Severe Handicaps* 13, no. 2 (1988): 87-99.

Scagliotta, E.G. *Special Education: As You Liked It.* North Branch, NJ: Midland Publications, 1993.

Schaeffer, B., Kolinzas, G., Musil, A. & MacDowell, P. "Spontaneous Verbal Language for Autistic Children through Signed Speech." *Sign Language Studies* 17 (1977): 287-328.

Schain, R.J. & Freedman, D.X. "Studies on 5-Hydroxyindole Metabolism in Autistic and Other Mentally Retarded Children." *Journal of Pediatrics* 58 (1961): 315-20.

Schickendanz, J.A., Hansen, K. & Forsyth, P.D., eds. *Understanding Children.* Mountain View, CA: Mayfield, 1990.

Schopler, E. "Autism Services: Past, Present and Future." In *Proceedings of the Eden Institute Foundation Princeton Lecture Series on Autism: Affecting the Research and Service Agenda* (pp.1-28). Princeton, NJ: Eden Press, 1995.

———. "Parents of Psychotic Children as Scapegoats." *Journal of Contemporary Psychotherapy* 4 (1971): 17-22.

Schopler, E., Brehm, S.S., Kinsbourne, M. & Reichler, R.J. "Effect of Treatment Structure on Development in Autistic Children." *Archives of General Psychiatry* 24 (1971): 415-21.

Schopler, E. & Mesibov, G.B., eds. *Communication Problems in Autism.* New York: Plenum Press, 1985.

Schopler, E. & Mesibov, G.B., eds. *Autism in Adolescents and Adults.* New York: Plenum Press, 1983.

Schopler, E. & Van Bourgondien, M., eds. "Critical Issues in the Residential Care of People with Autism." *Journal of Autism and Developmental Disorders* 20, no. 3 (Special Issue: Residential Services). (1990).

Schopler, E., Reichler, R.J. & Rochen Renner, B. *The Childhood Autism Rating Scale (CARS).* Los Angeles: Western Psychological Services, 1990.

Schubert, A. *Facilitated Communication Resource Guide.* Brookline, MA: Adriana Foundation, 1992.

Schwarzkopf, N. "Take Charge." *Personal Selling Power.* (July 1992).

Seiden, S.B. & Zirkel, P.A. "Commentary: Aversive Therapy for Handicapped Students." *West's Education Law Reporter* 48 (1988): 1029-44.

Semmel, M.I., Abernathy, T.V., Butera, G. & Lesar, S. "Teacher Perceptions of the Regular Education Initiative." *Exceptional Children* 58, no. 1 (1991): 9-24.

Sigafoos, J., Cole, D.A. & McQuarter, R.J. "Current Practices in the Assessment of Students with Severe Handicaps." *Journal of the Association for Persons with Severe Handicaps* 12, no. 4 (1987): 264-73.

Simpson, R.L. "Public School Integration of Autistic Pupils." *Focus on Autistic Behavior* 1, no. 6 (1987): 1-7.

Simpson, R. & Regan, M. "Focus on Autistic Behavior: Punishment as an Intervention Procedure." In *The Management of Autistic Behavior.* Edited by R. Simpson. & M. Regan. Rockville, MD: Aspen, 1986.

Smalley, S.L., Asarnow, R.F. & Spence, M.A. "Autism and Genetics: A Decade of Research." *Archives of General Psychiatry* 45 (1988): 953-61.

Sommers, R.K. "Language Assessment: Issues in the Use and Interpretation of Tests and Measures." *School Psychology Review* 18, no. 4 (1989): 452-62.

Sovner, R. & Lowry, M.A. "A Behavioral Methodology for Diagnosing Affective Disorders in Individuals with Mental Retardation." *The Habilitative Mental Healthcare Newsletter* 9, no. 7 (1990): 55-60.

Sparrow, S. & Zigler, E. "Evaluation of a Patterning Treatment for Retarded Children." *Pediatrics* 62 (1978): 137-50.

Sparrow, S.S., Balla, D.A. & Cicchetti, D.V. *Vineland Adaptive Behavior Scales* (Interview edition). Circle Pines, MN: American Guidance Service, Inc., 1984.

Spiker, D., Lotspeich, L., Kraemer, H.C., Hallmayer, J., McMahon, W., Petersen, P.B., Nicholas, P., Pingree, C., Weise-Slater, S., Chiotti, C., Wong, D.L., Dimicelli, S., Ritvo, E., Cavalli-Sforza, L.L. & Ciaranello, R.D. "Genetics of Autism: Characteristics of Affected and Unaffected Children from 37 Multiplex Families." *American Journal of Medical Genetics (Neuropsychiatric Genetics)* 54 (1994): 27-35.

Stainback, W. & Stainback, S. "A Rationale for Integrations and Restructuring: A Synopsis." In *The Regular Education Initiative: Alternative Perspectives on Concepts, Issues, and Models*. Edited by J.W. Lloyd, N.N. Singh & A.C. Repp. (pp. 226-239). Sycamore, IL: Sycamore Publishing Co., 1991.

Stainback, S. & Stainback, W. "Letter to the Editor." *Journal of Learning Disabilities* 21 (1988): 452-53.

Stanton, B.H. *Trustee Handbook*. Boston, MA: NAIS, 1989.

The Association for Persons with Severe Handicaps. "Resolution Calling for the Cessation of Aversive Procedures with Persons who are Handicapped." Seattle, WA: The Association for Persons with Severe Handicaps, 1981.

The Association for Persons with Severe Handicaps. "TASH Resolution on the Cessation of Intrusive Interventions." Alexandria, VA: The Association for Persons with Severe Handicaps, 1986.

Thompson, M. *Andy and His Yellow Frisbee*. Bethesda, MD: Woodbine House, 1996.

Tinbergen, N. & Tinbergen, E.A. *Autistic Children: New Hope for a Cure*. London: Allen and Unwin, 1983.

Tomchek, L.B., Gordon, R., Arnold, M., Handleman, J. & Harris, S. "Teaching Preschool Children with Autism and Their Normally Developing Peers: Meeting the Challenge of Integrated Education." *Focus on Autistic Behavior* 7, no. 2 (1992): 1-17.

Torisky, D.A. "President's Message." *Advocate: Autism Society of America* 3 (Summer/Fall 1990).

Touchette, P.E., MacDonald, R.F. & Langer, S.H. "A Scatter Plot for Identifying the Stimulus Control of a Problem Behavior." *Journal of Applied Behavior Analysis* 18 (1985): 343-51.

Towner, G., Malgady, R.G., Barcher, P.R. & Davis, J. *Vocational Adaptation Rating Scales.* Los Angeles: Western Psychological Services, 1989.

Tustin, F. "Revised Understandings of Psychogenic Autism." *International Journal of Psychoanalysis* 72, no. 4 (1991): 585-91.

Wacker, D.P., Steege, M.W., Northup, J., Sasso, G., Berg, W., Reimers, T., Cooper, L., Cigrand, K. & Donn, L. "A Component Analysis of Functional Communication Training Across Three Topographies of Severe Behavior Problems." *Journal of Applied Behavior Analysis* 23, no. 4 (1990): 417-29.

Wagner, M. *National Longitudinal Study: Transition Study of Special Education Students.* Menlo Park, CA: SRI International, 1993.

Watson, E. *Talking to Angels.* New York: Harcourt Brace & Co., 1996.

Weitzner, L. & Holmes, D.L. *The Eden Programs' Functional Communication Questionnaire.* Princeton, NJ: The Eden Press, 1990.

Welch, M.G. "Toward Prevention of Developmental Disorders." *Pre and Peri Natal Psychology Journal* 3, no. 4 (1989): 319-28.

Wheeler, D.L., Jacobson, J.W., Paglieri, R.A. & Schwartz, A.A. "An Experimental Assessment of Facilitated Communication." *Mental Retardation* 31, no. 1 (1993): 49-60.

Wilbur, R.B. "The Linguistics of Manual Languages and Manual Systems." In *Communication, Assessment and Intervention Strategies.* Edited by L.L. Lloyd. (pp. 423-500). Baltimore, MD: University Park Press, 1976.

Wilcox, B. & Bellamy, G.T. *A Comprehensive Guide to the Activities Catalog: An Alterative Curriculum for Youth and Adults with Severe Disabilities.* Baltimore, MD: Paul H. Brookes Publishing Co., 1987.

Wilson, W.C. & Sailor, W. "Service Integration in Public Schools." *School of Education Review* 4 (1992): 127-30.

Wimpery, D. & Cochrane, V. "Criteria for Evaluative Research—With Special Reference to Holding Therapy." *Communication* 25, no 2 (1991): 15-17.

Wing, L. "Sex Ratios in Early Childhood Autism and Related Conditions." *Psychiatry Research* 5 (1981): 129-37.

Wing, L., ed. *Aspects of Autism: Biological Research.* London: Gaskell, Royal College of Psychiatrists, 1988.

Wolfberg, P. "Enhancing Children's Play." In *Teaching Children with Autism: Methods to Enhance Learning, Communication and Socialization.* Edited by K.A. Quill. Delmar Publishers, 1995.

Wyatt v. Stickney, 325 F. Supp. 781, 334 F. Supp. 373 (M.D. Ala. 1972), *aff'd sub nom Wyatt v. Aderhalt,* 503 F. 2d. 1305 (5th Cir. 1974), *modified,* 344 F. Supp. 395 (1975).

Youngberg v. Romeo, 102 S. Ct. 2452 (1982).

Zigler, E. & Seitz, V. "On 'An Experimental Evaluation of Sensorimotor Patterning:' A Critique." *American Journal of Mental Deficiency* 79 (1975): 483-92.

Zimmerman, I.L., Steiner, V.G. & Evatt Pond, R. *Preschool language scale.* The Psychological Corporation: Harcourt Brace Jovanovich, Inc., 1979.

Index

About the Author

Dr. David L. Holmes received his undergraduate degree from Western Connecticut State University and his graduate degrees in special education and educational psychology from Rutgers University. He has been certified as a Professionally Recognized Special Educator (PRSE) in both special education and administration by the Council for Exceptional Children. He has attained Diplomate sta-

tus and is Board Certified by the American Board of Administrative Psychology (ABAP), the American Board of Forensic Examiners (ABFE), and the American Board of Psychological Specialties (ABPS). He is the author of numerous books, book chapters, and articles on autism, learning theory, and administration.

Dr. Holmes is the founding director of the Eden Institute and its affiliate agencies (Eden A.C.R.E.s, Eden W.E.R.C.s, Eden Institute Foundation, Eden Connecticut and Eden Florida) comprising the Eden Family of Services, headquartered in Princeton, New Jersey, and currently serves as President and Executive Director.

Dr. Holmes has served on the faculties of Rutgers University and The College of New Jersey and is Adjunct Professor of Psychology at Princeton University. Dr. Holmes is Co-Chair of the Panel of Professional Advisors of the Autism Society of America and a consulting editor for the *Journal of Emotional and Behavior Problems*. He has served as President of the National Association of Private Schools for Exceptional Children, as President of the Association of Schools and Agencies for the Handicapped, and as Chairman of the Board of the Center for Non-Profit Corporations. Dr. Holmes is a founder of the National Commission for the Accreditation of Special Education Services and is presently Chairman.